TINDERBOX

TINDERBOX

The Untold Story of
THE UP STAIRS LOUNGE FIRE
and the Rise of
GAY LIBERATION

ROBERT W. FIESELER

LIVERIGHT PUBLISHING CORPORATION

A DIVISION OF W. W. Norton & Company

INDEPENDENT PUBLISHERS SINCE 1923 • NEW YORK • LONDON

Map drawn by Jeff Ferzoco

Endpaper image: The Up Stairs Lounge crowd gathers in the bar's back
theater space. Patron Michael Scarborough poses, at lower left, with a drink.

For information about permission to reproduce selections from this book, write to
Permissions, Liveright Publishing Corporation, a division of
W. W. Norton & Company, Inc., 500 Fifth Avenue, New York, NY 10110

For information about special discounts for bulk purchases, please contact
W. W. Norton Special Sales at specialsales@wwnorton.com or 800-233-4830

Manufacturing by LSC Communications Harrisonburg
Book design by Brooke Koven
Production manager: Lauren Abbate

Library of Congress Cataloging-in-Publication Data

Names: Fieseler, Robert W., author.
Title: Tinderbox : the untold story of the Up Stairs Lounge fire and the rise
of gay liberation / Robert W. Fieseler.
Description: First edition. | New York : Liveright Publishing Corporation,
[2018] | Includes bibliographical references and index.
Identifiers: LCCN 2018004765 | ISBN 9781631491641 (hardcover)
Subjects: LCSH: Gays—Violence against—Louisiana—New Orleans—History—
20th century. | Mass murder—Louisiana—New Orleans—History—20th century. |
Gay bars—Louisiana—New Orleans—History—20th century. |
Arson—Louisiana—New Orleans—History—20th century. |
Homophobia—Louisiana—New Orleans—History—20th century. | Gay
liberation movement—Louisiana—New Orleans—History—20th century.
Classification: LCC HV6250.4.H66 F54 2018 | DDC 364.152/340976335—dc23
LC record available at https://lccn.loc.gov/2018004765

Liveright Publishing Corporation, 500 Fifth Avenue, New York, N.Y. 10110
www.wwnorton.com

W. W. Norton & Company Ltd., 15 Carlisle Street, London W1D 3BS

1 2 3 4 5 6 7 8 9 0

For Ryan, my lover,
who was born on the thirteenth anniversary
of the Up Stairs Lounge fire.
The fates are strange, even cruel,
and yet aware.

Louis
Armstrong
Park

Saint Louis
Cemetery

map on opposite page

Jackson
Square

Vieux
Carré

Up Stairs
Lounge

Superdome

Mississippi River

International
Trade Mart

Central
City

MCC of
New Orleans

Cooley   Larson

Broussard
and Mitchell

Doolittle
and Butler

Lower
Garden
District

Kubicki
and Everett

McCloskey
and Bailey

Datson

Rasmussen
and Fontenot

Alabama   Mississippi   Florida

Louisiana

Mississippi R.

New
Orleans

Gulf of Mexico

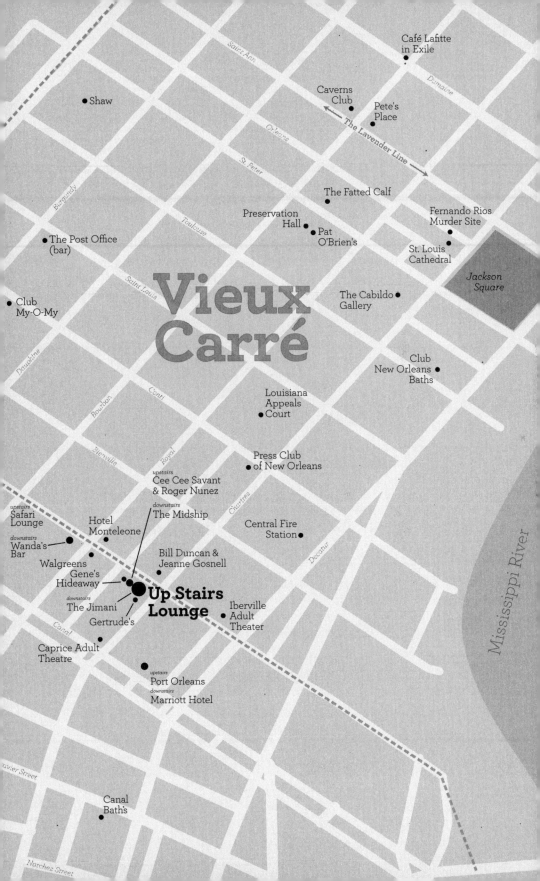

Café Lafitte
in Exile

Caverns
Club

Pete's
Place

Shaw

← The Lavender Line →

Saint Ann

Orleans

St. Peter

The Fatted Calf

Preservation
Hall

Fernando Rios
Murder Site

Pat
O'Brien's

Toulouse

St. Louis
Cathedral

The Post Office
(bar)

Burgundy

Saint Louis

Vieux Carré

The Cabildo
Gallery

*Jackson
Square*

Club
My-O-My

Dauphine

Club
New Orleans
Baths

Louisiana
Appeals
Court

Conti

Bourbon

Press Club
of New Orleans

Bienville

upstairs
Cee Cee Savant
& Roger Nunez

Royal

downstairs
The Midship

Chartres

Central Fire
Station

Mississippi River

upstairs
Safari
Lounge

Hotel
Monteleone

downstairs
Wanda's
Bar

Walgreens

Bill Duncan &
Jeanne Gosnell

Decatur

Gene's
Hideaway

**Up Stairs
Lounge**

downstairs
The Jimani

Gertrude's

Iberville
Adult
Theater

Canal

Caprice Adult
Theatre

upstairs
Port Orleans
downstairs
Marriott Hotel

avier Street

Canal
Bath's

Natchez Street

"We will be citizens."

—CURTAIN SPEECH,

Angels in America: Perestroika by Tony Kushner

Contents

Act III: Legacy

Historical Figures

GAY LIBERATION

Lucien Baril	interim pastor, MCC of New Orleans
Paul Breton	pastor, MCC of Washington, D.C.
John Gill	pastor, MCC of Atlanta
Morris Kight	president of Gay Community Services Center of Los Angeles
Morty Manford	president of Gay Activists Alliance, New York City
Troy Perry	founding pastor of MCC; based in Los Angeles
Bill Rushton	managing editor of *Vieux Carré Courier*

FRENCH QUARTER FIGURES

Roberts Batson	LGBT historian
Joseph Bermuda	owner, Cabildo Gallery
Dexter Brecht	pastor, MCC of New Orleans, 1994–2006
Gene Davis	Iberville Street businessman
Clancy DuBos	journalist; former *Times-Picayune* intern
Mark Allen Guidry	Iberville Street hustler
Milton Mary	French Quarter bartender
John Meyers	Catholic seminarian; Café Lafitte in Exile patron
Roger Dale Nunez	Iberville Street hustler

CITY/COMMUNITY LEADERS

Finis Crutchfield	bishop, United Methodist Church
Edwin Edwards	governor of Louisiana
Charles Ferguson	managing editor of New Orleans *States-Item*
Jim Garrison	district attorney of Orleans Parish
Philip Hannan	archbishop, Roman Catholic Archdiocese of New Orleans

Moon Landrieu — mayor of New Orleans, 1970–1978

William McCrossen — New Orleans Fire Superintendent, 1972–1993

Ernest "Dutch" Morial — Appeals Court judge; mayor of New Orleans, 1978–1986

Henry M. Morris — major, New Orleans Police Department

Bill Richardson — pastor, St. George's Episcopal Church

Clay Shaw — New Orleans businessman

Rod Wagener — local radio host

FAMILIES

Mary David — niece of Up Stairs Lounge victim Glenn Green

Anna Howell — mother of MCC pastor Bill Larson

Tina Marie Matyi — daughter of Up Stairs Lounge victim Bud Matyi

Duane Mitchell — son of MCC of New Orleans deacon Mitch Mitchell

Preface

Every social movement in American history has a body count. From Wounded Knee, a massacre of the Lakota by U.S. cavalry in 1890, to Emmett Till, a black teenager lynched in 1955 for supposedly whistling at a white woman, to the Triangle Shirtwaist fire, an industrial disaster in 1911 that killed more than a hundred people and exposed the slavish conditions of Gilded Age labor, it is routinely through death that we reckon with violations of our basic liberties. The full impact of these reckonings—for Native Americans, for the civil rights movement, for organized labor—often takes years or even decades.

On June 12, 2016, an American-born citizen named Omar Mateen stepped into a gay nightclub in Orlando, Florida, called Pulse. He entered the crowded room strapped with body armor, bulk ammunition, and a semiautomatic firearm. At twenty-nine years old, Mateen had already been investigated by the FBI, and some at Pulse thought they'd seen his face beforehand.[1] He was a rejected prison guard candidate, a one-time divorcé, and a devout Muslim who had performed the rites of hajj and seen Mecca. No doubt haunted by memories of his father calling him gay in front of an ex-wife, an accusation deemed abominable by his faith, Mateen had grown extreme in his politics and become desperate to purge the world of gays.[2]

After assembling a small arsenal through legal means, he acted on those beliefs. That Sunday in June, Mateen opened fire on the unarmed crowd in Pulse. He took the lives of his fellow Americans to punish their presence in a gay-friendly establishment—all during national gay pride week. He played executioner for hours, hunting men and women indiscriminately and taunting authorities by pledging allegiance to ISIS, until eight bullets from the Orlando Police Department took him down.[3]

His was an almost unimaginable field of slaughter, claiming forty-nine lives and injuring fifty-three others in what constituted one of the deadliest mass shootings of citizens *and* the largest mass killing of gay people in United States history. His attack seemed to defy the modern acceptance of homosexuality into mainstream society, a process that had permitted the once persecuted the right to live openly. Astoundingly, Mateen's rampage topped the body count of the most ghastly event that had previously struck the American gay community: the thirty-two burning deaths in New Orleans forty-three years earlier, at a bar called the Up Stairs Lounge.[4]

Disparities in the reaction to these two tragedies, the Up Stairs Lounge fire and Pulse, became apparent within minutes of the Florida attack. Orlando mayor Buddy Dyer rushed to the scene with emergency workers and comforted survivors. Florida governor Rick Scott, a staunch Republican, offered condolences to families. President Barack Obama made a statement that, four decades before, could easily have applied to the destruction of the Up Stairs Lounge: "For so many people here who are lesbian, gay, bisexual and transgender, the Pulse Nightclub has always been a safe haven, a place to sing and dance, and most importantly, to be who you truly are ... Sunday morning, that sanctuary was violated in the worst way imaginable."[5] Flags flew at half-staff over federal buildings. None of this happened for the bar-fire victims of 1973.

Yet stories of that incinerated building in New Orleans and faded pictures of a charred body dangling out a street window inundated media outlets in 2016 alongside news of the Florida shooting, with commentators in social forums citing that 1973 massacre as an antecedent to the homophobic, "lone wolf" ferocity made manifest at Pulse.[6] After the shooting, the New Orleans Superdome was lit up in all the rainbow of colors of the gay pride flag in recognition of the Orlando victims; days later, those same colors were lit again, to honor the Up Stairs Lounge victims.[7] In fact, more stories about the Up Stairs Lounge appeared in major news outlets *after* the Pulse shooting than in the previous four decades. The tragedy in Orlando had succeeded in shedding some light on the tragedy in New Orleans, just as that historic event was lending context to the present-day grief, which in turn made a reckoning with Pulse more immediate.

The story of the Up Stairs Lounge, by contrast, had disappeared willfully, hushed by a nation not ready to look. It was only recently revived by a persistent set of voices who paid a ransom's price for their work. Homosexuals, for decades if not centuries, existed in a lived lie called the closet,[8] that obscure place where men who love men hid their true selves. Edward Sagarin, who published under the pen name David Webster Cory in the 1950s to protect his life and livelihood, once observed, "Society has handed me a mask to wear."[9]

A gay publication called *Vector* described the pragmatic gradations of the closet in 1966: "We lie so that we may live. Whether it is to our boss, or the draft board, or the civil service, we rarely can afford to divulge the simple truth of our homosexuality. But this is merely the beginning. Lying begets lying: we have to cover up for so many of our activities and doings that we find ourselves in a mire of untruths."[10] If the closet began as a personal conspiracy to turn away from portions of the self, then the conspiracy metastasized when enough closeted citizens aggregated to form a societal illusion, a closet deep enough to create a secret world inhabited by a secret class of Americans.

The closet, thus, grew to function as a governing institution for nonheterosexual life in twentieth-century America, which explains precisely how a makeshift bar like the Up Stairs Lounge could burn to its foundations and, in so doing, disappear from memory. The closet had enough power to eat it up. This framework, by historic reflection, helps to illustrate how a gunman's slaughter of innocents in Orlando could no longer be silenced in the same way: by the second decade of the twenty-first century, the closet no longer prevailed as the governing institution for gay life. Something had irrevocably changed, and, true to the undulations of history, someone had died to change it.

This book, then, is about those generations who battered their heads against padded walls and fell so that events like the Up Stairs Lounge might be known and aligned with America's larger civil rights story.

TINDERBOX

History Reclaimed

June 25, 1995

W hat does it mean to remember? What does a memory give you license to do? Resurrect, retell, or embellish? Honor, avenge, or fume? Can we remember without an agenda, without an enemy to bury and shame? And when can yet another recollection of a bygone tragedy yield something new? Such were the questions reverberating in the mind of Dexter Brecht, a gay minister in New Orleans who in the summer of 1995 was about to reintroduce history to his small congregation.[1]

It was a Sunday morning in the Crescent City. The air felt sweet, fecund, almost fermenting—blue to the heavens and green to the earth, sunny from levee to levee. Inside the worn building at 1128 St. Roch Avenue, a flock of about forty members of the Metropolitan Community Church (MCC) scrutinized Reverend Brecht and waited to hear the holy man in white and red preach the good word. Today, his gentle voice seemed to quiver with an unusual anxiety. He clearly had something to say, beyond the ordinary sermon. His audience was not a wealthy assemblage, but a host of working-class gay men and lesbians who, as with most New Orleanians, took to gatherings and festivals like hot sauce to gumbo, but to politics like water to oil.

To be fair, Louisiana politics could be hard to fathom, whether one happened to be straight or gay. Sometimes, the particulars could be hard to stomach. A 1991 gubernatorial runoff had pitted the former Ku Klux Klan leader David Duke against ex-governor Edwin Edwards, an emblem of the Democratic machine who during his third term had stood trial on federal corruption charges. In the end, the election had tipped in Edwards's favor through the clever use of the campaign slogan "Vote for the Crook. It's Important."[2] Edwards remained the people's governor that June of 1995.

Brecht's congregation sat in folding chairs in loosely assembled rows: men and women, black and white and Creole. All were casually, if colorfully, dressed in summer outfits. The house of worship was an old storefront—small and bare save for a piano in the corner and flowers near the altar. The congregation couldn't afford to keep much more around, for fear of break-ins. A humble roost, their building was among the first real property to be owned by an LGBT-identified organization in the city.[3] Yet, according to some MCC members, the building itself was a sore spot—situated in a "less than desirable" neighborhood of déclassé groups, to which many of the faithful just wouldn't make the trip. New Orleans, after all, remained a stratified metropolitan area with rising crime rates. A record 424 murders had occurred in 1994—more per capita than in any other American city.[4]

Reverend Brecht, at thirty-seven years of age, gripped his lectern. Like so many preachers possessing charisma and a healthy mane, he styled himself after the image of Christ in Renaissance paintings. Long hair flowed from the top of his head to his thin shoulders. A mustache framed a sharp grin. Eyebrows angled to an aquiline nose. Brecht had all the bearing of a young idealist, a pastor on his first assignment with a flair for social crusading. In the back of the room stood Mark L. Thompson, a cub reporter from the *Times-Picayune*, New Orleans's major newspaper. A staff photographer had also tagged along.

Brecht found himself not alarmed but "excited that a reporter for the daily newspaper was willing to attend worship."[5] A newly minted Princeton graduate, Thompson had interned the previous summer at the political newsmagazine *The New Republic* for editor Andrew Sullivan. Sullivan was then a controversial figure: an Englishman who'd studied at Harvard and a gay Republican, he was said to be working on a book that made a conservative argument for gay marriage.

Reverend Brecht had sent an invitation to the *Picayune* for the day's events but hadn't expected any coverage. In many cases, his congregation shunned such attention from the press. Almost as soon as Brecht had taken the job the previous year, he risked it by penning a critical letter to the editor of *The Advocate*, the nation's premier gay and lesbian magazine. Brecht knew that his congregation had a mixed record with activist ministers, having heard about the pastor who founded the MCC of New Orleans back in the 1970s, David Solomon. Evidently, Solomon had been asked or forced to leave his post—no one could recall the exact details—after campaigning to become a delegate to the 1973 Louisiana state constitutional convention.[6]

"He stirred the shit," remembered Henry Kubicki, a longtime congregant and friend of David Solomon. "His activism was an affront to the congregation's closeted-ness." In his candidacy, Solomon had taken the radical step, no doubt natural to him and ghastly to his flock, of aligning his liberal politics with their religion. Solomon "feels that the church has always had a role in the shaping of society," read a candidate profile in the *Times-Picayune*, "and that his church, the Metropolitan Community Church, is a leader." But in fact, a reticence to engage the community soon muddled the church's mission and gradually the number of members dwindled. By 1994, when Dexter Brecht inherited the gay church's pulpit, only a dozen or so people regularly attended.[7]

The young minister's political salvo, published in the March 1994 issue of *The Advocate*, chided the magazine and its editors for ignoring or misrepresenting gay Christians. "The Universal Fellowship of Metropolitan Community Churches celebrated twenty-five years of ministry in 1993," wrote Brecht, "and there was no coverage in *The Advocate*. Could it be Christophobia? Get with the true spirit of pride."[8] Brecht's letter appears to have resounded with *Advocate* editor in chief Jeff Yarbrough. That December, *The Advocate* featured a front-cover illustration of a crucified Christ with the incendiary headline "Is God Gay?" Inside was a seven-page story on the MCC, Brecht's LGBT-friendly Christian fellowship with more than 42,000 members in sixteen countries.[9]

The issue had exploded off newsstands, demonstrating that gays were Christians too, and attracted the ire of Christian Right leader Jerry Falwell. "Advertisers pulled out," Yarbrough later recalled. "My publisher screamed at me and told me someone called in a death threat. Readers and a lot of nonreaders sent us hate mail. The straight press said we'd stepped over some imaginary line."[10] That imaginary line of decency—reflecting midterm elections in which Republicans had recaptured the House of Representatives in a fifty-four-seat swing that would elevate Newt Gingrich to Speaker when the 104th Congress convened in January 1995—conflated morality squarely with the "family values" of conservative Christian politics.[11]

Gay Christianity remained a lightning rod even for magazines with a stated mission to serve gay and lesbian interests. In publishing "Is God Gay?" *The Advocate* was baiting a cultural majority that continued to view homosexuality as an immoral choice and the path to perdition. When a Gallup survey in June 1992 had asked whether "homosexuality should be considered an acceptable alternative lifestyle or not," 57 percent of the respondents said that homosexuality was "not acceptable."[12] The uproar over "Is God Gay?," according to *Advocate* editor in chief Yarbrough, provided a "way to point out how marginalized we were at the time."[13] But at least, in Dexter Brecht's assessment, *The Advocate* was printing these words, these pictures. And, to think, the young preacher had played a small role in inspiring the noise.

This distant world of 1995, in which *The Advocate* boasted a regular circulation of more than 100,000 readers,[14] granted gays and lesbians the power to provoke but rarely to set the social agenda. Fear and condemnation of same-sex relations remained one of Western society's deepest and most irrational prejudices: the belief that acting on this specific biological impulse constituted a moral offense. This bias had roots in Christendom itself—dating to myths of Sodom and Gomorrah, the letters of Paul, and the Justinian code of Rome[15]—and leached into the foundations of our civil society. It was Thomas Jefferson who wrote the 1777 revision to Virginia law that sodomy should be punished "if a man, by castration, if a woman, by cutting thro' the cartilage of her nose a hole,"[16] and General George Washington who court-martialed a Continental Army lieutenant for "attempting to commit sodomy" with another soldier, which resulted in the lieutenant's dismissal by being marched out of Valley Forge "by all the Drummers and Fifers in the Army."[17]

In the late twentieth century, it was often easier to say you were dying of AIDS than to admit you were healthy and gay. In fact, the AIDS epidemic became a window through which many "straight" Americans found their compassion for so-called queer folk, although it was hardly a universal gateway. Celebrities, with legions of devoted fans, often found easier acceptance from the grave. In 1991, closeted Queen front man Freddie Mercury announced he had AIDS and expired but a day later. Before Mercury, actor Rock Hudson had died of AIDS, in 1985—ending the life of a Hollywood hunk long in the closet.[18]

Bucking this trend, as he did not contract the disease like scores of his closest friends, singer Elton John ended years of speculation by formally declaring himself to be gay. A friend of Princess Diana, he continued to be the most prominent out gay voice in the world.[19] Rock singer Melissa Etheridge was barely two years out of the closet, her release of the 1993 album *Yes I Am* a semaphore.[20] In 1987, U.S. Representative Barney Frank had become the first member of Congress to voluntarily out himself by identifying as homosexual.[21] Ellen DeGeneres, despite beginning her career out at Clyde's Comedy Corner in New Orleans, remained a closeted actress in Los Angeles. To even suggest that someone was gay, whether this was true or not, could generate a whisper campaign heard round the land and catalyzed on internet message boards, then in their infancy.

Brecht's experiment with the press in 1994, however, had a salutary effect in that it restored the faith of his congregants; by the early summer of 1995, the ranks of his New Orleans flock had grown to more than three dozen attendees. Consequently, Brecht spoke with credibility in front of his kin: a remnant church that had survived a catastrophic event—one that happened years before the ravages of the AIDS. Their house of worship had been forced to move many times and seen a long procession of ministers since suffering an act of devastation, which had occurred on a Sunday much like this one.[22]

There was a fire, Brecht began. It was a fire so horrific that Courtney Craighead, the church's deacon (who was standing nearby), couldn't even speak about his memories of the event. It was a fire set intentionally on June 24, 1973, resulting in the death of one-third of the MCC congregation at the time.[23] This fire, which had happened twenty-two years and one day before, at a hangout called the Up Stairs Lounge, remained so disturbing a memory that it never existed in the pages of American history. This tragedy, congregants knew, was in fact the only reason that the *Times-Picayune* had opted to send a reporter to hear their minister. "We gather here this morning to remember," Brecht continued. "Remembering, whether we like it or not, is part of the human condition. It is good as a way of acknowledging our grief."[24]

It was a horrific scene to relate: a fire in a busy bar on the fringe of New Orleans's French Quarter that was set with lighter fluid. On that evening, flames had invaded a sanctuary for blue-collar gay men. The fast-moving blaze overtook the second-floor bar with deep ties to the MCC faithful, but the destruction would extend well beyond church membership, claiming the lives of thirty-one men and one woman.[25]

Although it raged out of control for less than twenty minutes, the blaze left a fallout that shocked Carl Rabin, the coroner who would struggle to identify the bodies using jewelry and hotel room keys. Fingers and faces and bones were scorched beyond recognition. "They were just piled up," he said. "People in a mass. One falls, then another falls. It's just a mass of death. It's sickening."[26]

Then the story went silent. After a mere blip of coverage, it fell off the front pages of newspapers, and then from interior pages entirely. Local and national television channels would dedicate just a few minutes of on-the-scene coverage to the Up Stairs Lounge, in which survivors were interviewed with cameras to their backs, due to reporters' fear of legitimizing the gay lifestyle and victims' fear of outing themselves. Yet, in fact, the tragedy had affected nearly every segment of New Orleans's closeted gay community, estimated a month later by the local Gay People's Coalition to be from 40,000 to 100,000 of the city's then 600,000 residents. Most of the dead—educated and illiterate, young and old, white and black, including a hustler, a minister, and a dentist—perished within the fire's first 360 seconds.[27]

The Up Stairs Lounge, Brecht related to his flock, represented a moment that exposed a majority of citizens as at best apathetic toward homosexuals while also revealing that civil rights movements of the era were tone-deaf to homosexual plight. Indeed, civil rights and feminist constituencies in the 1970s did not leap to the defense of the Up Stairs Lounge victims.[28] The tragedy was not noted in *Distaff*, New Orleans's feminist magazine—it was a time when lesbians themselves were marginalized from "mainstream feminists"[29]—nor was there any mention in iconic black newspapers like *The Chicago Defender*, despite there being a black victim.

"This fire was a holocaust," Brecht intoned. "Perhaps not in the millions like in the forties, but surely just as devastating to the lesbian, gay, bisexual, and trans-gendered community." The immediate aftermath of this blaze—occurring on the last day of celebrations marking the fourth anniversary of the 1969 Stonewall Riots[30]—became a chilling moment of loss for those gay Americans who actually heard the story, who were long conditioned to the reality that their sorrows were quarantined from the heterosexual American dream. In a cartoon in the August 1973 issue of *The Advocate*, which was then a somewhat ragtag alternative newspaper, a man in a hospital bed was bandaged up like a mummy; in the background, his chart read "Up Stairs Bar Fire Victim."[31]

With its physical and emotional toll, the Up Stairs Lounge fire sat in stark contrast to the legendary riot that had taken place outside of the Stonewall Inn in New York City on June 28, 1969. On that day, homosexuals, transsexuals, and street kids had joined forces to resist New York Police Department officers who were raiding a gay bar and arresting the patrons. This act of defiance had become a wellspring for gay political recruitment.

In the wake of the Stonewall Riots, a new movement called Gay Liberation arose. It was a "radical thinking" and "militant" crusade—according to a newsletter distributed by the more conservative Homophile Action League—whose stated goal was "complete sexual liberation for all people" through the abolishment of institutions that forced homosexuals to "live two separate existences."[32] Gay

Liberation was a departure from the so-called homophile movement (the term derived from the Greek words *homo* and *phile*, meaning "same love"), which had led the fight for homosexual rights up until then. Standing in an oblique shadow of the Stonewall Riots, the Up Stairs Lounge fire would be a major test of Gay Liberation: Could the movement steward its people through a crisis? Would gay people recognize its right to lead?

Yet, as Dexter Brecht spoke twenty-two years later, the Up Stairs Lounge remained forgotten. Aspects of the fire were reminiscent of other notable events that had shaped social-justice movements. There was the Triangle Shirtwaist Factory fire of 1911, as previously mentioned, in which 147 people (mostly female garment workers) died in New York City. The owners of the Triangle factory had locked employees into the building to prevent theft and truancy—and thus imprisoned them in an inferno.[33] Similarly, at the Up Stairs Lounge, victims were trapped inside a burning structure because windows had been sealed with iron bars—bars overlooked in lax inspections by authorities.[34] Parallels could also be drawn with the 1963 firebombing of the Sixteenth Street Baptist Church in Birmingham, Alabama, which killed four young girls. Even though the Up Stairs Lounge fire was determined to be an arson—most likely by a disgruntled bar patron exacting revenge upon a rival gay clique—the homophobia that resulted from the tragedy and the conspiracy to erase its memory differed markedly from that outpouring of sympathy that accompanied those four deaths at the hands of the Ku Klux Klan.[35]

So why did the Up Stairs Lounge remain obscure? Brecht asked. While the Triangle fire had led to mobilization for the labor movement and the Birmingham bombing had served both as a rallying cry and an elegy for the civil rights movement, the Up Stairs Lounge fire had not been a turning point for homosexual rights in America. Civil rights leaders in 1963 had advocates in northern papers like *The New York Times*, and labor leaders in 1911 had political champions like New York State assemblyman Al Smith, who later ran for president.[36] By contrast, the Up Stairs Lounge fire received no political attention or investigative stories from a national newspaper.

The mainstream reaction to the fire ranged from silence and avoidance to trivialization and demonization. This response could be seen in the comedic quips of locals, in the refusal of state and local officials to issue statements of sympathy for victims and families, and in the abandonment of the investigation by the New Orleans Police Department, which led to no charges or prosecutions even though a prime suspect was taken into custody and then lost, due to carelessness. Other local disasters, such as a fire at the Rault Center office building that killed six people in November 1972, received greater news coverage for a longer period of time than did the Up Stairs Lounge.[37]

Long before the existence of the Up Stairs Lounge, forces had conspired to suppress homosexuals in New Orleans. In 1958, a New Orleans police superintendent sent a letter to forty-two fellow police chiefs inquiring about methods of combating the "problem of homosexuals and lesbians." Other undesirables throughout the French Quarter, he noted, could be handled with existing laws. But with homosexuals, the policeman complained, "most of them are gainfully employed, or have a source of income from their families, and are not engaged in crime for profit."[38] Twenty-four police departments, from Washington, D.C., to Chicago, responded to that letter with sympathetic suggestions.[39]

At Tulane University, the city's premier private educational institution, Dr. Robert Heath, chair of the Department of Psychiatry and Neurology, conducted "gay conversion" experiments, published in two medical research papers in 1972, with university approval and some state funding. Listed as a "mental disorder" in the *Diagnostic and Statistical Manual* of the American Psychiatric Association, homosexuality was a condition that fell well within Heath's purview to treat and investigate.[40] Heath's research on a homosexual patient codenamed B-19 was particularly grim. Heath described how he had drilled stainless steel electrodes into nine regions of patient B-19's brain, with wires dangling out of the man for more than ten days, and paired electrode stimulation with pornographic images of women to create sexual arousal, thus building a Pavlovian association that culminated in a bizarre lovemaking session between the gay man and a well-compensated female prostitute.[41]

The Roman Catholic Church of the time significantly contributed to the general air of homophobia. Two months before the fire, an interfaith group called Morality in Media of Louisiana paid for a half-page ad in the *Times-Picayune*, which called for the "deletion of obscene language and immorality" in the news. "The problems of homosexuality, prostitution, adultery, promiscuity, perversion," the ad read, "must not be treated as normal behavior."[42] Signing the message "Faithfully yours" was Archbishop Philip M. Hannan, head of the Archdiocese of New Orleans.

Thus did the city's civil, scientific, and religious authorities each perform a pivotal role in the oppression and censorship of gay life, which coalesced into successful campaigns to prevent them from organizing in the open. Gays were sinners, said religion, sexual psychopaths, said science, and sex criminals, said the law. It's no stretch to say that the media reflected the same bias. If one looks at the number of mentions in the *Times-Picayune*, the Rault Center fire had five days of front-page articles and twenty-one letters to the editor were published, while the Up Stairs Lounge—with five times the victims—spent only two days on page 1 and just two letters to the editor appeared.[43]

Likewise, the American public remained largely committed to a campaign of gay oppression. Seventy percent of Americans, according to a 1973 survey conducted by the National Opinion Research Center (NORC) at the University of Chicago, thought adult homosexual relations were "always wrong." By and large, the public viewed talk of sexual "orientation" with suspicion, believing that there was one true alignment for sexuality—heterosexuality—and all other alignments represented the blunders of heterosexuals needing intervention. "There are no homosexuals—only people with homosexual problems," wrote Dr. Daniel Cappon, a preeminent psychologist in the field of sexual deviance. Journalist Mike Wallace, in a 1967 CBS News special, "The Homosexuals," summed up prevailing attitudes as such: "Homosexuality is an enigma. Even in this era of bold sexual mores, it remains a subject that people find disturbing, embarrassing in their reluctance to discuss it." Another NORC poll said nearly 35 percent of Americans opposed the idea of allowing a homosexual to speak in public.[44]

It's little wonder that Gay Liberation attracted no political sponsorship following the Up Stairs Lounge. There was simply no support, certainly not in an era when more than one third of the public contested the idea of First Amendment rights for homosexuals. Moon Landrieu, the progressive mayor of New Orleans, remained out of town for several weeks after the incident—on vacation and supposedly unreachable in Europe. Governor Edwin Edwards—the self-declared "crook" of the 1990s—would studiously avoid phone calls and telegrams in 1973 from ministers asking him to declare a statewide day of mourning.[45] President Richard Nixon, perhaps not even aware of the tragedy, offered no condolences on behalf of the nation.

Speaking in 1995, Dexter Brecht told his congregants, "It is time to go back to the fire that the media and the historians have forgotten."[46] The preacher then recited the names of the thirty-two victims, pausing after each one—the rhythmical beat emphasizing that every name was that of a real human being:

Joseph Henry Adams
Reginald Adams Jr.
Guy O. Andersen
Joe William Bailey
Luther Thomas Boggs
Louis Horace Broussard
Herbert Cooley
Donald Walter Dunbar
Adam Roland Fontenot
David Stuart Gary
Horace Getchell
John Thomas Golding Sr.
Gerald Hoyt Gordon
Glenn Richard Green
James Walls Hambrick
Kenneth Paul Harrington
William R. Larson
Ferris LeBlanc

> *Robert Lumpkin*
> *Leon Richard Maples*
> *George Stephen Matyi*
> *Clarence Joseph McCloskey Jr.*
> *Duane George Mitchell*
> *Larry Stratton*
> *Willie Inez Warren*
> *Eddie Hosea Warren*
> *James Curtis Warren*
> *Dr. Perry Lane Waters Jr.*
> *Douglas Maxwell Williams*
> *Unidentified white male*
> *Unidentified white male*
> *Unidentified white male*[47]

More than a third were veterans, men who had served their country while risking the punishment of an undesirable discharge if they were discovered as gay. More than a third were under the age of thirty. More than a third were practicing Christians—baptized, confirmed, and active members of their religious communities. At least seven of the victims had been married to women prior to embracing their homosexuality; as a result, six men were fathers of young children, which defied prevailing stereotypes. Yes, Brecht noted, three of the victims were charred so horrendously that they could never be identified. For their loved ones, they had simply "disappeared"; they were buried without gravestones in the city's potter's field.[48]

In reading the names aloud, Brecht did not mean to belabor the tally of carnage. He didn't call out the fourteen men and one woman who had been injured by the fire, many grievously. But his recitation did move congregants to tears; their wails and sniffling were mixed with the muted sounds of the photographer's camera. Brecht had wondered whether he should have mentioned which of the victims were MCC members, but he'd decided against it when he considered the Catholic Church and its role in dismissing the tragedy. Despite pleas for the archbishop to do so back in 1973, Philip Hannan had not offered a resounding statement of sympathy for the (Stairs Lounge, although he had within hours of the Ra, the previous autumn.[49]

All events leading up to 1995 suggested that the Up St, had fallen by the wayside—a sad but seemingly isolated in spoke more to fire codes and public safety initiatives than to human rights in America. That the fire occurred at a gay bar, where homosexuals met and pursued each other sexually—as if the Lounge were a bathhouse where men paraded in towels and sodomized each other in stalls—seemed to diminish its power as a metaphor of injustice.[50] Some New Orleanians, of course, had made valiant efforts to revive the story.

Just a year before Brecht memorialized the dead, in 1994, the site of the fire became a stop on a "gay heritage" walking tour of the French Quarter, led by historian Roberts Batson, but it was hardly a point of pilgrimage or reflection for most who knew the story, much less the uninformed who passed by unaware. Between 1989 and 1991, Johnny Townsend, a local author, had heroically interviewed more than thirty Up Stairs Lounge survivors and then written a chronicle called *Let the Faggots Burn*. In conducting his research, he encountered widespread caginess and determined that there was still "such a strange feeling about the fire."[51] For example, Floyd Getchell, the brother of victim Horace "Skip" Getchell, sent Townsend a letter declining to speak about the fire. As explanation, Getchell expressed that he had no wish to "open an old wound" for himself. Townsend couldn't get a local book publisher, much less a national press, to take on his completed manuscript—"these people aren't very interesting," one editor told him—so copies of it circulated about town, passed from friend to friend like a message moved along an underground network.[52]

The deadliest blaze on record in New Orleans history, as well as the largest mass killing of gays and lesbians in the United States until the 2016 massacre at Pulse, had become so downplayed that a 1991 exhibit at the Louisiana State Museum about historic fires in New Orleans managed to exclude the Up Stairs Lounge entirely.[53] When Up Stairs Lounge survivor Stewart Butler and activist Rich Magill saw this display, they immediately brought the omission to the museum's attention. "Rich and I picked up on that and said, 'We've got to do something about this shit,'" recalled Stewart Butler. "So we started bitching and complaining." Museum curator Wayne Phillips now characterizes the interactions more diplomatically. "The curator of the time, who put together the exhibition, and the museum director were both terribly embarrassed and ashamed," he recalled. The museum's solution was to place a small, text-based placard on the wall until the exhibit was taken down.[54] No announcements or public apologies were forthcoming or considered necessary.

The Up Stairs Lounge was a tinderbox,[55] calling to mind the days of home hearths and fire lighters so unstable they had to be hid away in metal chests. The tragedy proved to be a literal tinderbox, an inferno that destroyed a location, as well as a political tinderbox in the repression it exposed, of a nation refusing to acknowledge the very fact that homosexuals existed, and, finally, a psychological tinderbox in its spotlighting of an underclass of closeted gays who feared defining themselves as a minority group, lest they attract attention. By degrees, some survivors of the fire faced a fate more scandalous than that of the deceased: outed after their names were published in newspapers, shamed into silence by straights and fellow gays wishing to hurry past the event and hobbled by post-traumatic stress.[56]

In 1988, *The Times-Picayune* dedicated just one-quarter of one page, in an interior section, to an article about the fire's fifteenth anniversary which included this blunt assessment from survivor Stewart Butler: "A tragedy that, as far as I know, no good came of." On its twentieth anniversary, in 1993, there were no public events memorializing the Up Stairs Lounge, and again the *Times-Picayune* had a single story.[57]

Admittedly, a strange and polemic history surrounded this event. In the twelve months before the fire, beginning in June 1972, the death penalty had been halted by the U.S. Supreme Court, abortion legalized through *Roe v. Wade*, and American ground troops withdrawn from Vietnam, at least in principle, at the Paris Peace Accords. It seemed like a time of fundamental change, and, in a coup for the free press, *The Washington Post* won a Pulitzer Prize for its unfolding coverage of the Watergate break-in.

Dexter Brecht had been in high school in small-town Iowa when all this unfolded.[58] Questions reverberated in his mind. How come he had never heard of the Up Stairs Lounge? Why hadn't everyone? Gaining momentum, he implored those gathered to bring the story to the attention of the wider public, just as Christ had revived Lazarus, a man dead and entombed in a cave for three days in the Gospels. "We demand that the stone be rolled away," proclaimed Brecht. "We must demand that it be unbound and set free."[59] The image of Lazarus emerging from the tomb in his burial shroud, foreshadowing the Resurrection, epitomized the journey of many MCC congregants—or gay Christians of any stripe—out of the darkness of the closet and into the light.[60]

With these words, Brecht announced the creation of a church committee to honor the fire victims. Its primary goal was to place a plaque or memorial at the site of the Up Stairs Lounge by 1998, the twenty-fifth anniversary of the tragedy. Such an initiative would elevate the legacy of the Up Stairs Lounge by making it one of just a few events in gay rights history to receive some form of permanent recognition before the millennium. Such a commemoration would also signify the attainment of an objective set forth by Troy Perry, the founding pastor of the Metropolitan Community Church, for a "living memorial" to ensure that the fire victims would never be forgotten—a call for public acknowledgment that had gone unanswered since 1973.[61]

As Brecht offered these views, he considered whether he wandered too far for his people to follow. Was he just refighting old wars? He wondered if his own deacon, Courtney Craighead, would abandon or support him in front of others. "He really didn't feel like he wanted to bring it all back up again," recalled Brecht. When the young minister had first come to New Orleans, he'd assumed "everyone involved would want to acknowledge and claim the significance of the event."[62] However, he met with reticence when he suggested the idea of memorializing the tragedy and rekindling its memory, an act that could potentially embarrass the city and its now vocal and tourist-friendly gay community. Every Labor Day weekend, tens of thousands of homosexuals poured into New Orleans to celebrate the festival of Southern Decadence.

Yet, unable to remain silent, the minister had chosen to speak his piece. "And let us hope there won't be another fire," he concluded. The man fell silent. The congregation was silent at first, too, then burst into applause. The St. Roch church was suddenly filled with a new-found energy, as well as the paradoxical euphoria that can flow from the venting of grief. Brecht ended the service with a blessing. Elated, he hugged Deacon Craighead and walked toward Mark Thompson of the *Times-Picayune*. The reporter had many questions. Although he had been born within days of this event, in July of 1973, and raised in New Orleans by liberal parents, he had never heard about the Up Stairs Lounge until this day.[63]

People crowded in, impeding Brecht's progress as they suddenly felt compelled to share stories and memories. Courtney Craighead reached Thompson ahead of Brecht and pulled him aside. "I spent most of that first night at Charity Hospital," the deacon volunteered, his voice soft, "consoling those who were alive and identifying the dead." He told Thompson that he would probably chair the committee to commemorate the fire victims. "This is really the first time it has been brought out," Craighead continued, reflecting on the novelty of discussing the tragedy in public. Curiously, Craighead used the word "out" as if the bar fire itself had been closeted to this point. Yet, even with this change, Courtney Craighead leaned in and asked Thompson not to publish his name in a story about the fire, for fear of harassment.[64]

: ACT I :
FIRE

CHAPTER I

Brotherhood of Men

June 24, 1973

Sunday started late that day, as Sunday mornings in New Orleans—then, and still now—tend to be annexed as part of Saturdays. Douglas "Buddy" Rasmussen, manager of a popular Iberville Street gay bar, didn't leave home much before noon. The day was roasting in a way distinct to the region, the sun beating on the clapboard Creole cottages of the Lower Garden District.[1]

Buddy's lover, Adam Fontenot, roused himself as his beau showered and shaved, preparing for what would be the busiest day of the week. Sundays had become madcap occasions at Buddy's bar since the establishment of a "beer bust" from 5:00 to 7:00 p.m. That drink special—two hours of unlimited suds for one dollar, plus a refundable fifty-cent deposit for the mug—had proven an irresistible affair for a certain cadre of gay men. Adam usually accompanied Buddy to beer bust night, but he tended to eschew draft beer for the harder stuff.[2]

Although both Buddy and Adam were in their early thirties, in many respects they were a joining of opposites. Buddy was tall and winsome, with a basketball player's physique. Adam, on the other hand, was short and a bit fey, as one said, more of a genteel Southern dandy. Their upbringings could not have diverged further. Buddy had left an abusive household in Houston at age eighteen and enlisted in the air force, while Adam hailed from landowners with a lineage that went back to the original French Acadians of Louisiana. Adam was university educated and spoke six languages fluently, while Buddy had managed a 7-Eleven. Buddy was out of the closet, while Adam remained conflicted about revealing his private life—even though Buddy had spent holidays with the Fontenot clan as Adam's "friend."[3]

Buddy always seemed to have a job, while Adam appeared, paradoxically, too smart for his menial work, which never lasted. Buddy made friends easily and told it like it was, while Adam was more of an acquired taste, a character who spoke with a faux-English accent to impress. Nevertheless, through some alchemy, the two men had met and fallen deeply in love. They were nearly inseparable in their four years of being together, buying a home and wearing rings to mark their commitment.[4] Other gay friends aspired to a love like Buddy and Adam's, even if their couplehood was not without risk. The boot heel of the law loomed as a constant threat to their acts of tenderness; either could be reported and arrested as sex criminals through various methods (for example, local ordinances made it unlawful to rent, lease, or buy a house for "homosexuals, lesbians or sex perverts").[5] Buddy and Adam's cottage on St. Andrews Street could, therefore, be declared a house of ill repute and repossessed, if anyone cared to do so.[6]

Their home was what was called a "double," with two front doors and two street addresses for the postman. Buddy shared half of the residence with Adam; they rented the other half to a redheaded welder named Linn "Rusty" Quinton, who was openly gay and wont to show off his work-hewn muscles in mesh T-shirts. Quinton, in fact, made extra cash by helping out on Sundays as a busboy for Buddy. The three housemates gravitated around the same scene—one that was sexually liberated if also community-minded, with singles and couples respecting each other's monogamy, if so declared.[7] Friends commonly used the word "lover," as opposed to "boyfriend" or "partner"—the latter coming into vogue in subsequent decades—to signify a committed relationship. The terms "husband" and "fiancé" were not used except in jest. In an era when same-sex marriage did not exist, mainstream society perceived gay commitment ceremonies as make-believe. By 1973, Buddy had started noticing the overtures of a bar regular named Bill Duncan, but he and Adam had remained true to their promises.[8]

Theirs was a close-knit brotherhood of men, what Stewart Butler jokingly called a coterie of "friends, tricks, and associates," in which almost everyone was gay and went by a nickname or slightly altered pseudonym to start fresh—away from their painful pasts.[9] Most saw one another regularly and dined at each other's homes. Many, as it happened, were also members of the nearby Metropolitan Community Church (MCC), but those who didn't cotton to the image of a gay-friendly Jesus still made their way to the French Quarter to raise a glass to the Roman god of parties, Bacchus.

Buddy and Adam's neighborhood boasted a protected society of gay men, whose proximity created a sense of family in a larger world dominated by prejudice. Just down the street from their home lay the cottage the MCC was then operating out of and, on the side, the rectory of gay pastor Bill Larson: a clean-cut, fatherly sort of fellow. A few blocks beyond that, MCC parishioner Ricky Everett—blond and petite, said to be precious-looking—was crashing at the apartment of Henry Kubicki, a proverbial tall, dark, and handsome sort. However, as only friends like Ricky knew, Henry's "quiet cool" disguised serious hearing and vision impairments, which frustrated and confused admirers who sought him out solely for his looks.[10]

After a sudden breakup, Ricky had moved in with Henry on Coliseum Street until he could find more permanent digs, and the two shared a queen-size bed platonically.[11] Ricky made the most of being unattached and had invited a twenty-year-old suitor named Ronnie Rosenthal to fly in from Atlanta that weekend. Ricky and Ronnie had hit it off at an MCC religious conference and wanted to explore their connection. They arranged for Ronnie to stay in a New Orleans suburb with Ricky's mother, who seemed to be oblivious of her son's sexuality. "It was no big deal," recalled Ricky. "My mother just took it as a friend of mine visiting."[12]

About a block away from Ricky and Henry stood a house on Prytania Street rented by Stewart Butler, the outspoken hippie of the group who grew hydroponic weed in the second story of his residence and listened to the Grateful Dead. "The shit that we've done, Lordy!" exclaimed Stewart's longtime friend and partner in crime Steven Duplantis. "We used to make a hobby of going out and seeing how many we could pick up and bring back to Prytania Street, who got all of 'em first or how many each one of us got." As a man who had only embraced his gayness in his late thirties, Stewart Butler was, in his own words, "making up for lost time." Stewart could often be seen, as they said, on the prowl with his lover, Alfred Doolittle, and joined by their dog, a mix-breed terrier.[13]

The home of Mitch Mitchell was also close to Stewart's domicile. A boisterous man, Mitch served as a deacon assisting Bill Larson at the MCC. Mitch had a garrulous, if not irascible, personality. Larger than life, he weighed about 300 pounds and proudly wore a necklace to notify medical personnel of his diabetes. Mitch's lover, Horace Broussard, was a barber and a confirmed "chubby chaser"—for him, someone like Mitch was a rare and ravishing catch.[14] In the promise of a new gay world in the early 1970s, Mitch and Horace made a nest like Buddy and Adam.

Living a bit farther north was MCC parishioner Herbert "Hugh" Cooley, who was probably still asleep in his apartment as the sun climbed to its apex. Hugh took over as bartender at 8:00 p.m. on Sundays, at the end of Buddy's shift.[15] All together, these men formed a makeshift family—singles, duos, and third wheels who conspired to hide one another's sexualities from biological family members, who drove each other to doctor and dentist appointments, who loaned one another money, and who even, when necessary, retrieved each other from police lockup.

IT WAS STILL before noon when Buddy and Adam ducked into their car, rolled down the windows, and left St. Andrews Street behind as they headed downtown. The scaffolding of the Superdome, a crown of a public works project for the city and state, immediately came into view.[16] About halfway finished, the football stadium's skeletal frame looked like a cross between a UFO and a mushroom.

Soon glass towers of the Central Business District loomed, the largest of which was One Shell Square, a business center for Shell Oil.[17] Fluorescent signs and department stores materialized as Buddy and Adam's car crossed Canal Street, a major thoroughfare with a center-laid walkway that once housed the streetcar tracks memorialized in movies, brochures, and Tennessee Williams's *A Streetcar Named Desire.* Canal Street dead-ended near the river and a recently installed statue of Joan of Arc, a gift to the city from Charles de Gaulle, the legendary leader of Free France. When the statue was unveiled in October 1972, Mayor Moon Landrieu hailed it for transforming what had been a "rundown area" into a "landmark showcase." This was but one instance of a city constantly slapping a fresh coat of paint on itself, lest it give in to decay and return to the state of nature; alligators would occasionally return through the drainage canals when the sluices were opened.[18]

Past Joan of Arc was the International Trade Mart, a riverfront tower and headquarters for the Port of New Orleans. Perched near the mouth of the mighty Mississippi, New Orleans had long been an entrepôt and the gateway to America's breadbasket. The busy port, where casks and bales had floated south on barges and were transferred to oceangoing cargo ships before the river split into a delta and ran into the Gulf of Mexico, was a major source of revenue for the city.

The International Trade Mart building had been erected in the 1960s under the direction of Clay Shaw. A man of aristocratic bearing who wore seersucker suits and lived in a French Quarter mansion, Shaw had counted himself among the New Orleans elite. Years earlier, he had organized the 1953 sesquicentennial celebration of the Louisiana Purchase, an event that had attracted the newly elected President Dwight Eisenhower. Shaw's position in the city seemed assured, having accompanied New Orleans mayors on trade missions. However, as only his close friends knew, Clay Shaw lived two lives: conservative businessman in public and homosexual bon vivant in private. His feat of compartmentalization had come crashing down when Jim Garrison, the Orleans Parish district attorney, bizarrely arrested him in 1967 and charged him with colluding to assassinate President John F. Kennedy.[19]

This would be the first and only trial brought against a living suspect for the killing of the president, and District Attorney Jim Garrison worked the limelight, as prosecutor, to his full advantage. Garrison postulated to the press, using defamatory tropes of the era, that Shaw's involvement made the assassination a "homosexual thrill-killing." The prosecutor loudly declared that an individual associated with the presidential assassin Lee Harvey Oswald, named "Clay Bertrand" by the Warren Commission, was none other than New Orleans resident Clay Shaw. Garrison's claim that Bertrand and Shaw were one and the same person, an apparent break in the case touted by the press as the final reveal of a "mystery man," ultimately turned out to be a dubious connection, at best, and a knowingly baseless one, at worst. In fact, Garrison happened to be a man with his own set of demons: during his crusade, Garrison was concurrently investigated by an Orleans Parish grand jury for allegedly molesting a thirteen-year-old boy at the New Orleans Athletic Club.[20]

Unfazed by his personal inquiry, Garrison continued to impugn Shaw. During the 1969 show trial, which lasted a month, Shaw would, as *The New York Times* noted in his obituary, "chain smoke filter cigarettes impassively at the defense table as prosecution witnesses described him as a flamboyant homosexual." Having raided Shaw's home and discovered private sexual paraphernalia, Garrison manipulated the businessman's secret, and his wish to remain closeted, to cast a haze of intrigue over the case. The foundation of Garrison's argument rested on a virtual clown parade of witnesses: the confessions left behind by a pilot named David Ferrie, dead from a cerebral hemorrhage that Garrison trumpeted as an "apparent suicide"; the hypnosis-induced testimony of a businessman named Peter Russo; the assurances of a convicted heroin user named Vernon Bundy; and the sworn statements of Charles Spiesel, a paranoid accountant who regularly fingerprinted his children to confirm that they had not been replaced by CIA doubles.[21]

"Gay people in New Orleans, after Clay Shaw was arrested, went into panic," noted local gay historian Roberts Batson, who happened to live near the Up Stairs Lounge crew. "Because if someone as prominent and important as Clay Shaw could be arrested and destroyed by Jim Garrison, who's next?" Clay Shaw, despite the humiliation, chose to provide his account of the ordeal to author James Kirkwood for the book *American Grotesque*: "In the early days after my arrest, Mr. Garrison said to a journalist that I'd never come to trial, I'd commit suicide first."[22]

Although the jury found Shaw not guilty after less than an hour of deliberations—an agonizing defeat for Garrison—the businessman suffered permanent damage to his reputation. His personal revelations, cast into public light, were not minor indiscretions but an imbroglio that created stigma and embarrassment.[23] Doubling down then on what seemed like less a prosecution than a personal vendetta, Garrison accused Shaw of several counts of perjury; a federal judge later dismissed these charges, ruling that they had been brought in bad faith,[24] but such a decision hardly provided solace or rehabilitation for the once accused.

The French Quarter beckoned ahead as Buddy and Adam continued their drive. This was New Orleans's oldest neighborhood—sometimes still called by its French name, Vieux Carré (literally, "Old Square")—which languished as a colorful ghetto in a city deeply at odds with itself. The Quarter was forever a place of the imagination, the home of wrought-iron balconies and Blanche DuBois, among other louche literary figures. On its pitched and gabled rooftops, said the legends, the Creole pirate Jean Lafitte leaped from house to house to ply his illicit business. The famously eccentric Ruthie "the Duck Girl" Moulin was constantly out walking her mallards, and the badly denigrated Clay Shaw still resided in the district on St. Peter Street.[25]

In the spiritual brew, voodoo spirits mixed with Catholic saints, houses of the "rising sun" with Gothic-inspired churches. Every Fat Tuesday was inevitably followed by an Ash Wednesday, just as mourners of the dead participated in gloomy-cum-joyous spectacles after burials called jazz funerals. Even the compass seemed to adjust to a different pull. A neighborhood called the West Bank lay east of the French Quarter. North, to any decent New Orleanian, was "lakeside" toward Lake Pontchartrain. South was "riverside" toward the Old Man. Reference to north, south, east, or west instantly revealed your status as a tourist. This amended sense of space reflected not just street lingo but reality for residents, who used these terms in police reports, land deals, and other legal documents.[26]

Scenery changed from steel and glass to stucco and brick as Buddy and Adam proceeded onward, but the French Quarter didn't officially begin until they crossed Iberville Street,[27] one block farther, which fell to the backside of Canal's swank hotels and department stores to offer the other side of commerce: twenty-four-hour bars and a drug fix, perhaps, or hustlers dabbling in the oldest profession for money, a meal, or both. Misadventures often ended on Iberville at gay-friendly establishments like Gene's Hideaway or Wanda's, both owned by an entrepreneur named Gene Davis, or around the corner at La Normandie Bar, where, in 1972, a gay bartender named Jerry Capplin had been found with his throat slashed and body stuffed into an ice cooler (as usual, the murder and trial had gone mostly unreported by the *Times-Picayune*). City institutions were attempting to downplay rising crime rates, which could easily stanch the procession of tourists.[28]

Buddy and Adam slipped into a ghetto sleeping off a routine hangover, but few streets on that Sunday were silent. Neighbors sipped coffee with chicory, an herbaceous additive brewed by New Orleanians for centuries, as they chatted on balconies and doorsteps. Bohemian artists took showers in art galleries. On nearby wharves, Greek and Norwegian sailors milled about barges that held the proverbial world's shipping. Down Decatur Street, the mealy aroma of grain wafted from the smokestacks of the Jackson Brewery, a local landmark known as the Jax. Tourists filtered down the pedestrian walkway of Royal Street, closed to daytime traffic by proclamation of Mayor Landrieu, and shopped for antiques.[29] Just a block south of Royal Street appeared the slightly more worn corner of Chartres and Iberville, Buddy and Adam's port of entry.

The couple parked and walked, crisscrossing the almost invisible border between rich and poor—the ivory tower of the new Marriott Hotel casting a shadow near their feet. Up ahead was the dark canopy they sought near the Chartres Street intersection. It bore the cursive words "Up Stairs." The text, partially blocked by the rain roofing of the bar next door, was intentionally easy to miss. The sign didn't offer a hint of impropriety or any enticement to enter, nor did it aim to titil-late with a turn of phrase. Instead, it appeared like a public notice of a place off the beaten path.

Buddy turned the key in the wrought-iron door, marked 604 Iber-ville Street, and started up the thirteen wooden steps, so old that they whined when you climbed them. The building dated at least to the 1870s, when Iberville had been called Custom House Street.[30] Some of its fixtures and systems looked to be plucked from a museum. There was room to climb the stairs two abreast, but not enough to extend your arms without clipping the pipes and wires running over brick. Buddy had made these eyesores more palatable by attempting to cover them in burlap fabric. Light barely shone inside this entry-way. Heading past wood-paneled walls and curtains was much like entering a portal—up, up, and away. This wasn't a saloon stumbled into by accident: the place was somewhat concealed, and only those in the know entered.[31]

Buddy pivoted at a landing with a small window and scaled the final steps. He unlocked a steel door to the bar appropriately called the Up Stairs Lounge. Empty, the bar possessed a hushed quality. Sur-faces gleamed in the light of windows and smelled of cigarette smoke. Buddy flipped on the lights. Red was the scheme: red-flocked wallpa-per, red indoor-outdoor carpeting, pink-orange laminate on the bar, red fabric streaming across the drop ceiling. Even the bar stools had red seats. The place looked to be cloaked in a velvet robe, giving what Susan Fosberg, the arts critic of the *Vieux Carré Courier*, a local alter-native weekly, called the impression of "discreet elegance." (Stewart Butler begged to differ with this assessment: "I don't know if it was elegant," he remembered. "Well, it just hid the bare walls.")[32]

The *Courier*, edited by Bill Rushton, an openly gay man, reviewed the Up Stairs Lounge as a "warm and congenial haunt" in its 1972 French Quarter bar guide, a "big intimate room" where "middle aged queens and their trade flock." *Times-Picayune* writer Howard Jacobs pronounced it a "first-class tonsil coolery." Stewart Butler thought of it as a "social club."[33] Tables and chairs were crammed, inviting ran-dom interactions; this was less an intended feature than a remnant of the pickup bar that had previously held the lease—telephone cords had run from table to table as a method of fostering hookups between business executives and ladies of the evening.[34] Buddy had removed the phones but not the furniture or wan sense of joié de vivre.

The Up Stairs Lounge was surprisingly roomy, linked across three contiguous buildings and wrapped by twelve-inch-thick brick walls. The bar itself, the locus of activity, was stationed parallel to Iberville Street in the first room.[35] Near one end of the bar was a small, elevated stage with a white baby grand piano. Its worn keys suggested that they had been frequently played. Adam Fontenot, a few drinks deep, would sometimes sit at the bench and come to life crooning jazz ditties. A jukebox situated nearby was loaded with contemporary hits, as well as records brought in by Buddy and regular patrons.[36]

Close by was a window overlooking a fire escape, which stood beside the entrance to the tiny bathrooms—the only commodes in the place. Lines frequently formed here that stretched to the front door. Often, the inconvenience provided an opportunity to make friends while commiserating over the call of nature. Behind the bar, among assorted liquor bottles, stood a decorative fountain. Regulars called this first room the "bar area," but there were other, quieter spaces in the Up Stairs Lounge.[37]

A long archway provided exit from the bar area, which was festooned that Sunday with Fourth of July decorations to publicize an upcoming party, into a parlorlike space, smaller than the first, with tables and a dance floor. This was called the "dance area," where bodies whirled and drag queens like Marcy Marcell performed on Sundays for charity shows. At the time, the Up Stairs Lounge offered the only drag revue in the Quarter other than Club My-O-My, whose previous location had burned down without explanation the previous year. Beyond the dance area stood an unmarked door to a final section, a theater space often locked up and overlooked by patrons. The New Orleans MCC had hosted prayer meetings there for a span. Patrons also put on theatrical performances there, sometimes for charity, at other times just for kicks.[38]

Adam parked himself on a stool while Buddy Rasmussen tallied the previous day's receipts and ducked out to make a bank deposit. The owner of the Up Stairs Lounge, a gay man named Phil Esteve, had basically handed Buddy the reins to the business. As the "heart and soul" of the bar, Buddy had managed the Up Stairs Lounge since its opening night, on Halloween in 1970. In fact, it was Buddy who had championed the beer-bust idea to Phil, and the drink special had grown in popularity; by the early summer of 1973, it drew a hundred or more people reliably each Sunday.[39]

Buddy ran the place efficiently—no small order by Iberville standards. His rules were clear and consistently enforced: no hustling the customers, although hustlers were allowed to drink *as* customers during breaks from work. Hustlers could even date patrons, but monetary solicitation was strictly forbidden. For example, a hustler nicknamed Napoleon, who dressed like the French dictator as a calling card, had met his lover, Stanley Plaisance, while nursing an after-hours drink at the Up Stairs Lounge. Napoleon had made romantic overtures to Stanley but wasn't soliciting him, and so the two hit it off as Buddy observed. Love followed, surprisingly, and Napoleon abandoned his career Iberville's "queer legionnaire."[40]

The Up Stairs Lounge banned "tearoom sex," the furtive encounters that often took place in dark corners or bathroom stalls of gay bars, frequently the only places where gay men could then steal a private moment. Nonetheless, according to patron Michael Scarborough, a "small hole" did exist in the partition between toilets stalls to facilitate peeping or previewing the so-called merchandise. Ricky Everett did not recall said hole, although he did remember a chalkboard, which Buddy had installed in the bathroom as a deterrent to patrons scrawling phone numbers and explicit messages on the walls. But Ricky could be rather innocent; although he had been the childhood best friend of Stanley Plaisance, and even had sleepovers with him when they were teenagers, Ricky professed to have no idea that Stanley might be gay, too, until he saw his old friend at the Up Stairs Lounge in the arms of Napoleon.[41] Although they'd drifted apart since high school, Stanley and Ricky hugged and burst out laughing. Charmed by this mutual revelation, they immediately reconnected.

In addition, no drug use or drug dealing was tolerated inside Buddy's bar. Nevertheless, if a patron like Stewart Butler came already high, well, that was his business. "It was off the beaten path," Buddy Rasmussen told a *Times-Picayune* reporter in the 1990s. He continued, "But the Upstairs had a regular, steady clientele. Mostly employed people, mostly gay, but some straight, some women, too." Ricky had similar memories: "It was just a wide variety of people," he said. "We had politicians who come in there. We had doctors, lawyers, everyday hourly-wage blue-collar people." Writing after the fire, *Vieux Carré Courier* editor and bar regular Bill Rushton attested, "The Up Stairs set out to give Iberville Street a new kind of anchor."[42]

Surprisingly for New Orleans, Buddy set a policy of no sloppiness due to overimbibing. Nights could end with Buddy calling a cab and serving a patron coffee or a soft drink. Buddy even stocked milk behind the bar, which he'd occasionally mix with a dollop of vodka and serve to Stewart Butler's dog, Jocko, the unofficial mascot of the place. "He used to sit up on the bar stool," Stewart recalled, laughing. "A bar-hound, literally," he continued. "Cause it didn't take much. He'd get a little smashed, and I remember one time he got out of the place, and, when we noticed, we had to run out and caught him down near Exchange Place."[43]

While this was a gay bar where people met and danced and dated, the staff did their best to encourage responsibility without being preachy. Perhaps this refreshingly sane attitude of fun within reason was why Bob McAnear, a plainclothes narcotics investigator working for U.S. Customs in New Orleans, had been visiting the Up Stairs Lounge both on and off duty from its inception. Bob often brought along his wife, Bettye, who had befriended Buddy Rasmussen years before.[44]

"Buddy and Phil [Esteve] invited us over to look at the proposed bar they were going to open," Bob McAnear recalled. "I helped tear up the linoleum covering the floor." Bettye had a passion for acting and directing in local theater troupes, and so Bob had, over the years, met countless gay men whom he deemed to be decent folk.[45]

The McAnears had grown particularly fond of Buddy and Adam as a couple and trusted them to babysit their kids whenever Bob was out on a case or Bettye was rehearsing for the New Orleans Opera. The couples became like family to each other—with a closeness that always extended into the Up Stairs Lounge. "The guys trusted me, and knew their being gay was not a problem," explained Bob. "Due to their trust, if I needed information, the guys knew everything that happened in the streets, and they would give me information that other lawmen couldn't get." He continued. "I never betrayed that trust."[46]

This was New Orleans, after all, a Mediterranean and Caribbean melting pot that preferred to be Janus-faced on a vast range of topics, including the factual validity of one's so-called racial makeup. This Creole culture would rather accept moral incongruities as part of human nature than try to root them out in a witch hunt. The Puritan mind-set never touched the Paris of the South.[47] Contradictory actions and beliefs could be sustained in one body so long as that person held them discreetly in two hands and—to borrow a phrase from Matthew 6:3—never "let your left know what your right hand is doing." Terrible things were known to happen in New Orleans when the left hand acknowledged the right, and no one wished for the trouble that could spoil the party, even for a moment.

Quickly drawn into the bar's inviting culture, Bob's wife, Bettye, directed several melodramas in the back theater hall. Art critics like Susan Fosberg and female friends like Jeanne Gosnell also made the Up Stairs Lounge their watering hole.[48] It was just the kind of neighborhood place that seemed to welcome all, its overt friendliness an antithesis to the hostility of the outside world. Several times, owner Phil Esteve invited female secretaries from Touro Hospital, his former workplace. Longshoremen working the river, known by nicknames like Smokie and Cocoa (probably racially inspired monikers), lived above the bar in a flophouse and became regular faces. And, of course, countless gay couples, like Deacon Mitch Mitchell and Horace Broussard or Michael Scarborough and Glenn Green, made the Up Stairs Lounge their base of operations, from which they'd make incursions into deeper parts of the Quarter.[49]

Perhaps because management made sure the bar's rules were obeyed, it had never been raided. Right after the fire, Sergeant Frank

Hayward, information officer for the New Orleans Police Department (NOPD), confirmed to *The Advocate* that "the department has no records of any arrests at the Up Stairs—for thievery or anything else." When the Up Stairs Lounge had opened back in 1970, it was the first gay establishment in New Orleans to receive a dancing license.[50] This official sanction was significant for the safety of patrons. Historically, gay men in New Orleans and elsewhere could be arrested for making physical contact or shaking hands in a drinking establishment. For example, Napoleon had once been arrested at Caverns, a Bourbon Street bar, and booked for "dancing with a member of the same sex in an intimate embrace." Buddy Rasmussen regularly sent the NOPD notice of upcoming events, a signal that he operated the place as a legitimate enterprise, not an underworld lair.[51]

This was also an era where phrases like "discretion assured" and "strictly confidential" proliferated as gay code words to ease the fears of closeted men and advise that their patronage at a bar or membership in a social club would not jeopardize their privacy. Informal surveys estimated that about 75,000 homosexuals lived in New Orleans in 1971, but fewer than 1,000 could be called "out," by twenty-first-century standards. According to *Bob Damron's Address Book*, an annual travel guide for the gay vacationer, in 1972 New Orleans boasted two gay bathhouses, twenty-four gay and lesbian bars, and three restaurants that were particularly gay-friendly.[52] Thus was the gay community expanding its footprint in a town where, paradoxically, most homosexuals continued to wear the mask of heterosexuality.

Accordingly, Buddy, Adam, and their circle regarded the involuntary exposure of anyone's sexuality as a serious problem, and they took measures to avoid its ever happening. Newcomers to the Up Stairs Lounge, especially those acting uncomfortably or unaccompanied by a familiar face, could encounter a few minutes of suspicion or wariness until sounded out. Buddy would loop such a customer in by asking him to carry a pitcher to the piano or a coin to the jukebox. "Request a song, honey?" he would ask. The point wasn't to be conspiratorial or clannish. Men of any stage of "outness" were welcome. But in an age when gay sex was still criminalized and stigmatized, it was important to protect customers from a mugger seeking a mark; a sexually conflicted, violent assailant; a con artist looking for a blackmail victim; or anyone from the outside world looking to prey upon a man with a secret.[53]

Indeed, blackmailing homosexuals was a form of con artistry that had thrived for centuries. As late as 1967, as the *Chicago Tribune* reported, federal authorities exposed a nationwide blackmail ring targeting homosexuals. Subsequently, at least thirty persons were convicted on charges of extortion when an unnamed member of U.S. Congress from an eastern state was shaken down for $40,000 (then several years' pay for the average person), on the threat that his homosexual activities would be otherwise exposed. Of course, in keeping with the mores of the era, the *Tribune* didn't reveal the congressman's name, nor did any other publication. Other victims, said the report, included "two deans of eastern universities, several professors, business men, a movie actor, a television personality and a high ranking military officer who committed suicide the night before he was to testify before a New York county grand jury."[54]

Up Stairs Lounge regulars, more vulnerable to predation than members of the social elite, feared the blackmailer seeking something other than money. Such paranoia became a noticeable part of the gay psyche. "It was S.O.P. [standard operating procedure] at the Upstairs [sic] to know your customers," remembered the longshoreman known as Cocoa. "The management required you to be there with someone they knew before they would serve you." And there was always the possibility of gay-on-gay betrayal. Unscrupulous individuals were known to engage in the practice of "dropping a nickel" on a fellow homosexual—a term that signified using a pay phone to anonymously call a person's employer or family and report their location.[55]

If a new patron pitched in when Buddy asked for help, he passed the initial test and was considered a friend until proven otherwise. Through Buddy's efforts, the Up Stairs Lounge had succeeded in becoming an oasis where regular customers felt safe, less a hookup space than a hangout where friends and lovers could exhale and be themselves. "There was a brotherhood there," wrote Susan Fosberg. "People who understood, people with whom you could let your hair down. A place, perhaps, to find love." Buddy kept a microphone behind the bar and would call the names of regulars as they entered in a style reminiscent of announcer Ed McMahon, a venerable late-night television fixture as second in command to Johnny Carson on *The Tonight Show*. Buddy would announce, parodying the jolly McMahon, "Heeeeeeeere's Luther Boggs!"[56]

When Buddy didn't know a patron's name, he'd call them "Honey" or "Sweetheart." He was also known to wear one-piece leotards to lighten the mood. "It was an unusual mix of people, both in dress and appearance," remembered Up Stairs Lounge regular Paul Killgore, "but, to be honest with you, there was kind of a sweetness." Patrons would compete in tricycle races over zigzag courses between the tables or try to win the Easter bonnet contest. David Stuart Gary—or Piano Dave, as he was dubbed—would march up to the baby grand and ready the room with his signature "Ready, kiddies?" Sing-alongs ensued.[57]

This rich social dialogue, a dominant feature of the Lounge, also reflected the expressive sexual mores of the decade. According to the *Vieux Carré Courier*, "As you walk in Up Stairs first thing you notice is a picture of Queen Victoria seated with the caption, 'Even a Queen can get the Clap.'" There was plenty of kissing and ducking out to get a room, but those practices occurred in a relaxed, unpressured atmosphere. "It certainly was more accepting than some of the other gay bars that were down along Bourbon Street," recalled Killgore, "where, at that time, if you were going out, you wanted to look good, or you wanted to be in the company of attractive people." By contrast, Killgore explained, "When you went into the Up Stairs Lounge, nobody gave a fuck about that. I mean, just enjoy yourself. Be nice. Be polite. Behave."[58]

As sex and sexual expression were not frowned upon per se, the Lounge's main room was decorated with suggestive and erotic imagery, such as a tiny replica of a statue called the Farnese Hercules, the disrobed Grecian hero leaning on a giant club with an apple tucked behind his nape.[59] On the far wall, a naked Burt Reynolds—his revolutionary *Cosmopolitan* centerfold from 1972 enlarged to poster size—

grinned on a bearskin rug with a hand suggestively draped over his crotch; Reynolds was a newly minted star who, only the year before, had shown off his acting chops in the movie *Deliverance*. Elsewhere, an image of Olympic swimming champion Mark Spitz appeared, smiling with his thin mustache and chiseled frame, his seven gold medals dangling just above his star-spangled Speedo. Around 2:00 p.m. that Sunday, Buddy opened the bar for his first customer, Adam Fontenot, and handed him a drink.[60]

Sunday Service

Afternoon

The church service at Magazine Street, down the street from Buddy and Adam's house, caused a stir but not for any religious reason. The summer solstice had occurred just three days before, and that meant long days. The faithful entered the church's front door expecting an hour of worship in close quarters, the proximity of bodies creating a pungent aroma. Circulation could be sparse in a "double" Creole cottage like this one, erected without insulation and elevated a few feet off the ground to prevent the slow decay of mold. Humidity, so thick with vapor that breathing air could feel like crying tears, would almost routinely reach 100 percent. Add the singing and sweating of congregants inside New Orleans's only gay-friendly church, and matters could become unbearable with larger groups. Despite such deterrents, worshippers made the best of circumstances, since this was a sanctuary of their own, long struggled for and prayed for, and the only one that they could afford.[1]

Imagine the surprise of attendees on this, the last Sunday of June, when they crossed the porch and entered their church to be hit with the hum of an electric organ and an unanticipated blast of frigid air. Someone had donated a relatively expensive item: a window-unit air conditioner. Pastor Bill Larson thanked the anonymous benefactor for the generous gift to New Orleans's own Metropolitan Community Church.[2]

The coolness felt new, even fancy, for these working-class men of faith, who, as if in a Tennessee Williams play, typically ventilated their homes with fans; air-conditioning was a luxury relished only in bars or at the office. Heading inside, worshippers took their seats in a room about twelve feet wide and twenty feet deep, flanked by folding chairs angled toward an oaken table that they used as an altar. This table and its five Gothic arches, reminiscent of the five candles of Advent, had been salvaged and repaired by the pastor himself.[3]

Indeed, Bill Larson was known as a carpenter of some skill. He had moved a load-bearing wall to free up room and convert this private residence, with a floor plan like Buddy and Adam's home, into a gathering space. The sanctuary was tall and bright, with sieves of light falling in from side windows. The effect was ethereal and peaceful. New Orleans excelled at making rooms of these sorts. Bill had also maintained for himself and future pastors a small living quarters in a back room, generously referred to as the rectory. Most of this work he did at personal expense—using money he'd earned working nights— and at some risk, since the MCC did not own the building yet. The church rented the cottage on a lease-to-own basis and was saving for the down payment.[4] Standing with grace behind the altar he'd saved, Bill Larson welcomed gay Christians to another Sabbath on this first Sunday of the summer.

The room was lively, but Bill commanded it. He evoked a parental presence with his blond hair, sharp nose, and square chin. Bill was a tall, soft-spoken figure in his late forties who seemed to exude Midwestern humility. Originally from Kentucky, he had been born with the name William Roscoe Lairson and raised in crippling white poverty.[5] Bill's parents had married when his mother, Anna, was only sixteen. They had six children, with Bill being the baby of the brood. Bill's father was a gambler who died from drinking poison whiskey when Anna was three months pregnant with Bill. Then the widowed Anna Lairson uprooted her kids to small-town Ohio.[6]

There, Anna waitressed and received a mother's pension for child-rearing expenses, yet often left the children alone to raise one another. In Anna's care, Bill's six-year-old sister Dorothy ran into the street and was crushed beneath the wheels of a car. This death occurred around the time of Bill's first memories. While Anna received a financial settlement, the money was squandered.[7] Receiving reports that Anna was neglecting her children and entertaining men, the county paid a visit and assumed responsibility. Though Anna remained local, her children became dependents of the state. Subsequently, Anna was arrested on statutory charges while living in a shack on the city dump with Troy Howell, a disabled World War I veteran with sizable debts. In a local scandal, a county official turned up at their residence and hauled them to a courthouse to be married, under the threat that the two would otherwise be arrested for the sex crime of adultery.[8]

Bill's new stepfather was not able to accept Anna's children into his home. Thus, from age three to fifteen, Bill would be raised as "Roscoe," in the Butler County Children's Home[9] (apparently, he became Roscoe because there were already too many Williams at the facility). Although Anna hoped to spring her kids from county care someday, she never was able to do so, and neither were any of Bill's elder siblings. When Bill was a junior in high school, he enlisted in the armed forces. He served in the European theater and got married to his church sweetheart when he returned to the States. He and his young wife were both likely virgins, at the tail end of puberty, when they made lifelong vows. Bill's wife bore him a son and then left abruptly because he wished to become a Methodist minister.[10] Evidently, she did not want to be a preacher's wife. Bill eventually did become a lay minister and youth fellowship leader, despite the toll of losing his family. Abandoned and eventually divorced for the official reason of neglect, Bill became free in his thirties to explore his once-latent attraction to other men. By then, he had changed the spelling of his name from William Roscoe Lairson to William Ros Larson,[11] a nonlegal gesture common for homosexuals in this epoch, when aliases served as self-protection, a means to embrace what was then a radical new identity and avoid being outed in a newspaper, were that radical new identity to spur an arrest.

Bill never abandoned his religious calling, although a divinity school education never became a reality for him. He did what one did in those days: apprenticed in a trade and then worked as a master carpenter for many years. Drawn to New Orleans, Bill eventually made peace between his orientation and his religion. He found his way to St. George's Episcopal Church, with a supportive minister named Bill Richardson, and then to the gay-friendly Metropolitan Community Church, which had formed in 1971 under Pentecostal minister Reverend David Solomon.[12] It is unlikely, by 1973, that even Bill Larson's closest allies in the MCC knew of his past or his birth name, but many gay men existed in this fashion: sloughing off previous identities to embrace their truer selves, much like Saul of Tarsus abandoning his given name to become Paul on the road to Damascus.

THE HISTORY OF the creation of the MCC of New Orleans bears telling. The church's original leader, David Solomon, stood in deep contrast to Bill Larson, who was no politico by any stretch of the imagination. Solomon was a small, mustachioed man with a thunderous disposition—a figure quick to blend social activism with matters of religion. In 1970, Solomon had helped found a short-lived chapter of a militant political group called the Gay Liberation Front (GLF) in New Orleans.[13] At the time, GLF organizations were popping up across the country and loosely networking with hubs in San Francisco and Greenwich Village.[14] Through the GLF, Solomon had led protests in response to the mass arrest of homosexuals at a French Quarter cruising ground called Cabrini Playground.[15]

As a fenced-in, unlighted space just a short jaunt from Bourbon Street, Cabrini Playground had long been fertile terrain for gay or closeted men looking for quick, anonymous encounters at a time before the internet obviated the need for public cruising. This fenced-in zone also made for easy pickings when officers of the NOPD vice squad came calling. In a four-day period in January 1971, thirteen gay men were lured, beaten, and arrested by plainclothes police officers posing as fellow "cruisers" seeking, and sometimes even accepting, sexual attention. "One brother, his head ripped by a billy club, was taken to Charity Hospital, given a tetanus shot and returned to his cell," read a report in *Sunflower,* New Orleans's first "gay newspaper," which had been started by the GLF. "Neither police nor (so-called) physicians cared about his bleeding head," the report continued. "We, the homosexual people of New Orleans, have been patient. We have suffered silently untold abuse at the hands of police. Now we draw the line." The establishment press, of course, barely covered the park raid or the subsequent protests.[16]

Fiery in tone, Solomon showed few qualms attacking the integrity of Louisiana officials and equating them with some of history's most notorious rogues. "The folks in GLF were antagonistic," remembered a gay New Orleanian named Roger Nelson. "They were stirring the shit. This had always been a very genteel city, and suddenly here were these insurrectionists." Following the Cabrini Playground arrests, Solomon led a group of seventy-five GLFers to City Hall and clamored to present Mayor Moon Landrieu with a list of demands, much in the style of the Black Panthers. Solomon wanted the mayor to immediately suspend Police Superintendent Clarence Giarrusso, a well-connected "top cop" who had inherited the post from his brother, Joseph Giarrusso, also immensely popular.[17]

Solomon's request was audacious, considering that most of New Orleans's closeted community had not exactly risen up in response to the beatings. Landrieu, a Democrat with civil rights credentials, was in the midst of racially integrating employment in his administration. He clearly felt he had bigger worries. "Before I got there, not absolutely so, but there was hardly a black above the broom and mop job in City Hall," Landrieu said in a 2009 interview for the Historic New Orleans Collection. "And I decided to go ahead and just get it done. So it wasn't just the tokenism." Landrieu declined to speak with homosexual activists of the GLF in 1971, even as they chanted outside of his office, his recalcitrance reflecting a widespread belief that gays were beyond the pale of America's civil rights debate.[18]

David Solomon, however, would not be deterred. "We will march daily until we get a redress and satisfaction," said Solomon. The next day, Landrieu again rebuffed the protesters. "The mayor had other things to do," reported the *Times-Picayune* without attribution, revealing the newspaper's sentiment.[19] Absent from headlines, however, a backdoor series of conversations did occur. Richard Kernion, an assistant to the mayor, met with GLF leaders and scheduled a meeting between the activists and the New Orleans police chief. A genuine cessation of hostilities followed, and the mayor's office made a statement that no newspapers chose to print: "Superintendent Giarrusso stated that no citizens would be harassed in any way provided that they were not molesting others or otherwise breaking the law."[20]

Without any publicity, this behind-the-scenes victory for the GLF seemed more like a defeat, which emboldened Reverend John Harrington, the self-styled "Chaplain of Bourbon Street," to challenge the gay radicals and praise police for protecting "the natural man against the unnatural." Other Solomon-led events, such as an attempted "gay-in" at City Park, met with apathy, even vituperation. Within the year, the New Orleans chapter of the GLF had faltered, losing the support of Lynn Miller, the group's female cofounder and financial sponsor.[21]

Changing tack, Solomon announced his intention to organize a gay-friendly Christian fellowship. "New Congregation Will Be Organized," read an April 17, 1971, headline in the *Times-Picayune*. The religious assembly "to be known as the Metropolitan Community Church" would be led by Solomon "to cater to the spiritual needs of those up to now neglected."[22] The phrase "those up to now neglected," instead of the obvious term "homosexual," can be read as the coded style of the time, since it remained provocative to reference homosexuality in print.[23]

Additionally, using the word "Gay" was widely considered to be an act of advocacy for Gay Liberation organizations. It was a social gesture that aimed to counter the image of a stigmatized group, since in the public's eye the term "homosexual" was virtually synonymous with "sex criminal."[24] In this era, where out homosexuals faced constant attacks on their characters, a happy term like "Gay" was a way to reject negative stereotypes, but acceptance of this substitute was rare. For example, in 1970, when Henry Kubicki declared to his father "I'm Gay," the man responded, "Well, I'm not very gay about it."[25]

When forced to acknowledge the existence of homosexuals, the average person, whether in New Orleans or elsewhere, tended to frame his or her language in a derogatory manner, lest he or she be accused of sympathizing or participating. "The word 'Gay' was not used, as it was sort of new," remembered Joseph Bermuda, an art curator and father of two who ran the Cabildo Gallery in the French Quarter in 1973. "They were called fruits, homos, tutti fruttis, and queers. The latter was the prevailing word: they were referred to as queers." According to Bermuda, the slur "faggot" was reserved much in the same way that the *n* word was reserved for blacks—for opportunistic delivery or deepest hurt.[26] In a city of southern gallantries, most recognized "faggot" as a term to be muttered under the breath unless challenged or provoked.

Despite efforts to veil the purpose of Solomon's new church, the coded announcement in the *Times-Picayune* caught the attention of gay Christians like Courtney Craighead, Bill Larson, and Mitch Mitchell. "The MCC was a church for everyone," explained congregant Henry Kubicki, "but it had an outreach to gays and lesbians. That's why they were there: because they had enough hurt from the denomination that they grew up with, but they were not about to be an activist or have anything that would bring harm to their comfort or sanctuary."[27]

Craighead, Larson, and Mitchell would attend the first MCC meetings led by Reverend Solomon in 1971, and they'd all be anointed as deacons in 1972. Courtney Craighead would often recall his ordination as the greatest day of his life. Reverend Troy Perry, the founding minister of the national fellowship of MCC churches, presided over the ceremony. "I was ordained as a deacon by the laying of hands," Courtney would tell fellow congregants and new pastors, "and you can't ever take that away from me."[28]

Perry, pastor of the original MCC church in Los Angeles (sometimes called the "Mother Church"), would pass through New Orleans on several more occasions in 1972 and 1973. Troy Perry was not just a minister of some renown but also a man whose name connoted social action.[29] He was the gay rights equivalent of either civil rights leader Dr. Martin Luther King Jr. or Black Panther leader Huey Newton, depending upon whether admirers or critics were describing him. With his Southern drawl, domineering height, and piercing blue eyes, Perry could hold a room with a spellbinding presence. He was a holy man, much in the American evangelical tradition, quick to shout and quicker to shed tears.

Troy Perry's origin story had become part of church legend. As an ex-Pentecostal minister from Florida, Perry had been ousted from a ministerial position in the Church of God of Prophecy in the early 1960s for his so-called homosexual sins. "They viewed homosexuality, in the South, as something heterosexuals did that was bad," he explained in an interview for this book. "They didn't view it as a separate orientation." Losing his church and a heterosexual marriage to the scandal of being outed, Perry left his home state. According to his controversial 1972 autobiography, *The Lord Is My Shepherd and He Knows I'm Gay*, he served in the U.S. army in Europe before resettling in California. In 1968, Perry posted an advertisement in *The Advocate* and founded the Metropolitan Community Church (MCC) as the first gay-friendly Christian fellowship in the United States.[30]

By April 1972, the MCC boasted twenty-four congregations and missions from California to Washington, D.C., the rapid growth reflecting a religious need. Perry's work was revolutionary in that he appended formal spirituality to a lifestyle that previously lacked a religious center. Much like the Southern Christian Leadership Conference, which imbued the civil rights movement with religious imperative, Perry and the MCC—with its avowed platform of social action—injected a Christian sensibility into the early character of Gay Liberation. He received some notoriety for performing the first public same-sex wedding—called a "holy union"—in the United States, although this ceremony was not recognized by any legal entity.[31]

In 1970, Perry teamed with an activist named Morris Kight to organize Los Angeles's first gay pride parade. Los Angeles Police Chief Ed Davis, predictably, opposed the parade vociferously. "We would be ill-advised," Davis told the police commission, "to discommode the people to have a burglars' or robbers' parade or homosexuals' parade from a legal standpoint."[32] Still, Perry and his team eventually received a permit to hold the event. Photographed for countless news articles, Troy Perry was among the few visible faces for homosexuality in America.

BY 1972, DESPITE the best efforts of men like Reverend David Solomon, New Orleans had witnessed no pride parade or equivalent act of gay mass expression. The city also lacked a visible leader like Troy Perry to serve as a spokesperson for gay causes. With a Pentecostal background similar to that of Perry, Solomon viewed himself as a leader of the same mold, with the same responsibility to buck the system. But Solomon faced a sizable challenge in the Big Easy, called by then the Queer Capital of the South by pro- and antigay groups, a place where most homosexuals felt the need to live secret lives.[33]

Values encoded in the region's French Creole heritage tolerated sexual "otherness" only so long as such behaviors remained immured in a private realm. In this neo-Victorian culture, built on overlapping private realms, homosexuals could be offered a closeted niche, similar to 1920s Berlin. Such was the bargain for keeping quiet. This quirky system had functioned for centuries, offering homosexuals the promise of safety in hiding, but it strained against the encroachment of America's broader sexual revolution.

Yet, in 1970s New Orleans, traditions continued to trump Gay Liberation. Only in New Orleans was the term "uptown marriage" popularly understood as two well-to-do aristocrats married to women while romantically involved with each other.[34] "In my world, and this is what's very hard to put across, there were definitely people who were gay, but they didn't live as gay 'out,'" explained New Yorker writer and former dean of the Columbia Journalism School Nicholas Lemann, who grew up in 1960s New Orleans and attended the private high school Country Day. It's important to note that Lemann was heterosexual, a sympathetic outsider who looked into the gay substrata early on. "Some were married. Some were quote 'confirmed bachelors,'" Lemann continued. "And, to the extent that you had a very hazy understanding [of their sexuality], it was that they had a kind of other side of their life that they kept compartmentalized and separate."[35] A homosexual, in these circumstances, would hardly ever be asked to speak about private trysts; most neighbors would be more upset at the person or institution asking the questions. For example, many New Orleanians grew angrier with Jim Garrison for discussing Clay Shaw's sexuality than with Shaw himself for being homosexual.[36]

In such a society, built not on morality or rule of law but on social exchanges, the closet came advertised as functional and preferable. Those who accepted closeted lives would resist even identifying with the closet. Most preferred more elegant labels, such as "disinclined to be identified as homosexual," according to John Meyers, who lived blocks away from the Up Stairs Lounge. The famously louche traditions of the city allowed for such broad types as the "dandy," the "millionaire bachelor," or two "longtime companions." As early as the 1890s, John McDonogh, a shipping titan and New Orleans philanthropist, for example, was widely reputed to be one of these "bachelors."[37] Therefore, a curious dichotomy pervaded in New Orleans that was hardly new to the twentieth century: the success of hidden gays could, in a sense, provide the closet's greatest defense.

Modern homosexuality posed a dilemma, however, in that it violated Creole discretion and triggered reprisals. Despite its flamboyant reputation, resulting from the presence of drag queens and men in extravagant costume during Mardi Gras season, New Orleans had witnessed frequent persecutions of openly gay residents, especially effeminate "jennie-men" or cross-dressers who could or would not conceal their differences.[38] A 1906 article in the *Sunday Sun,* a New Orleans morality newsletter, called homosexuals "its," as if they were beneath naming. Hostile attitudes were also common in the post-McCarthy era; a 1958 campaign led by prominent French Quarter resident Jacob Morrison, half brother to Mayor Chep Morrison, proposed several ordinances to "drive out the deviates," including decrees to fire immoral workers and the aforementioned statute to seize homes and property—all of which the mayor signed into law.[39]

Given these peculiarities, it shouldn't be surprising that New Orleans's closeted lineage tended to operate slyly—but in plain sight. One of

America's oldest continually operating gay bars, Café Lafitte in Exile, for example, had shelled out drinks to closeted celebrities and dignitaries from 901 Bourbon Street since 1953. A precursor to Café Lafitte in Exile, more efficiently known as Café Lafitte, had opened during Prohibition and catered to such "exotics." But when the original property owner died, new management barred such fraternization. Café Lafitte in Exile, flauntingly, opened up on the next corner, the "in Exile" referring to those "bachelors" and queens banished from their former domain.[40]

Café Lafitte in Exile, a tavern for the "genteel," not only survived but thrived in the wake of a 1969 incident in which Laisder Mendoza, the twenty-five-year-old gay son of a Venezuelan industrialist, had gotten into an argument with a lover, exited the bar, and then plowed his pickup truck through the building's front door, injuring three. Five years earlier, Mendoza had been arrested by the vice squad and booked for "attempted crime against nature," but, because he was a closeted member of diplomatic society, it does not appear that he received any comeuppance for that charge or for driving his truck through the bar.[41]

Tennessee Williams frequented Café Lafitte in Exile but avoided acknowledgment of his homosexuality because the content of his plays roused enough controversy as it was: he feared it would escalate if his "mad pilgrimage of the flesh" were to become common knowledge.[42] Some critics, such as *Time* magazine's Louis Kronenberger, were especially keen to goad Williams as an artist "obsessed with violence, corruption and sex" or a man whose "profanity often seems to relieve . . . [his] own feelings rather than his characters.'" Williams's dance between outness and closeted-ness created paranoia and psychological breaks. Consequently, the playwright suffered a diminution in self-worth. "I once had the idea, the hope, of being a major artist," he confessed to his lover, Frank Merlo, in 1957. "I know I am a minor artist who has happened to create two or three major works."[43] At the time Williams wrote these words, he had already won two Pulitzer Prizes for Drama.

Still, the playwright Williams, the shipping titan McDonogh, and the diplomat's son Mendoza had all been moneyed men with the means to live in a gray space. In a pinch, they could bribe or influence their way out of trouble with law enforcement or the press. Homosexuality, for the affluent, was often something to be managed and concealed like a drug addiction, a "social tic" that would only read on the surface of the deranged or confused. It was still relatively common, for example, for the closeted rich to "keep a boy" in the Quarter, a young lover well maintained, at least temporarily, for the wealthy man's own pleasure.[44] "It was more of a class thing," agreed Jane Place, who waitressed at a gay-friendly French Quarter diner. Upper-class gays could have their way in this world of complex graces. One gay fraternal order, for example, held a Mardi Gras ball at the luxurious Hotel Monteleone in 1970, but no pictures appeared in newspapers. "There were the high societies," Place noted, "and then there were the derelicts, that you knew they weren't going to live very long. It was very sad because you could almost pick their fate by the group they were in."[45]

Places like the Up Stairs Lounge and groups like the MCC, however, were havens for blue-collar gays and middle-class professionals: individuals without fortunes, who sometimes lived month to month. Patrons of the Up Stairs Lounge tended to be tolerated in establishments like Café Lafitte in Exile but rarely welcomed into the toniest cliques. The journalist and gay activist Bill Rushton, writing for *The Advocate*, observed this hierarchy in action, as well as the diminution in power and agency that came with descending the rungs:

> In the mid-Quarter gay bars on Bourbon Street and the surrounding gay restaurants, it's the "beautiful people" gays with their bow ties and bloody Marys and maybe brunch squeezed in between. On Rampart Street, it's countless refugees from small southern towns, middle-aged hairdressers and decorators who can't make it here and can't go home, repasting off buffet spreads like you'll only find elsewhere on Southern Baptist picnics. On Iberville, it's the hustlers and their johns staggering in from the night before, carousing at only a slightly subdued key. Except for the Up Stairs.[46]

The Up Stairs Lounge, actually, had provided a lifeline to the MCC of New Orleans at a critical juncture. In the fall of 1971, the growing congregation was evicted from its original gathering place.

The MCC approached Up Stairs Lounge owner Phil Esteve, who generously offered up the bar's back theater hall free of charge. Each Sunday for a long stretch of months, Buddy Rasmussen would let churchgoers in around 2:00 p.m., and they'd file into the back room to pray. Services often included an adaptation of the civil rights anthem "We Shall Overcome," with an added line: "Gay and straight together, some day." Afterward, the MCC would hold a reception of coffee and sweet rolls in the "dance area" that blended into more boisterous "fellowship" when the beer bust became roaring in the evening.[47]

It was at this time that the Up Stairs Lounge witnessed a transition in that MCC members played a role in expanding the Sunday beer bust from a gathering of several dozen friends to an end-of-weekend occasion for crowds. "Piano Dave" Gary would take requests and lead groups in song throughout the two hours of bottomless draft beer. Richard Robert Cross, an MCC member nicknamed Mother Cross, started a tradition of requesting the ballad "United We Stand" by the band the Brotherhood of Man.[48] The lyrics, extolling the virtues being "together, you and I," explored themes of unwavering loyalty. Pounded out from the bar piano, it seemed to sum up their lives.

"United We Stand" became the anthem of the Up Stairs Lounge, a metaphor for who its patrons were and what they meant to one another, a means through which gay men could temporarily express and escape their existential pain. Piano Dave received multiple requests for the ballad at each beer bust, and it became tradition to sing the song loudly, emotively, to the point of tears until seven, when beer bust ended. Moments like these raised the profile of the Up Stairs Lounge. In 1973, *Bob Damron's Address Book* listed the establishment with an asterisk for the first time, indicating that the bar was "very popular."[49]

But challenges arose. A bar that got hopping earlier in the afternoon made a poor location for a gay-friendly church seeking religious legitimacy. "If patrons of the bar are waiting for the service, and they're already getting their drinks," noted MCC congregant Henry Kubicki, "they're definitely 'feeling the spirit' but not necessarily holy." Some gay-friendly aspects of MCC worship could upset Christian traditionalists. For example, John Meyers, who happened to be a gay

Catholic seminarian, came to one service but was "mildly offended" when he saw the Eucharist broken into halves so that gay lovers could receive the same "Body of Christ" during communion. Additionally, the MCC was forced to share the bar's back theater hall with various nonreligious groups.[50] It was hardly a consecrated space, although they did their best to make it so.

Several bar regulars joined a growing troupe of actors who dubbed themselves the Up Stairs Players. The floors of the theater hall often became littered with peanut shells during performances of melodramas there, nicknamed "nellydramas" because of their cross-gender casting. Southern melodramas held proud traditions of being performed before raucous audiences, with crowds cheering on heroes and throwing popcorn and peanut shells at villains, and patrons took this heritage to heart. Bettye McAnear, wife of U.S. Customs officer Bob McAnear, wrote and directed several original melodramas as part of this effort. She initially had high aspirations for these productions, but the closeted stars of other acting troupes wouldn't audition, for fear of being outed by association with the venue. As such, amateurism became part of the charm. The Up Stairs Players were known to veer from her script in repeat performances by letting audience members interrupt the action to shout the big lines. In response, casts started ad-libbing to throw off the crowd.[51]

One night, when the actors thought that the McAnears were out of town, they abandoned the script entirely. "All of a sudden, midway into the play, Bettye stood up," recollected Ricky Everett, who was a frequent cast member. "She said, 'I did not write that.' She turned around and said, 'I don't have to sit here and watch this.' She stomped out of the little theater." Bob McAnear left with an apologetic look. He knew to follow or face her wrath. "And then some queen back in the back corner of the audience said, 'Well, if she wrote that, and she doesn't want to watch it, why should I?'" recalled Ricky. "And he got up and walked out, and there went the rest of the audience behind him."[52]

Proceeds from these performances went to support the local Crippled Children's Hospital, and many "nellydrama" performers were also MCC members receptive to the idea of having fun for a charitable cause. The melodrama *Egad, What a Cad* featured MCC members Tad Turner and Jason Guidry. In another performance, Ricky Everett brought the house down as the "Infamous Memphis Queen." Deacon Mitch Mitchell and Reverend David Solomon also participated, and it dawned on the congregation that there needed to be clearer boundaries between the bar and their church.[53]

By mid-1972, David Solomon moved the MCC from the Up Stairs Lounge to a side chapel of St. George's Episcopal Church in the Garden District. The MCC's temporary residence there, coming as a result of Deacon Bill Larson's close friendship with St. George's minister Bill Richardson, was not without controversy. One longtime congregant of St. George's had refused to return to worship until the gay Christians left and the chapel had received an exorcism. Eventually, Solomon brought the MCC to the cottage on Magazine Street, an affordable location closer to the apartments of many worshippers.[54] It was truly a home of their own, but, even though they'd migrated across town, the congregation kept close ties with the Up Stairs Lounge and maintained the tradition of fellowship.

The timing of these afternoon services made a meal in the Quarter, followed by two hours of beer bust at the Lounge, something of a routine. Solomon parted ways with the MCC shortly after his attempt to embrace politics, and church elders tapped Bill Larson to fill the position. Larson moved into the Magazine Street cottage and spruced up the location, while Solomon went into a kind of exile in rural Bogalusa, Louisiana.[55]

Bill Larson accepted the title "Interim Worship Coordinator" for a church that, by then, had expanded to roughly thirty gay men. In his liturgical style, Bill preferred "High Church," the traditional style of Christian worship common to Catholics and Episcopalians. He served communion with a calm demeanor he'd perfected years before as a lay minister for Methodists. There would be no more playing cute with communion hosts. Reflecting the transition to his new style of pastoring, Bill Larson adorned the Magazine Street sanctuary with such simple decorations as a tapestry of the Last Supper.[56] As Bill spoke, two candles would burn beside him in brass holders.

A congregant named Lucien Baril lent sobriety to these services. He often stood beside Larson, assisting while wearing formal religious attire—a cassock and skullcap. Baril had a great love of religious pageantry and served as what Henry Kubicki called "an adult version of an altar boy," having zealously purchased this spiritual clothing unbidden. No one remembers exactly what Bill Larson preached on these Sundays—his messages were, undoubtedly, tamer than his predecessor's—but congregants such as Ricky Everett expressed relief at the subtler expression of Christian faith. "His creed was innocent," said Courtney Craighead. "He believed in freedom and love. He wanted the right of individuals to make their own choice—without any harm to anyone." Larson had a stunning singing voice, honed performing at the orphanage and at churches over many years,[57] and he would often break into song from sermon.

Like Larson, Deacon Mitch Mitchell had received a promotion; he presided each Sunday as assistant interim worship coordinator. Mitch would lean on the podium and preached round-shouldered, round-bellied. He was a handsome man whose girth accentuated his message. "He had a wild and wooly manner," lovingly remembered Troy Perry, "and was far from sophisticated." At the Up Stairs Lounge, Mitch had famously dressed as Queen Victoria one Halloween, and photos of him in costume still circulated. Mitch worked weekdays as a salesman for Danos Beauty Supply Company. On the weekends, he was a church deacon and a devoted family man. Mitch and his lover, Horace Broussard, had, in 1971, been joined in a "holy union" ceremony at the Up Stairs Lounge to announce their fidelity and soulful love. Although not a civil marriage, their union represented a kind of spiritual conjugation sanctioned by the MCC, a promise until death did them part. These Christian "celebration of commitment" ceremonies between two men were then considered beyond the pale. In June 1973, a pastor in Boston was voted into forcible retirement by the United Methodist Church for the scandal of performing such a ritual.[58]

Much like Bill Larson, Mitch had tried his hand at heterosexual life as a young man. He had married a woman, become a father, and then divorced for reasons that became apparent. Back in his home state of

Alabama, Mitch's ex-wife, Vicki Tane, raised their two young sons, Duane and Stephen, during the school year. Unlike Bill Larson, however, Mitch stayed on friendly terms with his ex, and he often showed up on holidays to lavish gifts on the boys. Every summer, Vicki Tane shipped the kids to New Orleans to visit their dad and Uncle Horace. On Sundays at church, while Mitch preached, their family would sit in a back row. Horace often brought comic books to occupy the boys, who tended to be quiet and well behaved.[59]

Guy Andersen (sometimes spelled "Anderson" for anonymity purposes), a former teacher from Illinois, attended this June Sunday. Deacon Courtney Craighead—a heartfelt, if occasionally brash and self-proclaimed "Arkansas hillbilly"—sang loudly near Mother Cross and the rest of their gang. Glenn Green had traveled in from across the river to worship.[60] Likewise, Perry Waters, a closeted dentist living in the suburbs, and Luther Boggs, a businessman, counted themselves among the day's celebrants.

Ricky Everett and guest Ronnie Rosenthal, the friend visiting from the MCC of Atlanta, also sat and sang. Reggie Adams, an ex-Jesuit seminarian, notably bowed his head and adulated Christ. Reggie was one of the few black members of the congregation. Like many, he had arrived via a wayward path. Reggie had grown up in a shack near the housing projects on the west side of Dallas, Texas. He had demonstrated enough intellectual gusto to be accepted as one of the few black scholarship students at Jesuit College Prep. Eventually, Reggie decided to become a priest and moved to New Orleans.[61]

The Crescent City had been eye-opening in unanticipated ways. Reggie had caught the scent of a dashing young prospect at the Up Stairs Lounge. This person, born Richard Soleto, performed in charity drag shows at the Up Stairs Lounge and was trying on female personae. Reggie—from his Catholic background—was accustomed to being the only black man in a room full of white worshippers, and so he readily identified with Ricky Soleto's sense of individuality.[62]

It's remarkable that, in a city where relations between the races tended to be polite but at arm's length, Reggie felt as comfortable at the Up Stairs Lounge as he did at the Safari Lounge, a predominantly black gay bar on Iberville Street.[63] Hence, Reggie and Ricky Soleto were encouraged to flirt and date by other patrons. At the time, Reggie had been preparing for ordination with the Jesuits, but this new relationship provided a compelling reason for him to reject that path.

It was Reggie who suggested the new name "Regina" for Ricky Soleto; "Regina" meant "reigning queen," and Reggie often liked to call Soleto "my queen." Thus were Reggie and Regina (as Ricky was known from then on) an unmistakable pair—bridging race and gender. During MCC services, Reggie would fold his hands in prayer and reveal the gleam of a high school ring given to him by Regina—a symbol of their bond. They shared a French Quarter apartment and made a romantic ritual out of Sunday nights at the Lounge. The place held distinct memories.[64]

Bill Larson ended his service with a blessing. He bid his friends to go out and serve the Lord. But the congregants stuck around: for one thing, they were jubilant about the miraculous gift of an air conditioner.[65] As this was New Orleans, where merrymaking can happen especially on the fly, the group resolved that the surprise donation was right cause to celebrate. They agreed to meet later at the beer bust for extended fellowship.

Bill Larson, Ricky Everett, Ronnie Rosenthal, and their cohort trudged in punishing heat toward cars or the nearby St. Charles streetcar, the last working trolley line in New Orleans. By then, these trolleys had become symbols of the quaint character of a city that seemed to bathe in eternal lassitude. Indeed, the green, wooden coaches continued to be of practical use for MCC congregants like Henry Kubicki, who worked in the service industry. Puttering toward the French Quarter, the trolleys would pass through the turnabout of Lee Circle and its famous Robert E. Lee monument, a white pillar erected to honor the Confederate general (it was taken down in 2017). On January 19, 1972, a young Ku Klux Klansman named David Duke had been arrested for "inciting a riot" during which bricks had flown at a rally at this monument, as segregationists clashed with a local retinue of Black Panthers.[66]

At Canal Street, the trolley would halt. Doors would fling open, and people would exit into the French Quarter, toward dinner and the promise of a light buzz. A pink, crepuscular haze, beribboned with fumes from nearby oil refineries, framed the sky above. Some of their flock might already be at the bar, but Bill, Ricky, and Ronnie still had time to dine before catching the drink special. There seemed no reason to hurry. The Up Stairs crowd was hosting a benefit for the Crippled Children's Hospital later that evening, this one a drag show and piano sing-along, which might or might not serve as a preamble to a larger benefit that would incorporate the Up Stairs Players (of nelly-drama fame). No one could precisely remember the details, and no one sweated them.[67]

Slightly delayed, Mitch and Horace rewarded Mitch's sons for another peaceful Sunday by driving them to the Prytania Theatre, a historic movie house closer to home. Mitch and Horace knew the boys would be safe at these matinees for children supervised by the theater's owners and parents from the neighborhood. They got in line for tickets to the Disney blockbuster *The World's Greatest Athlete*, starring teen heartthrob Jan-Michael Vincent. The year prior, Vincent had gotten into some heat over a *Los Angeles Times* interview in which he'd reputedly used the word "fag," although the actor had disputed this. "I didn't say any of those things in the article, man," Vincent later told *The Advocate*,[68] and *The Advocate* had let the issue rest as a case of misquotation.

In *The World's Greatest Athlete*, a loincloth-donning Vincent starred as Nanu, the Tarzan-like athlete who "brings the jungle to the gym" by competing in every event of an NCAA track and field competition. Mitch and Horace, no doubt, chuckled at the irony of a homoerotic muscle man starring in a family-friendly flick. But the Disneyfied story line made excellent fodder for kids, and the movie house brimmed with high-pitched giggles, befitting the playground-like atmosphere. Mitch and Horace bid adieu to Duane, eleven, and Stephen, eight.[69] They left the children to watch the movie and drifted down St. Charles Avenue toward the beer bust.

They'd be back, they assured the boys, before the end credits rolled.[70]

CHAPTER 3

Gay Liberation

Evening

Bill Larson and Ricky Everett dug into burgers at the Fatted Calf, a gay-friendly diner located on a slip of St. Peter Street between the promenades of Bourbon and Royal. The din of this greasy spoon was paradoxically endearing for both tourists and locals: bells rang with orders, surly waitresses scribbled on pads. The Fatted Calf could turn over tables several times per hour, especially on a summer Sunday. Ronnie Rosenthal, the Atlanta native, was getting his introduction to this French Quarter institution, where burgers were named after characters from *Gone with the Wind*. It was already clear that emotions were ricocheting across tables. Through stealthy glances and body language, it became clear that this trio of gay men harbored several layers of affection.[1]

No one put it into words, but Ricky Everett was fast developing more than a crush on the out-of-towner, and Ronnie was returning the feeling. To complicate matters, Ricky also harbored some affection for Bill Larson, though the attraction that he and Bill shared remained unexplored. "We could have been partners, but I was in a relationship," Ricky remembered. "And he respected me and the relationship." Much of their connection stemmed from a mutual love of Christ. Raised Presbyterian in Monroe, Louisiana— deep in "God's country"—Ricky was both devout and devoted. He beamed purity and innocence, having grown up in what he called a "bubble of protection," despite his budding inclinations. But Ricky was hardly an ingenue, as he'd been around the New Orleans scene and was no stranger to its ways. Like untold Christians before him, Ricky found his pastor enchanting. "Bill was just a very legitimate person," remembered Ricky. "And I loved him very dearly as my very closest friend."[2]

Between bites, Ricky kept looking across the table at Bill. Though memory over decades can deceive, Ricky is certain that he voiced an unusual thought. "Bill, I don't know why, but I just have a bad feeling that you're going to die," Ricky remembered saying. Bill looked back with concern and slowly responded, "Yeah, I know." Overall, Ricky preferred to be honest to a fault with those he loved and trusted, and Bill was not shocked. Their conversation moved on, dissipating in a haze of laughter and flirtatious remarks. Eventually, they settled up with the check and left.[3]

Strolling through the Quarter, the three men passed Preservation Hall, the world-famous jazz venue, and Pat O'Brien's, home of a fruity drink called the hurricane. They then turned on Royal Street near the quaint, backyard garden of St. Louis Cathedral. This was the backside to the city's grandest church—situated before the expansive greenery of Jackson Square and framed by two stately museums. Glistening off-white above the cacophony of pedestrians, St. Louis Cathedral was the basilica for the Archdiocese of New Orleans. An ancient structure, it had been built, burned, and rebuilt several times over, with foundations dating to French governance in the 1720s and Spanish governance in the 1790s, shortly before New Orleans was passed back to France and then formally acquired as U.S. territory in the Louisiana Purchase of 1803. Mud-caked roads presently crossed in front of the cathedral as part of a film set for director Sergio Leone, in town shooting a western with Henry Fonda titled *My Name Is Nobody*.[4]

Bill and Ricky kept on Royal Street, thereby avoiding the movie set, but Bill seemed to be thinking as he moved. Perhaps he took Ricky's words as a premonition, or perhaps he was just aligning what he heard with something Ricky told him weeks earlier: "Bill, I have this feeling that you're not going to be on the pulpit much longer."[5]

———————— ᘺ ————————

BLOCKS AWAY ON Iberville Street, in the direction Bill, Ricky, and Ronnie were headed, a twenty-six-year-old man named Roger Dale Nunez was making a drunken scene at the bar Gene's Hideaway.[6] He hounded friends to head with him a few doors down to the Up Stairs Lounge. Drinks would be even cheaper during the beer bust.

Roger's brown hair looked to be slightly disheveled. A musty perfume of booze wafted from his pores. Known as a drifter, Roger's life seemed to exist in permanent transition. He hustled on the side, when he could. Gene Davis, the owner and namesake of Gene's Hideaway, had been shilling drinks and observing Roger's exploits for hours. Davis commonly wore bowling shirts over his swell of a belly and styled his hair in a gelled pompadour. A married man with children, he spoke with machismo and walked with some swagger, but he was no stranger to the affections of men. He was known to take home hustlers and pay for them out of the till from his bar. After all, this was New Orleans. Roger had briefly worked for Davis, and they remained friendly. The truth was that Davis pitied Roger enough to let him keep his clothing in the bar whenever the ragamuffin lost a job or ended a relationship and had no place to live.[7]

Gene's Hideaway was a sort of "last kind words" saloon for the downcast, the lost and the broken. Dust matted in corners, and the wallpaper bore clear signs of aging. Davis was reputed to be a minor figure in New Orleans's underworld, although no one really knew if they could believe these whispers. He had been arrested in 1958 for his involvement in taking pornographic photographs of a fifteen-year-old male runaway, charged with a "crime against nature" for illicit sex. His name had also surfaced in the 1969 Clay Shaw trial, when a local lawyer testified that Davis had once been introduced to him as "Clay Bertrand," the mysterious pseudonym that obsessed District Attorney Jim Garrison.[8]

Clay Bertrand's possible connection to Gene Davis, despite the testimony, led to no arrests and only added to the bar owner's mystique.

Many assumed that Davis was a protected asset, so to speak. He had audaciously sued NBC when a newscaster identified him as "the real Clay Bertrand," but that suit was ultimately dismissed. In 1970, Gene's Grill, another of his Iberville bars, suffered fire damage, with two related deaths, and he claimed $20,000 in water damage from the hoses that put out the blaze. Davis had chosen to run Gene's Grill with no insurance because, he explained, "They're always having fires."[9] Places like Gene's Grill and Club My-O-My just burned down in New Orleans.

At Gene's Hideaway, Roger Nunez had been hustling a "john," or prospective customer, in plain sight, but it caused no stir. This bar was devoted to such practices and served customers of "exotic" tastes— businessmen seeking cross-dressers, wives buying men for their husbands, etc. Roger's hustling prospect, Donald Landry, was an elderly gentleman who happened to be wearing a colostomy bag and seemed open to Roger's flirtations.[10] Initially, Roger had been doling out the sugar in exchange for free booze from Landry and the promise of future favors.

While flirting, Roger spoke with a deep Cajun accent. He was last employed as a custodian at the Marriott Hotel down the block, but no one knew whether he worked there anymore. Roger was currently spending his nights on the couch of an acquaintance named Cynthia Ann "Cee Cee" Savant. Roger had asked Savant this favor because she, having survived on Quarter streets as a thirteen-year-old urchin, possessed a reputation for being bighearted. Unfazed by Savant's criminal past, as his was no better, Roger had asked if he could crash at her place, and Savant had said yes, provided that he was a clean roommate. Still, Savant never quite viewed Roger as a friend. "I didn't know Roger," she would later say. "Nobody did."[11]

Born Rodger Dale Nunez, with a "d" in the first name, the man grew up in a place called Abbeville—a small town in bayou country where some preferred French to the English language. Abbeville, at the time, was associated with oil rigging, horseback riding, and the Cajuns—a rollicking rural society descended from the Acadians that had been popularized and even commercialized worldwide. The famous Tabasco factory peppered the air about twenty miles from Rodger's hometown. Local Cajuns held "fais do-do" dance parties for all ages and "boucherie" hog slaughters and feasts.[12] Carnival season held its own traditions, separate from Creole New Orleans, with the Courir de Mardi Gras being custom, when men in comical costumes ran between homesteads in search of live chickens for gumbo. Young Rodger, whose February 22 birthday often fell within Mardi Gras season, would have delighted in these pantomimes, proof positive that there were more ways to be rich in life than material wealth.[13] Shelton Nunez, a relative born the year before Rodger, was the right age to be Rodger's brother, but Shelton was actually Rodger's uncle, a phenomenon relatively commonplace in a bucolic region where infant mortality rates remained high and relations stayed put. Shelton's and Rodger's were both likely home births, and they grew up side by side. People in town tended to marry early, as religion dictated, and some began to whisper when Rodger never settled down like Shelton, but even sexual differences could be balanced in Abbeville if unique "tastes" could be kept a family secret.[14]

Rodger held the distinction of being both the elder boy and the middle child of his brood, the third kid of four. Rodger's father, Mansel J. Nunez, served with honor in the Coast Guard during World War II and was an exemplar of masculinity. Mansel fancied himself a bit of a cowboy and bragged about life in the saddle. Mansel and his wife Rose, Rodger's mother, divorced in 1963. During the split, Rodger stood in the prime of adolescence, and he took the breakup very seriously. His mother received custody of the children and did not remarry immediately.[15] There was great shame in reneging on one's vows in this heavily Catholic region. At some point after the divorce, Mansel decamped for other locales, and Rodger started to test his freedom.

Rodger began spelling his name without the "d" around this phase of his life, passing himself off as Roger Nunez. He applied for, and received, a Social Security number using this pseudonym. Few left the microcosm of Abbeville; as a Cajun, it would be akin to abandoning one's tribe, but Roger did choose to vamoose during high school—ahead of schedule. Something within him must have felt constrained by the world he knew. In June 1964, he applied to enlist in the navy as a seventeen-year-old minor with the consent of his mother. On his enlistment form, he answered no to the question "Have you ever suffered from epilepsy, fainting spells or dizzy spells?" Considering that Roger would eventually enlist in the U.S. army—a separate military branch—several months later, it's likely that navy recruitment discovered a problem with this questionnaire.[16]

From 1964 to 1967, Roger served in the army as a typist, first in Louisiana and then at the headquarters of V Corps in Frankfurt, West Germany.[17] Writing his hometown newspaper a letter to the editor from abroad, Roger described the heartsickness of being away. "I miss Abbeville very much," he pined. "It is my home and I love it. You can't possibly imagine how much something means to you until you no longer have it." Roger's posting in Europe proved fortunate, since the Vietnam War was at its height, with troop presence in South Vietnam soaring from 23,300 in 1964 to 485,600 in 1967. U.S. forces in West Germany were actively monitoring Soviet communications, and Roger won his spot away from battlefields either through luck or merit or due to medical restrictions that would have rendered him ineligible for combat.

Despite not being in a war zone, Roger was wounded in service. Following an unspecified injury, he received a transfer back to the States and recovered at a Georgia base. In Roger's military records, the transfer is marked as "CAS" (casualty), but the circumstances of this injury and transfer remain unknown. Roger served out the remainder of his career in Georgia and then transferred to the army reserve with a National Defense Service Medal and a good conduct award.[18] It's unknown exactly when he began acting on his feelings for other men, but one can presume that Roger found eager companions in warrens where gay servicemen congregated in West Germany.

Notwithstanding his public yearnings for Abbeville, Roger didn't settle home when he received his discharge. He was a haunted character to those who met him in 1970, around the time he emerged from a state mental hospital and resurfaced in New Orleans. At some point, he applied to become a candidate for the New Orleans Police Department, though he had a drunk driving conviction, and his application wasn't taken seriously. Roger was not one to discuss his past at length, but he gained a reputation for taking advantage of people and situations. On at least two occasions, in December 1972 and April 1973, he was arrested and charged with making illicit purchases using stolen credit cards. Roger, in fact, was already in violation of the one-year probation he'd received for pleading guilty to these charges as he drank at Gene's Hideaway. He had failed to report to his parole officer, and he'd given his parole board a fake address.[19]

THROUGHOUT THAT SUNDAY afternoon, Roger and Donald Landry do-si-doed between tables at Gene's Hideaway and Wanda's, the other bar on Iberville Street owned by Gene Davis, who continued to watch their dalliance. Davis recalled that Roger and Landry would lean close to each other and make eyes. But a younger, slimmer hustler staying in a nearby hotel named Mark Allen Guidry—supposedly, an acquaintance of Roger—walked into Gene's Hideaway and must have sensed an opening. While Roger was, as one might have said in that era, no slouch in the looks department, he was by no means a catch. He stood five foot eight and had a slight tummy. With a ruddy complexion and medium-length hair, he struck the eye as average.[20]

Yet in the eyes of an older man standing in a darkened bar, having already had too many drinks, Roger's averageness could mollify and become elevated. But Roger did lack a certain charisma to pull off the illusion. He took the medication Dilantin to treat his epilepsy and occasionally had seizures in public as a result of alcohol diluting its effect. Nevertheless, he tended to brush off these alarming displays and keep the party rolling.[21] Roger also occasionally attempted to date women, although these dates would end in utter failure.

Mark Allen Guidry, taking a seat in the bar with Roger, must have presented a striking contradiction to his friend. At nineteen, Guidry would have stood out as a more desirable catch for Donald Landry. In the terminology of the time, Guidry looked like a Peter Pan, and Landry was eager to find a young specimen. Guidry made eyes, and Landry bit on the metaphorical line, which resulted in Guidry "nipping the trick" from Roger. It became clear that Landry was now Guidry's piece of business. Hustler competition could indeed be so cutthroat. Guidry and Landry canoodled as Roger brooded. Eventually, the lovers-to-be left Roger to his cups, heading to a St. Charles Avenue hotel, where Landry procured food and paid for their lovemaking with a personal check. Meanwhile, Roger vented rage and stomped about Iberville Street. He reappeared at Gene's Hideaway around 5:00 p.m., just when Guidry and Landry had returned from their engagement.[22]

Although Landry—with his colostomy bag—was hardly dashing, and probably unused to being fought over by two younger men, Roger fumed over lost earnings. Incensed, he guilted a twenty-dollar bill (the contemporary spending equivalent of a hundred dollars) from Landry for services offered but unperformed. Roger then emptied his pockets of stray bills and coins onto the bar. He publicly counted his loot and demanded that a barmaid break the twenty-dollar bill into smaller increments, which she did. Next, Roger insisted, with some amount of aggression, that another dalliance was still possible. Their party would continue, Roger emphasized loudly enough to be overhead by Gene Davis, three doors down at the Up Stairs Lounge beer bust. By this time, Landry, well past slurring in his speech, kept falling off his bar stool, and Davis voiced concerns that Landry wouldn't make it up the stairs to the beer bust without injury.[23]

PERCHED ABOVE IBERVILLE STREET in the Marriott Hotel, Henry Kubicki dipped his hands into an industrial sink filled with soapy water. He tried to keep pace with the dinner rush and avoid invectives from coworkers and his boss. For months, Henry had worked as back-kitchen help in the luxurious high-rise restaurant called Port Orleans. His shifts ran from 4:00 p.m. to midnight, which meant that Henry constantly missed drink specials at the Up Stairs Lounge. Henry was making minimum wage, $1.65 per hour, and the Port Orleans effectively ran his life.[24] Hemmed in by ceramic tile, Henry's work space resounded with clatter, steam-cleaning machinery and dishes balancing in stacks. Henry, who was legally deaf, seemed to be the only worker who didn't mind the constant racket.

He would turn down his hearing aids and drift away into the swish of the water, following trains of thought over past and present. How did he get to this place? The year before, celebrities and heads of state had presided over the opening of this restaurant and hotel with Mardi Gras–like celebrations. Governor Edwin Edwards had attended the festivities, which started on Canal Street and rose forty-two stories to this top-of-the-city vantage point. According to a spread in the *Times-Picayune*, 175 business conventions had booked the Marriott, whose backside on Iberville Street—as the article failed to mention—abutted a sprawl of midcentury porno theaters and gay bars.[25] This juxtaposition was hardly unusual, for the well-heeled and the in-need of New Orleans often rubbed in close proximity.

A few years before, Henry had made the mistake of skipping town with an older man. He remembered meeting a sophisticate named Jeff when he was an eighteen-year-old runaway crashing at a New Orleans bathhouse. At the time, Henry had been feuding with his father, a former military man. As revenge, Henry vanished from the family home and took up residence in the Club New Orleans Baths, which had just opened on Toulouse Street. As bathhouses began proliferating in urban areas, the Club New Orleans Baths became the French Quarter's first official business devoted to hosting anonymous encounters between men around the clock. Stretching across numerous rooms, the "Club Baths," as the establishment was nicknamed, offered not just a pool area but also, ironically, a reading room, as well as a sauna, shower facilities, a living room with a television, and private rooms for the more inhibited. Indeed, "the bathhouse" became such a celebrated institution of the American gay community in the 1970s that these establishments would feature full gyms for working out, just as in Man's Country in downtown Manhattan. In these early days, before the scourge of AIDS, the Club Baths—like countless others—celebrated its orgy chamber, kept nearly pitch-black.[26]

When he met Jeff, Henry was exhausted from several nights of trying to sleep in a reading room chair, so he'd flopped onto a mattress in the dark room. Henry then felt hands unzipping his pants. "In the heat of the moment, I professed love, which is a crock of shit," recalled Henry. "Well, when the light came on, it was not exactly Prince Charming. It was more like Prince Charles of England." On his part, Jeff professed affection for the teen and prevaricated about his age, shaving off about a decade. Smitten, Henry followed Jeff all the way to Brooklyn Heights, New York, and then to Georgia—without alerting his family, of course, to the journey. Henry, with his sensory impairments, had trouble finding consistent work and became a financial burden on his beau. By 1972, Jeff grew tired of their May–December entanglement and ended the relationship. Afterward, Henry's handsomeness got him a job selling men's suits at Davison's Department Store in Atlanta. He rented a garage apartment, but his landlady, a churchgoing woman, saw him leave with Jeff for a late-night soiree. She reported Henry to the authorities for sexual immorality. The next morning, security guards at Davison's escorted Henry from the front doors to a manager, who fired him summarily.[27]

At the time, few legal protections existed to prevent the firing of gays and suspected gays. Only the municipalities of New York City and San Francisco offered employment protections to homosexuals in 1972. Private employers in Atlanta or New Orleans, or any other city in the United States for that matter, could do as they wished. So widespread was such discrimination that these practices were not challenged or seen as wrong by the vast majority of citizens; nor did any major civil rights group document or prevent employers from "cleaning out the riffraff" by firing the odd gay or lesbian. The federal government had explicitly endorsed this practice during the Lavender Scare of the 1950s, a protracted hunt for homosexuals in the Department of State that had led to the firing of approximately five thousand people. Common sense dictated that where one found a gay man, one had a duty to remove him from the situation. As late as 1967, the Supreme Court had validated this precept, when, by a vote of 7–2, it ordered the deportation of a Canadian national applying for U.S. citizenship purely on the basis that he said he was homosexual. In a dissenting opinion, Justice William O. Douglas wrote, "It is common knowledge that in this century homosexuals have risen high in our own public service—both in Congress and in the executive branch—and have served with distinction."[28]

Walking home after his dismissal, Henry pondered suicide. He found his belongings tossed out in garbage bags along the front driveway. A sheriff stood, like an armed sentry, next to his landlady. This county official was present not to protect Henry's property but to ensure that he wouldn't cause a ruckus as he left. Taking pity on an ex-lover, Jeff bought Henry a one-way ticket back to New Orleans.[29] With a new job at the Marriott and his apartment on Coliseum Street, Henry was attempting to reestablish ties at home and restart his life.

Henry's story of expulsion was relatively common among the so-called queer folk of New Orleans. His friend at the MCC, Deacon Courtney Craighead, had been exiled in a similar way from his Methodist church in Little Rock in 1967, when an associate pastor began spreading rumors that Courtney was gay. Courtney and Henry had both found refuge in Up Stairs Lounge society and sought lives at the level of their emotional states. They worked low-wage, low-skill jobs where an absence, even for illness, meant termination. Many gay men had similarly hardscrabble lives dominated by basic threats to their survival. Those who succeeded in advancing themselves did so, like Clay Shaw, at the risk of exposure. States and professional bar associations used licensing laws to prevent homosexuals from practicing as a doctor, a dentist, a lawyer, a pharmacist, or an embalmer. Thus were out homosexuals barred from many occupations associated with higher-income lifestyles.[30]

Henry often came home from the Marriott Hotel demoralized, shattered on the very nights that Ricky Everett came home with stories from the weekend. The pair had in fact met at the Up Stairs Lounge on a Saturday in 1971. A photo of the two that day by the bar's front door shows them smiling, with Ricky sitting demurely on Henry's lap. Henry sometimes fantasized about quitting his damn job at Port Orleans and taking the elevator down to meet Ricky at the Up Stairs Lounge. He'd have a great beer bust if he left tonight, but then, he reasoned, where would he be? "I had to work or be fired," he explained matter-of-factly.[31] His hands kept cleaning the plates.

———————— ✢ ————————

THE FRENCH QUARTER was a beehive of merriment that hazy evening, and Stewart Butler socialized in his element. Bourbon Street was a notorious bazaar of buskers and hustlers, peddlers and mendicants, an avenue that could hardly be imagined beneath America's Bible Belt. Most tourists kept to a tamer strip of bars located closer to downtown hotels, but a certain cadre of men dared farther, strolling past the invisible line at the intersection of Bourbon and St. Ann Streets. If you passed St. Ann, you would inevitably find a cloister of "exotic" establishments, like Pete's Place or Caverns or Café Lafitte in Exile, where Stewart Butler was currently imbibing.[32]

St. Ann Street was one of many markers for men whose tastes ran toward the unconventional. Every year, Carnival season brought money and majesty into the city, in addition to over-the-top galas and krewes, the private fraternal orders that sponsored nearby parades and crowned kings and queens of Mardi Gras. Many krewes were only beginning to racially integrate by 1973. Yet from the Twelfth Night after Christmas to Fat Tuesday in February, New Orleans would be consumed, and the gay community subsumed, in a dream state of masks and feathers and anything goes. For many celebrants, Mardi Gras signified not a pantomime but a culmination of real life, and the French Quarter seemed to savor this fantasia. The nation's oldest annual gay event, the Fat Monday Luncheon Club, had begun in the Quarter in 1949, while the Krewe of Yuga, New Orleans's first gay Carnival club (its initials, K.Y., a sly reference to the most popular sexual lubricant of the era), debuted in 1958. A young Stewart Butler, in town with his family, remembered attending his first Mardi Gras with awe and becoming aroused at the sight of the "flambeaux," or mirrored torches paraded by crews of muscular black men. Such was the spell of the season.[33]

By 1972, New Orleans had six gay krewes hosting ticketed balls for private members, with discretion, of course, assured and requests for "no pictures please."[34] The exhilaration of Carnival, with its masked traditions, facilitated the unmasking of otherwise captive aspects of the self, which called into question which one was the truer mask: the pious man or the partier. Alas, the dream of Mardi Gras was fleeting—and ended, always. Ash Wednesday stood as a Catholic roadblock to cut the fun short before Easter Sunday. Bourbon Street attempted to keep a small share of this merriment going year-round, although not always succeeding. Today, in late June, fun was achieved through the bonhomie of Stewart Butler.

Stewart held forth at Café Lafitte in Exile with twin "bombshells" on his arms: twenty-year-old Steven Duplantis, Stewart's "guy Friday," and thirty-something "baby doll" Alfred Doolittle, Stewart's steady boyfriend. Stewart had met and bedded Steven Duplantis first, when Steven was eighteen and he drove from Lake Charles to New Orleans for the first time. This was Mardi Gras 1971, and Steven had been accompanied by a few young drag queens from his hometown. They'd all set up a tent on the riverfront parkway, as one could do in this era, but the group had split off and shacked up throughout the first day of partying.[35]

Steven was left alone, bereft of companionship and down to his last two dollars at Café Lafitte in Exile. He bought a final drink and resolved to spend the rest of the night in a stinking hot tent. Just then, Stewart Butler, sitting in the back corner of the bar, persuaded a friend to taunt Steven by extinguishing a cigarette in the teen's drink. When Stewart's friend did so, Steven became enraged, and the situation escalated. "Well, here comes Butler to save the day," remembered Steven Duplantis. "He says, 'Oh, I tell you what, why don't you come back to the house, and we'll smoke a joint, and I'll fix you up all the cocktails you want.' And I said, 'Oh thank you, God!'" Stewart and Steven became involved physically, even somewhat romantically. But Stewart was in his forties, and Steven was barely an adult. Given their age difference, postcoital conversation could only progress so far.[36]

After graduating from high school, Steven enlisted in the air force in 1972 and was stationed at Randolph Air Force Base in San Antonio, Texas. He knowingly entered the service as a gay man. "I went through basic training," he recalled. "I went through computer train-

ing in Biloxi, Mississippi. The whole time, I kept my 'straight face.'"
Steven knew that the unmasking of his "straight face," the detection
of his inner world, would lead to a dishonorable discharge and his
blacklisting from countless civilian careers. Distance and fear, however, couldn't fully extinguish Steven's desire for fun. Once a month,
sometimes more, Steven would sneak out of his military barracks and
drive his 1969 Buick Wildcat the eight hours across Texas and Louisiana to Stewart's house. With a four-barrel, 440 engine, the car could
eviscerate the highway with a top speed of 140 mph. One time, Steven
got pulled over in Bienville, Louisiana, at three in the morning, but he
avoided a speeding citation by giving the cop a blowjob.[37]

New Orleans had long been a sexual oasis for members of the
armed forces like Steven. As a port city, like San Francisco or New
York—where generations of "undesirably discharged" homosexuals
settled after being kicked off transport ships—New Orleans boasted
a lineage of military men on leave seeking gay sex. In fact, Tennessee Williams's first homosexual encounter was with a G.I. in New
Orleans.[38] In 1966, W. F. Charles of the Armed Forces Disciplinary
Control Board wrote the proprietor of Café Lafitte in Exile: "Inspection reports presented to the Board indicate that your establishment
is a known hangout for persons of undesirable character." This letter
had the reverse of its intended effect. Tickled instead of intimidated,
the owners of the bar framed the letter and put it on display near the
front door.[39]

Nothing could keep Steven from drinking with Stewart that Sunday. Unbeknownst to them, their revels coincided with national gay
pride celebrations—observed in different ways across American cities
since the uprising at the Stonewall Inn four years before, when homosexuals had resisted police and demanded visibility. That Saturday in
1973, gay and lesbian New Yorkers had marched from Central Park
through midtown Manhattan to Washington Square, evidence that
a gay political revolution was very much on the horizon. According
to reports in *The New York Times*, police barricades stretched fifteen
blocks to contain gay revelers, with thousands chanting in unison,
"Out of the closets and into the streets!" These festivities marked the

fourth annual "Christopher Street Liberation Day" parade to commemorate Stonewall.[40]

The political ferment was also evident in San Francisco, where "Gay Freedom Day" had attracted more than forty thousand people. In Chicago, three thousand marchers braved a heat wave to parade from the Loop to Lincoln Park. Ripples of Stonewall were also visible in Los Angeles, though the Christopher Street West association's parade had been canceled due to infighting among gay groups, but Troy Perry and the Metropolitan Community Church of Los Angeles had stepped in to preserve the gay pride sentiment.[41]

Few American cities with sizable gay populations could escape the fervor set off by Stonewall, but New Orleans had managed to do so. Many New Orleanians hadn't even heard of the Stonewall Inn or, if they had, questioned the relevance of "pride" to lives they knew and enjoyed. At Café Lafitte in Exile, gays and lesbians celebrated their "pride weekend" rather mutely, if at all, with obligatory cocktails. There would be no marches in the streets, no posters, and certainly no speeches. As Gay Orleanians well knew, their alternate system balanced on a knife edge and wasn't always foolproof. Police had raided a gay Mardi Gras ball for the Krewe of Yuga eleven years before, in 1962, and arrested ninety-six for "disturbing the peace."[42]

Still, bars like Café Lafitte in Exile were places where gay men like Stewart Butler could cut loose with a modicum of safety. "Modicum" was the key word, as fraternities from Tulane University were still said to practice their longstanding tradition of "rolling a queer." These college boys would "roll" a gay man by luring him from a gay bar, beating him senseless, and stealing his wallet.[43] Hunting gays in this way offered fraternity brothers safeguards from getting into trouble, in that one's prey possessed little means of recourse. The assault and theft would go unreported because doing so would implicate the victim in a sex crime.

Even though fifteen years had passed, the cautionary tale of Fernando Rios lingered in memory. A Mexican tour guide visiting New Orleans, Rios had been lured by Tulane student John Farrell from Café Lafitte in Exile in 1958. Farrell and two friends then ambushed and attacked Rios in a secluded walkway next to St. Louis Cathedral. In a horrific scene, Rios's echoing whimpers went unheard, even by priests in the rectory mere steps away. Rios lay bleeding until about 6:00 a.m. the next morning, when he was found, and he died at the hospital. Subsequently, the undergraduates beat the murder rap with high-priced attorneys, who argued that Rios's cranium was "egg-shell" thin, too weak in constitution for an attacker to suspect it would crack from a pummeling. Legal notes indicate how attorneys questioned the coroner about the hormonal implications of an "egg-shell" cranium or "anything else abnormal about [the] body to suggest to show homosexuality."[44]

This bit of convoluted logic—using an autopsy to make a character insinuation—appealed to the jury, which acquitted these students and served as broader confirmation that homosexuals, when exposed to the light of justice, lost their basic inalienable rights. But, alas, the danger of the Quarter remained part of its allure. *New York Times* reporter Roy Reed called it "an enchantress who always keeps her secrets" in a 1972 travel piece. And the Vieux Carré continued to be a beacon for celebrants like Stewart Butler and Steven Duplantis. After each of his New Orleans soirees, Steven needed to be back at his base in Texas on Monday morning. He recalls changing from his street clothes into military dress while driving down the highway. He would report bleary-eyed at 7:30 a.m. and do his utmost to pass as the masculine norm.[45]

Once he had settled into this arrangement, Steven began exploring gay life in Texas, but he did so cautiously, never bringing any identification to bars in case of a police raid. On one of these excursions, Steven accidentally befriended an Office of Special Investigations (OSI) officer from the air force investigating homosexual cases. Introduced by a mutual friend, the man had sat and flirted with Steven for several hours. The OSI inquisitor eventually divulged that he was homosexual himself and used his position to provide advance warning of raids and investigations to gay friends like Steven. For months now, the eight hours between New Orleans and San Antonio put time and miles between Steven's two lives, but Steven felt the distance closing.[46]

Occasionally that Sunday, as Stewart and Steven laughed and

clinked their glasses, Steven's eyes would wander off vacantly, and Stewart had to ask what was wrong. Nothing, Steven would respond, flashing a grin, but Stewart surmised that something weighed on him. Starting during Mardi Gras 1972, Stewart and Steven had entered more of a "friends who drink together sleep together" phase of their relationship, but they still teamed up to lure unsuspecting thirds. That's how they met Alfred Doolittle.[47]

It had rained torrentially during much of February 1972, more than any other Mardi Gras in decades. The typical 4:00 p.m. drizzle of "holy water" in New Orleans had turned that year into an unrelenting tempest. Stewart and Steven had already ducked into Gertrude's, a gay bar located a few doors down from the Up Stairs Lounge. They noticed Alfred, whom they took to be a baby-faced hustler, shivering outside. "He's standing in the door out in the rain sopping wet, crying," remembered Steven. "I said, 'Stewart, look at that poor boy.' He was beautiful." Alfred had chin-length dark hair that fell in his face. He reminded Stewart of the comic strip character Prince Valiant. Alfred's cherry-red lips matched his maroon shirt, the polyester so wet it was nearly see-through. Stewart went out and cajoled Alfred into joining their table.[48]

They hit it off, and the group soon headed for a second stop at Café Lafitte in Exile, where the flirting escalated. A photo taken at that bar that night shows Alfred hugging Stewart from behind. In the picture, Alfred is catching Stewart off guard as he snuggles his nose into Stewart's ear. If Alfred looks smitten, Stewart looks to be lovesick, his eyes closed. He's leaning back into Alfred's embrace with a cigarette dangling from his lips. "He came onto me like gangbusters," recalled Stewart. "On the way to the car, he says, 'Well, you'll probably throw me out tomorrow like everybody else does.'" The next morning, Steven drove back to San Antonio, and Alfred stuck around with Stewart for the rest of the day. "During the following months, it became obvious that oh no, that was it!" said Steven. "Alfred's going to be there forever."[49]

Alfred Doolittle, as it turned out, wasn't so clueless as he first appeared. He wasn't even a hustler. As a trust-fund recipient in his thirties with mental health difficulties, "Alfred was a little bit screwy in the head," agreed Stewart. "People would say, 'What's his diagnosis?' And I would say, 'All of the above.'" Alfred was heir to a family fortune built on the ambitions of James "Jimmy" Doolittle, a celebrated World War II hero. He had grown up attending General Doolittle's military balls with the rest of the family and felt the pressure of regimentation crash against his wild sexuality. Now an outcast from his San Francisco–based upper-class family, and to their chagrin, Alfred received regular checks from his trust fund, which he squandered on books, boys, and booze, among other indulgences. Fortunately for Alfred, Stewart was a man without the usual moral or sexual hang-ups. Stewart never wanted the party—or, in fact, the orgy—to end. He craved more than a little eccentricity in his bed, and he sensed in Alfred not just a romantic prospect but also, he admits, a financial sponsor.[50]

But Stewart's life had always muddled the pragmatic and the romantic. Stewart had a unique upbringing—spending his formative adolescent years at the National Leprosarium, a self-contained medical campus in Carville, Louisiana, for individuals suffering from leprosy (now known as Hansen's disease). Carville, as it was nicknamed, was one of only two lazar houses—isolation facilities for patients with leprosy—in the United States. Between 1942 and 1949, Stewart's father worked at this remote sanatorium as a maintenance and supply officer. Thus, from the ages of eleven through eighteen, Stewart and his family resided on the hospital campus, living across a dividing line that quarantined the patients away from staff and their families.[51]

Stewart remembered how the place operated as a kind of happy prison. Some of his friends, children suffering from disease on the "patient side," were abandoned by their parents and assigned surrogates. They'd receive little access to education. Stewart, on the other hand, had attended a special school for the children of Carville staff. Guards patrolled patient corridors from 9:00 a.m. to 6:00 p.m., when gates to the patient buildings were closed and locked. But Stewart always ran free of those restrictions. Even when he was young, Stewart possessed a demeanor that foreshadowed some degree of isolation in his uniqueness—in the form of his budding attraction to other boys, some of whom were ill. Stewart saw the centuries-old stigma, which predated biblical accounts of lepers, at work in various ways in front of him. These people, thought to be highly contagious in a millennia-long misunderstanding of the slow-spreading illness, were society's untouchables. More than sympathizing with Carville patients, he related to them. What if anyone discovered his disorder? His family observed Catholic mass, and communion at the hospital church was always served from separate chalices for the diseased and the well.[52] The hypocrisy was patent and painful.

In fact, as a teenager, Stewart zoned in on those disparities and used them to reject organized belief systems. A quarter century later, not even the MCC of New Orleans, with its gay-affirming message, could coax Stewart back to Christianity. He was a man of strong principles but largely without creed. After what he'd witnessed, moral purity seemed sanctimonious. So, as an adult in his forties, Stewart had no qualms taking charge of Alfred's trust-fund checks and ensuring that the money lasted for the both of them. After a few months, the Doolittle family reached out to Stewart with a supportive letter, saying that they were impressed with how he'd managed Alfred's affairs. "They knew that if Alfred had his way, in ten years he'd be out of money," explained Steven Duplantis. Although Stewart didn't believe in monogamy, Alfred didn't either, and so their union blossomed—together, and with Steven, and with other hookups and runaways whom they unofficially adopted.[53]

In their couplehood, Stewart continued his work as a draftsman at an engineering firm, where he wasn't open about his sexuality, while Alfred seemed to occupy his time decorating their apartment and cheerfully writing letters to world leaders. The relationship of Steven, Stewart, and Alfred had deepened into a genuine ménage à trois by the summer of 1973, and the trio would sleep in the same bed on weekends when Steven visited. And they seemed to be having a proverbial ball that Sunday, Steven's small bouts of silence notwithstanding. Steven would soon have to leave for his long drive back to San Antonio, but Stewart suggested that they stop at the beer bust for one last drink.[54]

CHAPTER 4

United We Stand

Twilight

Adam Fontenot was visibly sauced. Having imbibed hard liquor for more than five hours without a bite to eat, Adam took on the role of a resident lush at the Up Stairs Lounge. He was, witnesses recall, able to giggle and nod in agreement with a speaker's words but unable to participate more in the conversation. Nor did his compromised balance enable him to stand or move much from his bar stool. Buddy Rasmussen was busy, if also slightly annoyed with his lover. He was accustomed to seeing Adam in such a stupor, but he also felt partially responsible for serving him too many drinks this afternoon.[1]

Buddy and his busboy, Rusty Quinton, had their hands full tending to the crowds, facing the ceaseless call for pitchers and mugs, and they soon forgot Adam. The beer bust was in full swing, with ninety or so patrons laughing and carousing on a carefree Sunday evening. Some patrons needed babysitting more than others. Plus, those not satisfied by bottomless beer were placing drink orders that needed to be filled. During hectic hours at the Up Stairs Lounge, one had to shout drink orders to Buddy, but they needed to be simple. Anything beyond a rum and Coke, a Bloody Mary, or a Cape Cod (vodka, cranberry juice, and lime juice) would be laughed off.[2]

Nursing a drink, Steven Duplantis ran his eyes over the bodies around him, looking for a new squeeze. Prospects abounded, many in a condition that made them amenable to a pickup line. Steven tended to drink straight rum, as did many in the armed forces. Stewart and

Alfred drank whatever and whenever the fancy struck them, but they usually sprang for vodka. Above their heads, a haze of cigarette smoke hung in bilious clouds that wafted just below the ceiling tiles. Window units pulsed with air conditioning, and Buddy tried to preserve the coolness by shouting "close the door" whenever patrons entered. Coins jangled in pockets or rolled across the bar, as many paid the beer bust fare in change.[3]

It felt like everyone was at the Lounge tonight. Robert Vanlangendonck, a newbie, wore gold-rimmed glasses and introduced himself warily as Bob Vann. Maybe he was closeted, some guessed. He used the nickname to protect a corporate job at Shell Oil. Vanlangendonck's friend Jim Hambrick, a toupee-wearing regular who looked more than a few decades Robert's senior, had provided a ride to the French Quarter and was ordering drinks. Seeing a crowd form at the bar, Hugh Cooley agreed to pitch in a few hours early as a second busboy for Buddy. The MCC crew arrived in trickles: Deacon Courtney Craighead, around 5:00 p.m.; Deacon Mitch Mitchell with Horace after they'd dropped the kids off at the movies; and Pastor Bill Larson and the rest from the Fatted Calf. Witnesses recalled how they all looked primed for fun.[4]

Ricky Everett, with out-of-towner Ronnie Rosenthal, snagged a table in the dance area so that they could talk with fewer interruptions. In an era when televisions had fewer than eight channels, bars were forums where people commonly struck up banter easily with strangers. "I just never could sit still in a bar," explained Ricky. "I was too hyper. I would have a cocktail and, if I was not having a conversation, then I'd drift off to another bar." Bartenders would often serve as conduits by making quick introductions. Ricky called Buddy Rasmussen a renowned "promoter" of dialogue, capable of juggling multiple exchanges and a telephone conversation at once. Buddy's talents worked to Ricky's advantage. Ricky's mother, who lived across the river, was known to call the Up Stairs Lounge with messages. As a self-confessed "mama's boy," Ricky was still in and out of the family home as a tenant, and his mother insisted that Ricky give her a place to call when he was out, in case of emergencies. Despite all the shenanigans surrounding him in the bar, Buddy was known to play it cool when the phone rang. He kept people's cover. One time when Ricky was out barhopping, Ricky felt a tug on the shoulder from a cute stranger—just over from the Lounge—who leaned in and whispered a message from Buddy Rasmussen: Call your momma, Ricky.[5]

Today, Ricky relaxed in a nook with Ronnie. Closer to the bar, Luther Boggs leaned on Jeanne Gosnell, his best friend and occasional beard—a female companion used as a ruse to conceal one's homosexuality. They sat near the couple Reggie Adams and Regina and the inebriated Adam Fontenot. Perry Waters, the gay dentist, joked with a group. Was that sweet-voiced Francis Dufrene in from Harahan? Dufrene was known to catch two buses from the suburbs to reach the bar. He lived for these nights. And there was Willie Inez Warren, a gay mother "hen," and her two "gay for pay" sons, the part-time hustlers Eddie and James; they were considered shabby but honest folk, always off duty at the beer bust.[6]

Worlds inevitably intermixed. Stewart Butler chatted with Horace Broussard, Mitch Mitchell's lover and Stewart's regular barber. "That's where I'd make a barber appointment," recalled Stewart. "I'd just made an appointment with him that night." Jason Guidry, sometimes called the "bar dingbat," was present as well (Guidry was a very common surname in Louisiana, and Jason was no relation to the hustler Mark Allen Guidry). The place seemed to darken a bit toward the grand piano in the corner, which was lit up to provide a stage for performers. Some of the windows on the Chartres Street side were shuttered to accentuate the feeling of privacy. Patrons like John Golding, who'd recently celebrated twenty-five years of marriage to his wife, appreciated these precautions.[7]

John had much to lose by drinking at the beer bust. He was a prototypical blue-collar breadwinner, working as a salesman at a cigar shop and living with his family near the Lower Garden District. For decades, John and his wife, Jane, had had an understanding. She didn't venture with him downtown, and he didn't let his fun creep back into their marriage. "She clearly accepted Dad for who he was," explained their son, John Golding Jr., who was eleven years old in 1973.

"Yes, there was this void of homosexuality linked to Dad. That was always there, but Mom was accepting of it and clearly very attached to him. They shared a bed. It wasn't just a black-and-white, 'it-was-all-deception' dynamic."[8]

Although their arrangement was loving, it wasn't ideal. Months before, John had been fired from his well-paying job at a public utility after being caught in a homosexual act. This wasn't his first such incident, but luckily this one stayed out of the newspaper and didn't become neighborhood gossip. That night in June, Jane had served her husband spaghetti as part of their family's Sunday ritual. Before he walked out the door for the evening, they kissed goodbye. They had three children together, but two were already out of the house. With John off to do whatever he did, Jane readied John Jr., their youngest, for sleep. Now John Golding mingled at the beer bust with Dr. Waters and other men, whom John called "lovers" but Jane thought of as her husband's "friends."[9]

These patrons wished, beyond all else, to avoid public declarations of their lifestyle. Individuals caught by the police and charged with offenses would be outed when their names were routinely published in the "Orleans Parish Records of the Day," a popular section of the *Times-Picayune*. In this police record, names would be listed beside alleged crimes and alleged attempted crimes—indeed, according to Louisiana's criminal code, an *attempted* crime against nature could be prosecuted.[10] A gay man didn't actually need to commit a homosexual offense to face a penalty; conspiracy, or intent to commit, could be sufficient, if proven. The state's sodomy law, ostensibly on the books to prosecute any type of nonmarital sex from adultery to bestiality, was most often employed to prosecute same-gender sex and at one time prescribed a mandatory penalty of life imprisonment with hard labor for a single offense. By 1973, the charge had been reduced to a felony with a minimum two-year prison sentence. And, even in the event that a charge was dropped due to lack of evidence, a name would often still appear printed in the newspaper beside the annotation "nol prossed," meaning not prosecuted. "That pretty much ended your life in New Orleans," recalled John Meyers, the gay seminarian who lived near the Up Stairs Lounge.[11]

These were the stakes, pressing in from the outside world. But all seemed different inside the Lounge, as if freedom reigned to the tune of David Stuart Gary's piano. Piano Dave was tearing it up to the delight of partygoers. A crowd gathered as melodies poured forth. The twenty-two-year-old performer paid his rent through the tip jar, posted on the bench, as well as through a steady gig across the street at the Marriott. He took some gigs for the money and others for the soul—the Up Stairs Lounge was clearly such a soul gig. Dave grooved on his instrument. Notes reverberated into the dance area, where Ricky and Ronnie laughed and boogied. A gay pied piper, Piano Dave played, and New Orleans's gay working class turned out in force. Rooms overflowed, though the Lounge always seemed to keep within its fire code capacity of 110 people.[12]

Circulating closer to the piano was George "Bud" Matyi, a semi-famous musician who performed under the name "Buddy Stevens" and appeared with the house band on *The Tonight Show Starring Johnny Carson*. Bud Matyi was what was considered an "A-gay," a sophisticate who owned a condo near the lakefront. Bud's lover, folks whispered, was Rod Wagener, an afternoon talk show host on radio stations WDSU and WGSO. Given their public personae, Bud and Rod were forced to hide their relationship from fans. Most who knew them understood that public exposure of their lifestyles would destroy their careers. Nevertheless, Rod and Bud lived in conspicuous luxury. They drove a 1966 Chevrolet Camaro convertible, a "muscle car" that turned heads. According to a blurb in *Billboard* magazine, Bud Matyi had just signed a management and recording deal.[13] Not unlike Clay Shaw before his downfall, Bud was a man on the verge of celebrity, a person with something to lose.

As Rod steered their convertible down Iberville to drop off Bud at the Up Stairs Lounge, he couldn't hide his agitation with Bud's desire to visit such a dingy block. Of course, there were personal complications. Despite being only twenty-seven, Bud Matyi had three young kids—Tina, Todd, and Shawn—back in California from two previous marriages. Bud had, in fact, parted ways with his second wife, Pamela Cutler, when he met the handsome Rod Wagener. "She said my dad left her for a guy," Tina Marie Matyi recalled her mother telling her. "And I feel that she felt betrayed in that aspect of it." As an innocent lie to help the children, Pamela Cutler explained that Rod Wagener was now important to their father because he was a "business manager." Bud Matyi filed for preliminary divorce in 1972, but the proceedings were still pending. Emotions stayed raw as Bud and Rod attempted to negotiate some form of custody arrangement with Pamela. All the while, Rod formed emotional attachments on the phone with Bud's kids. "I was told by my grandmother that Rod and my dad were going to come and get us," recalled Tina Marie. "And they were going to take us and fight for custody for us. And they were going to raise us."[14] This impossible dream of a gay family made whole, with gay lovers at the helm, seemed tantalizingly within reach.

But Bud had promised that he'd pitch in on the piano that night. Unable to dissuade his lover, Rod had slowed to a stop beneath the Up Stairs canopy. They kissed before Bud hopped out. A medal of a dove clutched by two hands, the Catholic symbol of the Holy Spirit, swung around Bud's neck as he climbed the stairs.[15]

POLYESTER, THAT MAINSTAY of 1970s fashions, clung to male bodies as patrons sized one another up and likely chatted about such topics as Secretariat's recent Triple Crown triumph; *Deliverance*, a hit movie from the previous year starring the hirsute Burt Reynolds (whose arousing poster in the bar made "purty mouth" jokes a go-to); or whatever cantankerous jibe Archie Bunker, a beloved if also bigoted character, had gotten away with on *All in the Family,* the top-rated series of the season. Maybe they chatted about the movie being filmed down the street, *My Name Is Nobody*. Or about effete television personalities like Paul Lynde on *Hollywood Squares* or Charles Nelson Reilly on *Match Game*, game-show contestants whose double entendre–laden wisecracks helped them play the "nancy," a vaudeville-era term for an effeminate male jester. Nancies were, in fact, caricatures that society had been trained to laugh at: fey, limp-wristed, speaking with a lisp, with no social defense but a quip. Lynde, particularly, had perfected his shtick and made it family friendly enough for the sitcom *Bewitched*. Even though Lynde's sexuality might have seemed obvious, especially in retrospect, many of his fans lacked the context in his heyday to question whether he was actually gay. There were few other gay icons to chat about. David Bowie's audacious claims of bisexuality, recently said while wearing epicene attire, were more the mechanisms of courting controversy than candid affirmations of difference. In the literary world, Gore Vidal and Truman Capote both walked a clever line and played off their affectations as the eccentricities of brilliant minds.[16]

Roger Dale Nunez stumbled through the door of the Up Stairs Lounge and into the beer bust. Through his forays in and around Iberville, Roger had visited the Up Stairs Lounge on several occasions, although the regular patrons, nonjudgmental as they were, hadn't exactly welcomed him. Roger, who was more of an outsider in a jovial society of buddies, functioned better in the hustler bars, where men went alone. Although many on Iberville had seen his face, few had taken the trouble to learn his name. Ricky Everett vaguely remembered seeing Roger at the Lounge, but it's telling that even kindhearted Ricky didn't consider Roger a friend.[17]

Roger looked rough and drunk enough that night to be a hassle. Steven Duplantis remembered hearing an audible reaction to the guy's presence, as if people were saying, "He's here again?" Behind Roger walked Mark Allen Guidry, the younger hustler. Ignoring the wisecracks, Roger headed straight for the bathroom before he could be served, which left Mark Allen Guidry standing alone. Mark must have felt stranded, socially speaking, after the less than enthusiastic reception, and he didn't stick around long. Roger didn't seem to notice. He stationed himself in one of the two men's room stalls and began gawking through a peephole at patrons using adjoining facilities.[18]

According to those present, Roger whispered comments of encouragement or harassment to those in the neighboring stall, perhaps hoping to win a friend or torment a quick lay from someone with a fragile ego. But his tactic created a bottleneck. The line to the bathroom soon backed up past the bar, and patrons began to get testy. Buddy seemed preoccupied. An eighteen-year-old named David Dubose, a youngster not in the bar's employ, was gathering empty beer mugs and attempting to return them en masse. Dubose wanted to claim the fifty-cent deposit on the mugs and use the proceeds to further imbibe. But Buddy and Hugh caught him in the act and refused the extra coinage. In retaliation, Dubose began "pouring beer on the floor, kicking the customers, and being loud."[19] It was teenage revenge.

After a raucous but hardly uncommon afternoon-into-evening session, the beer bust ended at 7:00 p.m., and people stood and sang "United We Stand." Beer pitchers returned to ordinary prices, and half of the crowd had departed as Dubose headed for the bathroom. He cut in line, to the chagrin of other patrons like Robert Vanlangendonck, who had been waiting his turn. Dubose began pounding on the occupied stall door, the one holding Roger Nunez. He repeatedly cursed at whoever was inside and refused to come out, but then he noticed Steven Duplantis standing at the sink.[20]

Dubose grabbed at Steven and proposed a blowjob for five or ten dollars. Although they were around the same age, Steven was unimpressed. Steven rebuffed him with a "No, you're just trash," but Dubose failed to take the hint. "He wouldn't leave," remembered Steven. "So he stayed in the bathroom. I went straight and told Buddy."[21] Hustling was a rule violation, and Steven's report would mean immediate ejection. However, just as Steven blabbed, Michael Scarborough entered the empty bathroom stall and heard Roger Nunez's whispers.

Evidently, Roger said the wrong thing to Scarborough, a man who had grown up tough. Michael's father was one of the biggest bail bondsmen in the city, a strongman who made employees call him "sir." Having learned to stand up to that domineering figure, Michael wouldn't just accept the taunts of a drunken stranger. Enraged at the Peeping Tom, Michael left the bathroom and reported the conduct. Buddy Rasmussen weighed whether to act first on the Peeping Tom gumming up the bathroom or the hustler pouring beer, and decided to start by clearing Roger out. Buddy and Hugh Cooley entered the bathroom, pulled Roger Nunez from the stall, and told him to leave people alone.[22]

Suspicious of a snitch, Roger began looking for Michael Scarborough. Spotting Michael by the piano, the highly inebriated Roger ran at him. Michael was sitting at a table with his lover, MCC patron Glenn Green. Born on All Saints Day, Glenn was a gentle soul and the steadier of the two lovers. He had grown up in Michigan with two macho older brothers serving in the army. Glenn himself enlisted in the navy. He'd been stationed in Okinawa and spent three years in the service of a high-ranking admiral. But, according to Glenn's sister, Naoma McCrae, he was caught having sex with another man and discharged for "medical reasons." Now in New Orleans, Glenn worked as a clerk at the International Trade Mart. On his off days, he helped elderly neighbors.[23]

Glenn Green likely tried to ignore Roger. Michael, however, would let no one insult him. So when Roger shouted a few epithets, Michael stood up and leveled Roger with a punch to the face. "He came over and started agitating me," Michael said later, "so I jumped up and just knocked him down." Roger fell to the floor and, groaning in pain, stayed on his back for a minute, until Buddy and Hugh gathered him up. Now Buddy had another decision to make: eject Michael for fighting Roger, or eject Roger for inciting the fight. Since Michael was popular at the bar and Roger was too intoxicated to be served anyhow, Buddy moved to eject the injured man, who would probably bother more patrons if they let him stick around. Before he could stand up on his own, Roger yelled something Michael heard as "I'm going to burn you all out." Close to the altercation, Steven Duplantis heard Roger say, "I'm going to burn this place to the ground." It's worth underscoring that, even above the teeming noise of the bar, both men heard the word "burn." Buddy and Hugh proceeded to drag Roger toward the bar entrance as Roger kicked and spat. "It took two or three people to get him to the upstairs door," recalled Steven. "There was an altercation to get him out," Steven continued, "even out on the landing."[24]

The violent scene shook Steven out of his reverie. He checked his watch and realized it was time to leave. He knew he had to go right then to reach San Antonio by sunrise. He'd be driving at top speed through the night to make it back to base, but something about that guy screaming "burn" felt wrong. "Especially the way that he said it," Steven remembered. He turned to Stewart and Alfred and told them, "Y'all need to leave here," to clear out and head elsewhere. "Stewart was having fun and hearing none of it," Steven continued. Alfred took Steven's side immediately, but Alfred suffered from frequent bouts of paranoia that made Stewart roll his eyes. "Alfred says, 'I want to leave,'" recalled Stewart. Steven tried to persuade Stewart further, but he couldn't wait any longer. Having passed the message, Steven kissed his friends and took off. With Steven gone, Stewart tried to dismiss any notion of leaving, but Alfred persisted until Stewart had to listen.[25]

Meanwhile, Buddy and Hugh dragged Roger down the staircase and out the front door by his shoulders. They returned to find David Dubose, the teenager, as defiant as ever, dancing with two beer mugs that he hadn't paid for. Having hustled and attempted to steal, Dubose was clearly not welcome anymore. They dragged him, mugs in hands, down the front stairs. Buddy told Dubose to "leave and never return" and tossed him onto Iberville Street. Realizing that he was still holding the mugs, Dubose threw them at Buddy in a rage. They shattered in the bar's entryway, littering the inside foyer with glass.[26]

Dubose stumbled away, and Buddy asked Hugh to sweep the entrance while he went back upstairs to man the bar. Perhaps sensing an opportunity in an out-of-control teen, an older man named James Smith left the Lounge and caught up with Dubose. Smith proposed a sexual fling, and Dubose accepted. They staggered back to his apartment, where Smith cooked Dubose a meal and then gave him a blowjob for ten dollars. Eventually, Smith drove Dubose to the Golden Slipper Lounge on the northern edge of the Quarter.[27]

Back upstairs, the Nunez altercation and Dubose's ejection had certainly caught the attention of patrons and become fodder for conversation, but the ruckus in no way ruined the evening. No one would mistake the Up Stairs Lounge for a high-toned establishment, and Buddy and Hugh had handled things quickly and efficiently. "The fight was over just like that," recalled Buddy. Still, Mitch and Horace must have been glad that they dropped off the kids. They tended to think of the Lounge as a family place and, the previous year, had held their holy union ceremony and reception in the bar area. As such, they sometimes brought Duane and Stephen along on beer bust night,[28] but this evening's violence would have been confusing for children to witness.

DOWN THE STREET, at the Walgreens on the corner of Iberville
and Royal, a white man in his midtwenties walked through the doors.
He had dark brown hair, a ruddy complexion, and a medium build.
Standing behind the register, cashier Claudine Rigaud made a practice
of greeting her regular customers by name, but she'd never seen this
man. He walked directly to the counter and asked to buy a can of
lighter fluid. He appeared to be heavily intoxicated. Rigaud showed
him where the fluid was kept and noted the sizes available. Ronsonol,
the iconic lighter fluid in a yellow can with blue letters, had long been
sold at French Quarter drugstores. It's a petroleum distillate commonly used as fuel for Zippo-style lighters.[29]

Rigaud thought nothing of the man's request. This store did a
good bit of business in tobacco products, in this era when smok-
ers could light up almost anywhere. But something else did pique
Rigaud's attention: the man's hands were visibly shaking, and he
seemed to be, in her words, "emotionally upset." No stranger to Iberville Street culture, Rigaud assessed that this man—soft-spoken and
"feminish"—might be gay. Nevertheless, a customer was a customer,
and Rigaud was about twenty minutes from her evening break.
Apprised of the can sizes, seven and twelve ounces, the man asked
Rigaud if a smaller can was for sale, but she informed him that the
smallest and cheapest of cans, four ounces of Ronsonol, had recently
sold out. So the customer reluctantly purchased the medium-size
can and left.[30]

Meanwhile, aggravated to be departing from the bar so soon, Stewart tramped down the staircase with Alfred, whom Stewart thought
must be experiencing another emotional episode. They halted at the
landing and shouted in a couple's row very likely witnessed by William White and Gary Williams—two teens poking their way around
wild French Quarter bars. White and Williams, jittery youths, bolted
as Stewart and Alfred took their argument down the stairs. Trailing
them all was Regina, born Richard Soleto. She and Reggie had dinner

plans with Buddy and Adam, but they needed money. Reggie offered to run back to their apartment, but Regina insisted that she do so. They pecked, and she left.[31]

At the bar, Buddy counted out his register and prepared to formally hand over duties to Hugh Cooley at 8:00 p.m. The night had been wild, and Buddy just needed to go to the storeroom, secure his money in the safe, and call it a day. By the Chartres Street wall, Piano Dave was chatting up patrons, perhaps speaking with a few frequent tippers who had taken a liking to him, and Bud Matyi played exuberantly at the bench. A few of the drag queens scheduled to perform for the charity benefit for the Crippled Children's Hospital had yet to arrive, but time was loose on beer bust night.[32] Matyi's hands danced across ebony and ivory. Hammers hit piano wires as, down below the Up Stairs Lounge, someone stood at the base of the stairs. This person—very likely the Walgreens customer but unwitnessed in the act—proceeded to empty seven ounces of lighter fluid from a yellow Ronsonol can onto the left side of the second step and then drop the canister. The porous wood of the staircase, more than a hundred years old, drank the fluid effortlessly. The red carpeting, running like a ribbon over lumber, sopped up the rest. On the second step, a patch of wet carpet sat ready like a wick. Searching pockets for a lighter or match, the assailant then dropped two ten-dollar bills, which floated down unnoticed. A spark was lit. Then the unmistakable smell of smoke.[33]

Harold Bartholomew, an attorney, was driving his kids from a downtown event when he hit traffic on Iberville. Bartholomew laid on the horn until he noticed the driver in front of him gaping and pointing. With his car windows rolled down, Bartholomew heard someone shout, "I'm telling you, you better get out of here!" Bartholomew saw a white man in his midtwenties come out from beneath the dark canopy marked "Up Stairs." A second man, wearing a T-shirt with writing across the back, approached the first man and slapped a hand over his back to hurry him along. "That'll fix the mother-fuckers," Bartholomew heard one of them say as they ran. An unnamed witness in a neighboring building thought he saw the two men get into a honking car. Everything was happening at high speed. Continuing to beep his horn to move traffic along, Bartholomew pulled his vehicle almost parallel with the canopy. His kids screamed. Acrid black smoke suddenly bellowed from the entryway. Across the street from the Up Stairs Lounge, Katherine Kirsch hit a commercial break on her TV program and ducked out for a pack of cigarettes. Her feet hit the sidewalk, and Kirsch heard someone say "fire" as she crossed Iberville toward Walgreens. She looked into the doorway of the Up Stairs Lounge. Flames gathered on a front step. It was about 7:53 p.m., and the sun had yet to set.[34]

Kirsch started yelling and ran into the nearest bar, the Midship, to sound the alarm. A retired soldier sprinted out to assess the emergency situation. Maybe he could douse the flames with a pitcher, but the blaze crackled stubbornly in a small pool that looked to be fueled with oil. The fire spread from the second to the third step as the veteran ducked back into the Midship. He shouted for the barmaid to call the seven-digit emergency fire number (911 did not yet exist in New Orleans). It was 7:56, and help was already en route from the Central Fire Station, which was located just two blocks away. The soldier ran back to see the fire snaking aggressively up to the top of the stairwell. "It sounded like firecrackers going off in there," he later told the *States-Item* (New Orleans's other daily newspaper at the time), perhaps hearing the shorting out of electrical wires. "That stairway was gone."[35] No one was going into the Up Stairs Lounge now, nor was anyone coming out.

Harold Bartholomew would later describe this staircase as a "door to hell." The smoldering scent, stirred by a northerly wind in gusts of five to ten miles per hour, wafted all the way down Chartres Street to the Cabildo Gallery off Jackson Square. "The smell of smoke and a taste of barbeque," remembered curator Joseph Bermuda, who found the odor odd. People drinking across the way left their tables, saying, "There's a fire, there's fire!" The smell became pungent. "I came out in the middle of the street," said Bermuda, "and I could see five blocks down: smoke. I realized it was serious, and I walked all the way down the street to see what was going on." Bermuda headed briskly past the Club New Orleans Baths on Toulouse Street, then past the state Fourth Circuit Courthouse toward he knew not what.[36]

At the top of the bar's landing, a window flickered light through gloom and soot. Exposed to flames below, this tiny aperture now acted as a vent to a chimney. Witnesses watched as the staircase became fully engorged and began to project heat in waves, like a makeshift furnace stoking temperatures above 1000 degrees Fahrenheit. What wasn't yet burning on the walls and stairs through direct contact released volatile gases, in the process that solid matter takes to heat up to its ignition temperature. Flammable, poisonous vapors rose and gathered in an air pocket—right near the metal door to the Up Stairs Lounge. Trapped in the enclosure of the staircase and with nowhere else to vent, these gases increased in pressure and sank deeper toward the wood embers.[37]

The now-raging conflagration threatened to become what fire marshals would call a "flashover," when a room ignites floor to ceiling. But there was a slight cessation to the fire when the cramped stairwell abruptly ran out of air. Here was the chance, if any, to douse the flames. Having consumed all the oxygen in the space, the fire now struggled to suck wind down through the window and up from the street.

Trapped behind the metal door, patrons of the Up Stairs Lounge had no clue what awaited them. They milled about. There was a sudden ringing inside the bar. Buddy knew the sound. It came from a buzzer installed at the street level to notify him of morning deliveries or the presence of a taxi. Buddy looked around the bar. This buzzer felt odd. No customer had asked him to use the bar phone to call a cab, and the piano was loud. "Who's hitting that buzzer?" Buddy yelled. "Go check to see who's hitting that buzzer." The sound continued. Buddy wondered if it was one of those troublemakers he'd kicked out. The drone was relentless, triggered he thought by an electrical short, by a prankster, or some combination. Back in the storeroom, Hugh Cooley counted out a register and opened the safe. Buddy shouted to a nearby patron, MCC congregant Luther Boggs, to open the door and yell down.[38]

Luther turned the knob and pulled inward. As he did, air slid into the staircase. Touched with oxygen, superheated gases detonated on contact. Luther, in disbelief, pulled the door ajar, and the explosion rushed through in a fireball. Fire flew down the length of the bar in a backdraft that resounded like a cannon. The flames cleaved forty-four feet across the room—past the archway and into the crowd singing at the grand piano. Already burning, some began screaming on the spot. Others dove haplessly under chairs or the piano for cover. Glasses fell. Tables tipped over. The blast knocked Luther to the floor.[39]

MCC member Frank Dean, who'd been in the military for fifteen years, described it as "a flame shot from a flamethrower." Another customer called it a "big block of fire." Hearing desperate yelling, Buddy turned his head as the lights went out. He remembered what he saw as "a blast furnace." Then soot and smoke took care of visibility. People began stampeding.[40]

"Don't panic!" Buddy shouted as he flicked on a flashlight and hopped over the bar. "Adam was sitting right where Buddy jumped over," recalled Ricky Everett, who was looking into the first room. "And he yelled at Adam to follow." Ricky then saw fire peel a length of carpet off the floor, which seemed to hang in the air. Used to taking charge in the bar, Buddy moved with purpose. He grabbed people by the collar, the elbow, the arm, anything to shake them as they looked transfixed. "Come with me," he said as he headed toward the archway to the second room. "Follow me, follow me, follow me." Darkness enveloped the space, inciting "smoke blindness," a form of claustrophobia from sudden light deprivation (imagine losing your primary sense when you are intoxicated and at the peak moment of an emergency). Buddy physically dragged Ricky Everett from his chair.[41]

Intense heat shattered lightbulbs. Fire licked its way up the wallpaper and chased decorations across the ceiling. Within seconds, a ten-foot-tall plume lifted a ceiling tile, which exposed the pocket of air above the bar and created a second rush of flame toward every corner of the room. A plastic-fed firestorm blew over the heads of patrons, who couldn't see the blaze moving faster than they could sprint. It chewed up walls like linen. It whooshed across the tinder-dry space—snapping and sizzling in its thrust. A line began to form behind Buddy as Jeanne Gosnell scooped up Luther Boggs near the doorway and headed for a window.[42]

Robert Vanlangendonck had finally gotten into a bathroom stall when someone shouted, "Oh, they've started a fire out there." He backed out of the stall and saw a glow reflecting beneath the door. Then three or four men ran into the bathroom. One said he planned to wait until a fireman came and got him. Robert decided to get out. The hallway dead-ended in a rolling darkness. He took a breath and entered smoke. He waved his arms in front of him, attempting to feel his way forward. His hands touched a nearby window, next to the restroom door. Just then, another patron threw a chair through the glass and cut Robert's hands. A burst of air from the outside world coaxed flames into a vortex, burning his arm. The first man hopped through, ahead of everyone, onto the fire escape. He looked for a street ladder—only there was no ladder to take them down to Iberville. This particular fire escape led only toward the rooftop. From down on Iberville Street, looking up from his car, Harold Bartholomew saw the window shatter and this man rush out.[43]

Glass showered onto Bartholomew's windshield as he told his kids to duck down. Before he could blink, Bartholomew saw the man leap a metal railing and fall twelve feet. Air burst from his lungs when his feet hit concrete. Men ran over to pour pitchers of ice water onto his back, extinguishing flames.[44]

Robert prepared to follow this escapee's lead. He sat on the metal platform with his legs dangling. Strangers shouted, but he couldn't slow his mind to hear what they were saying. Desperate, Robert gripped a metal rod on the fire escape and swung down. "It started bending," Robert remembered. "And I just sort of floated down to the sidewalk." Sensing danger for his kids, Harold Bartholomew pressed the accelerator and pulled his car out of range.[45]

Back upstairs, limping toward the window, his back aflame, Luther Boggs panicked and shoved Jeanne Gosnell forward in an attempt to save her. The maneuver stripped Jeanne of her balance and pushed her face into the broken window casing. Her front teeth shattered, but Jeanne pulled herself up. She emerged onto the fire escape and heard cries coaxing her down. But she couldn't make herself jump. The world started spinning, and she ran up the fire escape toward the third floor. When she ran out of stairs, she paused at the top and sheltered—unable to move further—and gasped for air.[46]

Luther made it out behind her. With burns across half his body, he flailed into and over the railing and fell like a human torch. Passersby tried to catch him, and then sat him down as his body continued to emit steam and smoke—literally, cooking as they stripped him nude.[47] He cradled bits of flesh that dangled from his hands as these strangers smothered him in a blanket. The blanket clung to his wounds, and he could not adjust or remove the blanket again for risk of reopening them.

Blocked by four bodies in the bar's Iberville Street window, hemmed in by crowds following Buddy, lovers Eugene Thomas and Fred Sharohway found themselves trapped near the blazing doorway, which wasn't closing. They'd been standing near Luther when the inferno began, but now they couldn't see but for flashes of orange through pitch-black. They faced a choice: stand and die or try something, try anything. What happens in that moment when the floor is fire and the walls are fire and the ceiling begins to rain fire? The couple looked at each other and nodded their heads and proceeded to sprint into the fiery stairwell. They burned themselves down the length of the staircase and appeared in the faint light of Iberville. Their burns bubbled. Blinking, they screamed and gagged, alive with ashen faces, their clothing scorched and hair vanished.[48]

About thirty seconds had passed when Buddy reached the door to the theater hall, the entrance to the oft-forgotten back room, through the dance area. A line of bodies snaked behind him, from the dance floor to the archway that led into the bar area. Buddy fumbled with his keys to unlock the door. Behind their burning backs, bottles popped like corn kernels. Friends cried out to find one another, but the crackle of flames was deafening. Few could fathom what was happening or knew what Buddy was up to. They'd simply heard him say "Come with me."[49]

The bar's back Exit sign, positioned near the theater door, was nonfunctioning and therefore couldn't advertise its route of escape. Ronnie Rosenthal grabbed Ricky Everett. With the place suddenly illuminated, Ronnie had turned to his new friend, sensing death. He assumed they were jammed, entombed, but now they crushed against each other and waited. In line behind Buddy stood Courtney Craig-head and Jason Guidry with Mitch Mitchell—MCC congregants all. A man named Albert Monroe, scorching his face as he passed through the archway, moaned aloud. He'd gone for the fire escape, like Jeanne and Luther, but had to turn back.[50]

Richard "Mother" Cross stood behind Monroe, closest to the bar area, and debated trying another route. Then flames filled the arch-way behind him, which separated patrons in the bar area and the dance area. Hugh Cooley had run out from the storeroom amid the chaos, but must have bumped past Buddy in all the confusion. Men now gathered around Hugh in the back corner of the bar area as he tried to get them out through the far windows facing Chartres Street. "I just run [sic] over there and started breaking glass," remembered Michael Scarborough.[51]

Buddy then opened the metal door to the theater hall, and men pushed as he ran ahead of them. Twenty patrons shoved into the cool room as Buddy ducked behind the stage curtains. He threw props aside. He must have looked crazed as he moved a giant spool and then unlatched a hidden means of egress. Dusk light flashed onto faces, revealing the Up Stairs Lounge's unlikely second emergency exit. "This way," Buddy implored.[52] He pulled person after person across the small threshold onto a rooftop. It was 7:57 p.m., one minute since the first alarm.

The escapees wiped their hands and tried to catch their breath. They blinked and regarded one another for the first time since the commotion began. Most men on the rooftop were not burned, not even hurt, but terror set in when many couldn't find lovers and friends. Some tried to take a tally. Most huddled and coughed uncontrollably until someone found a way down. Evidently, a nearby window led to a neighboring building, one that could take them to Iberville Street and safety.[53]

Back in the theater hall, three MCC members returned from the relative safety of the roof: Mother Cross, Mitch Mitchell, and Ricky Everett. No one inside knew this way out, they figured, and some-one had to tell them. Together, they reentered the Up Stairs Lounge. When Mitch Mitchell couldn't find his lover Horace Broussard, he knew what he had to do. Balling hands into fists, Mitch trudged into the second room as it burned. Perhaps he couldn't fathom the danger unleashed in the place where he and Horace had spoken their vows. Likewise, Ricky Everett had lost track of Ronnie. "Going out, there was just so much confusion," recalled Ricky. "I couldn't remember if Ronnie was in front of me or behind me, and I looked behind me, and I didn't see him." Ricky chased after Mitch, but something stopped him short in the doorway. Standing in the wind tunnel, he watched Mitch—not even five feet in front of him—disappear in a mosaic of amber heat.[54]

Wind pulsed around Ricky's body, sucked from the theater hall into the swirling red of a room engulfed—a pyrogenic mass that swayed in what looked like slow motion. To Ricky, a religious man, it felt like a "moment with God," as if some divine presence was cloaking him in a blanket of protection and holding him safe. "It was a physical feeling that covered me," he insisted, "from the top of my head to my feet." Staring into fire, Ricky was struck with a strange certainty: Ronnie was safe while his pastor, Bill Larson, must be a goner. In shock, Ricky stumbled backward through the door. The entire interlude took but seconds. "I did not have one burn or a singed hair or any of that," he said. "I was perfectly protected." He found Ronnie waiting for him on the rooftop. Ricky cried as Ronnie held him up and guided him over the windowsill into the building next door.[55]

Mother Cross, the last of the MCC trio who reentered the building, lay on his stomach and inched toward the second room. The crawl was almost too hot to undertake, but he was determined to find his lover, Dean Morris. Mother Cross had metal braces on both of his legs from an accident years before, and he knew that heat could easily melt the hinges and prevent his own escape. From the floor, he searched for feet, for legs, for anyone he could reach with his hands. He saw nothing.[56]

Meanwhile, having guided the mass of people outside, Buddy backtracked into the theater hall for stragglers. He grabbed Mother Cross off the floor and tossed him back. When Cross stood his ground, ready to fight his protector, Buddy delivered what must have felt like miraculous news. Dean Morris was waiting outside.[57]

Buddy then shouted into the dance area through the open door. There was no response. He shouted several more times. Still no response. Remembering training he'd received in the air force, he closed the fire-rated door and put a latch in place, locking it shut. The second room was burning, but he knew that the third room would be protected by this act. Buddy had helped more than twenty people, spared the third room from all but smoke damage, maybe even saved the block by containing the blaze. However, he did not know that Mitch Mitchell had reentered the bar and was now barricaded inside.[58]

Buddy finally exited the theater hall, found his way across the roof, and descended to street level. No longer in danger, he joined the gathering mass of spectators and Good Samaritans attempting to help. Patrons from the Jimani—the first-floor bar located directly below the Up Stairs Lounge—were just then evacuating as smoke massed on the ceiling above them. They'd heard an eerie "pounding noise" from above—likely, people trying to break through the floor. No fire truck was present in front, not yet, as sirens screamed and the equipment wound toward them on one-way streets. Severely burnt men were sprawled on the sidewalk, while Buddy tried to provide comfort. But he could sense that something was catastrophically off. He scanned the faces again. Then it dawned on him: no Adam. No Adam Fontenot.[59]

Back upstairs, in the burning Lounge, those who hadn't seen Buddy or hadn't caught his words "Come with me" gathered with Hugh Cooley in a clump of about thirty in the back corner of the bar area. They sheltered there—as far as they could retreat from the advancing flames. It must have felt like the smart move, with Buddy guiding others in the direction of the fiery doorway to reach the theater. They'd only had seconds to make a decision, and there had been no Exit signs to call attention to Buddy's wisdom or arrows to guide their steps.[60] In fact, this group had backed into a death trap. Brick walls around them held in heat like an oven. Their means of escape, through three windows fronting on Chartres Street, was ramshackle, involving pushing, shoving, and stepping on broken glass.

Each of these massive windows, taller than a man, had been enclosed by iron burglar bars like a grille. These bars, spaced ten inches apart to prevent partiers from falling to the street below, now held them prisoner. The metal seemed strong, but Hugh found that men with thin frames could narrowly slip through one by one. Rusty Quinton squished himself out. He grabbed the corner sign of the Jimani bar and hung from it perilously before wrapping his hands around a pipe and shimmying down the building. Quinton ran yelling into Gertrude's, the nearby gay bar, on Chartres Street. It was 7:58 p.m.[61]

Upstairs, flames drew closer to the corner, and while larger patrons attempted to push themselves through the bars, some got stuck. Flames audibly choked out the oxygen, causing men to faint and gag. The floor became embers beneath them, burning through the soles of shoes. Ceiling tiles dripped molten Styrofoam on their heads like napalm, with the same horrific capacity to bury into flesh as in Vietnam.[62]

Oblivious to what was happening, Adam Fontenot sat on his stool. He felt a nip at his heels, somewhat muffled by the booze. The nip rose to his legs like the sting of a hot poker. It must then have crawled up his back and onto his head until everything was unimaginable pain and panic.[63] He rocked back and forth. How does one process the thought that I am burning, that my life may not end in bed as an old man but right here?

As one response, many froze in place. Most could not believe how the room that once protected them, existentially it had seemed, now engulfed them. Their Sunday beer bust was a charnel house, an auto-da-fé. The fire department's Flying Squad arrived outside in a red engine. A hook-and-ladder unit specially trained for rescue, they'd flown down one-way streets from the firehouse. Helmets on, men ran hoses from hydrants and raised an extendable ladder. Donning fire suits, several firefighters prepared to run up the front staircase. Just within eyeshot on the corner of Iberville and Royal, Roger Nunez walked into the bar Wanda's. Panting deeply and out of breath, he announced to the bartender, "Thank god, I just made it, from the fire." Roger looked, as bar patron Jackie Bullard would later describe, "filthy, covered in black."[64] Patrons cocked their heads, confused about what fire he was talking about.

Rusty Quinton ran back from Gertrude's to a spot on the sidewalk under the Chartres Street windows of the Lounge, opening his arms to break the fall of friends who'd slid through the bars; several smacked into him. Milton Mary, a bartender on his way to work nearby, turned a corner and saw men stacked against the windows, pressing away from death. "I kept thinking, throw some grappling hooks up there, tie it to the bumper of the fire truck, and take off to rip those bars out so those men could spill out," Mary recalled.[65]

Those metal grilles glowed orange-hot. Touching them meant scalding flesh, but the alternative was being scorched to death. Phillip Byrd, with burns on his hands, Francis Dufrene, with burns on his face, and Adolph Medina all jumped into the firefighters and bystanders desperately trying to catch them. A splay of legs kicked through the paneling of other windows. The men were running out of room, arms tangled, necks outstretched. Seven more bodies inched through the bars until Glenn Green had his turn. With no time to think, he grabbed his lover, Michael Scarborough, and pushed him through. Or maybe Michael just thought that Glenn was pushing him when he was only heaving himself. Michael felt a whoosh and struck the sidewalk hard. He looked back but couldn't see anything. "He saved me," Michael thought or may have said aloud—he couldn't be sure. He couldn't stand for all the people smacking at his back. His body smelled of cooking. He had been roasting. "He saved me."[66]

Glenn Green, who'd been holding his breath, must have inhaled with utmost exertion. It would have felt natural to take such a breath after expending all his strength. First, the superhot gases would have singed his lungs and rendered them useless. Then, the poisons he'd been inhaling reached his head: carbon monoxide, hydrogen cyanide, phosphine. Suffocating, he doubled over on the floor and lost consciousness. Jim Hambrick was the last patron to fall out of the windows, sheaves of muscle exposed beneath flaps of skin, like shirtsleeves pulled back. Hambrick's toupee had melted into his scalp. Plummeting face first, he cracked his head on the concrete, spewing blood into a gutter filling with hose water.[67]

Joseph Bermuda, having walked from nearby Jackson Square,

reached the pandemonium. "All I could see is young people trying to get out of the railings of the window," Bermuda remembered. "I remember very clearly the young fellow, holding this thing shaking it and screaming, 'Help, help!' "[68]

Lambent flames reached the back corner of the bar area, and the street lit up with the sound of seventeen people shrieking. Seeing faces burn in the windows, Rusty Quinton yelled for them to jump. Fire ate them up. "My friends are up there!" Quinton screamed. Men coughed up parts of themselves and dropped to the floor, one atop the next: Clarence McCloskey and his lover, Bill Bailey, who'd attended church that day; Dr. Perry Waters, with burns over 75 percent of him; Reggie Adams, too tall to fit through the bars, who had once wanted to be a priest; Hugh Cooley, who tried to play the rescuer; and Mitch Mitchell, with charring so bad his face would be unrecognizable. Mitch curled into the fetal pose of fire deaths immemorial. Bodies piled grotesquely on the floor, bones searing and blood boiling. "[After] all those screams and yells for help, everything got quiet," recalled Milton Mary. "And all you could hear were the firemen shouting orders. It was very eerie. It just went from a cacophony of noise to very quiet, and I realized then that all those people stacked like cords of wood against those windows were dead."[69]

In a standard "flashover," poisonous gases are enough to kill before a fire victim can burn to death. But this Sunday evening fire had progressed too quickly; it could not be so merciful in each case. Whoever had hidden in the bathroom perished from smoke inhalation. Bud Matyi, with Rod Wagener across town and three kids in California, lay burned beneath the grand piano. In his last act, it seems that Bud threw his body atop Willie Inez Warren, the gay mother hen, attempting to shield her. He smoldered while she suffocated. Sensing death in seconds, Bill Larson surged with adrenaline and ripped off a piece of the wall. Exposing a new window, he leaned into open air and edged himself between the bars. It looked as if he just might make it, just might squirm free until an air conditioner dropped on his head and a piece of window casing penned him in place. Fire burst through the gap of air he'd miraculously created, devouring his clothes and hair.[70]

Witnesses could do nothing but gape. Buddy Rasmussen looked on as a second burst engulfed Bill Larson with a commanding fury, which withered the skin on his face. So much seemed to happen simultaneously, but Buddy swears he could look past Bill a bit, to where Adam sat burning on his bar stool—just as he'd left him. Buddy watched a hose pierce the wave of flames and knock what had once been his lover to the floor.[71]

Bill Larson drooped his head against the window ledge.

His strength had not saved him.

"Oh, god, no!" he shouted.

It was 7:59 p.m.[72]

: ACT II :
FALLOUT

CHAPTER 5

Mayhem

Dusk—June 24, 1973

Up Iberville at the next corner, Royal Street, Stewart Butler and Alfred Doolittle drank and caroused at Wanda's, the Gene Davis–owned hustler bar. Their tempers had cooled after Stewart's little flare-up with Alfred on the Up Stairs Lounge staircase, and they were back to being relaxed in each other's company. More drinks, of course, helped to pacify the rage. Sirens blared a few blocks away, but Stewart thought nothing of them at first. Alfred was in good spirits, seemingly pleased that Stewart had finally listened to his entreaties. Sounds of alarm grew, interrupting their conversation as a red firetruck sped within feet of Stewart and Alfred—the engine from the Central Fire Station screeching as it plowed a taxi aside to reach the one-way of Iberville.[1]

Down at the next intersection, nearer to the scene of horror, a district chief of the fire department waved the engine forward. Metal scraped metal as the truck smashed yet another car to the curb and rushed toward the Up Stairs Lounge in a blur. Something horrific clicked in Stewart's head, a realization overriding the warm buzz of booze: Alfred, crazy fucking Alfred, had been right. "Alfred didn't, but I went out there on the street," recalled Stewart. He walked toward his favorite saloon, which he had left only minutes before. "I kind of approached it slowly," he said. "And all this [he throws up his hands], gradually." As Stewart headed toward the Lounge, Roger Nunez passed and entered Wanda's from the direction of Walgreens. Roger made the strange announcement: "Thank god, I just made it, from the fire."[2]

His blackened appearance, covered in what looked to be soot, likely provoked this declaration—a means to explain his condition and win sympathy from patrons who might otherwise regard him strangely. Roger kept repeating these words as he wandered into and out of the bar to peer down Iberville. When someone later asked how he escaped the burning bar, Roger replied that he "got out the back exit door," perhaps wagering that no Wanda's patron could discern how his previous front-door ejection by Buddy Rasmussen made this means of egress impossible for him. Clearly, Roger's story was evolving with the scene down the way.[3]

A smell like charcoal increased as Stewart Butler neared the flashing lights. The walk, 145 steps from Wanda's, took less than two minutes. What Stewart encountered looked like a war zone. The street reflected the blowout of an explosion: fire leaped from windows and smoke wafted off bodies, with friends pointing and officials yelling. Everything seemed to shout for Stewart's attention; few details connected or made sense.[4]

Fire engines stretched from street to sidewalk, which was littered with bits of glass, flakes of ash, pieces of acrid flesh, and pools of human fluid. Drunken sightseers ambled forth curiously between the casualties as firemen and policemen tried to hold them back. Indeed, a virtual cross-section of New Orleans society coalesced on Iberville, hugging the sides of the street. Guests exited from two pornographic movie houses near the burning bar. They coalesced with businessmen wandering from the Marriott's Levee Bar or sauntering from the upscale Hotel Monteleone. Gripped by the flames, their eyes reflected a mixture of horror and fascination.[5] Cinders fluttered like bright moths, threatening to light the entire French Quarter.

Firefighters aimed a hose into a window, while others chased and tackled a man trailing smoke signals—hands slapping flames on his head, red running down from the burn. Courtney Craighead and Ricky Everett struggled to breathe, and Rusty Quinton cried repeatedly, "My friends!" Strangers echoed names of people trapped upstairs. Some cries, they tried to persuade themselves, answered in response. Milton Mary scooped water from a gutter and ladled it onto a soot covered figure, who lay facedown with a gash on his head. Grabbing a fireman, Mary asked, "Can you put some water on this man?" The fireman answered, "He's gone," even though the man—most likely Up Stairs Lounge patron Jim Hambrick—was not actually dead but in a state of catatonic shock; he would later be discovered alive and rushed to the hospital.[6]

Regina Soleto, bearing a checkbook and a hat borrowed from her friend Jeanne Gosnell, wandered back from her errand toward the Up Stairs Lounge. Minutes before, she'd left her lover, Reggie Adams, at the grand piano, close to Adam Fontenot and Bill Larson. Moving through rescue workers, she heard a distant yelling that she soon realized was the sound of her own screaming voice. Regina kept thinking she saw Reggie in the crowd, but each time it would only be a stranger's face. She saw what looked to be an air conditioner detonate and fly from a window.[7]

A silver ladder stretched toward her friend Jeanne, who was up on the fire escape.[8] A white-helmeted man yelled for her to reach farther. Grabbing the handles with singed fingers, Gosnell ran down the makeshift stairs, which bounced in the air, and met the fireman halfway. Buddy Rasmussen stomped about angrily, as if he were looking for some culprit. He ran into Bill Duncan, an Up Stairs Lounge regular and close friend, and the two hugged in silence. From his nearby apartment, Duncan had heard yells and run outside. "Thank god," Buddy said, not having known if Duncan had perished in the bedlam. Closer to the parking lot, Francis Dufrene sat stunned on the curb. Other survivors, like Robert Vanlangendonck, deputized themselves as medics.[9] Somewhere down Chartres Street, an ambulance peeled away.

Firemen dragged those survivors who'd fallen from the windows and lacked the strength to move another inch. "The guy's skin stuck to the fireman's hand," recalled a witness of one victim. Survivor Phillip Byrd was physically thrown into an ambulance, where a man on a gurney begged him to remove his scalding clothing. Byrd burned his hands more trying to do so: the rags were hot enough to cauterize flesh. In a helpless moment when the vehicle accelerated, Byrd realized that he had defecated in his pants.[10]

When Stewart Butler turned right onto Chartres Street, he saw something heartrending. It was "Bill Larson's corpse," recalled Stewart, who noticed the green fabric of Larson's shirt clinging to pink flesh. Stewart gagged and cried at the same time. The watch on Larson's wrist, cracked from heat, stopped just a few minutes past 8:00 p.m. One patron from the Jimani pleaded for firefighters to help the man. "He was caught and trying desperately to get out," the man later told the *States-Item*. "The firemen said he was dead. But he wasn't. I saw him move."[11]

A boot with a buckle, connected to a body bent in fetal position, hung from another window. This man was clearly dead. A few feet behind the boot, in clear visage, was a face scorched beyond recognition. It looked to be made of stone, unrecognizable as a human form except through prolonged observation, which provoked a shudder. Also visible inside, above the bodies, was the tiny statue of the Farnese Hercules. It was the only piece of the Up Stairs Lounge that survived the night intact.[12]

Fire Superintendent William McCrossen, arriving on-site, readied his men to storm the front doorway, which smoldered and steamed beneath the shredded "Up Stairs" canopy. Flames, raked by winds, periodically gusted and swelled against their hoses, which painted the neighborhood in blood hues. Trained rescuers slapped on layer after protective layer, and a fire captain in a gas mask entered the stairwell to test the air. Heat temporarily stopped him in his tracks. Lifting his mask, he smelled what he thought to be the odor of gasoline residue.[13]

Other firemen pressed forward, hopeful there was a life to save beyond the burning stairwell. They placed their weight on sieves of char and ascended, trusting the steps to hold their weight. What they found at the top, through the door, was everyone in piles, carbon mounds that were hard to describe. In the farthest corner, a stack of what appeared at first glance to be gnarled lumber sprouted arms and heads; it was the worst thing some had ever seen. "When I first saw the fire victims, it was kind of sickening," admitted rookie fireman Rodney Gillespie to the *Daily Record*, a small New Orleans newspaper.

Veteran firefighters, who typically deployed the "thousand-mile stare" as a psychological barrier between their minds and absolute chaos, broke down. "We were within eighteen feet of rescuing them—yes, we got that close—but it took time to work our way up there," Fire Superintendent McCrossen later recalled. "I saw firemen throw up and cry when they saw those people dead."[14]

Additional emergency calls for aid brought engines and equipment from every corner of the city, which created a traffic jam of emergency units. Thirteen fire companies, including four hook-and-ladder divisions, brought eighty-seven firefighters to the scene.[15] Ladders hung in the air like construction cranes as firefighters extinguished the blaze by 8:12 p.m. The fire had burned within the staircase for around nineteen minutes, inside the bar for little more than sixteen minutes.[16]

Night descended, revealing a half-moon in the firmament. Higher in the darkness, stars burned cold and distant. Major Henry M. Morris arrived and took charge of law enforcement. Police tape was rolled out to protect the crime scene as the chief detective conferred with the fire chief, who couldn't yet speculate how many had perished inside. It wasn't obvious with all the bodies fused together. It was still too hot to bring the coroner, or anyone but a firefighter, upstairs. Cops hustled around paramedics and patients. On a curb, Luther Boggs sat beside Jeanne Gosnell, his best friend. A white compress hung from Luther's head, and he held his neck slack, as if broken. Jeanne gasped for breath behind an oxygen mask and looked blue, fogging up the plastic. Luther could neither hug nor comfort her: his skin dangled like papier-mâché from his hands, which he curled up like talons to avoid the contact of exposed nerves with anything but air.[17]

HIGH ABOVE THE devastation, in the dishwashing room of the Port Orleans, Henry Kubicki worked through stacks of pots and pans. Roused from his lonely trance, he received an order from a chef to retrieve supplies from the hotel commissary, which resided in a basement level of the sprawling hotel complex. Snagging an elevator to the subterranean level, Henry navigated his way through cool cellars and eventually handed his order to a man of Cuban descent who managed supplies for the various restaurants in the Marriott. This man, speaking to a coworker, laughed and yelled, "Oh boy! We are having barbequed queens' asses tonight!"[18]

The words startled Henry. Had he just been outed as a "queen's ass"? Hoping the joke wasn't about him, he played it safe by not lingering for long. He loaded a cart and took it back to the elevator. Up again in the Port Orleans, Henry noticed waiters and customers gathering in the northeast corner of the floor, looking down and pointing. Curious, Henry wandered over and attempted to peer down, too, despite his having poor vision. All he thought he saw were darkly clouded streets. Must be a fire, he thought, before heading back to his dishes.[19]

Down on the street, Ronnie Rosenthal guided Ricky Everett from spot to spot. Ricky was unable to see for the tears clouding his eyes. "They had all that space for people lying there," recalled Ricky. "And they were pulling the burning clothes off of them." By some strange fate, neither Ricky nor Ronnie turned the corner onto Chartres to witness Ricky's best friend, pastor Bill Larson, in his final repose.[20]

Courtney Craighead, however, did so and became dumbstruck. The legendary essayist Michel de Montaigne once described this traumatic condition as the body's inability to express that "torpor that paralyzes us when events surpassing our capability overwhelm us." Indeed, Courtney Craighead struggled to inhale and exhale alongside Rusty Quinton and the other survivors who, by some miracle or some curse, were forced to look up at carnage also intended for them. Their guilt was sudden and uncontrollable.[21]

Courtney moved like a stranger in his own limbs. Dropping all of his social defenses, which had protected him from the dangers of wayward openness, he inadvertently used his real name when answering questions from bystanders and police.[22] Just then a throng of reporters and news crews seemed to materialize, among them John LaPlace of the *Times-Picayune* and Bill Elders of the CBS-affiliate WWL-TV.

They showed press credentials, and police lifted the tape to allow them immediate access. In this era, little adversity between police and the press seemed to exist. It was Frank Hayward, the police information officer serving as the department's liaison to City Hall, who managed the list of journalists approved to receive official press passes.[23] In the competitive field of breaking news reporting, one's holding of a certified New Orleans press pass, which provided entrée to everything from crime scenes to city-sponsored galas, had become table stakes for working in the industry. If a press pass was denied or revoked, a journalist ran the risk of getting scooped, and thus could members of the press be favored or squeezed by the gatekeepers.

En masse, reporters rushed survivors like Courtney. The cacophony of voices made it difficult for survivors to hear orders from police and firefighters. As the ranking officer on the scene, Major Henry M. Morris made a statement to the *States-Item* about the Up Stairs Lounge. "Some thieves hung out there, and you know this was a queer bar," he said. A second police officer, perhaps attempting to qualify Morris's comment, explained how it was "not uncommon for homosexuals to carry false identification."[24]

Ronnie LeBoeuf, a photojournalist, captured images of the dead and despairing. "Fire came up the stairs fast," Courtney muttered to the *States-Item*. "Two guys told me to jump, and I was small enough," survivor Adolph Medina said to the Associated Press. "What was done was done intentionally," an anonymous man, interviewed with his back to the camera, told Elders, the WWL reporter. Seeing the macabre, ashen-gray face of Bill Larson in the window, photographer Pat Bourke of the *Daily Record*, displaying a gallows humor common to newsmen, took a picture and jested, "At least it was only a mannequin factory." "Those aren't mannequins," someone else told him.[25]

A nearby tourist provided testimony to the *Daily Record*: "We watched those people burn before our very eyes, and we couldn't do a thing to help them. Don't use my name. I just won't think about it, it never happened, it never could have happened." Down the street, an Associated Press reporter watched a bartender set up a drink station on the sidewalk and do "a brisk business with spectators."[26]

BUDDY RASMUSSEN WOUND through the crowds looking for a person of interest. Something instinctual told Buddy that the destruction of his bar was connected to the ruckus that happened earlier. "I had already in my mind," Buddy later told investigators, "and said to myself that it was arson because of the way this fire started." Buddy ran into Mark Allen Guidry, the nineteen-year-old hustler who'd come to the beer bust with Roger Nunez, and it was Guidry who directed Buddy toward Wanda's. At the corner of Royal and Iberville Streets, Buddy spotted his man. He ran up to Roger, who was drinking a cup of beer, and grabbed hold of him.[27]

"Where have you been?" Buddy asked.

"At Wanda's," Roger answered.[28]

Buddy attempted to drag Roger toward a plainclothes policeman.[29]

"Why are you holding me?" Roger yelled as he struggled to get away.[30]

Reaching the officer, Buddy tried to explain that this person he was restraining had been causing trouble at the Up Stairs Lounge just before the fire. Buddy demanded that Roger be held for questioning. Given the era, this policeman had probably never had any interactions with homosexuals other than arresting a few. At first, the officer feigned distraction, ignoring the hubbub as these two gay men struggled and shouted in front of him. After a few minutes, the officer looked Buddy in the eyes and gave him the proverbial "move along." Buddy released Roger, who stumbled a few steps and just stood there, watching the calamity. "I couldn't convince the policeman that he should hold this person, and I let him go," Buddy later told investigators.[31]

Moments later, Courtney Craighead ran up to Buddy and pointed accusingly toward Roger. Buddy threw up his hands and explained what had just happened. The deacon walked over to that same officer and attempted to clarify the matter. According to the fire marshal report, "The police officer told [Courtney Craighead] that he didn't have the authority to restrain the subject and referred him to the lieutenant that was standing across the street from them, in front of the Walgreens."

Courtney and Buddy then approached the lieutenant and told the same story. "You think you know police business better than I?" the officer yelled. After muttering something into his walkie-talkie, he turned back and told them, "Go back across the street, you're in the way."[32]

Courtney and Buddy obeyed, lest they be arrested. The deacon and barkeep watched helplessly as Roger Dale Nunez slowly disappeared into the masses.[33]

Roy Reed of *The New York Times* reached the intersection just as the firefighters were packing away their hoses. Reed was a reporting legend, the lone member of *The New York Times* Southern bureau. He had achieved a rare level of journalistic fame by reporting civil rights events throughout the South, like the 1965 march by Dr. Martin Luther King Jr. on Selma, Alabama.[34]

Reed focused on the scene at hand. "The first thing that hits you was the odor, burning flesh," remembered Reed about the Up Stairs Lounge. "Then the sight of the man in the window, the expression of horror on his face." Reed interviewed Buddy Rasmussen and Fire Superintendent McCrossen. The veteran reporter spent about thirty minutes around the intersection and even spoke to a news photographer who'd been permitted upstairs to document the mass grave. Aware of a 10:30 p.m. deadline, Reed knew that he had to rush home to a typewriter and telephone if he was going to dictate a story that would make it into the *Times* morning edition. Driving back, Reed attempted to outline the story in his head. The scene had been as gruesome as some of the church burnings he'd covered during the civil rights era. Then it dawned on him: this was the first assignment he'd ever received from *The New York Times* involving homosexuals. The Up Stairs Lounge was a gay bar. Reed knew this fact from his interview with Buddy Rasmussen. The sexuality of victims and survivors could prove a crucial detail. This was an undertone that his editors had likely missed when they'd assigned him to report yet another disaster to strike downtown New Orleans.[35]

Reed would be bound by the ethics of his profession to print an unmistakable and provocative fact, one that would likely irk his editors at the national desk of the *Times*: the Up Stairs Lounge served a "homosexual" clientele. It was a fact that, Reed recalled, "could point to motive in the event of a crime."[36]

CLANCY DuBos, an eighteen-year-old reporter six weeks into a summer internship at the *Times-Picayune*, stood in the Accident Emergency Room of Charity Hospital as Up Stairs Lounge victims arrived. At least fifteen people were brought to this facility. Blood smeared across tile as a nurse's aide attempted to mop the floors. A physician drew fluid from a festering arm. Earlier that night, DuBos had caught himself lolling in the *Times-Picayune* newsroom. A night editor named Frank Martin shouted, "Come on, let's make some news happen," and everyone chuckled. Tedium had broken when a colleague came barreling in after hearing the word "fire" on police radio.[37]

Now, at the hospital, DuBos watched doctors in tennis shoes cut dead skin from the chest of a middle-aged man who hemorrhaged with pain. Friends and family members hovered nearby, watching until orderlies cordoned them into a visiting area, where DuBos heard them praying loudly. "Nursing divided themselves into teams," DuBos would later write. "Some gathered blood, others tried to get names from those who could talk." DuBos observed Phillip Byrd, a nineteen-year-old moving somewhat freely, asking for help making a phone call because his fingers were so badly burned that he couldn't take a nickel out of his pocket.[38] DuBos noticed the age similarity between himself and the boy, whose hands trembled uncontrollably. "David? Listen, I've had a sort of accident," Byrd spoke into the receiver. Sights and smells began to overpower the young reporter. In front of him lay Eugene Thomas and Fred Sharohway, the couple who had plunged down the burning staircase to save their lives. There was Francis Dufrene, with scalds on his temples from what looked like a backyard grill.[39]

DuBos saw two Catholic priests arrive and attempt to provide spiritual succor. Visitors grew so voluminous in the waiting pen that a supervising social worker, identified only as "Ms. Schwarz," cleared a separate hospital wing to hold them. According to *The Advocate,* Schwarz "persuaded the dietary department to provide coffee" and described the handling of the emergency by some police officers and staff as "dispassionate." When the critical patients, like Luther Boggs and Jim Hambrick, arrived, the hospital director took one look and opened the new burn unit—an unstaffed, state-of-the-art facility weeks away from its official unveiling.[40] An emergency of this magnitude, quite simply, forced an early opening.

Names and numbers of fire victims floated about, but no could say for sure who was dead or who was merely missing. "Confusion seemed to reign," DuBos would write. Medical personnel became so preoccupied with saving lives that DuBos walked into an operating room and observed a surgery. "All these doctors came in," recalled DuBos. "And they were dressed in the same street clothes as I was." DuBos eventually left, having witnessed all the gore that he could stomach.[41]

Returning to the *Times-Picayune* newsroom, DuBos headed straight for a typewriter, which ignored the newspaper's established protocol of conversing with the editor on duty, Frank Martin, to frame the story and its angle. A few minutes later, Frank Martin noticed the young intern at work and glanced at the first draft. Martin clapped a hand on DuBos's shoulder. "That's what I want," the newsman said.[42]

HOMICIDE DETECTIVES Charles Schlosser and Sam Gebbia of the New Orleans Police Department strode through the hospital doors around 9:00 p.m. Notified of six persons dead at the Up Stairs Lounge and one alive at Charity Hospital, these detectives had rushed to the infirmary hoping to interview the lone witness. Obviously, they were operating on faulty information—a bad start to their investigation. What Schlosser and Gebbia found at the hospital made their stomachs churn. Tom Carr, a firefighter who had hopped into an ambulance with paramedics, told detectives that several survivors were now being released. These men, Carr said, were cognizant enough to be questioned.[43]

Clicking into action, the officers took statements from Rusty Quinton, Adolph Medina, and Phillip Byrd. Interviewing—but not arresting—homosexuals would have represented new terrain for these detectives. In their defense, few—if any—policemen in America had received official guidance for investigating gay crimes. Indeed, the novelty of dealing with homosexuality would lead to their compulsively citing who was homosexual in their reports, reflecting an inability to recognize and offset what was then a commonplace bias. Nor had the officers been briefed on up-to-date studies for "pathological firesetting," which would have given them a suspect profile for a potential arsonist: a white male between the ages of sixteen and twenty-eight with a chronic condition or physical disability and divorced parents. As a result, they didn't know that the desire for revenge was what made a so-called firesetter snap in more than one quarter of such cases. Nuanced concepts such as homophobia, internalized self-hatred, or even the closet were absolutely foreign to them—for this was a law-breaking group with whom their profession spurned relations. Law enforcement officers could in fact be punished for simply knowing a gay person. In January 1972, for example, three sheriff's deputies in suburban Jefferson Parish had been fired from their jobs for merely associating with "a known homosexual," a man not under arrest for any crime and who turned out to be the hairdresser of the deputies' wives.[44]

These detectives, to put it plainly, approached the task ill equipped. "There were some very fine officers on that force," said Bob McAnear, who as a criminal investigator with U.S. Customs had ample experience with the NOPD, "but there were so many more that looked down on gays as less than humans." Schlosser and Gebbia left Charity Hospital at 9:20 p.m. to scope the scene on Iberville Street. At the site, they met fire officials conducting a concurrent investigation. Indeed, because of the profound levels of death and destruction at the bar, and the distinctive possibility of arson, the NOPD investigation would occur simultaneously with an inquiry compiled by the New Orleans Fire Department and an arson investigation conducted by the Louisiana Office of the State Fire Marshal (a law enforcement agency with authority to investigate crimes involving fire).[45]

Schlosser and Gebbia found and interviewed Harold Bartholomew, the lawyer who had been driving his kids home; he recalled what the men said as they ran from the burning staircase. They also questioned the nineteen-year-old hustler Mark Allen Guidry, who said that he'd gone to the Up Stairs Lounge with a "male he did not know." Perhaps abiding by the code of no snitching among Iberville hustlers, Guidry then further protected Roger Dale Nunez by misremembering his name and contact information, stating that he knew the guy "only as Gerry or Johnny" living "somewhere in the 2700 block of Esplanade Street."[46] The NOPD pursued this false lead, which would take them away from Iberville.

⚭

DUANE AND STEPHEN MITCHELL waited in the lobby of the theater long after the movie ended, as if forgotten. The showing of *The World's Greatest Athlete* had been thrilling, but when neither their dad nor Uncle Horace arrived with the car, the kids began to feel unsafe. Duane knew his father as a reliable man who kept his promises, a salesman who made regular appointments. Duane hid his anxiety by keeping his brother distracted with another showing of the film.[47] Fortunately for them, the G-rated feature was playing in a loop that Sunday, first at 3:15 p.m. and again at 5:10, with the last showing at 9:00 p.m.

What a treat, Duane tried to convince Stephen. "I was trying to look after him," Duane recalled, "and scared to death myself." The boys again took in the story of Nanu, the title character, who left his jungle home to enter an American athletic competition against all odds. But when the end credits rolled, once more, and their father didn't pull up with the car, their world seemed to fall apart. "Where's Dad at?" Stephen asked. "I don't know, he'll be here," Duane answered. Today, Duane swears that he watched *The World's Greatest Athlete* seven times with his brother, but it's just as likely that these repeat viewings, under such duress, tattooed the movie in his brain.[48]

Stephen cried as Duane struggled to explain that their father would soon arrive. But when the clock passed 11:00 p.m., which signified a later hour than Duane and Stephen Mitchell had ever been awake, theater attendants began to eye the boys with concern. Duane broke down in tears in front of strangers. He pleaded for help. Eventually, a manager called the Mitchell residence. No answer. The manager also tried the Up Stairs Lounge. No answer, again. Lastly, the manager tried a neighbor. Luckily, this woman picked up, and agreed to collect the boys. Perhaps, Duane told himself, nothing was wrong. Then the neighbor showed up with a police escort. "She knew that we were going to the movies," explained Duane. "And she knew something happened."[49]

CHAPTER 6

Call for Aid

Night—June 24, 1973

oroner Carl Rabin crossed the threshold of the Up Stairs Lounge. The structure had cooled enough by then for him to safely enter the second floor and pronounce those who had not been able to flee dead. His go-ahead signaled police photographers and coroner's assistants to spring to their work. Together, the staff combed the premises to make a meticulous record of where everyone and everything was positioned. They commenced the gruesome process of finding and tagging bones beneath layers of human cremains. "The charred, still-oozing remains filled the air with a stench difficult to bear," noted the *States-Item.*[1]

Because the electricity was out, firemen shined klieg lights up from the street. As they noted, none of the bar's supposed safety features had worked. The fire-rated front door, rigged to close on a spring, had crumpled on contact with heat, as if patently defective. Several Exit signs, supposedly connected to an emergency power system, had not functioned.[2] While measuring the stairwell, Major Henry Morris discovered an item of interest, an empty seven-ounce can of Ronsonol lighter fluid. The yellow can lay right side up, the blue writing on it legible and the top pointing toward Iberville; the plastic spout of the can was missing, suggesting that it had been pulled off in haste. Nearby, police also found two half-burned ten-dollar bills, which were scorched enough to be worthless but just intact enough to display their monetary increments.[3] The police sent the can to the lab for fingerprints.[4] Maybe, they figured, they'd get lucky.

"Coroner's assistants would untangle bodies two at a time," wrote the *Times-Picayune*. They took breaks to retch out nearby windows. Prying the stack of seventeen corpses in the corner, and deciding which piece went where, was a horrific task—in fact, a guessing game.[5] Firemen and policemen pitched in to help the coroner and his team. They began by clearing the front door and bathroom of bodies and proceeded through the bar area toward Chartres Street, gathering and reassembling body parts on top of the bar. Each carcass, completed as best they could, was then photographed and searched for identifying artifacts—jewelry, trinkets, or pieces of wallet. Each was then zipped in a bag. A fire engine with a sixty-five-foot arm raised and lowered a metal basket, and black rubber sacks descended, one by one. Three Catholic priests turned up on the street in time to offer "conditional absolution" over the bags as they were lowered. They made a sign of the cross in the air more than twenty times.[6]

After the priests performed their duties, authorities piled the body bags into ambulances and drove them to the Charity Hospital morgue. Since this was an unconventional destination, drivers radioed back several times to make sure. Generally, victims of a disaster or mass incident went to the public morgue; however, the coroner shrewdly assessed that that facility lacked the space to handle this volume of death. Removing bodies methodically, starting with sections nearest to the front door, resulted in leaving the shriveled remains of Bill Larson exposed in the Chartres Street window for more than four hours, from 8:00 p.m. until after midnight.[7] Hundreds of onlookers saw him in that state.

When Buddy Rasmussen and bar owner Phil Esteve were finally permitted inside, they could barely recognize the place. But they did notice something peculiar. Evidently, even though only police, fire, medical first responders, and news reporters were allowed inside the structure, the night's earnings had gone missing. "Phil said the cash register, juke box, cigarette machine and some wallets had money removed," recalled Bob McAnear, the former U.S. Customs officer. "Phil wouldn't report it because, if he did, the police would never allow him to operate a bar in New Orleans again." Up Stairs Lounge historian Johnny Townsend, who interviewed Phil Esteve in the 1980s, in part corroborates this account in his *Let the Faggots Burn*: "Phil Esteve rushed over to the bar that evening but couldn't go in until the following day. Then, he says, he watched as investigators tore names off of checks and took money from the cash register which they never turned over to him."[8] Esteve is now deceased and unable to speak to these details himself.

But money was indeed unaccounted for. "Whether it was because it was a gay bar or that insurance would cover it, so it wouldn't be missed, there are those who would take advantage of the situation," McAnear contended. "It would be difficult to break open those machines without more than one person being aware." The night's monetary haul from the beer bust was gone, not in the safe. Buddy and Phil both felt the pressure to pretend that no other crime, other than the fire, had occurred that Sunday night.[9] Besides, if anyone had filed a complaint about such missing funds, it would have been the word of two homosexuals against the officials.

RONNIE ROSENTHAL KEPT faithful watch over Ricky Everett that night, although neither of them had suffered physical injuries. Pale and faint, Ricky had at times seemed functional in his conversations with the police. Smoke stuck to his clothing, and black ash hid in his hair. As soon as Ricky found his composure, shock would hit him again, and he'd almost collapse in a surge of grief. At 7:00 p.m., Ricky had a bounty of friends. An hour later, so many had vanished. Ricky wasn't sure which pals, besides pastor Bill Larson and Deacon Mitch Mitchell, he'd never see again.[10]

The police told Ricky that if he was up to it, they'd need his help identifying the bodies. Ronnie and Ricky caught a ride in a squad car and wandered down into the Charity Hospital catacombs. The room was cold and quiet but for the tremor of refrigeration equipment. Each numbered corpse was removed from its transport bag and placed on a six-foot-long metal tray.[11]

Ricky tried his best to match these bodies with friends he had
known hours before. Unfortunately, most faces were melted away.
Only three or four were recognizable. Ricky had to examine carefully
to notice details like tattoos.[12] The coroner's reports don't reveal how
much Ricky aided this process, but by Monday morning a tentative
list of thirteen victim names would be released to the public.[13] The
roster included Ricky's friends John Golding, Horace Broussard, and
Mitch Mitchell. They were thus outed in death. Many of the injured,
forced to show IDs to receive treatment at Charity Hospital, were also
named in morning coverage in a story cowritten by the closeted *Times-
Picayune* journalist John LaPlace, who would have agonized over the
repercussions of printing surnames and ages.[14]

Ricky called his mother from the hospital to let her know that he
was alive. "She knew I was going to the bar," said Ricky, "but she
hadn't seen the TV yet, and so I thought, 'Oh, I better call her, just
in case.'" Reports of the bar's incineration were circulating widely.
Though Ricky's sexuality remained a matter undiscussed, his mother
was familiar with men like Buddy from calling the Up Stairs Lounge,
and Ricky suspected that some part of her must have guessed his
inclinations. Ricky had planned eventually to come out formally, but
the fire had forced his hand. Telling his mother what had happened
would result in her asking why he frequented such a place. The truth,
Ricky felt, would come easiest from him. He dialed her number, and
she sounded relieved at first.[15]

Afterward, Ricky and Ronnie went to the MCC church, where survivors and friends were gathering for an overnight vigil. Ronnie telephoned his employer in Atlanta. Choosing his words carefully, Ronnie
informed the man that he'd be out of town for a few extra days. "I
told him that I was in a fire in New Orleans," Ronnie recalled, "a lot
of people died, and I'm here to help out for right now." His employer
didn't take the news happily, but agreed to his request for extended
time off. "I didn't tell him about it being a gay bar or anything like
that," Ronnie noted. Like most gay men of the time, he wasn't out to
his employer, and avoiding this detail very likely saved him his job.[16]

Ronnie then dialed a second number long-distance. He knew so few people in New Orleans. The fire survivors needed more help than he could provide, so he called his pastor, Reverend John Gill of the MCC of Atlanta. "He couldn't have called his mother in those days because his mother didn't know he was gay," explained Dan Bugg, later Ronnie's partner. Gill's booming Georgian congregation, with more than two hundred members and a twenty-person gay men's choir, happened to be holding a "movie night" in their church at that late hour. In Atlanta, a phone rang in the vestry, and the person who answered rushed in to summon the minister. The disturbance drew murmurs, but Reverend Gill could immediately hear the anguish in Ronnie's voice.[17]

Steven Duplantis felt power beneath his feet as his Buick Wildcat purred down the interstate. He was young and handsome, and he had just gotten away with yet another rendezvous off base. Dials glowed on the car stereo. He passed by Lake Charles and didn't think twice about stopping home. There was no time, in any case.[18]

As he sped over a bridge, a newscaster interrupted the music to announce that there had been a fire in the French Quarter. "Oh no!" Steven thought. The music resumed, and anxiety crept in slowly as Steven turned the facts over in his head. He couldn't shake what that guy had said before Buddy threw him out of the bar: "I'm going to burn this place to the ground." Had anyone else heard it? Steven had passed the message to Stewart and Alfred, but did they really listen? Five hours into the drive, Steven hit the outskirts of Houston, and another newscast broke in to report that the fire in New Orleans had hit the Up Stairs Lounge, with many dead. Steven's eyes blurred instantly. He steered to the shoulder to avoid sobbing himself into a highway accident.[19]

"That was the hardest drive I've ever had to go through, from Houston to San Antonio," Steven recalled. "I was crying. I didn't know at the time that I heard this that Stewart and Alfred had left [the bar]." There was no question in Steven's mind exactly what had happened. That guy, after being punched to the floor, had gotten up and done exactly what he'd threatened. "I knew for a fact that it was that guy," Steven insisted. "I knew it was the fire that that guy said he was going to do. That was a given: I never, ever doubted that."[20] Had Stewart and Alfred left before it all went down? Steven replayed their last conversation in his mind, as best as he could remember.

Steven had told them, "Y'all need to leave here." Stewart had responded, "Oh, you're crazy!" But Steven retorted, "Stewart, not this time." Next, Steven turned to Alfred, and he listened intently, though with a glaze in his eyes. Steven remembered kissing them both and skedaddling down the staircase.[21]

Survivor's guilt was inevitable. Why did he have to abandon them, just then? Steven tried calling Stewart's house from a pay phone along the highway, but no one answered. He didn't know how to help. He couldn't just go to the police with an anonymous tip. His testimony was far too specific. "There was no way I could do it," said Steven. "I felt bad about not being able to do it. But I knew that if I did that, everything for me would have just stopped, with the military and all that." The night advanced as Steven drove farther from New Orleans and back to his other life. Any statement to the NOPD, he knew, would make his clandestine trip a matter of record. He was already skirting trouble.[22] Steven, despite Stewart's invitations to share his troubles, had managed to keep a secret from Stewart and Alfred over the weekend. Steven had kept quiet because every trip to New Orleans functioned as respite from his worries. But, in fact, he was under investigation in Texas—he had pushed the fun too far.

Back in May, something had happened to Steven on the border road at Randolph Air Force Base. Military policemen (MPs) had entrapped him with another man using a common deceptive tactic that involved deploying a military spy, who pretended to be homosexual, against a suspected gay person.[23] If a gay serviceman like Steven took the bait, and was drawn into a sexual encounter, MPs would then charge the suspect for criminal sexual behavior.

Steven's lure was a strapping, straight-acting officer who had suddenly transferred into his department. The spy, with a face like a porcelain doll, took a sudden interest in his coworker. He and Steven made eyes and flirted and eventually found time alone in a car. "It was a beautiful, star-filled night," Steven recalled. "Out in the middle of nowhere on the end of the Air Force base in Seguin, Texas. Oh, lord, it was beautiful. Course, all he wanted was a blowjob, and he was good. Oh, I gave it to him."[24]

Early the next morning, Steven received a phone call at his desk. It was his buddy, the closeted Office of Special Investigations (OSI) officer, who asked him pointedly, "What did you do on the perimeter road last night?"[25] Steven was taken back. How could anyone have guessed what happened in the dark just hours before? Then Steven stood up and noticed how his admirer, the straight-acting officer, was missing from work. It dawned on him. Steven's tryst-mate, who willingly accepted the oral gratification, had set him up.

In military logic, receiving fellatio from another man didn't make the *recipient* a suspect; only the giver was the target. Odds are, the spy had neglected to report how he had been fellated to climax. Steven surmised that the guy hadn't acted out of hate: "It was more like, 'Okay, well, I can get a promotion for doing this, all right? So I find somebody who's gay, they're going to reward me.' And they would."[26]

"I'm going to have to really work to keep you out of this," the OSI officer continued, "but, if you're going to continue, better get out." Steven knew his friend meant, by "better get out," better leave the air force. Because this conversation took place on an official telephone line, and could possibly be tapped or overheard, so much else was left unspoken. Later, over beers at a gay bar, the OSI officer made things more explicit. "They set you up," he told Steven. "There's somebody on your base that set you up. They're trying to prove it. They are after you."[27]

As Steven drove that final leg to San Antonio, his friend's words came back to him, intermixing with the radio announcement about the Up Stairs Lounge as well as that weirdo's use of the word "burn." Night then became twilight, finally dawn. Heeding his friend's warning, Steven earlier that June had submitted a request for transfer to the Louisiana Air National Guard, an air force reserve unit headed by the state governor. "Air Guard don't care about gays," Steven explained bluntly. The Vietnam-era draft had ended in early 1973, and Steven could technically do as he wished with his military career. But papers were still pending. The only thing gumming up the works was the signature of his commanding officer. "All that was going on," recalled Steven. "So that was a really hard weekend."[28]

FAR WEST OF NEW ORLEANS, turmoil marked the emergence of a gay political consciousness in Los Angeles. The Christopher Street West parade, Los Angeles's annual gay pride march down Hollywood Boulevard, had, as previously mentioned, been called off. The cause was infighting—chiefly, the sparring between parade cofounder Morris Kight and conservative allies of the Mattachine Society, a California-based homophile group, over how to censor content and tame such displays as had defined previous parades.[29]

The 1972 Los Angeles pride parade had been a social and moral free-for-all, and the result was some notoriety. Marchers embraced public nudity, and spectators waved banners depicting graphic sexual images. Risqué outfits proliferated in a game of erotic one-upmanship. These boisterous expressions created friction with gay parents and their children, who also attended. The pièce de résistance had been a float called the Cockapillar: a giant, papier-mâché monument to the phallus that stretched, like a Chinese dragon, the length of several cars. The Cockapillar even emitted white fluid onto spectators, forcing media outlets to censor their coverage of the day's events.[30]

These expressions of merriment clashed fundamentally with traditionalist gays who sympathized with the Mattachine Society, an older gay group emphasizing public sobriety, which aimed to present homosexuals as suit-and-tie wearing citizens bearing a reasonable argument for "first-class citizenship." By contrast, Kight and members of Gay Liberation favored a flagrant revolution that would overturn oppressive institutions. Throughout Kight's long career as a civil rights crusader, he had lived as an out man and put fellow activists "on notice" that they were dealing with a Gay Liberationist.[31]

This squabble over the 1973 parade, a contest between two generations of homosexual advocates, ended in stalemate. Once Kight resigned as parade chairman, the parade committee canceled all plans for events that year. Venomous gay conservatives attempted to blame Los Angeles's lack of a gay parade squarely on Morris Kight. After the cancellation, Kight received an invitation to serve as grand marshal of New York City's 1973 Christopher Street Liberation Day parade, and he jumped at the opportunity.[32]

Similarly, the national consolidation of Gay Liberation remained slow going as hundreds of far-flung organizations, many inspired by the Stonewall Riots, struggled to align politically. The importance of Stonewall as a symbol for gays finding common cause with other gays continued to be debated. A 1973 op-ed in *The Advocate*, "Stonewall 'Historic'?," questioned whether the site of the Stonewall Inn was worthy of memorial status. *The Advocate*, having expanded from a Los Angeles newsletter to a national newspaper by then, boasted a readership of fewer than 35,000.[33] Such was the state of Gay Liberation, where small tribes fought protracted turf wars.

This enmity could filter to the street level, where many gay men still refused to defend one another from physical assault. At 8:30 p.m. on June 21, 1973, for example, a young gay man in Griffith Park, a popular Los Angeles cruising area, was brutally beaten by three attackers while more than a dozen witnesses stood dumbstruck. One assailant shouted, "We're gonna kill you, fag," as he stomped the young man in the face. Cruisers scattered rather than help. "We had the bastards outnumbered four to one," recalled an anonymous witness to *The Advocate*, "and no one had the balls to organize assistance."[34] The paralysis felt by observers was emblematic of a moment in which many gay Americans suffered an oppression so ingrained that they could not identify with others like themselves, even those with whom they were physically intimate. The isolation of the closet had reinforced, for many, that theirs was an individual burden.

The 1969 police raid on the Stonewall Inn might have ended in a similar way, just like the Griffith Park beating, had a New Orleans transplant and drag king named Stormé DeLarverie not seen a policeman kick her friend onto the cement of Christopher Street. According to DeLarverie's account, a cop then said, "Move, faggot." When the officer shoved her, she decked him in the face and drew blood. This punch represented a breach of historic protocol. Police had been a common sight at the Stonewall Inn after all. "The cops would come in and flirt with the drag queens at the bar and then take their take," recalled Brendan Flaherty, who was an eighteen-year-old coat-check boy at the Stonewall Inn in that era, referring to the payoff arrangement police had with the bar's owners.[35]

Gays, much like blacks in the South, were expected to accept their place and never fight the police, not to mention the mobsters running the bar as an illegal gambling front. "There were people who were beat up," admitted Flaherty. "But they were beat up by people who owned the Stonewall, and there was some condescension like that. You could feel the hostility. Like, these men were making money off of people that they detested." One's favorite gay bar was inevitably a dangerous setting. Flaherty recalled a friend, a drag queen known as Barbara Eden, remarking of a line outside Stonewall: "Can you imagine standing in line to go inside a concentration camp?"[36]

According to gay lore, DeLarverie's very punch outside the Stonewall Inn sparked a revolt against the New York Police Department in what became a violent demonstration. It drew hundreds of supporters and lasted for several days. Sundry groups, representing the bar's fractured culture, rallied in defiance of their persecutors.[37] The anger that had ignited the Stonewall Inn differed markedly from the camaraderie of the Up Stairs Lounge, whose patrons were more content and wished to have fun in their out-of-the-way refuge, until that refuge was obliterated.

ON THE PHONE to Atlanta, Ronnie Rosenthal spoke frantically to his pastor, Reverend John Gill.[38] The two were close, and Ronnie broke down as he recalled details.

Dozens of gay men had burned, Ronnie related, in a blaze that appeared intentional. People had only seconds to get out, though many didn't. Gill listened without interrupting. Once Ronnie finished, the pastor hurried back into the church hall and announced to the MCC of Atlanta that a disaster had befallen their gay brethren in New Orleans. All joined hands in a communal prayer. But Gill couldn't hazard what to do next. He had never confronted such a catastrophic situation as a regional leader for the MCC, a role that had broadened his pastoral duties beyond Atlanta to gay churches across the Deep South.[39]

He picked up the phone again and dialed the only man he knew with such expertise, calling upon the founder and leader of his church, his friend and mentor Reverend Troy Perry. He had to try several times. Then, realizing the time difference between Atlanta and Los Angeles, Gill realized that Perry wouldn't be home because it was still gay pride Sunday in California.[40]

THOUSANDS GATHERED WITH the MCC of Los Angeles at Santa Monica State Beach. Waves crashed, and gay lovers chased each other in the surf. Some strummed guitars and sang songs by a campfire. Troy Perry's impromptu "free wiener roast," it seemed, had succeeded in restoring a semblance of goodwill.[41] Attendees recall men suggestively licking ice cream cones or chomping on hot dogs. There would be no Christopher Street West–sponsored parade this year, but Perry gazed at the men and felt some modicum of gay pride.

He arrived home around midnight to find a note thumbtacked to his door. "Where are you?" it read. "They had a fire in New Orleans. People from all over the country are trying to get in touch." The phone rang, as if on cue, as Perry entered his living room. It was John Gill, his pupil: "Troy, at last! I'm about to catch a plane to Louisiana." Gill told him what he knew, mentioning the fire was at "a place called the Up Stairs." Perry froze, remembering a visit he'd paid to that very bar a few months before. Indeed, he had stopped in New Orleans to support the interim MCC pastor there, Bill Larson. Perry could picture the red interior of the bar, where congregants had brought him after some good Sunday "fellowship."[42]

"Oh, God!" Perry exclaimed. This was only the latest in a spate of fires—often deemed "of suspicious origin"—of MCC buildings around the country. First, the mother church for the MCC of Los Angeles had been burned to its foundations in late January, with arson suspected. In March, the MCC in Nashville had gone up in flames, with arson again a possibility. The Up Stairs Lounge, Perry figured, would make the third such location to vanish since the New Year. He recalled how the Up Stairs Lounge had held frequent prayer meetings. Throughout 1972, the MCC's national newsletter *In Unity* had listed 604 Iberville, the bar's street address, as the place to send church mail.[43]

For Perry, the inspection of such burnt-out rubble, the causes of which "couldn't be determined," was becoming a regular task. He collected his emotions and listened to John Gill, but in his head he was already running with the presumption that the Up Stairs Lounge fire was yet another arson.[44]

"Can you meet me in New Orleans?" Gill asked.

"I'm on the first available flight," Perry answered.[45]

Perry called Delta Airlines to reserve a seat for a morning flight and packed his bags. When he couldn't sleep, he picked up the phone and started dialing. He phoned one of his contacts at the *Los Angeles Times*, who assured him that the paper was covering the tragedy.[46]

By 1973, Troy Perry was no stranger to the press. He had been featured and quoted in at least two nationally reported stories: "Homosexuals in Revolt," which appeared in *Life* magazine, and "The Militant Homosexual," for *Newsweek*. That kind of visibility made him an anomaly among gays, who would mostly equate a call from a journalist with a visit from the Grim Reaper. Perry was one of the few homosexual Americans unafraid of his name and picture appearing in print. He dialed *The New York Times* after *The Advocate,* aware that sunlight would soon reach the Eastern Seaboard. He called through the night, alerting those on his Rolodex of the crisis in New Orleans.[47]

Perry tried his ally Morris Kight at home. Then, remembering the rigmarole with Kight and New York City, he attempted to track him down on the East Coast. In Manhattan, the Christopher Street

Liberation Day parade had been a marked success. Parade master of ceremonies Vito Russo introduced Morris Kight to New Yorkers as "the dean of the Gay Liberation movement, the silver thread which stretches from L.A. to New York." Kight had taken the podium and brought greetings from *Advocate* publisher Dick Michaels and Reverend Troy Perry. In a stirring speech, Kight memorialized dead brothers and sisters of the gay struggle and cried out, "Never again, never again can they take our children, our lives, our houses, or deny us a job." Feeling celebratory, Kight pulled an all-nighter at gay bars across town. Around five in the morning, he headed back to the apartment of fellow gay activist Morty Manford in Greenwich Village.[48]

Marty Manford's work with the Gay Activists Alliance had led to coordination and outreach between Manhattan's gay community and the West Coast, as well as the South. The twenty-two-year-old New Yorker had been present at the Stonewall Riots and the gay student protests at Columbia University in 1968. Manford was also by then no stranger to conservative forces attempting to beat back any political display. In April 1972, while protesting an event at the New York Hilton, Manford had been assaulted by Uniformed Firefighters Association President Michael J. Maye.[49]

In an attack witnessed by no fewer than four New York City officials, Maye had kicked and shoved Manford onto a downward-moving escalator, where Maye then stepped onto Manford's groin and ground his boot heel several times. Manford subsequently had filed assault charges against Maye, but a local criminal court judge had thrown out the case before it reached a jury, acquitting Maye due to "variances, incongruities, differences" in the brave testimonies of city officials who came forward to testify against him. Manford had called the decision "an affront to the American principle of equal application under the law."[50]

Manford, by serendipity, was the person Troy Perry reached on the phone while attempting to contact Morris Kight. When Kight returned to the apartment, it was Manford who delivered the news about the Up Stairs Lounge. Kight was due back in Los Angeles that evening, but he agreed to change his plans. "I used my airline ticket that took me to New York, which had been contributed by friends . . . to bring me and Morty Manford to New Orleans," Kight explained to *The Advocate*. "We had $6 left when we got there."[51] Thus, in a roundabout way, Ronnie Rosenthal's call to John Gill for aid had alerted a national network.

Sympathetic publications were now on alert, and prominent leaders from some of the most visible gay organizations in the United States— Troy Perry, Morris Kight and Morty Manford—were en route. Such a response was unprecedented. Before this horrible fire, local gay populations had each been responsible for advocacy in their respective turfs, with little overlap. But that was about to change, with leaders from across the United States wanting to help. Activists agreed to rendezvous in the afternoon at the Marriott on Canal Street.[52] The organizers of Gay Liberation were set to descend on New Orleans—a city with no visible gay leadership, little taste for activism, and less experience with modern gay politics.

SOMETIME IN THE wee hours of Monday, New Orleans police detectives Charles Schlosser and Sam Gebbia detained David Dubose, an eighteen-year-old Up Stairs Lounge patron. Police had located Dubose at the Golden Slipper Lounge on Rampart Street, precisely where James Smith had dropped him following their romantic rendezvous at Smith's apartment. Dubose admitted to throwing beer mugs at the Up Stairs Lounge, and the detectives brought him in for questioning. At New Orleans Police Department headquarters—a bunkerlike building on South Broad Avenue, located near the criminal courthouse—officers interrogated their suspect.[53]

Speaking without a lawyer, the young interviewee broke down and confessed his involvement in setting the Up Stairs Lounge fire. For a brief moment, Schlosser and Gebbia thought they had Dubose on the hook for the crime of arson and many more cases of involuntary manslaughter. They had an admission from a chief suspect, case closed. Something, however, must have sobered in Dubose before he signed a written confession, because the eighteen-year-old then recanted, denying that he was aware of or had played any part in the deadly fire.[54]

Having verbally confessed but then denied his confession, Dubose placed himself in a tenuous position. Police administered a polygraph test to clarify the matter, and the results showed conclusively that Dubose "was telling the truth in that he had not set the fire or brought any gasoline to the Up Stairs Lounge." In their report, the detectives noted that no other evidence, besides his being ejected from the bar, existed to implicate the teenager in the crime. With no probable cause to hold Dubose, they released him. Later, the NOPD visited the Walgreens on Iberville and interviewed the cashier Claudine Rigaud about the gay man with shaking hands who'd angrily purchased the medium-size bottle of lighter fluid, because the smallest size was sold out. Her description of a male in his midtwenties did not match David Dubose.[55]

REVEREND JOHN GILL's plane from Atlanta touched down in the Big Easy shortly before dawn. Passing a newsstand, Gill scanned the early editions and saw headlines about the Up Stairs Lounge. He dashed to a cab and headed toward a totally unfathomable situation.[56]

That Monday began like any other day in New Orleans. Streetcars rolled down St. Charles Avenue, hauling commuters and the odd tourist. Workers lit industrial boilers at the Jax Brewery. Twenty-four-hour bars[57]—the mainstay of a city with an altogether different relationship to alcohol than most—flipped off their fluorescent signs and opened their doors for the pre-work rush.

There were no top-of-the-morning press conferences from city officials to discuss the previous night's calamity. Winston Lill, director of public relations for City Hall, was preoccupied with plans for his daughter's wedding at the Trinity Episcopal Church the next Saturday. Announcements and pictures had been posted in the *Times-Picayune*, and Lill described himself, in a letter to a local bank executive, as "worn out, broke, and emotionally exhausted."[58] Journalists accepted this distraction and knew to lay off him. Such was their esprit de corps.

Mayor Moon Landrieu, Lill's boss, was out of town. Subordinates knew to treat that time away as sacrosanct. The mayor was not to be roped into a local mess. And New Orleans residents weren't rushing to Charity Hospital to donate blood for the fifteen injured at the Up Stairs Lounge in the same manner that crowds had overrun the facility that January to provide blood for thirteen wounded following a disaster called the "Howard Johnson's sniper incident."[59] The straight world, which had momentarily gazed into the abyss, regained an air of detachment.

Reverend John Gill proceeded to the MCC church. He reached the Creole cottage on Magazine Street a little before 6:30 a.m. From the rectory, he phoned *The Advocate* in Los Angeles. Gill put Lucien Baril, a lay leader of the congregation, on the line and introduced him as the man who would be "basically taking over leadership of this church." The boyish-looking Baril, who wrote under the name Thomas L. Baril, gave Gill the impression of being a long-standing member of the flock, although, in truth, he had been an MCC member for only a few months. Baril reiterated to *The Advocate* how "I will be worship coordinator . . . on John Gill's recommendation, waiting for confirmation from Reverend Troy Perry." Apparently, upon hearing through the grapevine of the fire and pastor Bill Larson's death, Baril had seized the moment by packing a bag and moving into Bill Larson's rectory—claiming that he had been living there all the while, with "Rev. Larson, myself and my lover," as a renter.[60]

STEWART BUTLER, WHO wasn't out with coworkers at the engineering firm where he worked, showed up at the office that morning and attempted to conceal his sorrow with busywork. "It was a hard, hard thing to do and not show any reaction," Stewart recalled. News reports on the fire came hourly, with likely names of the dead. "Everybody in the office is fucking talking about it," recalled Steven Duplantis. "And Stewart's got to listen to it like he doesn't know nothing about it."[61]

Meanwhile, Steven himself had made it back to Randolph Air Force Base and dashed into the office tower where he worked. Although his uniform was impeccably clean, he had not had time to shower. Fortunately, no one at the base had heard about the Up Stairs Lounge yet, so he had nothing but private thoughts to plague him. "That was a hell day," he recalled. When Steven finally got back to his barracks, he made the phone call he dreaded. Stewart picked up, and Steven bawled into the receiver. He started apologizing before Stewart could even understand what for. Steven reiterated what he had heard out of the mouth of that guy, who'd been ejected by Buddy Rasmussen and Hugh Cooley right before he left for Texas.[62]

Then Steven tried to explain to Stewart the mitigating circumstances in his life, with the May setup and his commanding officer possessing the power to deny his transfer and commence a court-martial for a sex crime. No one could catch wind, Steven told Stewart, of his being in a New Orleans gay bar on the night of June 24. "Stewart begged me to come back over and talk to the police," recalled Steven. Steven cried all the more: "I said, 'Stewart, if I do that, my military is finished.' "[63]

HENRY KUBICKI OPENED his eyes to another day. He firmly believed that his universe remained fundamentally unchanged. The night before, Henry had been exhausted when he finished his shift at the Marriott. He used the employee exit and sprinted to catch the St. Charles streetcar home. This route had caused him to bypass the fire scene at the corner of Iberville and Chartres. "I still had no idea what was going on," Henry recalled. Ricky Everett hadn't been home when Henry reached the apartment, but Henry had just assumed that his roommate must still be "trolling the bars" with Ronnie Rosenthal, the out-of-towner.[64]

So Henry casually readied himself for work. He showered and shaved. Nothing could prepare him for what happened as he walked to a newsstand for the morning paper. Henry read and reread the headline "Twenty-Nine Killed in Quarter Blaze," emblazoned on the front page of the *Times-Picayune*. The words stung. Accompanying the text was a picture of Rusty Quinton wiping ash from his face.[65]

That image of his friend, reified in black and white, assaulted him. Henry wandered home in a daze. He sobbed alone with his coffee and eggs. Even if he could help, he didn't know how. Henry grabbed for the telephone, which Ricky had installed about a week before to talk to boyfriends. Henry's income was too meager to pay for even a portion of a phone bill, and so the phone was exclusively for Ricky's use. But the emergency situation warranted a breach of roommate etiquette. Henry phoned the MCC church. The line was busy. He dialed another number. "I couldn't find Courtney Craighead, cause he was working, or he died," recalled Henry. "I couldn't get ahold of Ricky Everett. I couldn't get ahold of Bill Larson. I couldn't get ahold of Mitch Mitchell."[66]

Panic mounted with each failed attempt. Henry knew that he couldn't spend all day on the phone. He had to leave for work within minutes, to punch his time card or lose his only source of income. Hoping that Ricky wasn't dead, Henry left a frantic note for his roommate to call him at the Marriott immediately. He dabbed his face and tried to put himself back together as he threw on his work uniform. Though his hands were shaking, Henry knew that, as a dishwasher, he wouldn't be able to get time off today, no matter the circumstances.[67]

So Henry Kubicki, Steven Duplantis, and Stewart Butler all clocked into work that Monday. They kept their "straight faces" intact and minimized chitchat, with Stewart slumped at a desk, Steven punching digits into a military computer, and Henry lost at a kitchen sink. Most painfully, Stewart and Henry were forced to mask their emotions as coworkers joked crassly about the fire—they couldn't risk being outed by association.[68]

CHAPTER 7

Liberation Descends

Monday Morning,
June 25, 1973

As the week began, media establishments grappled with how to report a calamity involving a community that wasn't supposed to exist. The sexual "otherness" of the Up Stairs Lounge victims flummoxed editors and journalists, challenging a taboo about whether to hide or include homosexuality as a story element and then what precise language to use. Journalists struggled to perform their due diligence in reporting the high death count, even as articles lit up newswires and traveled across oceans, as far as *The Irish Times* in Dublin, *The Times* in London, the *International Herald Tribune* in Paris, and the *Sydney Morning Herald* in Australia.[1]

Some publications chose to play it safe by avoiding all mention of homosexuality. *The Oregonian* in Portland, the *State-Times* in Baton Rouge, and *The Times* in London each declined to do so. Egregiously, the *Times-Picayune* did not print the word "homosexual" in any of the three front-page stories on the Up Stairs Lounge it ran in its Monday morning edition. "The *Times-Picayune* was a very, very conservative paper, both politically and in terms of how it approached things," noted Clancy DuBos, who was interning there that summer. "They didn't take risks at all, and, it [the word "homosexuality"] should not have been a risky thing for them, but they would have seen that as taking a risk at the time or just something that they don't do."[2]

Journalist John LaPlace, DuBos's mentor at the *Picayune*, wrote two Up Stairs Lounge stories but failed to disclose to readers that he frequented the Lounge while making his regular rounds through gay establishments in the Quarter. Such information would have revealed his status in the closet and endangered his career, and so he concealed his personal connection to the victims as he covered the story dutifully and sympathetically, though occasionally outing men and pretending that his subjects were not also his friends.[3]

Some publications relied on euphemistic language to convey the nature of the bar in question. For example, the front-page story in the *Los Angeles Times*, "Twenty-Nine Die in Bar Fire," relied heavily on a dispatch from the Associated Press newswire, which had avoided using the word "homosexual." Instead, the *Los Angeles Times* called the Up Stairs Lounge "a popular place on Sundays," which left open the anachronistic suggestion that its vigorous business on the Lord's day might attract a clientele at odds with the Christian faithful. In other words, "a popular place on Sundays" provided a means for the conservative reader to suspect that the bar was less than reputable. The same phrase "a popular place on Sundays" also appeared in the Long Island newspaper *Newsday* and the *Chicago Tribune*.[4]

Only a few publications elected to print the then-controversial word. With Roy Reed's special report, entitled "Flash Fire in New Orleans Kills at Least Thirty-Two in Bar," *The New York Times* joined *The Washington Post* as the only major newspapers to convey the bar's "homosexual" clientele that morning. Through Reed's story, the *Times* also became the only paper outside the state of Louisiana to assign a reporter to the unfolding incident. Other major-market publications relied on commercial newswire services—printing articles directly from the Associated Press or UPI under contractual agreement, which was common practice for smaller publications with limited budgets but more questionable for publications with resources for national reporting like the *Chicago Tribune*. By contrast, just seven months earlier, when a fire claimed the lives of two men and four women—whose sexualities weren't in question— at the Rault Center in New Orleans, the Illinois newspaper had found the budget to send staff to Louisiana for original reporting.[5]

This time, on June 25, 1973, the lead story in the *Tribune*, entitled "Twenty-Nine Die In New Orleans Fire," knitted together dis-

patches from multiple newswires to deliver an account of the Up Stairs
Lounge blaze that included no unique quotations or enterprising coverage. At the time, the *Tribune* was known to be conservative, and it
had barely covered Chicago's own flourishing homosexual community.
For example, the city's first gay pride parade, in 1970, had received just
three inches of text on the paper's twenty-seventh page.[6]

There was a certain distaste in newsrooms across the United States
when dealing with the topic of homosexuality. Even in Roy Reed's
report in *The New York Times*, the single mention—"A neighboring
bartender said the place was frequented by homosexuals," a sentence
that sounds innocuous today—must have resounded negatively with
his editors. According to former *Times* journalists Jeff Schmalz and
Russell King, most gay and lesbian journalists in the *Times* newsroom were deeply closeted in the early 1970s. Managing editor A. M.
"Abe" Rosenthal was known to intimidate reporters covering the
homosexual community. "We'd done a piece about a gay cruise on
the cover of the travel section; there was a lot of shouting about it,"
Schmalz told *The Advocate* in 1992. "Abe thought it was a total mistake, and that we never should have done it. And we'd used the word
gay. He said we could never use that word again." In defense of the
Times, its coverage of the Up Stairs Lounge was far more exhaus-
tive than its coverage of the Stonewall Riots in its own backyard: just
four years earlier, in 1969, the paper's headlines had bemoaned, "Four
Policemen Hurt in 'Village' Raid," and scolded the "Hostile Crowd,"
while the stories discussed how "hundreds of young men went on a
rampage" that blameless cops were forced to rout.[7]

Whether because of their own biases or in an effort to spare the
sensibilities of its readers, the *Times* editors buried that sole mention
of "homosexual" in Roy Reed's story by placing it ten paragraphs deep
into the article, where—according to the "inverted pyramid" format
of newswriting—the least important information should appear. In
so doing, they also ensured the offending sentence would not appear
in the portion of the story on the front page, but after the "jump,"
or continuation of the story in a deeper section of the paper. In this
case, the jump was to page sixty-six, and many readers would not be

interested enough to shuffle the sections, find the rest of the story, and follow the tale to its finish. In exactly the same way, *The Washington Post* subverted the importance of the word "homosexual" through the page placement of its front-page story on the New Orleans tragedy: the term appeared only after the jump to page twenty-two.[8] Using this layout technique, a casual reader skimming headlines and perhaps only reading the front-page text wouldn't have to stumble upon the disconcerting term.

This sensitivity surrounding a word that, as Roy Reed later observed, was "a crucial detail" revealed prejudice in shaping the public's understanding of a national incident. That a specific group had possibly been targeted, by whom, and for what reason were not questions that readers could ponder as they learned about a random bar fire.[9] Deprived of the homosexual context, readers could not be expected to glean anything from the graphic pictures of burnt corpses, which, astonishingly, did not pose the same threat to so-called considerations of taste as one printed word.

Locally, most New Orleanians absorbed the homosexual subtext from barroom humor and corner gossip—jokes that portrayed the fire victims as incompetent criminals or femme clichés dying in caricaturish ways. "I remember, at the time, people called it the 'gay bar fire,'" said Clancy DuBos, "as opposed to just a fire at a bar." Just as Henry Kubicki had heard the Cuban man at the Marriott commissary laughing about "barbequed queens' asses," similar quips spread from block to block. "Did you hear the one about the flaming queens?" and "I hope they burned their dresses off" both circulated widely. One punch line involved the Up Stairs Lounge and a popular brand of children's breakfast cereal, through which a few fairies had burned into some Crispy Critters. Several morning radio listeners recalled a popular news/talk personality suggesting that the best way to dispose of the dead "fruits" was to "bury them in fruit jars."[10]

Obviously, much of this humor revealed homophobic feelings. "I was out of town on a case when the fire occurred," recalled Bob McAnear, the U.S. Customs officer who knew the Up Stairs crowd. "A large part of law enforcement officers made derisive remarks based on what they knew of the reputation of the gays that most people encounter in the Quarter." *States-Item* reporter Lanny Thomas observed how, although "the fire, to no one's surprise, has been *the* conversation topic in bars throughout the Quarter—straight, gay, hippie, dives, the jet set," the chatter "has not really touched the hearts of the city because it did happen in a gay bar." The prospect of vaudeville "nancys" dying in a fiery panic provided comic relief for New Orleanians, who were otherwise unable to face the discussion of "out" homosexuality in their town. "Most of the people were glad," remembered Joseph Bermuda, who opened his Cabildo Gallery to the usual cast of bohemians that Monday. "They were not charitable. They didn't feel sorry or bad about it. It's like, 'Oh, they got burned, *welllll*.' The feeling was they had it coming. There was no regret. That's what I remember from the people around my shop, 'They deserve it; those fruits, they deserve it.' "[11]

Such sophomoric attitudes were hardly anomalous in the early 1970s, or even offensive to the tastes of the era. In 1969, *Time* had published a poll in which 63 percent of Americans surveyed considered homosexuals to be "harmful to American life." Four years later, attitudes had hardly changed. Meanwhile, *Deliverance*, the hit 1972 adaptation of James Dickey's novel, had included perhaps the most prominent depiction of male-male sodomy in a piece of American art to date.[12] In its visceral homosexual rape scene, a pair of backwoods mountain men hold at gunpoint two "city boys" on a canoeing trip. One mountain man then forcibly sodomizes his victim while demanding that he "squeal like a pig." The trauma ends when the rapist is felled by an arrow from the bow of a friend (Burt Reynolds), another of the quartet of weekend adventurers roughing it in the wilderness. After the rapist dies, survivors of the ordeal choose to bury the stranger and continue on with their trip rather than report the incident and spark a scandal.

That the first prolonged and vivid depiction of male-male sex in a major American film was a terrifying rape, the payback for which was death, confirmed the image of same-gender sex as strange and frightening intercourse, performed by the wicked upon the unsuspecting. *Deliverance*, it should be noted, continued to play in New Orleans into June of 1973. The *Deliverance* rape sequence "contributed to an enduring popular association of homosexuality with sexual deviance and violence," writes historian Thomas Borstelmann in his *The 1970s: A New Global History from Civil Rights to Economic Inequality.*[13]

That media professionals and members of the public then be asked to express sympathy for a bar full of so-called sex predators struck many as hypocrisy. The fire had not just claimed lives, the logic went; it had fleeced out criminal wrongdoers in the midst of their iniquities.

AFTER HIS INITIAL phone call with *The Advocate*, Reverend John Gill attempted to notify sympathetic organizations of his presence in town. He called Tulane University's Gay Student Union, the city's one active Gay Liberation organization, and discovered that the group went dormant over the summer. Gill did reach Bill Rushton, the twenty-five-year-old editor of the *Vieux Carré Courier.*[14]

Gill alerted Rushton, who was an outspoken homosexual, to the groundswell of activism building around the fire. Rushton hurried over to the church on Magazine Street to cover events as they unfolded. Gill didn't have much luck with his other contacts. The Women's Work Collective of Louisiana didn't step forward to offer assistance. Local lesbian leaders had distanced themselves from the politics of gay men following the collapse of the New Orleans chapter of the Gay Liberation Front (GLF) in 1971. "Gay women active in the GLF felt a void," wrote Mary Gehman in the New Orleans feminist newspaper *Distaff.* "The organization addressed itself mainly to the problems of male homosexuals, the vice squad (which did not threaten lesbians) and the gay male bars. When the women's movement began to appeal to women of all backgrounds, gay women joined in large numbers. They saw themselves oppressed first as women and secondly as lesbians."[15]

National and local civil rights organizations didn't raise a commotion over the Up Stairs Lounge either. The *Chicago Daily Defender,* one of the nation's premier African American newspapers, neglected to report the Up Stairs Lounge as news, although there was a black victim: Reggie Adams. By contrast, earlier that year, the *Defender* had chosen to report news from New Orleans: the Howard Johnson's sniper incident, which involved a black shooter. By 1973, many black leaders in the Big Easy had been loosely assimilated into City Hall through the Human Relations Committee, a civil rights commission that Moon Landrieu had championed into being. By design, half of the committee's appointed members were black, although the presiding chairman, Monsignor Arthur T. Screen, was a white Catholic priest appointed as representative of the archdiocese by Archbishop Philip Hannan himself. The Human Relations Committee, which maintained an answer desk at City Hall, in Spanish and English, for housing or immigrant issues, did not exactly leap at the opportunity to help gay fire victims or the MCC. New Orleans's contingent of Black Panthers, following an armed standoff with the NOPD in 1971, ran a covert operation not easily contacted by outsiders, much less white homosexuals without black power credentials.[16]

Quickly exhausting his list, Gill understood the stark degree of isolation of the local gay population. Even though open avenues of communication between black and white residents had been established by 1973, none existed between out homosexuals and heterosexuals. It was obvious to Gill that, besides the ragtag members of the city's decimated MCC church, there would be no organizations with which to coordinate. He and Troy Perry would be alone in their management of the crisis.[17]

When Perry landed in New Orleans that morning, Gill drove out to meet perhaps the most recognizable gay man in America, with his dark pompadour and pork-chop sideburns. Perry, who was thirty-two, looked younger in person. "Gill informed me," Perry later wrote, "that in New Orleans there was a near vacuum of gay leadership that needed to be filled." Local constituencies would later disparage Perry for this assessment, but he remains adamant about the state of gay New Orleans in 1973. "There was nobody else," he insisted in an interview for this book.[18]

Meanwhile, as Gill was picking Perry up, reporter Eric Newhouse of the Associated Press appeared on the porch of the MCC cottage and talked his way through the front door. Deacon Courtney Craighead gave Newhouse an interview on a set of lawn chairs by the empty altar. Newhouse was curious about the personal life of pastor Bill Larson, the man reputedly photographed in the Chartres Street window. "What was he doing at the *bar*?" Eric Newhouse asked Courtney. "Had he made arrangements to go see friends?" Recoiling from these questions, which baited Courtney into admitting that Bill Larson was a homosexual hanging out at a gay bar, the deacon answered noncommittally, "Oh . . . I don't know." Then a crew from WWL-TV was at the door, and Courtney had to plead for no cameras.[19]

CONFUSION STILL REIGNED at Charity Hospital, where friends and family members awaited answers. Concerned parties, often refusing to give their names, overloaded the phone lines with questions about who had died. "The principal problems came from hysterical parents suffering from poor communications with reclusive sons," explained Bill Rushton in *The Advocate*, "whom the parents feared might be among the victims." A librarian working at the Historic New Orleans Collection in the French Quarter received a call from a woman who wouldn't identify herself but kept asking about the fate of her estranged gay brother. This caller believed her brother was employed at a local museum, and she wanted to know if her brother was at work that Monday. Sadly, the librarian couldn't help with such vague information, nor could she make an accusation that would possibly out a colleague.[20]

Throughout New Orleans and the rest of the country, it wasn't uncommon for gays to be so alienated, especially from blood relatives. Many homosexual adults had been teenage runaways, adolescents who left home without a forwarding address or a note of explanation. Cities, particularly, had long been places where the banished sought relief. Some clans had gladly parted ways with troubled offspring. For example, Brendan Flaherty, the eighteen-year-old coat check boy at the Stonewall Inn, had originally fled his hometown of Boston. "I was just so relieved I wasn't in that oppressed world," he said. "My parents had put me into two mental institutions and put me in prison and then put me into a school for incorrigibles, which were runaways, which you could do back then in the sixties." Others had escaped sexual abuse. For example, David Williams, who tended bar in New Orleans gay hangouts starting in the 1970s, recalled his father lending him out as a six-year-old "lot lizard," or rest-stop prostitute, in rural Georgia to truckers who would pay for the privilege of "being nice" to him.[21] Other gay men and women had run away preemptively, before conservative family members could discover what they were and attempt draconian measures through doctors. Most who went running did not wish to be found.

Some connections between gay men and their families were severed on moral grounds. For instance, MCC pastor Bill Larson had suffered a difficult relationship with his mother, Anna Howell. Despite losing custody of her children to the county and the scandal of her forced marriage to Bill's stepfather in 1930, she had seemingly reformed and been welcomed into sewing and artistic cliques for upright women in Hamilton, Ohio. Howell nonetheless renounced her son upon his 1947 divorce: having never been divorced, only widowed, she considered the dissolution of a marriage to be a disgrace. Strikingly, she made this judgment despite her failure to raise Bill from age three to fifteen—even though, according to public records, she seemed financially able to do so during much of this period.[22]

During the boy's long stay at the Butler County Children's Home, Howell showed little interest in fostering her son. Time and again, she offered excuses when the boy asked to visit her in town. The boy struggled in the context of a communal upbringing. As a ten-year-old, he was frequently disciplined for early signs of a "sex problem," with a penchant for "wrestling," being "particularly disgusting while boys are waiting for baths," and being the sort of "sissy" who "abuses himself." Not all, however, was misery for the "artistic boy." Young Bill displayed an early flair for singing and composing on the piano, wrote original plays, and exhibited a passion for the Bible that led a staff member to testify, "He really seems quite interested in doing some type of religious work in his adult life."[23]

After his divorce, Bill moved to Chicago and reinvented himself as "Ros Larison," nightclub singer and entertainer,[24] but Howell's disapproval of her youngest child only deepened. Ros Larison's final transformation to Bill Larson, the gay pastor in New Orleans, likely occurred years after their severance of relations.

Other gay men had been exiled for similar issues. For example, after Up Stairs Lounge victim Glenn Green's "undesirable discharge" from the U.S. navy, Glenn had attempted to return to his family in Walled Lake, Michigan. He was rebuffed, however, by his older brother Mahlon, a local politician who viewed Glenn's record of sexual immorality as a scandal that could be used by political opponents of his "Go for Green" campaigns. Glenn had ended up moving to New Orleans without prospects, but he made quick friends and began a habit of regularly telephoning his niece Mary David long distance to show that he was okay.[25]

Admittedly, other cases of estrangement could not be blamed entirely on the families. Up Stairs Lounge victim Ferris LeBlanc hadn't spoken to his relatives in California since 1970 because of a financial dispute. Although the LeBlanc clan had accepted Ferris's homosexuality and even welcomed one of his previous lovers into the family—a gesture of openness rare at the time—trouble began when that relationship ended and Ferris started courting a new gentleman named Rod. A dispute involving Ferris and Rod's failure to honor debts to Ferris's grandfather caused a falling-out that ended in small claims court. Ferris and Rod skipped town rather than pay a settlement. Although the gay couple eventually split up, Ferris's sister Marilyn LeBlanc suspected that her brother was still ashamed. She hoped and wished that time would heal the rift.[26] Sadly, that was no longer possible.

REVEREND TROY PERRY rushed into the double-parlor of the MCC of New Orleans. The AP reporter had cleared out by then, and Perry assumed the stance of a shepherd protecting his flock. The rumble of the air conditioner provided an eerie hum for the room, which was now occupied by about a dozen "fire-stricken" men slumped in folding chairs.[27] Deacon Courtney Craighead, as well as Lucien Baril, greeted the preacher.

In the back rectory, a telephone rang incessantly, and volunteers like Ronnie Rosenthal answered the succession of calls. Each new voice came with the alarm and paranoia of an uncle or a mother posing almost unspeakable questions. These were family members who might have a son in New Orleans, a son who, they hinted, might be a member of their church. Many admitted that they had dialed the MCC because it was the only number in the phone book for a gay-affiliated organization that wasn't a gay bar.[28]

To help these families, the MCC kept a running file of confirmed survivors and victims. Ronnie Rosenthal also took on the unenviable duty of calling families to inform them that their son was dead or missing. "The saddest part," said Ronnie, "was when we tried to call someone's parents to let them know what happened, and they could care less." Some families just couldn't face the shame of claiming a homosexual loved one as one of their own. "All of us understood why a lot of the families didn't come forward," recalled John Meyers, the Café Lafitte patron, "bemoaning it but, nonetheless, understanding it."[29]

For local gay men, the telephone became a preferred means of getting updates, given that city departments were refraining from comment and the news media seemed more intent on appeasing conservative tastes than providing clarity. "There was a dearth of information as to what exactly had happened," admitted Meyers. This phone network became a vital tool for friends and for parents of gay or suspected-gay children. Word spread far and fast. "I know that we first found out about it from phone calls," recalled former Up Stairs Lounge patron Paul Killgore, who resided with his boyfriend about eight miles from the Quarter.[30]

George Robert Sirois, a closeted construction worker in Massachusetts who made pilgrimages to the Big Easy with his mutually discreet "buddies," got the call from more than fifteen hundred miles away. His friends at the Up Stairs Lounge had perished. Some of these acquaintances, Sirois was told, hadn't yet been identified. Sirois was devastated, but he was also a married Vietnam veteran with a child. To come forward with any possible names would be to out himself. Larry Bagneris, a New Orleans native who had fled to Houston to embrace a fully out lifestyle, received an unexpected phone call from his mother in the Big Easy, filled with spoken and unspoken meanings. "I remember my mom saying to me on the phone," he said, "when she was telling me this awful story, 'But these were people that shouldn't have been treated that way,' which was encouragement to me to come out [of the closet]."[31]

Along with filling gaps in information, these phone calls heightened fears and engendered accusations of discrimination by religious groups when it came to delivering death rites for the deceased. "We started getting phone calls that there were families of Catholic victims that were upset because they were being denied opportunities to have funerals in their parish churches or even being denied burials in Catholic cemeteries, where they had their plots," relayed Paul Killgore, who recalled these rumors with the caveat that he had heard them second- and third-hand. "I never spoke to any family members that relayed that to me," he continued. "I was getting that from friends of mine."[32]

TROY PERRY ESTABLISHED his lead status among the local MCC congregants. Outranking Courtney Craighead by several echelons in the church hierarchy, Perry assumed this leadership role without debate—a peremptory gesture that, no doubt, displeased Courtney. The deacon, however, preferred to remain in some gradation of the closet, and even he had to admit that a tragedy of this magnitude required a spokesperson. Perry asked for testimony about the fire, and congregants, perhaps more than a little star struck by a preacher they'd read about in magazines and in the autobiography he'd published the previous year, shared what they knew. Lucien Baril gave his account of the past twelve hours.[33]

Many were moved by Baril's eloquence, even though he acknowledged that he had not been at the Up Stairs Lounge because of a "toothache." His speech must have impressed Troy Perry and validated

John Gill's faith in the young man he called "deacon exhorter." On the spot, Perry accepted Gill's recommendation that Baril be elevated to interim worship coordinator for the MCC of New Orleans—Bill Larson's former role. It was a position that, by rights, could have gone to Deacon Courtney Craighead. But, since Courtney didn't wish to make his sexuality an issue by becoming a "gay minister," he didn't object.[34]

Perry learned from Baril how, earlier that morning, Courtney Craighead had contacted Reverend David Solomon, the congregation's former pastor, and made arrangements for Solomon to conduct a memorial service for fire victims at nearby St. George's Episcopal Church that evening. Perry announced that he would also lend his voice to the service. He and John Gill then led a group prayer for strength in the days to follow. There were so many unknowns. Folks hadn't seen Deacon Mitch Mitchell since his rooftop escape, although Ricky Everett insisted that Mitch had gone back into the bar. Nor could they remember whether a congregant named Tad Turner had visited the Up Stairs Lounge that Sunday. Someone remembered seeing Rusty Quinton limping down Canal Street after the fire, as if lost.[35]

MCC congregants invited Troy Perry to stay in the rectory, but he declined. "We decided any efforts on our part to assist the local gay community would be better undertaken where the atmosphere of grief was not so overwhelming," the preacher would later write. Gill and Perry headed downtown and checked in at the Marriott Hotel on Canal Street. Their view from the tenth floor overlooked Iberville Street, so they faced the husk of the Up Stairs Lounge. Wisps of ash and smoke still rose from the building, kicked up by the occasional breeze.[36]

For the next few days, their pair of adjoining rooms would serve as headquarters for an ad hoc team of gay leaders, who dubbed themselves the New Orleans Emergency Task Force. They would attempt to bring prominence to a tragedy that, it soon became clear, most preferred to hustle past. Soon Morris Kight and Morty Manford, invigorated from their travels, arrived at the hotel. When Manford had told someone at the New Orleans International Airport that he was in town for the tragedy, the person had responded, "Only some faggots got burned." Morris Kight waved a copy of the *States-Item*, New Orleans's afternoon newspaper, which enjoyed a more liberal reputation than the *Times-Picayune*.[37]

Kight thrust the paper into Troy's hands. Emblazoned in large text was the headline "Twenty-Nine Dead in Quarter Holocaust." The story used hyperbolic language and metaphors to evoke the visceral horror, with phrases like "bodies stacked like pancakes" and workers struggling "late into the night pulling the bodies apart." The *States-Item* took the additional step of flouting local mores by printing the word "homosexuals" on its front page, in the process becoming the first local newspaper to do so.[38]

The featured photograph was that of an unidentified male hanging lifeless, seared to a window. Perry knew, from what he'd heard at the MCC church, that this was pastor Bill Larson. Cameras had flashed over Larson's corpse, Perry reflected. People had recorded these images in a near-automatic series of clicks and flashes that neither the police nor the fire department had tried to stop. They let the man hang exposed to the elements, and here he was: burnt up and on display without name. In a column beside the picture, thirteen tentatively identified victims were listed—Bill Larson was not among them. Inside the paper, the injured were also tallied.[39]

Reading further, Perry saw no words of indignation from civil rights groups like the Southern Christian Leadership Conference or Jesse Jackson's Chicago-based Operation PUSH (People United to Serve Humanity). But Perry had grown accustomed to fellow human rights movements giving little or no support to homosexuals. Larry Bagneris—a black as well as gay New Orleanian—cited antigay Christian dogma as partial explanation for this oversight. "There was no acceptance of gay rights because of the black churches," he said, yet "the civil rights movement began in the black churches." Bayard Rustin, who was known as the Socrates of the civil rights movement and who organized the 1963 March on Washington, remained a closeted homosexual—mum about his private affairs—almost a decade later.[40]

Perry seethed when he saw the language used to describe fire victims. "We don't even know if these papers belonged to the people we found them on," said Major Henry M. Morris, who complained about the subversive nature of gay culture. "Some thieves hung out there, and you know this was a queer bar," the police officer continued. Providing context to these "queer bar" claims, another officer offered, "It is not uncommon for homosexuals to carry false identification, which could complicate the identification procedure." Would such accusations against the dead be tolerated if the victims had been considered upstanding? "This slander," said Morris Kight in his professorial style, "must not go unchallenged." Kight called around to local television stations and scheduled a press conference for five that afternoon.[41]

Equally deplorable to Perry was something he'd expected to see in local coverage but did not: comment from city leaders about the death toll that Fire Superintendent William McCrossen had already pronounced "one of the worst in New Orleans history." Yet, even though McCrossen would call the fire gruesome and deadly, his public statements fell short of defending the dignity of those who had died. Mayor Moon Landrieu had offered no statement of sympathy for the victims. Louisiana governor Edwin Edwards was also wholly missing from coverage, and Archbishop Philip Hannan, whom Catholic admirers sometimes called the "Pope of New Orleans," offered no prayers or condolences. "Many gays held prominent positions in city and state offices," explained Bob McAnear, the U.S. Customs officer. "This [their closeted status] may have been the reason none of the city or state officials would make any public statements of empathy relating to the victims or survivors."[42]

Such silence from on high struck Troy Perry as suspicious— particularly for Mayor Landrieu, whose personal politics and past responses to local disasters merits deeper analysis. After more than a decade in elected office, Landrieu had established proficiency in crisis management. A charming fixture of liberal New Orleans, he was so beloved by civil rights groups that Ku Klux Klan sympathizers had nicknamed him "Moon McCoon" and subjected him to death threats.[43]

Landrieu dressed the part of the pragmatic dreamer, a principled man who made things happen, with glistening blue eyes offset by a seersucker suit and thick glasses. Following the Rault Center fire in November 1972, the mayor offered heartfelt remarks of sympathy for victims ("Mourned not only by those who knew them, but by New Orleanians in all walks of life") and left a U.S. Conference of Mayors meeting in Indiana—"one day early," according to the *Times-Picayune*—to lead his grieving city.[44]

During the January 1973 Howard Johnson's sniper incident, Landrieu participated in on-the-ground efforts to end the standoff between policemen and the disaffected gunman, who was shooting from the rooftop of a Howard Johnson's motel steps from City Hall. This shooter, a former military serviceman named Mark Essex who'd attended Black Panther meetings in New York, was on a mission to kill. Bullets flew around the mayor, one of which struck and killed Deputy Police Superintendent Louis Sirgo. Landrieu called Essex's mass shooting of civilians and law enforcement officials "perhaps the most tragic criminal act in the history of New Orleans," declared a citywide state of mourning, and proclaimed that January was National Volunteer Blood Donor Month "in lieu [sic] of the emergency situation that occurred Jan. 7."[45]

Almost six months later, in the wake of the Up Stairs Lounge fire, Moon Landrieu remained in Europe, on vacation during those first critical hours after the city's deadliest fire on record. As Landrieu was reachable via telegram or long-distance telephone call to hotels on his itinerary, it's difficult to conceive of a circumstance in which neither members of his office nor his fire chief, William McCrossen, failed to inform him of the situation. Furthermore, even if Landrieu were inaccessible by these methods, both the *International Herald Tribune* (an American-owned and -oriented, Paris-based newspaper) and *The Times* of London reported on the fire and were available on European newsstands.[46]

AT THE TIME, Moon Landrieu was a man on the rise—included as a possible vice president pick for George McGovern's 1972 ticket. His name was included among the most powerful Democratic circles. Indeed, through hard work and a knack for making friends, Moon

Landrieu had climbed far from humble roots; he'd gone to law school at Loyola University in 1952, when the school integrated by accepting its first black students, Norman Francis and Ben Johnson. Landrieu had been raised to believe that segregation was the norm, but his time in law school with Francis and Johnson became an epiphany, splitting his views from widely accepted racial theories. "I had come to the conclusion that segregation made no sense," Landrieu said. "It was contrary to Christian charity, contrary to my Catholic beliefs."[47]

Still, Landrieu hesitated to declare himself a civil rights advocate early in his career. "I was smart enough," he explained in an oral history interview, "to not to want to give my enemies a chance to kill me politically." Nonetheless, it was Landrieu who led clandestine efforts to remove the Confederate flag from the New Orleans City Council chamber in 1967. He also championed the unanimous passage of the Public Accommodations Ordinance in 1969, which ended the right of local restaurateurs, hoteliers, and bar owners to refuse to serve black customers. As a candidate for mayor in December 1969, Landrieu was asked in a televised debate if he intended to include blacks in top positions of government. "Yes, I do hope to appoint a Negro as a department head," he responded, "perhaps more than one."[48]

Moon Landrieu had also made small, albeit deniable, gestures in support of closeted gays, coded signals that would have been branded as extreme or even harmful if detected by his opponents. When campaigning on Bourbon Street in 1969, Landrieu had walked into Café Lafitte in Exile and shaken hands with bar patrons. During that campaign, one of Landrieu's top fund-raisers was Leon Irwin III, a man known—in an open secret among local Democrats—to be gay. "Leon was a much-beloved and flamboyant uptown character," wrote the local chronicler Dan Baum. "Everybody knew he was homosexual, but nobody ever mentioned it." As a reward for Irwin's abiding loyalty, Landrieu included the closeted insurance executive on his confidential "must invite" list of special guests for all functions sponsored by the mayor's office.[49] Irwin's appearance on the list, as a "bachelor" among married couples, stood out.

In 1972, Landrieu threw his support behind a successful campaign to elect Leon Irwin III to the Louisiana Democratic National Committee. Thus, one of the most powerful Louisiana Democrats at the time of the fire happened to be a closeted person.

That same year, Landrieu appointed the outed businessman Clay Shaw to the French Market Corporation, which provided Shaw with a respectable post that could help repair his reputation and pay his mounting legal expenses. "I knew if I could put him back in public life," recalled Landrieu, "I would let him [have] or give him back some of his dignity." Because many homosexuals in New Orleans perceived Shaw's persecution as a warning of what could happen to them, Landrieu's appointment of the businessman was seen as form of redemption. "Landrieu's support of Shaw shines as a beacon," wrote gay New Orleans historian Roberts Batson in a column for the New Orleans gay weekly *Impact*, "arguably the most significant political act for gay people in that entire decade."[50]

Nevertheless, Landrieu did not hurry back to New Orleans after the Up Stairs Lounge fire, declare a state of mourning for the victims, or encourage support in the form of blood donations for the injured. Nor did he call for the establishment of a city-supported victims fund, as he had after the January Howard Johnson's shootings. In fact, he did nothing about the Up Stairs Lounge for weeks—eschewing opportunities to even send a message from afar. Nor did any representative of Landrieu's administration make any such gesture in his stead. Their restraint from speech took the guise of hierarchical paralysis, as if speaking about the topic would be speaking out of turn. Winston Lill, the City Hall press secretary, didn't make a statement, and neither did a member of the Human Relations Committee, which was charged with expediting requests for human rights assistance. Unlike the two previous disasters, the city did not plan a public memorial or send representatives to private funerals.[51]

For decades, Landrieu has declined to say how he occupied his time in the days after the Up Stairs Lounge fire. There is little archival record of the 1973 disaster in his papers at Loyola University and a blank page for the events of June 24, with materials evidently redacted, in the scrapbook of newspaper clippings collected by the mayor's office. It seems that the mayor was in town on Friday, June 22, when he signed a letter to the IRS about the French Market Corporation. He declined invitations to attend events the next day, saying he'd be out of town—so it's probable that he left New Orleans by June 23. Chances are, he reached his travel destination by that Sunday, June 24.[52]

Although several articles described Landrieu's trip as "vacationing," one *Times-Picayune* story eleven days after the fire provided additional information: "Mayor Moon Landrieu spent his fourth of July in Europe where he is reviewing plans for a memorial park for Louis Armstrong." These circumstances—a public works project to honor a legendary black musician—represented a confluence of Landrieu's political interests: civil rights and revitalization. A few years before, Landrieu had spearheaded plans to rehabilitate a section of the Tremé—a predominantly black neighborhood adjoining the predominantly white French Quarter—that had been razed to the ground by a previous mayor. Seizing upon the 1971 death of the New Orleans–born Armstrong, Landrieu proposed converting this area into a memorial for the jazz icon. He appointed Ernest "Dutch" Morial, a popular liberal black judge, and a *States-Item* editor named Charles Ferguson to head up the Armstrong Park citizens' committee.[53]

Researching park designs, Morial and Ferguson were inspired by the Tivoli Gardens in Copenhagen, Denmark, which led to Landrieu's summer trip to see it firsthand. A June 11, 1973, letter from an Armstrong committee member to the deputy director of Tivoli Gardens describes Landrieu's travel plans and reveals that Ferguson would accompany him. The Tivoli director confirmed arrangements with Winston Lill. On Thursday, June 28, Lill sent a telefax to Ferguson at the Parkhotel in Lübeck, Germany. Landrieu, therefore, was reachable by senior staff and select members of the media during the week after the fire.[54] Politician and newspaperman were on a city-funded jaunt together, which consumed their attentions abroad.

AT AROUND 4:30 P.M., Troy Perry, John Gill, Morty Manford, and Morris Kight walked the short distance from the Marriott to the Up Stairs Lounge. They examined the rubble and scrutinized the scorched windows and marks of boiled blood. Stains marred the sidewalks, while passersby gawked and made faces at acrid smells. The *Times-Picayune* would print a picture around this time of a curious tourist in a candy-striped shirt poking his head into the charred staircase. "Rubbernecking spectators converged on the spot Monday," the caption read, "as though it was yet another tourist attraction in the City That Care Forgot." Perry placed a bouquet of yellow chrysanthemums on a makeshift "people's shrine" of candles and blooms rising beside the entrance to the bar and led a group prayer before rushing back to the hotel to meet the press.[55]

Some journalists arriving at the press conference voiced suspicions about Perry. One reporter called the gay leaders "fairy carpetbaggers." Overhearing this comment, Perry flew into a rage. He had grown up in Florida, where that Reconstruction-era slur signified the lowliest of low characters. "I want to tell you something," Perry said as he opened the conference. "I've seen yellow journalism before, and quotes from cops in your newspapers and on television about the Up Stairs being a queer bar and a hangout for thieves won't do." His voice rose, engaging rhythms that he typically used as a preacher. "The time in history for calling people niggers and kikes and queers is over in the United States of America. And it's high time that you people in New Orleans, Louisiana, got the message and joined the rest of the Union." This rebuke from a stranger to the Crescent City left the room of reporters flabbergasted. Moving on quickly, Perry castigated members of the closeted press for reporting the fire dispassionately. With that setup, Morris Kight leaped in and demanded an apology from the New Orleans Police Department for Major Morris's published statement about thieves and queers.[56]

As the news conference wound to a close, New Orleans's WVUE, the ABC affiliate, went live across town. On air, newscaster Alec Gifford took a call from an anonymous woman who said that she had vital information about the Up Stairs Lounge. "The fire last night was set by a vigilante group which has declared war on homos," she declared. That supposed vigilante group, which the caller identified as

"Black Mama White Mama" (an obvious homage to a 1973 action film of the same name), claimed credit for the Up Stairs Lounge as an act of revenge against *Deliverance*-style assaults upon innocent heterosexuals. More attacks were in the works, the caller declared before hanging up. As could be expected, this scoop incited anger and panic.[57]

Perry responded to the sensation with a plan to keep the peace. He escorted Up Stairs Lounge survivor Ricky Everett to a competing station for an interview. WWL agreed to interview Ricky on live TV, but under certain conditions. "Troy Perry kind of arranged that," Ricky recalled. "And he wanted them to do it with my back to the camera to portray the poor little gay man who can't come out cause he's afraid of being hated." News producers were wary of revealing the face of a confessed gay, to risk normalizing such an image, but Perry believed that the petite Ricky Everett, by virtue of his voice and body language, could serve as a nonthreatening exemplar. Ricky has only vague recollections of this TV appearance, during which he argued that many homosexuals were Christians and nonviolent citizens. "You have to remember, I'm in shock," recalled Ricky. "All of us were—total shock—and I was in shock for weeks after. You could point me in a direction, and I would go and not ask questions."[58]

Shortly after Ricky left the studio, WWL aired another report that lamented the losses at the Up Stairs Lounge without using the word "homosexual." Instead, the station categorized the incident as a public safety issue: "Louisiana cannot continue to ignore these fire deaths. Something must be done to make buildings safer." This safety angle provided a welcome way to universalize a narrative of twenty-nine deaths without delving into unsavory details. As a result, an antiseptic debate about "firetraps" and building codes gained currency. Nevertheless, watching one of these reports, Clayton Delery, a closeted teenager living in suburban New Orleans, recognized the gay subtext instantly. Bullied in school as "Gay Clay," he possessed a heightened alertness to homosexuality, a subject he knew precipitated attacks, and could decipher it on television. "They're going to kill me," Delery told himself, which eventually motivated his writing a book to explore this arresting thought.[59]

Outside of New Orleans, CBS and NBC national news desks ran segments on the Up Stairs Lounge that evening. Both of these reports, slotted near the bottom of the evening newscast (when minor stories aired), framed the narrative in careful terms. The NBC segment lasted less than twenty seconds, several of which were lost to a suggestive cough by the newscaster; it didn't include the word "homosexual" in its description of the bar. The CBS piece, lasting about a minute, featured reporter Bruce Hall cribbing heavily from the *States-Item*'s story. Hall said, "Police say the bar is a hangout for homosexuals, and homosexuals frequently carry false identification papers."[60]

CHAPTER 8

Visions

Monday Evening,
June 25, 1973

"Some said it was just a bunch of faggots," preached Troy Perry to the fifty or so gathered in the chapel of St. George's Episcopal Church. "But we knew them as people, and as brothers and sisters, and we will never forget them." The sun was setting, as seen through the bay window of the tiny room, as Perry held forth. It was 8:00 p.m., precisely twenty-four hours since the fire had changed the lives of those gathered at the memorial. "This isn't the end," Perry said, his voice booming in the very room that had held Sunday services for the MCC before they opened their Magazine Street church.[1]

Perry cast his eyes upward and then looked outward to his flock. While this side chapel was full, the vaunted sanctuary of St. George's (separated by a thin, white door) stood empty in contrast. Many chapels like this one, accessed by a side entrance from the street, had previously served the religious needs of black domestic workers employed by whites since early Reconstruction.[2] Reporters from the *Times-Picayune* and *The Advocate* stood in back, deferring to attendees, who included Ricky Everett and Ronnie Rosenthal. "The individuals who did this act, we have to pray for them because they have to live with themselves," stated Perry. Reporters from the New Orleans *States-Item* and the Associated Press also listened attentively; these venues' publication of the word "Gay" in headlines the next day would reflect an immediate change in comportment following Perry's castigation of their bias. Seated among the mourners was Reverend Bill Richardson, the minister of St. George's Episcopal Church, who nodded and prayed aloud. "All of us there at MCC who were regular members knew Father Richardson," recalled Ricky Everett. "And we loved him so much."[3]

As the rector for St. George's, Richardson lent dignity and authority through his presence. Yet he accommodated these guests at grave personal risk. Richardson had been devastated to learn of the fire. "My phone rang at 3 a.m. telling me of this," wrote Richardson in remembrance. "I was grieved greatly, for included among those burned to death was Bill Larson, my friend." Richardson had agreed to host a memorial "providing they [the gay activists] would not make a big splash over it." He cautioned local TV stations against taking pictures and asked the journalists to keep things low-key. Plans were so improvised that several MCC congregants, like Henry Kubicki, learned about this memorial only the next day.[4]

Richardson, a widower in his sixties, had enjoyed a close spiritual friendship with MCC pastor Bill Larson. He knew of Larson's homosexuality and was accepting. Although homosexual acts were decreed as sins by the American Episcopal Church (a member of the worldwide Anglican Communion, led by the Church of England), Richardson had flouted these rules and preached compassion for the sexually oppressed. In 1972, he had caused a commotion by letting Bill Larson and his MCC use this chapel. In the wake of the day's "Black Mama White Mama" scare, Richardson once again opened his doors.[5]

After Perry's sermon, Richardson himself addressed the chamber. He gave a homily for Bill Larson and openly wept. Reverend John Gill of the MCC of Atlanta then attempted to rouse the congregants to political action: "New Orleans should not be the City That Care Forgot but the city that God remembered." Reverend David Solomon and Deacon Courtney Craighead also spoke.[6]

Perry closed by calling for a so-called national day of mourning for the Up Stairs Lounge victims on Sunday, July 1, exactly one week after the tragedy. He asked that local gay bars and clubs mark the occasion by closing for one hour at 8:00 p.m. He also announced that funds would soon be solicited for a new gay church in New Orleans, one that could serve as a "living memorial" to the fire and its victims. "This is a most tragic ending of Gay Pride Week," he noted. Hearing this statement, many congregants expressed puzzlement about how the burning of the Up Stairs Lounge had anything to do with gay pride.[7]

Once the service ended, Troy Perry and the other leaders rose to tour bars along Bourbon Street. Feeling that his presence might be a boon, Perry visited Pete's Place, Caverns, and Café Lafitte in Exile to counsel locals and make his presence known. Many New Orleanians were, in fact, stunned to see him in person. "People were really scared," Perry observed. John Meyers said, "The reaction of all of my friends was pretty much he was capitalizing on this, that this was part of his own agenda to advance a church, really, that didn't have much of a following or a lot of respect among gay people here in the city. But that also fits in with the fact that we really didn't want any trouble stirred up."[8]

As PERRY CIRCULATED throughout the Quarter, Roger Nunez tossed fitfully on the couch of his friend Cee Cee Savant at 606½ Iberville Street—just two doors down from the Up Stairs Lounge. Pungent odors wafted through the open windows as Roger attempted to sleep. His dreams were night terrors, and he periodically yelled in his half-awake state, drenched in sweat. The night before, Roger's roommate had found him drunk on the street and guided him home.[9]

In testimony she would give to deputies from the Louisiana Office of the State Fire Marshal, Savant recalled a knock on her apartment door early that Monday morning. Two plainclothes officers, she remembered, flashed their badges and asked to speak to Roger Dale Nunez. She said that one of the officers had questioned Roger out in the hallway, while the other man kept her away. When the conversation with Roger got loud, Savant grew enraged, and the officers agreed to leave. This entire episode supposedly lasted less than thirty minutes. "They think I started the fire, but I didn't," Roger Nunez told Savant afterward, and she quieted him with two sleeping pills.

Later, Savant awoke half-sober and noticed that Roger's jaw was swollen. He claimed to have a toothache. She asked if he'd been in a fight, and he replied woozily, "I don't want to talk about it."[10]

In his sleep, Roger saw a horrible, violent blaze that he kept reliving in a loop. At the end of this dream, he was met by a row of accusers, who told him that he had set the Up Stairs Lounge fire and wouldn't accept his denials. He'd wake up shouting things like "I didn't do it!" and "Help me, I didn't start it!" and "Tell them I didn't." Although this behavior might seem incriminating, what exactly went on in Roger's sleep is hard to decipher. Fire had already played a significant role in Roger's life. His arrest record, in fact, noted a burn scar on his right elbow, a place where heat had met flesh and scalded deeply. No one knew how or why. Moreover, Shelton Nunez, Roger's young uncle and contemporary, had perished by flame in a terrible explosion on an offshore oil rig three years earlier.[11]

SOMETIME AFTER THE memorial, Courtney Craighead got a phone call from home. Evidently, a newspaper back in El Dorado, Arkansas, quoted his name in breaking news about the Up Stairs tragedy. His parents read the story and wanted answers. Courtney barely remembered speaking to reporters on Iberville Street, like Angus Lind of the New Orleans *States-Item* and Eric Newhouse of the Associated Press. Within hours, it seemed, his comments appeared—attributed—in papers distributed from coast to coast. The *Monroe News-Star* of Monroe, Louisiana, and the *Argus* of Fremont, California, quoted him by name. A *Boston Herald American* article, "Deacon in Tavern Blames Arsonist," printed Courtney's full name in the same column of print that included the term "gay bar."[12]

These quotations meant that Courtney was unequivocally outed to everyone he knew. Newspapers confirmed, to his devout Methodist parents, an "aberrant" sexuality that their son had made great efforts to mask. Courtney's father and namesake, Joseph Courtney Craighead Sr., was a banker and World War II veteran. His mother, Dorothea, was a schoolteacher.[13] An only child who was still in his thirties, Joseph Courtney Craighead Jr. bore expectations of passing on the family name.

Courtney's parents felt humiliated. Instead of expressing relief about their son surviving an ordeal, they expressed some anger at what they felt was a genuine betrayal. His mother had been diagnosed with breast cancer earlier that year, and the possibility lingered that Courtney's little "revelation" could worsen her condition. This reaction created a lasting psychological wound. Courtney's parents faced a choice in a moment between an expression of compassion and an exclamation of disgust for their child. Examined through the climate of the 1970s, the Craigheads' phone call might have seemed not like a choice at all to them but rather a refutation of sin.[14] Perhaps they thought they were saving him in this way. Furthermore, they just couldn't find the sympathy to console and comfort him about lost gay friends.

On Tuesday morning, Reverend Paul Breton of the MCC of Washington, D.C., arrived in New Orleans at the invitation of Troy Perry. At the airport, Breton noted a headline blaring from the front page of the *Times-Picayune*. "Devastating French Quarter Fire Probed by Three Agencies," it read. The story called the Up Stairs Lounge fire "catastrophic" and a "holocaust" but failed to mention the sexuality of bar patrons until the text jumped inside the paper. Two of the victims, the article reported, had been positively identified at this time, which set in motion the process of next-of-kin notifications: "Clarence McCloskey, 48, 816 N. Gayoso St.; and George Matyi, 27, 130 Mickal St. Slidell." Seeing that McCloskey actually resided at 1232 St. Andrews Street, according to the NOPD report, it seems that someone at the paper may have been cracking a sly joke—at the expense of the deceased—by printing the alternative street name.[15] McCloskey was identified quickly and quietly by his brother Bernard, a New Orleans fireman who learned of the death through his colleagues in the force. Vouching for the body, given Clarence's homosexuality, could have

cost Bernard his job if it became widely known, so Bernard's affil-
iation with the NOFD appeared in no reports or death notices for
Clarence. He was simply "brother."[16]

Next, coroners identified Bud Matyi's body through the religious
medal dangling on his neck—noticed in the morgue by Rod Wagener,
Matyi's closeted lover. Because Bud Matyi had not yet finalized his
divorce in California, Charity Hospital called Bud's soon to be ex-wife,
Pamela Cutler, with the news. "They called my mother, and I just
remember her screaming, and I just heard her saying 'No, no!,'" Tina
Marie Matyi recalled. Tina was only four, and this became her one of
her first clear memories. "Your dad died in a fire," Cutler later told her
daughter. Rod Wagener made no statements regarding the loss and,
according to recollections of several New Orleans residents, continued
to make appearances on his WDSU radio talk show throughout the
week. In written reports, the coroner respected Wagener's request for
closeted-ness by declining to name him as the source of the ID.[17]

REVEREND PAUL BRETON joined the task force at the Marriott.
He hugged Troy Perry and introduced himself to fire survivor Ricky
Everett, who still appeared dazed. "I remember being with them a lot
and staying at the hotel with them," recalled Ricky, "I don't know how
many nights. Anyway, I was kind of like, how you say, the pawn in
their hand." With Breton in tow, the group of leaders drove to Charity
Hospital to minister to the dying.[18]

These terminal patients remained in the newly opened burn ward.
Their condition was so dire that they could not be transported. Five
survivors had already been treated and released from Charity Hospital,
including Rusty Quinton. Seven others, who continued to require inten-
sive care, had been shuttled elsewhere throughout the state. For example, Michael Scarborough went to West Jefferson Hospital across the
Mississippi, while Jeanne Gosnell was taken to the U.S. Public Health
Service Hospital in the Uptown district, near the Audubon Zoo.[19]

Gosnell had lost consciousness several times, and she hadn't seen
her best friend Luther Boggs since she'd gasped into an oxygen mask

while sitting beside him on Iberville Street. No one would update Gosnell on Luther's condition for fear that the shock would kill her. Hospital orderlies were instructed to not bring her any newspaper clippings as she underwent a series of painful skin-graft surgeries. Before the fire, Gosnell had a well-paying job as an office manager in a real estate firm. Over the weeks to come, news would reach her through coworkers paying occasional visits that her old position was being filled. "I'm not gay," Gosnell later told *The Advocate*. "I found I didn't have any [of my] so-called straight friends coming to ask me if I needed money, or what they could do to help."[20]

Back at Charity Hospital, Paul Breton and the other gay leaders registered as chaplains. They walked to the burn unit, where the conditions of survivors Luther Boggs, Jim Hambrick, and Larry Stratton, who all happened to be military veterans, were alarming to behold. "They told me," recalled Perry, "and they told others, 'You can pray, but you can't touch them.'" The men gasped for breath beneath germ-protected tents, with large portions of bone and muscle tissue exposed. Like punctured gloves, their bodies leaked blood,[21] which orderlies struggled to refill in an endless process of dripping fluids that reddened the bandages and gauze.

Breton and Kight donned sanitary masks as they prayed with twenty-four-year-old Larry Stratton, whose open wounds covered 80 percent of his body surface. Dabbed with salve, this survivor of the fire seemed to glow in fluorescent light. "Next time I go out drinking," Stratton joked, "I'm wearing an asbestos jock." Jim Hambrick, in critical condition, flowed in and out of consciousness. The gay leaders learned that he was scheduled for surgery to remove both of his hands, which were blackened by gangrene.[22]

Near Jim Hambrick lay Luther Boggs, who at forty-seven had recently left the employ of the Pan American Life Insurance corporation. This was terrifying for a man with flesh dangling from his face, and he repeatedly voiced anxieties over his mounting medical expenses. Fluids building in his skull caused brain damage and memory loss, which resulted in Luther's continually forgetting that he was a military veteran entitled to federal benefits. Boggs asked Paul Breton if someone could help him with arranging job interviews from the burn ward so that he might find new employment. Perry and Breton humored him by agreeing to make inquiries.[23] Nearing death, it was clear that a man of industry like Luther Boggs did not want to be perceived as a burden.

IN RESPONSE TO CALLS for an apology from Major Henry Morris's comments about "queers" and "thieves," the New Orleans Police Department assigned Frank Hayward, the information officer and City Hall liaison, to discuss the Up Stairs Lounge. "They got their PR person out in front of it," recalled Perry. Behind the scenes, the city Human Relations Committee sent a note of admonishment to the police chief for Morris's "queer bar" quotation in the *States-Item*.[24] These back-of-the-class messages between city agencies demonstrated how City Hall was, in fact, cognizant of the fire but unwilling or unauthorized to speak openly.

In response to the note of censure, Officer Frank Hayward opened his first press conference about the fire with a statement that declared the *States-Item* attribution to be false: Henry Morris, he claimed, never said what reporters had heard and written down. This accusation of journalistic malfeasance occurred despite *Times-Picayune* reporter Chris Segura having also heard the remark from the mouth of Major Morris. Indeed, when Segura's own publication declined to print the exact quotation, Segura chose to tell *The Advocate*, which published the phrase in a follow-up story several weeks later.[25]

Next up at the conference, a second police officer, who went unnamed in newspapers but admitted to making the comment about homosexuals carrying "false identification" to the *States-Item*, apologized to the gay community and attempted to clarify his words: "The 'transient' lifestyles of many of the bar's patrons might make identification difficult." Evidently, this officer felt that the presumption of homosexuals living in a "transient" manner—a term commonly applied to vagrants—was less mendacious than the claim that homosexuals hid their law-breaking habits. The denial of Morris's statement, followed by the apology from the unnamed officer, who framed his regret as a case of misunderstanding, gave the NOPD the appearance of propriety while avoiding any admission of wrongdoing.[26]

Officer Hayward then made an announcement that seemed to pacify nerves. He unconditionally repudiated WVUE's "scoop" from the previous evening: there was no merit, Hayward said, to the "Black Mama White Mama" report, declaring it a hoax. Law enforcement had not been in communication with any multiethnic vigilante groups. The anonymous tipoff, WVUE's Alec Gifford would later admit, turned out to be nothing more than a crank call. After this admission, there would be no protests of WVUE by greater New Orleans. The station would not swiftly move to correct the misreport or offer an apology to homosexuals.[27] Some members of the public were, in fact, appreciative that someone had tried to scare the gay activists into silence.

That a local news station possessed free rein to broadcast a blatant falsehood one day after a deadly event further established the degree to which homosexuals were not afforded the deference of average citizens or considered to be part of the body politic. Meanwhile, at City Hall, PR Director Winton Lill seemed preoccupied with getting away from New Orleans after the family wedding. On June 26, 1973, he submitted a proposal for a city-funded road trip to conduct research on domestic "pleasure parks" for the Armstrong memorial project. While men were agonizingly dying at Charity Hospital, with bodies unnamed and unclaimed at the morgue there, these were the concerns that took priority.[28]

CHAPTER 9

Fun House

*Tuesday Afternoon–Wednesday Morning,
June 26–27, 1973*

Troy Perry and the others left Paul Breton, a pastor skilled in the administration of last rites, at the hospital to minister to the terminal patients. Breton's assignment was a grim one: to offer comfort to men in agonal states while colleagues attempted to heal the rest of a fractured community. Morris Kight returned to the Marriott determined to invent a new system of emergency assistance. On a piece of Marriott poster board, which served as the place mat for his hotel desk, he sketched an outline for what he called the New Orleans Community Disaster Relief Committee.[1]

Kight envisioned a grand union, the first of its kind during Gay Liberation, which would integrate the work of MCC churches with various gay and nongay political groups to merge community organizing with a national fund-raising operation. Perry enthusiastically signed on with Kight's expanded plan and phoned *The Advocate* to describe the founding of a National New Orleans Memorial Fund for gay fire victims, which would pair with his "National Day of Mourning, for this coming Sunday in all gay organizations all over the country."[2]

Meanwhile, the struggle to identify bodies in the hospital morgue exhausted authorities, who were loath to spend the extra time on the deceased. NOPD Sergeant Joseph Vitari told the press exasperatedly that "dental charts, that and fingerprints, would be the only true way to identify these people." Describing efforts to coordinate with the FBI in Washington, D.C., Vitari continued, "It's impossible for a mother to look at her son and say that's her son; that's how badly burned the bodies are." Paul Breton, having worked with the government of the District of Columbia and, in his words, "knowing the standard percentages of successes in cases of this sort," estimated that the Orleans Parish coroner would be "very lucky to identify fifteen of the victims" and would be "very lucky in being able to have ten of the fifteen bodies claimed for burial."[3]

Buddy Rasmussen, the bartender of the Up Stairs Lounge who had saved twenty-odd patrons, disappeared after giving his full account of the blaze to police detectives. Buddy was emotionally crippled, and he spent most waking hours with Bill Duncan, a close friend.[4] Buddy barely left Bill Duncan's apartment, which was situated on Iberville Street catercorner from the blackened edifice of his former workplace.

An entire chapter of Buddy's life—his triumph in building a profitable business with the bar's owner, Phil Esteve—had been reduced to cinders. Adam Fontenot, his great love, was also gone forever. Through the dull throb, Buddy could hear the hubbub at the Chartres Street intersection, where the detritus and rubble of the Up Stairs Lounge attracted large crowds. Motorists in packed cars drove past the site as if it were a fun house. Tourists lined up and nosed past the doorway to the stairwell holding cups of open liquor, a practice synonymous with New Orleans. The Jimani bar, untouched on the first floor directly below the rubble, had already reopened to serve passersby.[5]

A man by the nickname of Chuckie reportedly went up and down Iberville collecting donations for fire victims and then pocketed the proceeds. In the midst of this bedlam, Morris Kight attempted to hold a wreath-laying ceremony. "More flowers have been arriving, just anonymously arriving," Kight told *The Advocate*. "People have begun bringing them from their gardens." The longshoremen Smokie and Cocoa, whose third-floor residences sustained heavy smoke damage from the Up Stairs Lounge fire below, began posting a guard to prevent acts of vandalism.[6]

Spectators argued with one another. "It's the Supreme Court caused that," opined a tourist to a *Times-Picayune* reporter. "That's right. That's right. They gonna have to start shooting them to stop that, and the Supreme Court won't let them."[7] The man's comments, a propos of which Supreme Court ruling or who needed to be shot, were unclear, but his outrage affirmed the belief that no good came from pandering to homosexuals. A woman of about fifty openly criticized Up Stairs Lounge patrons in front of a *States-Item* reporter:

> I understand they could eat and drink all they wanted up there for $2.00 and Lord knows what other activities. The Lord had something to do with this. He caught them all in there and punished them.[8]

A second woman interrupted and contended, "They were human. God made them, too, and they didn't deserve to die like that no more than you." Despite this rejoinder, the overriding notion that justice had been served in the bar's obliteration was typical and acceptable. In 1973, only about one in ten Americans perceived homosexual relations to be "not wrong at all," according to a University of Chicago survey.[9] Few ideas could be called less popular.

Reactions of the survivors differed. For Buddy Rasmussen, the prospect of going home to his residence at 923 St. Andrews Street, where he had shared a domestic world with Adam Fontenot, remained too agonizing. Ricky "Regina" Soleto took the opposite tack: she fled from the fire scene and took refuge in the apartment that she had shared with Reggie Adams at 1017 Conti Street. There, she kept laying her lover's clothes out on the bed, expecting him to return each morning. All the while, just a few buildings down from Buddy on Iberville Street, Roger Dale Nunez shivered on Cee Cee Savant's couch.[10]

At 2:00 p.m. on Tuesday afternoon, Perry and the other gay leaders held a second news conference at the Marriott. Lucien Baril, the newly named MCC pastor, described the devastation to his congregation, while Morris Kight announced that the American Red Cross had agreed to a "blood banking" system through which any concerned person could give blood at any Red Cross facility in America and credit the donation to "Holocaust Victims, Up Stairs Lounge, New Orleans, care of Charity Hospital."[11]

Then Kight took a breath and changed subjects: "We are creating a National Memorial Fund and asking people who have human concerns to donate." No campaign in the history of Gay Liberation had previously requested funds explicitly or created a national infrastructure to receive them. The move would make gay leaders instantly accountable. The homophile movement, after all, had virtually imploded through the backbiting that sprung from a smaller drive for a failed U.S. Supreme Court case in 1970. Vouching for Kight, Perry reiterated that the editorial board of *The Advocate* had agreed to act as custodian for the National New Orleans Memorial Fund and accept emergency donations. "We've been building for five years," Kight said. "We've been building to a sense of national brotherhood and sisterhood, and that has happened. And now we have that strength. We've taken that space, that room, and when this enormous tragedy occurred, we came from all over."[12]

With this statement, the Gay Liberation movement transcended regionalism and rancor to reach cohesion on a single topic, other than the Stonewall Inn, for the first time. Political groups, including the Gay Activists Alliance (GAA), joined forces with service groups, including the Gay Community Services Center of Los Angeles (GCSC), and religious networks, extending from the MCC to the recently formed New York Gay Synagogue. They harnessed the platform of *The Advocate*, the most read gay news source, while allying with nongay relief organizations like the American Red Cross.[13]

A moment of national unity soon appeared in response to this announcement. A red flyer circulated around New York City. "Tragedy in New Orleans," it read, "thirty-two Gay people were killed," with calls to "give blood" at the Sixty-Seventh Street center or "give money" to *The Advocate*. A National Day of Mourning flyer was seen in Los Angeles, with news that "the GAA of New York City, The GCA [Gay Callers Association] of Chicago, and the GCSC [of Los Angeles] are contacting gay brothers," with invitations to attend memorial services. In Boston, the newly established *Gay Community News* made the "Upstairs Tragedy" its top story.[14]

UNAWARE OF TROY PERRY'S activities at the Marriott, Henry Kubicki arrived home from yet another shift at that hotel to find an empty apartment. Eerily, all of Ricky Everett's clothing and possessions were now missing from drawers and cupboards. While Henry was gone, Ricky had returned and taken everything he owned. "That was not a good time for me. I was not responding as well as I should," Ricky explained, looking back. "It was rather abrupt, and I do remember he was a bit surprised." Henry's note to Ricky in the kitchen sat untouched. Either Ricky hadn't seen it or he couldn't bring himself to face the darkness by writing a response. "I couldn't think about it without crying," Ricky recalled.[15] His inability to relate to such devastation was quite natural.

Henry, sadly, wouldn't see or speak to Ricky Everett again until 1978, and only then in a chance encounter on Canal Street. For Henry, it was as if the fire had raised a psychological barrier between them— one that severed his dearest friendship. Unbeknownst to Henry, Ricky was in need. Ronnie Rosenthal, Ricky's primary pillar of support, flew back to Atlanta that Tuesday: Ronnie just had to get back to work or lose his job. Alone, Ricky confronted a world that seemed to be carrying on without any of the pain that consumed him. "When I'd go to sleep, as soon as I'd fall asleep," recalled Ricky, "all of a sudden, I'd start dreaming and start seeing those people burning again."[16]

Plagued by nightmares, Ricky sought refuge with his mother in the suburb of Gretna. "When I got home, we had that talk," said Ricky. "You know, 'Are you gay?' 'Yeah, obviously.' But she accepted me. She loved me even more, I think." Ricky agreed to keep his things in her home, which, for Ricky, became a place of convalescence when he wasn't meeting with Troy Perry. Unlike Stewart Butler or Henry Kubicki, Ricky Everett had coworkers who were considerate of his trauma, even after some of the staff at Schweggman's grocery chain recognized Ricky's voice during his Monday TV interview. "They were all sympathetic to me, my employer and fellow employees," recalled Ricky. "I was fortunate. I've been fortunate like that all my life."[17]

Unlike Courtney Craighead's parents, Ricky Everett's mother was able to take the shock of her son's revelation in stride, after tears and some religious debate. She did not make a gesture of revulsion, which, in Ricky's forlorn state, could have pushed him away. She was undoubtedly grateful to have her son in any condition, even if something of Ricky's trusting manner now seemed injured, even if he asked why God had spared him from the flames that claimed Bill Larson. "Thank you for saving me," Ricky would say in his prayers, "but, next time, please let me burn up."[18]

By Wednesday, June 27, the Up Stairs Lounge fire had been dropped from the front page of the *Times-Picayune*. What was international news only days before now didn't merit an oversize headline on a local broadsheet. Top stories now focused on Watergate, the possibility of "gas limits" in the upcoming oil embargo, and the passage of a U.S. Senate bill to cut off bombings in Cambodia.

"The culture at the *Picayune*, in the newsroom, was very antigay," recalled Clancy DuBos, the *Times-Picayune* intern. "There were so many harsh attitudes expressed among old reporters, the old farts I guess." The fact that Charles Ferguson of the *States-Item* was traversing Europe with the mayor left that newspaper, and its sister publication the *Times-Picayune*, open to accusations of bias in that Ferguson, or his editorial colleagues, might not want to portray the mayor's absence negatively, lest they reveal how a member of the press was involved in delaying him. In the following weeks, Landrieu would maintain such an excellent relationship with the media establishment that he would pay a visit to the Press Club of New Orleans at 339 Chartres, located two blocks from the Up Stairs Lounge catastrophe.[19] It's unknown if the mayor passed the fire site to reach the party.

On that Wednesday, some younger reporters appeared to be in open rebellion with editors about the loss of front-page coverage. In a little-seen article buried on page fourteen, *Times-Picayune* journalist Vincent Lee reported on the founding of the National New Orleans Memorial Fund and used the word "gay" three times in his first one hundred words. This story was the newspaper's first use of "gay," outside of a proper noun (such as Gay Liberation Front) or quotation marks, a break from restrictive style conventions.[20]

From New York City to Chicago and Los Angeles, news of the Up Stairs Lounge all but disappeared, and the Associated Press and UPI newswires redirected their reporters to other stories. "Because these were negligible people of society, people just didn't seem to care," commented the fire witness Milton Mary. "I often wondered, 'What happened to them?' 'Did they arrest anybody?' There was not that much news that I can recall." *States-Item* photographer Ronnie LeBoeuf remembered the sudden diminution in coverage. "Oh, they buried it," LeBoeuf insisted. "They buried it."[21]

Troy Perry was moved to make a grand appeal to Edwin Edwards, the Democratic governor of Louisiana. The previous day, Edwards had offered a nonspecific statement about fire safety in an article about the Up Stairs Lounge.[22] The gay leaders sent a long telegram to the governor:

June 27, 1973

Governor Edwin Edwards,

   The tragic fire of June 24th in the Up Stairs Lounge
in the French Quarter which has taken the lives of 29
women and men shocked and now saddens the nation.

   Many of the fatalities were Gay women and men who compose
an important part of the human community. Consequently, Gay
churches and organizations as well as non-Gay churches and
organizations around the country will be observing a national
day of mourning Sunday, June 1, 1973. Money is coming
from all over the world to help bury the dead, pay the hospital
expenses of survivors and build a memorial chapel. Blood is
being collected all over the nation and shipped into New Orleans

for the disaster survivors. The heartfelt sympathy and love of
America has focused here in Louisiana at this time of need.
　　We respectfully call upon you to join in this spirit of compassion
and love by declaring Sunday, June 1, 1973 a state-wide day of
mourning for the victims of the New Orleans fire catastrophe. . . . [23]

Edwards, who while a congressman had bravely voted to extend the Voting Rights Act to safeguard the black vote in Louisiana in 1970, did not respond to this telegram, and so Morty Manford telephoned him personally. A secretary for the governor answered, and the conversation became stilted when Manford identified himself as a gay activist.[24]

At first, the secretary informed Manford that the governor's office hadn't received the telegram. Manford offered to read the text aloud for dictation. As if avoiding a trap, the secretary then told Manford that she had just found the communiqué. When asked if the governor had an official response, the secretary answered that Governor Edwards did not. When Manford requested to speak to the governor himself, the secretary told him that the governor was not in the office. When Manford finally asked if he could arrange a phone call with Governor Edwards at a future date, the secretary told him that the governor would not be in the office next week. As Paul Breton noted, "Newspapers in the following week reported several items on the governor's actions from his office in Baton Rouge."[25]

This pattern of obfuscation made it clear to Manford and Perry that the governor had no interest in joining their cause. Edwards's circumvention of the New Orleans Emergency Task Force—with maneuvers requiring more legerdemain than Mayor Moon Landrieu's avoidance from Europe—came after the governor had already associated himself with fire safety. However, in Edwards's careful framing of the issue, he did not state precisely which fire had motivated his concerns, nor did he utter the words "homosexual" or "gay."[26]

As negotiation sputtered with the governor, a group of gay entrepreneurs reached out to Troy Perry and insisted upon a face-to-face meeting. After Monday's "Black Mama White Mama" report, a series of threatening calls resulted in policemen being stationed near French Quarter gay bars. Gay patrons at these "guarded bars" reported harassment from the officers. This atmosphere of hostility metastasized to the point where some patrons no longer felt safe, and bar crowds decreased to about one half of their usual size. "My concern was that if people started raising holy hell about all this," remembered Café Lafitte patron John Meyers, "and Troy Perry came down and did this that and the other, that we were going to risk the unspoken agreement we had with city authorities and the police."[27]

Perry and Morris Kight presented themselves at the appointed place and hour. They were eager to meet New Orleans's gay businessmen but shocked by what they encountered. "How dare you hold your damn news conferences," one business owner shouted, censuring the activist leaders from the get-go. Perry had, by his very presence, flaunted a counternarrative about sexual liberation that upset the predominant hierarchy. The minister, who had hardly slept since Saturday, was encountering gay-on-gay oppression of the kind he'd once faced as a closeted youth in Florida. These reprimands, Perry admits now, struck a sore spot. He called the men "greedy" and reprimanded them for aligning themselves with the authorities, much like how the mob-related owners of the Stonewall Inn—prior to the Stonewall Riots—had ingratiated themselves with the New York Police Department.[28]

Indeed, many gay entrepreneurs in New Orleans kept their businesses operational in defiance of local law by accepting the occasional police raid and agreeing to pay bribes, which owners justified disbursing, and officers justified accepting, through the incongruous logic that only well-run gay businesses could afford to make payments. Putting a hand on Perry's shoulder, Kight stopped the preacher from shouting and redirected the conversation back to the "people's shrine" growing outside of the Up Stairs Lounge—attempting to rouse a sentiment about New Orleans having heart. Yet the meeting ended with no accord between Gay Liberation and the gay businessmen. Perry wouldn't attend a secret summit again, while Kight traveled back to Los Angeles to open a checking account, register a post office box, and sign the legal documents that officially created the memorial fund.[29]

CHAPTER 10

Firetraps

Wednesday Afternoon Through Friday,
June 27–June 29, 1973

Agitated by his meeting with the gay businessmen, Troy Perry made new plans to hold a larger Up Stairs Lounge memorial on Sunday, July 1, his proposed National Day of Mourning. Perry asked Reverend Bill Richardson for permission to hold a second event at St. George's Episcopal Church. "I had to decline," wrote Richardson in a 1991 letter of remembrance about the fire. For Bill Richardson, a pastor at loggerheads with his flock, the request seemed just too burdensome.[1]

Earlier that week, as a result of his hosting the first memorial in the chapel, Richardson received an unexpected call from his boss, Bishop Iveson B. Noland, the head of the Episcopal Diocese of Louisiana. Noland, a signatory member of the antihomosexual organization Morality in Media of Louisiana, began their conversation by crinkling a newspaper into the phone.[2] Richardson recalled the discussion:

"Is it true that the service was at St. George's Episcopal Church?"

"Yes, Bishop, it was."

"Why didn't they have it at their own church?"

"For the simple reason their own small church holds about eighteen persons. Without any publicity we had over eighty present."

"What am I to say when people call my office?"

"You can say anything you wish, Bishop," he replied, "but do you think Jesus would have kept these people out of His church?"[3]

With that comment, the bishop cut in and chastised Richardson, a cleric who had acted against superiors. Noland issued a stern warning to other Episcopal churches: none was to host another gathering for the MCC. Condemned from above, Richardson was also besieged from below when his church board pulled its support and censured him for his moral leniency. Only one member of St. George's vestry of elders supported his decision. He received "hate calls" and threatening letters.[4]

Pilloried by his flock, Richardson decided to pen an open bulletin. In writing, he acknowledged the "uproar caused by the Memorial Service" for those "who died in New Orleans worst fire last Sunday night." Still, Richardson argued, "God's Church exists to help all people, regardless of who they are or what they do." The pastor ended this letter with an ultimatum to church members, many whom he had pastored since the 1950s:

> If any considerable numbers of St. George's members
> still feel that our Church is to minister only to the select
> few, and not the whole community, then I shall seriously
> consider resigning as your rector in the near future, so as
> the Bishop and the Vestry can look for someone else.
>   William P. Richardson, Jr.

> P.S. I love you all, even if you violently disagree
> with me. But remember, we must try not to be
> Pharisees, thinking we are better than others.[5]

WITH RICHARDSON STEPPING out of the fray, Perry began to search for another house of worship—ideally, a church in the Quarter willing to host several hundred outspokenly gay men. It was a tall order, but he first approached the Roman Catholic Archdiocese of New Orleans. After all, several of the dead had been baptized Catholic, Perry argued.[6] Ed Martinez, a journalist for the alternative weekly *Nola Express*, quoted an anonymous New Orleans priest as saying,

"The rules are the rules; if they find one Catholic, or several, among the dead, we'll bury *them*. But that's all." The archdiocese was not interested in performing any such services for non-Catholic Christians. Neither Archbishop Philip Hannan, the three Catholic priests who had provided "conditional absolution" rites outside the Up Stairs Lounge right after the fire, nor any of the Catholic chaplains who'd ministered to survivors in Charity Hospital had commented publicly about the incident. The Archdiocesan Human Relations Committee, a religious group that adjudicated Catholic civil rights matters (and not associated with the municipal body of the same name mentioned earlier), told journalist Bill Rushton that "they had seen no reason to issue any sort of statement on the matter and that they had no plans to do so." In this way, the archdiocese denied the use of Catholic facilities and refused to hold funerals for the non-Catholic dead—and then denied their denials by refusing to acknowledge their decisions as named sources for the record.[7]

Silence and inaction was generally out of character for the archbishop. Philip Hannan was a man of high principles drawn to the limelight on momentous occasions. While serving as an auxiliary bishop in Washington, D.C., he had become spiritual advisor to President John F. Kennedy. After Kennedy's assassination, Hannan had delivered a moving homily at the requiem mass on November 25, 1963. Following the Rault Center blaze, he had offered effusive sympathies in the *Times-Picayune*. Less than six weeks later, in the standoff between the gunman and police at Howard Johnson's, Hannan proffered himself as an intermediary for a potential hostage exchange and, afterward, spent nine hours at Charity Hospital consoling survivors and comforting families. By all accounts, he was a remarkable human being.[8]

Yet, when the gay leaders called the archbishop's office to request a consecrated space for a memorial, they were met by what Paul Breton described as an "officious priest." This subordinate denied all requests abruptly and refused them the opportunity to speak to the archbishop. John Meyers, then a Catholic seminarian, recalled these events with indignation. "It was the demeaning of these deaths," Meyers agreed.[9]

A Vieux Carré Baptist church likewise rejected Perry's entreaty for use of their building. Perry recalled how they "laughed in my face." The board of a nearby Lutheran church, according to Paul Breton, "pompously informed our contact that . . . [they] would not authorize the usage of their church for our people, but to contact the comparative black congregation well outside the French Quarter since 'they are more tolerant of aliens there.'" Denied a house of worship, Troy Perry briefly considered performing the service outside. While exploring this possibility, Clay Shaw stepped forward.[10]

Arguably the most famous homosexual in New Orleans, Shaw was aware of the destruction of the Up Stairs Lounge. Having judiciously sought a quiet life after his trials, Shaw had initially chosen to remain silent as controversies swirled about the fire victims, and by this point he was also fighting lung cancer. Still, he was attempting to make a final mark upon his city through the opportunity afforded by Mayor Landrieu to work on the French Market Corporation. Overcoming legitimate anxieties, with French Market renovations beginning soon on July 13, Shaw notified Perry that, if no other alternative could be found, his contacts at the Vieux Carré Commission (VCC), a municipal body that oversees the French Quarter, were willing to close off a block of Iberville Street and permit the delegation to hold a memorial near the bar.[11] Such a bold move was not just professionally dicey, in that it could imperil his post with the French Market Corporation, it was also a political risk. Shaw's outreach was not echoed by Leon Irwin III, the closeted Louisiana Democratic National Committeeman, or other closeted gay men who benefited from the power structure.

Troy Perry thanked Clay Shaw and let him know that he intended to honor his gesture by using the VCC only as a backup option.[12]

ON THURSDAY MORNING, June 28, the Up Stairs Lounge returned to the front page of the *Times-Picayune*. This time it was a different sort of story—absorbed into a public safety debate about fire hazards and deathtraps in old neighborhoods. The front-page headline read, "Disaster Waiting to Happen: Quarter Firetrap Crackdown." It suggested, without attribution, that the Up Stairs Lounge was but one of "literally dozens of firetraps, unsafe buildings and unsound structures." Commenting on the deterioration, Assistant State Fire Marshal Timothy Driscoll blamed the VCC, the local preservation commission that also happened to support Clay Shaw and his efforts to rehabilitate the French Market.[13] The VCC's jurisdiction extended from the west side of Esplanade Avenue to the east side of Iberville Street.

Driscoll issued several jeremiads against the VCC, portraying it as an organization that endangered citizens by preventing efforts to condemn unsafe structures. As a prime example of VCC ineptitude, Driscoll pointed to the Safari Lounge at 706 Iberville—a popular black gay bar (according to the 1972 edition of *Bob Damron's Address Book*) that the *Times-Picayune* described as "a second story walk-up similar to the ill-fated Up Stairs Bar where 29 persons were killed in a Sunday night fire." Tellingly, the Safari Lounge's even-numbered address placed it on the west side of Iberville Street, like the Up Stairs Lounge, and outside of VCC influence. Driscoll's linking the Safari to the VCC constituted an obvious glossing of fact. "Life is more important than the preservation of old bricks," Driscoll added.[14]

In response, VCC Director Wayne Collier told the *Times-Picayune* and *States-Item* that forces were "trying to pass the buck for a fire that occurred outside of the Vieux Carré Commission's jurisdiction." Focusing on the Up Stairs Lounge, Collier paid no heed to Driscoll's attacks on the Safari Lounge, which was ordered closed by inspectors despite the bar owner's insistence that his business had received no code violations and was not under investigation. When backed into a corner by a state agency, VCC director Wayne Collier then became the first public official in Louisiana to make a statement about the Up Stairs Lounge. He called it a "hideous fire" and claimed that the attacks "divert positive attention from the holocaust."[15]

It's worth noting that the assistant state fire marshal did not include gay-friendly bars closer to the Up Stairs Lounge, like Gene's Hideaway or even Wanda's, in his attacks, but these were establishments owned by Gene Davis, the well-networked businessman (nonetheless, Davis had operated another Iberville Street bar without fire insurance in 1970). In effect, the immediate response to the Up Stairs Lounge fire was the closing of a nearby bar known to black gay travelers, which even *The Advocate* did not suspect might be a gay establishment. Reports also surfaced of Blake Arrata, the New Orleans city attorney, suing the two pornographic movie houses near the Up Stairs Lounge for obscenity. One of these theaters elected to shutter permanently rather than face a legal case.[16] A cleanup of the Quarter seemed imminent, either through a firetrap investigation or morals crusade.

In the meantime, the New Orleans police investigation hit a snag when test results came back from the crime lab. Specimen 4, which consisted of "one metal 7 oz. container marked 'Ronsonol Lighter Fluid'" found and tagged in the Up Stairs Lounge staircase by Major Henry Morris, which could potentially link a source of accelerant to a person, dusted "negative for fingerprints." No one who touched that can had left any traceable residue. With this finding, Specimen 4 was reduced to circumstantial evidence, disconnected from human contact. In the police report, it was never underscored how the policeman who had called the Up Stairs Lounge a "queer bar" was the same one who managed this vital piece of evidence, which ultimately proved useless. Even though the can had been found on a staircase step, a clever defense attorney could now argue that it may have been dropped there at any time and date prior to the catastrophe. Strangely, there is no record of the two ten-dollar bills, found half-burned near the can of accelerant, ever being tested for fingerprints. (These bills would sit in an NOPD evidence locker until August 2005, when they were contaminated in the flooding that followed Hurricane Katrina.) Whoever set the fire, in other words, got lucky several times with forensics.[17]

UNIDENTIFIED BODIES FROM the fire remained at Charity Hospital, although Coroner Carl Rabin had managed to positively identify twenty of the deceased people. Nine remained in question, of which several seesawed between being identified or not. One of the coroner's tentative IDs, a white male named Norman LaVergne, later permanently disappeared from all lists.[18] No one could be certain why LaVergne was finally ruled out: the authorities offered no explanations.

Dental records from the practice of Perry Lane Waters—the dentist himself, sadly, confirmed among the fire dead—arrived and proved critical for identifying Glenn Green and Adam Fontenot. Buddy Rasmussen received notification that his lover, Adam, was what the coroner had been calling Body 26; Adam's corpse would be released to the Fontenot family in Ville Platte, Louisiana. Despite their wearing commitment rings, one of which one was used to corroborate Adam's ID, Buddy possessed no legal right to Adam's remains. According to Up Stairs Lounge historian Johnny Townsend, and confirmed by cemetery records, Adam received a Catholic funeral at Sacred Heart of Jesus Church, the family's home parish, but was not buried in the church cemetery.[19]

Instead, Adam Fontenot was laid to rest in the Old Ville Platte Cemetery—a community burial ground. "It was reported to me that at the funeral of one of the deceased," Paul Breton wrote, "the deceased was denied a church burial by his priest, and the priest made comment in a derogatory manner during the brief funeral service to the deceased's homosexuality." Considering the conditions of Adam's internment, and the multigenerational legacy of Fontenots at Sacred Heart of Jesus, it is likely that Breton was referring to events that occurred at Adam Fontenot's funeral.[20]

Not all would be so degraded. Mary David, niece of Up Stairs Lounge victim Glenn Green, was made to wait several days in New Orleans before viewing her uncle's body in the morgue. After Glenn's expulsion from Michigan by his brother in the late 1960s, Mary and her uncle had grown closer through letters and phone calls. At one point, Mary had asked her uncle point-blank whether he was homosexual. "I love with my heart, Mary," she remembered his telling her, "not with my eyes." Offhandedly, Glenn had mentioned that his regular bar in the Quarter was called the Up Stairs Lounge. So when Mary first saw news reports of the Up Stairs Lounge burning, she'd booked an emergency flight on a credit card and arrived with but ten dollars.[21]

Mary stayed with the parents of Michael Scarborough, Glenn's lover, and got rides around town from her uncle's old friends. "I couldn't sleep," she recalled. "I couldn't eat. I was just a knot most of the time." Mary finally did receive the call to come to Charity Hospital and tour the row of cadavers. Corpses, she recalls, were arranged beside small packets holding artifacts found near each person. "When we got to Body Number 11, it was just a small envelope," she recalled. "It couldn't have been more than six inches long, three inches wide, just a little postcard envelope. Yellow." Opening the packet, she glimpsed a ring that she instantly recognized to be the wedding band of Glenn's deceased father, Forest Green. It was a family heirloom. Mary asked the coroner to compare her uncle's dental records with those of Body 11. They were an exact match. Straightaway, orderlies zipped up the man who was her uncle in a white, satin bag and placed him in a pine casket.[22]

Mary flew home that evening, with her beloved uncle's remains in the cargo hold. Back in Michigan, the Greens were arranging a full Catholic service at St. William's Church, the local parish. Indeed, Michigan was too far from New Orleans for word of the scandal to permeate homeward, as it had for victims like Adam Fontenot. Several of Green's friends from New Orleans attended as proxy for Michael Scarborough, who could not travel due to his life-threatening condition. Glenn Green would be praised posthumously as a navy veteran and a small-town hero by the more than forty mourners who signed the guest book at his wake.[23]

BACK IN NEW ORLEANS, as bodies received names and Perry sought a willing church, Jim Hambrick, one of the three most critical survivors at Charity Hospital, finally expired in the presence of Reverend Paul Breton and family members. The burns across the forty-five-year-old's face, scalp, torso, thighs, and back were too extensive for Hambrick to survive. His throat had been incised at the midneck for the insertion of a tracheotomy tube, and both of his hands and wrists had been removed, cut to halt the spread of gangrene.[24]

His wounds had bled for five days straight, and he'd died slowly, his agony subdued only by a morphine drip. Hambrick's passing raised the death count of the Up Stairs Lounge to an even thirty. The family scheduled a wake in town the next day and notified the local veterans association. Jim Hambrick, who had served in World War II, would receive full military honors at his funeral.[25]

Pastor Bill Larson's body also left Charity Hospital at this time. He was positively identified only through his dentures. Despite the testimony of Ricky Everett and the insistence of MCC members that their pastor had perished in the Chartres Street window, and despite the fact that four separate newspapers had run stories attesting to Bill Larson's demise, official confirmation took almost a week. It appears that officials had trouble believing the witnesses.[26]

When she was reached, Anna Howell, Bill Larson's mother in Ohio, declined to accept the remains of her son. But the circumstances remain extenuating: Anna was now eighty years old and widowed twice over. It's not entirely clear if Anna's refusal was morally or financially motivated, although the contention circulated among MCC members that if she had never been able to accept her son in life, how could she in death?[27]

Bill Larson, William Lairson, Roscoe Larison, Ros Larson—whatever his assumed name—was not a child Anna Howell had raised. Bill left his mother's arms when he was three, and the state took over from there as the instiller of daily values. Repeatedly disciplined for his early gay proclivities in his twelve years at the children's home, the boy somehow managed to blossom on his own. He loved music, plays, and Easter Sunday and was eventually confirmed at the First Reformed Church of Hamilton, Ohio, in April 1939. Thereafter, he displayed a remarkable passion for delivering sermons. In retrospect, all seemed to prepare the way for when the boy became "Ros Larison," the Chicago nightclub performer, and then Bill Larson, the pastor.[28]

Feeling a wellspring of gratitude, Bill took the step of writing his former caretakers as an adult to thank them: "The Butler Co Children's Home. Who through patience and never failing trust, taught me obedience, trustworthiness, and the courage to face life. Who encouraged me in those things I set out to do no matter how large or how small."[29] These were Christian words from someone raised so harshly.

According to Troy Perry, who spoke with Anna Howell, she was distressed at having seen her deceased son associated in newspapers with homosexuality. The *Hamilton Journal-News*, her local newspaper, had picked up the Up Stairs Lounge story from the AP newswire and published the name Bill Larson in connection with the tragedy. Although the article did not declare Larson or other bar patrons as homosexual, Anna Howell nevertheless did not want the remains of her unrecognizable child sent back to Ohio. "She made it clear," said Troy Perry, "that she could not face her neighbors if his funeral or burial was held in her small hometown." Subsequently, Anna released Bill's remains to the MCC of New Orleans for cremation and permitted them to keep his ashes.[30]

The MCC agreed to inter their former pastor and assume all responsibilities for his funeral expenses. "His legacy is our action," wrote Paul Breton. "His estate is our commitment." Breton held a quiet service and gave the eulogy, in which portions of Larson's past were laid bare: "His father is deceased. His mother, two sisters and one brother still live. His child is deceased. His lover lives." Many expressed shock to learn that Larson had a large family or a child that predeceased him. And who was this lover? Lucien Baril told *The Advocate* that he "was on board [a] ship" at the time of the tragedy because he "works for a shipping line," but some were beginning to question the veracity of Baril's assertions. Breton concluded the service with this thought: "I sought my God, but I found him not. I sought my soul, but my soul alluded me. I sought my brother, and I found all three."[31]

Unable to afford internment, the MCC chose to store Bill Larson's urn in the wooden altar that the pastor had salvaged. Considering that the MCC would unsuccessfully file for death benefits from the Veterans Administration to cover burial expenses for a "William Ros Larson," it's unclear whether anyone in his church—even Ricky Everett—knew the pastor's birth name, William Roscoe Lairson. Filing the paperwork under his legal identity would have granted the man not just a private funeral but also burial in a national cemetery or a headstone in a private cemetery. "Due, I believe, to lack of identification, the Veterans Administration was not able to locate records on military service," Breton would later write to Morris Kight. "Therefore, funds proceeding from the Veterans Administration for his burial are not available."[32]

With the Up Stairs Lounge funerals ongoing, the *Times-Picayune* chose not to publish an obituary feature story for any of the fire victims—not Adam Fontenot, Glenn Green, or Jim Hambrick. The paper also did not deem pastor Bill Larson a figure warranting such a "death feature," although Bill Larson's picture in the window had circulated internationally. "They probably didn't want to publish anything that might remotely give any respect toward Bill because of his sexuality, if anybody even suggested it," observed Ricky Everett. The *Picayune,* however, did provide a standard amount of space for William Ros Larson's death announcement: a legal paragraph that called him by this alias and provided public notification of his passing and funeral information. A portion of this notice read, "Relatives and friends of the family are invited to attend."[33]

It is unknown if any of William Roscoe Lairson's relatives accepted this invitation.

In Memoriam

Friday Through Sunday,
June 30–July 1, 1973

Clay Shaw's proposal for an outdoor service proved to be unnecessary when someone asked Troy Perry if he had tried St. Mark's United Methodist Church, an ultraliberal French Quarter congregation.[1]

Standing on the edge of the Vieux Carré, with its notable cream-colored tower, St. Mark's had long housed a ministry eager to support social causes. In 1960, when six-year-old Ruby Bridges became one of the first black children in the American South to attend an all-white school—New Orleans's own William Frantz Elementary School—Reverend Lloyd "Andy" Foreman of St. Mark's had bravely crossed racial lines and brought his own daughter, Pamela, to school as Bridges' classmate. In retaliation, members of the White Citizens Council had heckled Reverend Foreman as a "nigger-lover" and vandalized his church by climbing onto the bell tower and tarring the building in creosote.[2]

By 1973, St. Mark's had a black clergyman named Reverend Edward Kennedy, whom Troy Perry approached with his request. Kennedy was impressed. Seeing similarities between Perry's gay Christians and black Americans seeking equality, Kennedy approved the use of the church, which he said could easily seat several hundred mourners. The St. Mark's board of elders, composed of five white women, also lent their support, which flouted decrees in their church's *Book of Discipline* declaring homosexuality to be "incompatible with Christian teaching."[3]

Perry notified media of the plans and printed three thousand flyers to advertise the event. The leaflet proclaimed a National Day of Mourning that Sunday "in memory of the New Orleans Fire Victims," with an ecumenical service taking place at 2:00 p.m. According to Paul Breton, so as not to embarrass anyone, "because not all of the deceased were gay, and because the committee was opposed to the labeling process that had taken place," the delegation printed these announcements without any mention of homosexuality.[4]

Eager to spread the word, Perry and Breton headed down Bourbon Street with several stacks of flyers. Gay-friendly businesses refused to post them for fear of being firebombed. Walking into Café Lafitte in Exile, Perry handed leaflets to several "A-gays" before John Meyers entered the establishment and saw who was present. "I did go up to Troy Perry and confront him," recalled Meyers, "and say what he was doing was not helpful and was just going to raise a lot of problems for local gays."[5]

Perry listened incredulously, having heard the same argument from gay businessmen. "He wasn't exactly cordial, but he heard me out and was very strong in his disagreement with me," said Meyers. "I recall telling him personally that I thought that he was doing that more for himself and his church than for the city of New Orleans, that he knew nothing about New Orleans."[6]

Thus, despite attempts to thwart Perry's service, Stewart Butler, Ricky Everett, and Henry Kubicki were among the 250 people who sat in polished pews at St. Mark's Methodist Church on Rampart Street on Sunday, July 1. This was the largest public gathering for a gay cause in the city's history. St. Mark's looked to be filling up, although "it wasn't packed," according to Paul Killgore, who attended with his boyfriend.[7]

The mood was solemn. Several bouquets of flowers—including an arrangement of pink and aquamarine carnations—had been donated by a French Quarter vendor. "It was quiet, it was orderly, it was respectful," remembered Killgore, who readily admits that he and many others came curious to see Troy Perry, the famous preacher: "To me, he was a celebrity." Stewart Butler agreed with Killgore's assessment: "They had a star attraction, Troy Perry," Stewart recalled.[8]

As organ music played, Stewart draped his arm over Alfred Doolittle's shoulders—a radical gesture in a religious setting. Ricky Everett, still in a haze, sat in front with the national celebrants. Henry Kubicki took his place hurriedly in one of the back rows. He couldn't see or hear much due to sensory impairments, but he did his best to follow along. "Because I had profound hearing loss," recalled Henry, "I was there, but yet I wasn't there." Even though he and Ricky were just a few rows apart, there was no way that Henry could distinguish his missing best friend among the blurry shapes.[9] Ricky did not seek him out.

Steven Duplantis remained in Texas, despite Stewart Butler's entreaties for him to return and give a statement to police. They both knew that Steven could never do so, that he could never divulge what he'd heard from Roger Nunez. Buddy Rasmussen remained sequestered: he didn't wish to attend any spectacle, even one that commemorated Adam's death. Regarding Buddy, Lucien Baril told *The Advocate*, "He wanted no special recognition."[10] In spite of his saving so many patrons, he resisted efforts to label him as a hero.

Troy Perry, resplendent in full clerical collar, stood at the altar alongside Reverend Kennedy of St. Mark's. Seated close by, to the surprise of many, was Bishop Finis Crutchfield of the United Methodist Church of Louisiana, a man of serious bearing. After voicing approval for Reverend Kennedy's decision to host the memorial service, the bishop had evidently felt the need to make a personal statement of support, and traveled to New Orleans specifically for this purpose. Perplexingly, Crutchfield was also a member (along with Archbishop Hannan and Episcopal Bishop Noland) of antigay Morality in Media of Louisiana, the group that had opposed homosexual obscenity. The bishop's presence at the service suggested that, at least in private (and without the glare of the news), he had a more nuanced relationship with gay Christians than many assumed. "By my presence," Crutchfield told Troy Perry, "I want every Methodist to know Reverend Kennedy is not a renegade pastor acting without permission." No other churches in New Orleans sent a representative member of their clergy, despite invitations.[11]

MCC of Washington, D.C., pastor Paul Breton opened the service with a solemn prayer: "Almighty God, we have come together in peace and harmony as mournful people to worship and to make a living memorial for your children."[12] After MCC of Atlanta pastor John Gill read from scripture, Gay Activists Alliance cofounder Morty Manford made a political speech:

Many of our sisters and brothers who died at the Upstairs bar were Gay. They know what it was like to live in a condemning society where churches called us sinners, psychiatrists called us sick, legislators called us criminals; where capitalists denounced us as subversives and communists denounced us as decadent.[13]

Notably, Deacon Courtney Craighead did not rise to speak. It's not clear if Courtney could or would not address the crowd. The deacon was at that point half himself, devastated by how his father had critiqued his very being. Lucien Baril, the interim MCC of New Orleans pastor, read a series of telegrams from churches and organizations around the country, including an unexpected message of sympathy from American Baptist Churches in the U.S.A. Many joked that, because of the Baptists' conservative reputation, this telegram might have been sent in error.[14] With a two-sentence message, the Louisiana State University in New Orleans's Young Democrats became the first and only political body in the country to support the MCC's National Day of Morning. The Young Democrats acknowledged "the national day of mourning Sunday July 1st in memory of the victims of the 'Upstairs' fire disaster." The group also called for a "complete rewriting and strict enforcement of state and local fire codes."[15] The Louisiana Democratic National Committee—with its closeted membership—did not acknowledge this statement from their fellow party members. Yet, Tom Bradley, the new mayor of Los Angeles, sent a personal message, as did California senator Alan Cranston and John Burton, a member of the California State Assembly. These messages were, no doubt, stirred up at the request of Angelenos Troy Perry and Morris Kight. The words of these faraway politicians stood in contrast to the muteness of Mayor Moon Landrieu and Governor Edwin Edwards.[16]

By the time Troy Perry took the pulpit, there was a palpable sense that something momentous was about to occur. He thanked Bishop Crutchfield for "having the guts to be here today," and then expounded on a theme of gay oppression. "As long as one brother or sister in this country is oppressed, it's our problem," Perry preached. He declared such names like "faggots, queers, freaks" were "labels (which) will never put me down" and further advised mourners that "you can have dignity as a human being and hold your head high." Perry related stories of men and women who had frequented the Up Stairs Lounge. "It was no den of iniquity," he insisted. He roused the crowd with familiar memories. "The last song they ever sang was the one they always sang at the end of Sunday brunch. They all held hands and sang, 'United We Stand.'" Perry went on to quote from that emblematic song, which patrons had once sung together, locked arm in arm. With these words—spoken rhythmically, reflectively, with reverence—the entire church broke into a powerful, communal sob.[17]

According to witnesses like Stewart Butler, who recalled being overcome with emotion, it was a disembodied cry that echoed in the sanctuary, as if grief had taken on a voice. "There was a deep, respectful, caring emotion that was palpable," recalled Paul Killgore.[18]

Troy Perry then yielded the pulpit so that John Gill could lead a final hymn, but Perry rushed back in alarm. Interrupting John Gill, he advised everyone in the church that television and press cameras had set up across the street. Evidently, according to *Nola Express* reporter Ed Martinez, WDSU, the local NBC affiliate, was spotted "out front getting footage before the funeral." *The Advocate* and the *Vieux Carré Courier* said that *Times-Picayune* cameras were also present. Gay New Orleanians, it seemed, were being surrounded by hostile parties.[19]

A buzz filled the chamber, followed by protestations from people who said that the cameras should be forcibly taken away. Henry Kubicki recalled becoming frightened at the prospect of losing his job at the Marriott. Troy Perry informed the crowd of a contingency plan, through which Reverend Kennedy could guide anyone who didn't wish to be photographed, out of fear of being exposed as a homosexual, out a side door onto Governor Nicholls Street. According to the

Times-Picayune, Perry called this alternate exit an "escape hatch" to be used "in case there were those who would be embarrassed." A loud debate ensued, with one man saying that the cameras were already gone and others wondering if Troy Perry was arranging a stunt and several more insisting that they should all walk out together, come what may. Paul Killgore described it as the "one dramatic incident, which has been reported over and over; it is just like folklore."[20]

Then a "butch-looking woman," whom Killgore recalled as sitting behind his right shoulder, stood up and shouted, "I came in the front door, and I'm damn well going out that way!" Her statement roused many. In an unprecedented act, the crowd rose and headed with the woman down the front steps of St. Mark's—prepared to face the cameras. "I looked at [my boyfriend], and he looked at me," recalled Killgore. "I said, 'Are you okay with this?' and he said, 'Yeah.'" So they marched. Even Bishop Finish Crutchfield walked outside with the worshippers as they left. "That was the first time, for a lot of people, they had ever joined together with other gay people, gay and lesbian, in the light of day, though they'd known each other at night," recalled Perry.[21]

This sudden act of defiance seemed to symbolize the challenges that lay ahead: that gays and lesbians could never hope to gain their equality and become part of a human rights movement unless they were willing to be seen in public. Neither Henry Kubicki nor Paul Killgore, who each left through the front door, remembered seeing any cameras on Rampart Street. They recalled rejoicing among a teeming crowd of gay men and lesbians, who exited into a beautiful afternoon. Perry stood in front to corral reporters and body-block cameras, if necessary. He told the Associated Press, "In light of the real fear of recrimination felt here, I'm jubilant." Ed Martinez of *Nola Express* wrote how WDSU reporters seemed to vanish: "Mercifully, they were gone by the time the service was over, and the mourners were not subjected to the sight of a camera grinding away."[22]

No news photography or video footage of the exterior of St. Mark's would surface in news coverage, and so local gays came to question the veracity of this liberating moment. Years later, Troy Perry would even question their presence to the Up Stairs Lounge historian Clayton

Delery: "In a very real way, it doesn't matter that there were no cameras. People had believed they were there." And yet, a recently resurfaced film log for WDSU, recording its news cameramen's locations on July 1, 1973, states, "Memorial—held for 30 homosexuals who died in F.Q. fire."[23] Not only had a news cameraman been present outside of the church with heavy equipment, but the sight of that equipment seems to have been expunged, even gaslighted, from the minds of men who encountered it.

Immediately after the memorial, Troy Perry, who would not return to New Orleans for several years, flew to Los Angeles to attend a more public service for the Up Stairs Lounge victims. While no major news stories about Perry would appear in the *Times-Picayune* until July 1977, his national prominence would increase throughout the decade. Among other things, he would bring lesbian leaders into the fold of the MCC; crusade against the Anita Bryant antihomosexual movement; and tell the story of the Up Stairs Lounge to a personal advisor for President Jimmy Carter. Perry's memories of this time in New Orleans would always be nuanced. "I'm a Southern boy, and when I left home, I left home," he recalled. "I thought, 'I will never live like I've seen people have to live.'" The Dixie closet had almost killed him in the 1960s; he once attempted suicide because of it, worried that his first, ill-fated gay relationship was his only chance at happiness.[24]

Of the gay leaders who traveled to New Orleans, only Paul Breton and Morty Manford would stay behind to continue their grassroots work. Breton continued to minister to the dying, while Manford spent a few weeks organizing recently emboldened homosexuals into a political Gay People's Coalition. "We are aggrieved," began the group's first letter to City Hall.[25] These simple words were, in fact, a revolutionary proclamation.

: ACT III :

LEGACY

CHAPTER 12

Deliverance

July–September 1973

A National Day of Mourning for the Up Stairs Lounge was observed at the MCC chapters of no fewer than forty-six American cities, as well as in Great Britain. News of the fire inspired a collective grief that extended far beyond Rampart Street. Some 500 mourners gathered at the San Francisco memorial, according to figures published by *The Advocate*, as did 400 in Los Angeles, 125 in New York, 120 in San Diego, 100 in Washington, D.C., 80 in Denver, 65 in Milwaukee, and 45 in Miami. Those nineteen minutes of hell that devastated a community resulted in collective action on a level not seen since the Pride parades that commemorated the Stonewall Riots.[1]

Gay bars, nightclubs, and bathhouses in Atlanta, Boston, Chicago, Los Angeles, Miami, New York, San Francisco, and Washington, D.C., all went dark at the appointed hour. In San Francisco, some straight bars belonging to the local Tavern Guild followed suit out of mutual respect. However, in New Orleans, sympathies for the Up Stairs Lounge were mostly limited to the St. Mark's event. Café Lafitte in Exile on Bourbon Street continued business as usual, with registers ringing. Ignoring the lack of response from greater New Orleans, *The Advocate* devoted several pages to the Up Stairs Lounge memorials and called them a "rare showing of national gay togetherness."[2] The establishment media ignored these postfuneral observances: neither *The New York Times*, the *Chicago Tribune*, the *Los Angeles Times*, nor *The Washington Post* reported on any such event in its city.

In San Francisco, Jim Foster, a gay leader who in 1972 spoke as part of the first openly homosexual delegation invited to a Democratic National Convention, delivered an impassioned tribute to each of the Up Stairs Lounge victims. In Seattle, Scott Lewis, an MCC layperson, eulogized the loss of Bill Larson. In San Diego, MCC Reverend John Hose gave a sermon on the theme of freedom. In Manhattan, a representative of the New York Gay Synagogue, which would officially become Congregation Beit Simchat Torah in 1975, read a mourner's kaddish.[3] Although few people around the country knew the victims personally, many still felt it necessary to mourn.

In Los Angeles, Jim Kepner, a pioneering journalist and gay historian, delivered a speech citing Lazarus from the Gospels. "As the Son of Man raised up Lazarus from the dead with a kiss," Kepner said, "so must our incandescent love, our devotion, our commitment, commemorate and resurrect those who were so monstrously burned." He rebuked the millions of closeted Americans ignoring the Up Stairs Lounge. "Inescapably," Kepner implored, "for each of us, a part of our souls was ignited, and a part charred in the Up Stairs bar last Sunday." Likewise, at the Metropolitan Community Temple of Los Angeles, a call for unity went out: "If I am for myself only, what am I? And if not now, when?"[4]

Morris Kight, who'd helped to organize these Los Angeles events, addressed a crowd. He told the story of the New Orleans Emergency Task Force and its efforts to make a difference. Kight provided a rousing introduction for Troy Perry. At the sight of familiar faces, Perry burst into tears. He delivered yet another version of his "United We Stand" eulogy. He and Kight lit thirty votive candles, one for each person dead in New Orleans at that time.[5]

OTHER EVENTS, QUITE pertinent to the case, were transpiring in New Orleans, where investigators from the Louisiana Office of the State Fire Marshal, not the city's police force, finally located Roger Dale Nunez. Acting on the false lead fed to police by the nineteen-year-old hustler Mark Allen Guidry, Deputy State Fire Marshals Edward Hyde and John Fischer canvassed Esplanade Avenue for several days seeking the "Gerry or Johnny," identified by Guidry as the patron violently ejected by Buddy Rasmussen prior to the blaze. Unsurprisingly, the pair came up empty-handed. So Hyde and Fischer circled back to Iberville on Monday, July 2, to seek out Mark Allen Guidry. Finding him, they demanded that he come with them to Esplanade Avenue. Guidry broke down and confessed. "He told us that the subject's name was not Jerry [sic] or Johnny, but was one Roger Nunez and that he lived in the 600 block of Iberville St," the deputy marshals reported.[6]

In the company of the young hustler, Hyde and Fischer headed to Cee Cee Savant's apartment. There, they found Roger Dale Nunez sleeping on the sofa. The marshals observed immediately that Roger fit the profile of a "pathological firesetter" as determined by major studies of the time: a white male between the age of sixteen and twenty-eight with physical injury and a criminal record. "This subject was questioned about a swelling that he had on his jaw," reported the deputy marshals, "and he stated that he had had a fight with three Negroes on Iberville Street the night before who took his wallet and knocked him down."[7]

The investigators asked Roger about the Up Stairs Lounge, and he admitted to having been present in the bar "prior to the fire during the Beer Bust and that he did not have any trouble in the lounge prior to leaving." The marshals already possessed testimony about a fight inside the Up Stairs Lounge, which challenged this account.[8] Roger was likely misstating how he hurt his jaw—blaming black attackers instead of a fellow patron—and the circumstances of his expulsion. The marshals must have sensed they had a man who could spontaneously weave a tale and distort a violent incident to portray himself with pathos.

Hyde and Fischer asked Roger Nunez to come with them to make an official statement. Once Roger agreed, he started dressing. Meanwhile, the marshals phoned their NOPD counterparts, Charles Schlosser and Sam Gebbia, who were still assigned to investigate the case. When the detectives turned up, they observed the "white male subject, 25–26 years old, 5'8" tall, medium build with black medium length hair which appeared to be dirty." The deputy fire marshals were excited. Standing before them was the most viable suspect since David Dubose, the drunken teenager, had confessed and recanted on June 25.[9]

Schlosser and Gebbia gleaned from the marshals that the suspect had just experienced an epileptic seizure, with limbs and arms akimbo. Then something occurred with police in the room, and at whirlwind speed. Roger Dale Nunez, detectives determined, needed urgent medical assistance, and they radioed for two police patrolmen to immediately whisk him to Charity Hospital, taking him away from the arson specialists.[10]

Roger would not be questioned as he rode in the police car. In the admitting room of Charity Hospital, he suffered what appeared to be a grand mal seizure. He looked to lose consciousness while convulsing. Treating Roger for epilepsy, doctors heard him complain of a separate pain in his chin, although how Roger could verbalize pain after a grand mal seizure was a wonder. Taking X-rays, they discovered a fracture in Roger's jawbone and admitted him for surgery. He was now being treated at the same hospital where fire victims Luther Boggs and Larry Stratton still lay in the burn unit.[11]

Schlosser and Gebbia finally arrived in the emergency room to question the suspect, but they found Roger "unable to speak to detectives due to his prior seizure." This combination of delay and impairment prevented further casework. How could Roger not speak if he had just been complaining to the doctors of jaw pain? And how could he make complaints after a grand mal seizure, which commonly results in a so-called postictal state affecting verbal and visual memory? Nevertheless, the quartet of police officers left the hospital "after informing personnel that upon completion of oral surgery and release that they were to notify detectives." Curiously, the NOPD chose to leave Roger Dale Nunez without guard, presuming that he would stay put in his injured state. Later, the NOPD detectives would criticize Deputy Fire Marshal Hyde for his performance on this same day, July 2, by noting how Hyde "more or less led" one witness into making a statement, thereby casting doubts on the abilities of their state counterparts.[12]

DEACON MITCH MITCHELL was pronounced dead over the weekend using his commitment ring to Horace Broussard, the symbol of their holy union, which had taken place at the Up Stairs Lounge. News trickled back from New Orleans to Jamestown, Alabama, where Mitch's son Duane recalls spending the week with his paternal grandparents.[13]

In a confusing sequence of events, Duane and his brother, Stephen, identified by the *States-Item* as "two Alabama youngsters," had spent the day after the fire with their father's neighbors, who preoccupied the boys with streetcar rides and a trip to Pontchartrain Beach. Strangers they barely knew had told them their dad was in an accident. Then the kids flew back to their grandparents and stayed in their father's boyhood home. Old pictures of Mitch were still on display throughout the house, and some of the portraits looked uncannily like Duane. Distraught, Duane had tried to distract himself by riding his bike, a Christmas gift from his dad and Uncle Horace. Then the telephone rang with confirmation that Mitch Mitchell had lost his life. So ended more than seven days of uncertainty, during which adults had not wanted to traumatize the children by tipping their hands about a death prematurely.[14]

Duane's grandparents took him and Stephen onto the porch— away from cousins—so that they could hear the news directly from people they loved. Duane recalls them weeping, crushed not just by the weight of losing their son but also by the sad duty of having to tell the news to his children. "They just came up and said that there'd been a terrible accident, and he was dead," remembered Duane. "My granddaddy said, 'I'll do the arrangements and everything,' and I said, 'No, I want to go.'" Duane went with his grandfather to the local funeral home to choose a casket. "I went and called the preacher to preach the service," Duane continued, "and I also picked out a place for him to be buried." Duane found comfort in these actions. It made him feel grown up.[15]

"The [casket] couldn't be opened or anything," recalled Duane. "He was burned so bad. They put a picture of him on top of his casket. That was it." Mitch Mitchell's death notice in the *Birmingham News* (like Bill Larson, he was not deemed important enough to merit an obituary) provided no advance notice of the service and made no mention of the Up Stairs Lounge or of Horace Broussard, the lover for whom Mitchell had sacrificed his life.[16]

Relatives whom Duane had never met before traveled vast distances to pay their respects, and Duane's mother, Mitchell's ex-spouse Vicki Tane, helped by bringing food for guests. According to Duane, a lot of people attended. "My dad was real well liked," he recalled. Horace Broussard wasn't mentioned in the eulogy at Pleasant Valley Baptist Church, and nobody thought to explain to Duane how his father had been romantically involved with Uncle Horace. Their holy union from the MCC revealed itself to be legally meaningless once each of their remains were transferred to biological next of kin, who did not confer or even consider the idea of a joint funeral for two grown men. They were buried in separate states.[17]

Duane wouldn't understand the circumstances of his father's death for decades. "Nobody ever said anything about who did it or if anybody was arrested," Duane stated, which felt underhanded to him. "It was a gay thing that wasn't to be heard of at that time. They put it under the rug and left it there." Duane's aunts and uncles then forbade him from visiting his father's grave in the cemetery, largely because it brought back gruesome thoughts, and nobody wanted him to mention the loss. "I didn't find out he was gay until I asked my mom," he explained. "I was fifteen or sixteen."[18]

After their father's death, Duane and Stephen were expected to behave like small adults to make things easier on caretakers. Vicki Tane, their mother, worked hard in a hosiery mill, so the brothers would be stewarded into manhood by a network of relatives. Tane periodically brought boyfriends into their lives and attempted to forge new households, but Duane would express fury at anyone attempting to take the role of his father. Fortunately, Mitch Mitchell had had a small life insurance policy, and his sons were the beneficiaries. Their grandparents kept that money in a trust until the boys turned eighteen. In the meantime, Duane and Stephen lived off of Social Security survivors' benefits. "Me and my brother [would] draw a check off of him," said Duane. "And that's what we grew up on because that's all the money that we had."[19]

༄

In New Orleans, reports surfaced that authorities had not inspected the Up Stairs Lounge for more than two years. Although fire prevention experts recommended an inspection of structures every six months, the New Orleans Fire Department (NOFD) cited a staffing shortage to explain why the burnt-out bar had last been inspected in March 1971. Simultaneously explaining and excusing their shortfall, NOFD representatives complained that the entire French Quarter was allotted just one inspector. "Decorations in the Up Stairs Lounge, I'm sure, were not fireproof," fire examiner Norman J. Guererra told the *Times-Picayune*. "If the inspector had been able to get there, I'm sure he would have tested the decorations and made them change them."[20]

Most New Orleanians seemed willing to accept this pretext: a holocaust of flame in a tinderbox lit by an arsonist could never have been prevented or minimized. The front fire door that didn't close when exposed to heat, the rayon wallpaper that went up within seconds, the window bars trapping people inside, the back entrance without a functioning Exit sign—all of this was, officials implied through the media, neither the responsibility nor the liability of city or state agencies doing their best.[21]

The only semblance of blame leveled by authorities continued to be directed at the Vieux Carré Commission. "They're only concerned with design authenticity," railed Assistant State Fire Marshal Timothy Driscoll, "and to hell with safety." Driscoll's campaign to clean up the "firetraps" resulting in an unprecedented series of inspections, with nearly one hundred French Quarter buildings visited and more than a thousand violations cited. Exit signs would receive new lightbulbs. Fines would be paid. A letter to *Advocate* editor Rob Cole described how "Alice Brady's bar (gay) had to remove some grill work that was in front of a window," in addition to how "Lafitte (gay) put in a new side door so now it has three exits." The Central Business District, the neighborhood that actually contained the Up Stairs Lounge, escaped inspectors' attentions throughout the month of July.[22]

Speaking in the defense of this misdirection, Mayor Moon Landrieu would explain to the *Times-Picayune* that, even though the Up Stairs Lounge was not officially in the French Quarter, "the fire there did alert inspectors to the dangers of fire in any area congested with people and buildings." Indeed, the mayor had returned to his offices at City Hall without ceremony on Monday, July 9. He landed more than two weeks after the deadly fire, having completed his European trip by spending a final night in the Kong Frederik Hotel in Copenhagen. Back at his desk, Landrieu answered official letters and made proclamations. He gave a statement to *Living Magazine*, but his office rebuffed the *Vieux Carré Courier*'s attempts to speak to him about the fire, claiming that the mayor was still out of the country.[23]

Landrieu thus did not offer comments on the Up Stairs Lounge case, even though a decidedly laissez-faire attitude characterized his police department's investigation following the July 2 discovery of Roger Dale Nunez. On July 6, according to the state fire marshal's report on the Up Stairs Lounge, John Perino of Charity Hospital security notified the NOPD that Roger had recovered from surgery and was ready to be released. The fracture in the suspect's jaw had been closed with sutures on July 2. Four days later, he displayed no trouble speaking, even though police claimed to be making "periodic checks on Mr. Nunez," during which they were told the patient was "unable to converse due to the operation on his jaw." Nonetheless, "the New Orleans Police Department didn't send anyone to take a statement from this subject," reported the security guard to deputy state fire marshals. Nor did the NOPD send an officer to detain or supervise the suspect until detectives could arrive. Meanwhile, Roger phoned his mother, Rose Choate, in Abbeville, Louisiana, and requested that she make the long drive to pick him up.[24]

Thus, when no officer from the NOPD turned up to delay Roger, and with no instructions to do otherwise, Charity Hospital discharged the patient to his mother's care. Theirs was a medical facility, after all, not a prison. Roger wandered into sunlight with a partially wired jaw. He set free foot in front of free foot. He hopped into his mother's car and directed her through the miasma of New Orleans in the full daze of summer. They drove to pick up his things at Cee Cee Savant's on Iberville Street. Roger was now informally "at large" from several authorities, who wanted him for active investigations.[25]

According to the NOPD report, Detectives Schlosser and Gebbia arrived at Charity Hospital on July 7 and were flummoxed to learn that Roger had already been released "on July 6"—or so the detectives insisted in their account. The NOPD report includes a parenthetical note: "Detectives Schlosser and Gebbia were not notified of his release as requested." But hospital records reviewed by the state fire marshal said otherwise, with Roger Dale Nunez released on July 7 and police notification the day prior. Police were informed, according to Charity Hospital security, and Roger Nunez left on July 7 before Schlosser and Gebbia arrived and claimed to discover the suspect's supposed "early" release.[26]

Schlosser and Gebbia's police report makes a special point of blaming hospital security, much in the same manner that they critiqued Deputy State Fire Marshal Edward Hyde on July 2. However, after discovering Roger's discharge, the detectives failed to immediately notify other law enforcement agencies of the missing man. Investigators for the state fire marshal, in fact, wouldn't learn that Roger Dale Nunez had eluded police custody until July 11—four full days of noncommunication, during which Schlosser and Gebbia claimed to be "making attempts to locate Nunez," who by then had fled New Orleans.[27]

On July 9, the detectives interviewed Gene Davis, Roger's former employer. In an official statement, Davis claimed to have sat on the hood of a car with a view of the Up Stairs Lounge on Sunday, June 24, and was certain that "nobody was in front of the building for ten to fifteen minutes, maybe even twenty minutes before [the fire]." This account seemed to squash the possibility of arson. But Davis had, in fact, contradicted this testimony more than two weeks before, on the night of June 24, when he told a UPI reporter how he came upon the fire. "I heard all the commotion and ran out into the street," said Davis. "There was Luther Boggs—I cash checks for him—dancing at the window with his clothes on fire." How could Davis hear the commotion and run into the street if he was already in the street and facing the bar?[28] Nonetheless, detectives did not explore why Davis might have changed his story.

In the midst of these snafus, Sergeant Frank Hayward, the information officer assigned as the NOPD mouthpiece for the Up Stairs Lounge case, was suspended from the force pending an investigation into his acceptance of illicit moneys from the film crew during the late June production of *My Name Is Nobody*. Evidently, a producer working for Sergio Leone had written Hayward a $300 check to avoid "a great deal of trouble." Hayward admitted to accepting the check on June 21 and cashing it thereafter. Mayor Landrieu felt compelled to speak in Hayward's defense. "I have great respect for Officer Hayward and they are going to have to prove to me he tried to shake somebody down," said the mayor, while demurring that perhaps some mistakes "may have been made." A grand jury subsequently exonerated Hayward, even though his unreported "financial reward" for off-duty work was against NOPD rules.[29]

YET ANOTHER FIRE survivor became a fatality on July 10, when Luther Boggs succumbed to his wounds at Charity Hospital. A World War II and Korean war veteran, Luther died holding the hand of MCC minister Paul Breton.

Having opened the door to the bar's front staircase that Sunday night in June, Luther's skin had melted away, and third-degree burns covered nearly half of his body surface, including his lips and face. Clinging to life for sixteen days, he developed bronchopneumonia and cerebral edema—a swelling of the brain tissue—inside his sterile tent as ministers watched on and prayed. He expired through brain failure, while choking on his own blood, having never again seen his best friend, Jeanne Gosnell, who was still healing at the U.S. Public Health Service Hospital.[30]

The day after Luther Boggs's death, Mayor Landrieu held his first press conference of the month. Speaking from his office on Wednesday, July 11, Landrieu addressed the pressing matters of government. He criticized a property tax plan proposed by the Louisiana Assessors' Association. He opposed efforts to ease so-called corruption by placing the city's police and fire departments under state jurisdiction. And he issued his first words about the Up Stairs Lounge, advocating for sprinkler laws to be instituted statewide "on a reasonable basis." Landrieu seemed ready to change the subject when Bill Rushton pressed the mayor with a pointed question about the "homosexual angle," which drew eye rolls from the establishment press.[31]

"I'm just as concerned about that life as any other life," Landrieu responded. "I was not aware of any lack of concern in the community." These comments must have lacked fundamental newsworthiness to *Times-Picayune* and *States-Item* reporters, who either did not deem them important or attempted to include them in the day's coverage but were overruled by Landrieu-friendly editors like Charles Ferguson at the *States-Item*.[32]

At 6:45 a.m. the following morning, Up Stairs Lounge patron Larry Stratton also died in Charity Hospital. Burns covered 80 percent of his body.[33] Stratton had spent two years in the marine corps, from August 23, 1967, to November 26, 1969. His time in the marines, America's "first to fight" military force, included a tour of duty in Vietnam during the Tet offensive. The deaths of these two veterans, Luther Boggs and Larry Stratton, thus coincided with Mayor Landrieu's statement of absolution.

Larry Stratton was the Up Stairs Lounge fire's final and thirty-second victim—and one of its youngest. At the time of his death, Stratton was twenty-five and weighed just 113 pounds. His had been a fledging life in New Orleans, but he had clung to it for weeks after falling from the windows of a burning bar. No one really knew how to eulogize him, other than perhaps noting his time in the military. Some whispered about a lover, a devastated young man named Lynn

Cobb, but whatever stories or secrets held the keys to Stratton's past, whoever he'd loved in his home on 2719 Burgundy Street, vanished unrecorded with his last breaths.[34]

Between July 10 and July 17, NOPD detectives continued to search for Roger Dale Nunez or anyone with information pertaining to the fire. "However," they noted, "all attempts were to no avail." During this period, deputy state fire marshals received a tip from Morgan City, Louisiana. On July 13, the police there pulled over a person named Roger Dale Nunez during a routine traffic stop related to a local burglary. That officer from Morgan City, a bayou town located about seventy miles west of New Orleans, could not have been aware that Roger was wanted for questioning by anyone and simply let him go. At the time, Roger was driving a 1966 Plymouth Fury registered to his name and the address 305 South Valery Street in Abbeville—the home of Roger's mother.[35] It was apparent that Roger Dale Nunez had not fled the state of Louisiana.

As ROGER CONTINUED to evade law enforcement, the cremains of Up Stairs Lounge victim Bud Matyi were interred in Glendora, California, at a service attended by friends, ex-lovers, and children. Rod Wagener, still at odds with Matyi's spouse, Pamela Cutler, was openly discouraged from attending, and therefore did not make the trip. "I think it's because of my mother," insisted Tina Marie Matyi. "My grandmother said his 'manager' would not be coming because of the confrontation with my mom." For Rod Wagener, Bud's loss was calamitous. He would relinquish their lakefront condo and move to the Irish Bayou in eastern New Orleans, where he isolated himself outside of work hours and mourned privately for several years.[36]

On a verdant summer day, a small crowd gathered before an urn. Matyi's wife, Pamela Cutler, and his ex-wife, Mary Griego, sat in positions of honor. Tina Marie Matyi, only four, was old enough to understand some of what was happening at the burial. "You do feel that you get robbed of your childhood," recounted Tina. The little girl could not stop dreaming about her dad dying at the piano, as people had told her. She did not know—and would not know for years—how he perished while likely attempting to sacrifice his body for another in the midst of an inferno, how they found him 95 percent burned on the piano stage protecting Willie Inez Warren, who was only 35 percent burned but nonetheless became the fire's lone female victim.[37]

Although Tina had few recollections of her father, she could vaguely remember the song her dad liked to sing most at the piano, because it was also her favorite: "The Impossible Dream" from the musical *Man of La Mancha*. In the weeks that followed, she asked her mother to play that song repeatedly on the record player. She did not know why the part of the song about "unreachable stars" could make her cry.[38]

ENCOURAGED BY THE memorial service, gay leaders increased their focus on the Up Stairs Lounge. Morris Kight dispatched New Orleans Emergency Task Force member Morty Manford on a "national tour to mobilize gay organizations in major cities to form support groups." On July 16, Manford met with the Gay Coalition of Denver. According to the press release, "many in attendance that night learned of the tragedy in detail for the first time and realized that this was an event every gay person must respond to." The very next day, Manford rallied a massive assemblage in Chicago, representing the city's United Front of Gay Organizations. Chicago groups volunteered to use their mailing lists—their primary means of connecting with closeted ranks—to conduct fund-raising. "These lists range in size from a few hundred to several thousand names," said the press release. A front-page headline then appeared in the *Chicago Gay Crusader*: "Chicago Gays Mobilize to Aid Fire Victims."[39]

On July 18, Manford spoke in Washington, D.C. On July 19, he was in Philadelphia. Following Manford's tour, MCC Pastor Paul Breton made a similar trip around New England. "The most enthusiastic group so far has been the Homophile Union of Boston," Breton wrote Dick Michaels, editor of *The Advocate*. Attracted to the cause but unable to donate money, gay prisoners at the Federal Correction Institution in Lompoc, California, and the California Medical Facility in Vacaville went on a two-hour hunger strike for the Up Stairs Lounge victims. Around the country, concerned citizens gave enough blood to the American Red Cross's "New Orleans Catastrophe" account to raise the possibility of a "blood credit" for future gay emergencies.[40]

Checks poured forth into the National New Orleans Memorial Fund as *The Advocate* ran a series of Up Stairs Lounge stories and appealed directly to readers for donations: "We ask all who can to help with whatever money they can spare." Money started arriving as early as June 30. By July 19, more than eighty checks—ranging from $5 to $334—had reached the magazine. Organizations in Oklahoma City, Tampa Bay, Jacksonville, Detroit, and Boston pitched in. These sums, small and large, represented nothing less than a countrywide outpouring.[41]

ON TUESDAY, JULY 31, the Orleans Parish coroner released the last fire victims to the city for public burial. In the end, Coroner Carl Rabin was able to positively identify twenty-nine of the fire's thirty-two dead. The New Orleans Emergency Task Force viewed this percentage of identified bodies as remarkable, given the initial states of the bodies. The coroner also succeeded in moving twenty-eight of the victims out of the morgue and into funeral homes, where families (or, in Bill Larson's case, the MCC of New Orleans) could make arrangements.[42]

The final four victims became property of the city, despite attempts by the MCC to claim them. NOPD Sergeant Joseph Vitari, speaking for the Coroner's Office, told the *Vieux Carré Courier* that he was unable to release bodies to the MCC without a letter of exemption from Blake Arrata, the city attorney. When the MCC sought out Arrata, his office told them that such an exemption "might open up possibilities for later lawsuits by relatives against MCC, the city, and the Coroner's Office." Arrata then denied the church's request and condemned four people to public graves. Three of the bodies—numbers 18, 22, and 28—were burned so badly that they could never be given names.[43]

Additionally, the body of Ferris LeBlanc was identified at the eleventh hour using an antique ring made from a silver spoon. The Coroner's Office made this connection after an anonymous caller tipped them off about this piece of jewelry. "Authorities are requesting that the unknown caller contact police to provide further information on LeBlanc," said a report in the *States-Item*. Sadly, the caller never reached out again. In an unfortunate coincidence, LeBlanc was a common French surname in Louisiana, and authorities grew frustrated with attempts to contact local households, ultimately abandoning their search. No one in the LeBlanc clan in California ever spoke to an official or received news of the death.[44]

Ferris LeBlanc's sister, Marilyn, went on believing for decades that her brother was alive but not in touch due to the grudge he bore about moneys owed to their grandfather. Through a mix-up of surnames and fear of an acquaintance who would call authorities but not risk outing himself, Ferris LeBlanc received burial alongside those without kin. A fifty-year-old World War II veteran who fought in the Battle of the Bulge, he was interred in a plywood box. Though federal agencies assisting the city could have accessed military records to prevent this oversight, LeBlanc was buried without military honors in Panel Q, Lot 32 of Resthaven Memorial Park, a city-affiliated cemetery for indigents. As LeBlanc and the three unidentified bodies were lowered into the ground, MCC pastor Lucien Baril stood over them reading scripture. Ceremoniously, he blessed the caskets while wearing his red and white cassock.[45]

The bodies were then carefully covered with earth and left without markers. The trio of unknown victims would forever remain question marks to loved ones and friends, who would miss them without any certainty of being able to grieve. Body 18, an over-eighteen-year-old white male, for example, had no identifying tattoos and burns over 70 percent of him. Body 28, over 60 percent of his body charred, met his final resting place with pants and an undershirt still grafted to his skin. Body 23, 90 percent burned, was the most unrecognizable figure who had been pulled from the ruins. All that is known is that he met his end wearing brown shoes and black socks.[46]

With the last bodies laid to rest, the story faded from minds. "I remember distinctly on a Monday running into gay friends on the street [Iberville]," recalled John Meyers of the local gay gentry, "cause I was living in the Quarter at the time, and these were gay people, and nobody said a thing about the fire." Silence extended to fire survivors and friends of the deceased, a response not unusual for victims of trauma. "The following weeks, months and years afterward, I don't remember much," wrote Henry Kubicki in a self-published account of the tragedy. "It is as though I stepped out into limbo, not connecting with anybody or events. The malfunction of my memory occurred as though a safety valve had exploded."[47]

The Up Stairs Lounge became a nonentity. People who passed the structure told themselves that there was no tale to be heard about the wreckage. It says something profound that, in a natural story-telling community like New Orleans, one story remained off limits. "I started coming to NOLA [New Orleans, Louisiana] in the mid-1970s," wrote New Orleans gay Carnival historian Howard Smith. He continued, "The fire was *never* a topic of conversation." Louisiana governor Edwin Edwards, for whom the fire barely registered, would never reexamine his conduct. "I have a vague slight memory of the event," Edwards wrote in an email for this book, "but frankly do not remember that gays very [much] amount [to] the people involved."[48]

On July 17, New Orleans detectives Schlosser and Gebbia received yet another tip. That day, according to the police report, Deputy State Fire Marshal Edward Hyde notified detectives that an Up Stairs Lounge survivor with critical information had been located and interviewed at a Baton Rouge hospital. The survivor's name was Michael Scarborough. To pique police interest, arson investigators showed the detectives a typewritten statement from Scarborough, in which the witness admitted to a physical altercation with someone in the bar just prior to the blaze. While being ejected from the establishment, Scarborough had heard this person say something to the effect of "I'm going to burn you all out." Looking at a series of mug shots following this interview, Michael Scarborough identified Roger Dale Nunez as the person with whom he had fought.[49]

After driving to Baton Rouge, Schlosser and Gebbia met with Scarborough, who gave testimony consistent with his prior statement and described Roger Nunez as a "white male, with medium dark complexion, brown hair, not real long" who was thrown out from the bar "thirty or forty five minutes prior to the fire being discovered." The NOPD now had a witness from inside the Up Stairs Lounge who could describe suspicious behavior pointing to motive (anger) and opportunity (timing) to set the fire, as well as a description that closely matched with Claudine Rigaud's description of the suspicious customer at Walgreens. Schlosser and Gebbia concluded their interview with Scarborough, noting that the witness "could add nothing further" and then concluded their investigation. As detectives, they simply stopped pursuing new leads.[50]

In the final pages of the New Orleans Police Department's "General Case Report," filed on August 30, 1973, the detectives describe no attempts to locate Roger Dale Nunez outside of New Orleans, even though a lead available to the state fire marshal on July 13—an address used to register a vehicle owned by Roger—existed. For reasons ultimately unknowable, the NOPD closed a criminal case having never interviewed a person whom a witness identified as screaming "I'm going to burn you all out" moments before a fire and who multiple witnesses identified as saying "I just made it, from the fire" or "I got out of the fire" afterward while covered in what looked to be soot.[51] That the twenty dollars gifted to Roger Nunez by Donald Landry, which Roger had drunkenly accepted and then broken into smaller increments, matched the amount dropped in the Up Stairs Lounge staircase never interested detectives or became an avenue of inquiry. These oversights call into question whether the missing testimony of Steven Duplantis would have changed the police officers' actions. Instead of locating Roger at his mother's house in Abbeville, the NOPD would spend the next six weeks compiling a report. The final, sixty-four-page document, which could be described as rigorous prior to Roger Dale Nunez's discovery on July 2 and cryptic thereafter, seemed incomplete.[52]

On the report's final page, in the concluding paragraph, the NOPD blamed witnesses who came forward for providing testimony that was "conflicting in content" and filed away the "fire of undetermined origin." Despite the discovery of a canister of lighter fluid in the bar stairwell, this official document declined to acknowledge that the fire was "deliberately set," a piece of language later used specifically in a separate report on the Up Stairs Lounge by the National Fire Protection Association, a trade association providing standards for fire safety. In addition, the police report wildly mischaracterized the testimony of attorney Harold Bartholomew, who attested to suspicious characters shouting "I'm telling you, you better get out of here!" before running away from the Up Stairs Lounge, when they concluded, "with all the persons interviewed, none observed anyone leaving or entering the stairwell just prior to or after the discovery of the fire."[53]

The NOPD's closing of the Up Stairs Lounge case drew no headlines, however, as the report was not made available to the public and would not be for several years. Soon afterward, in a criminal courthouse located across the street from police headquarters, Judge Frank J. Shea issued a warrant for the arrest of "Nunez, Roger Dale." This order of the court authorized state and local authorities to locate and make a lawful arrest. However, this warrant wasn't for anything to do with the Up Stairs Lounge. Evidently, the slow gears of justice had been grinding to address the violation of Roger's one-year probation from early 1973, following his guilty plea for the "unauthorized use" of a credit card and subsequent failure to honor terms of parole. Nunez, sought for questioning in relation to the June fire, was now officially declared a "probation absconder" for a completely different crime.[54]

AROUND THIS TIME, New Orleans Archbishop Philip Hannan published his first words about the Up Stairs Lounge. Coming unexpectedly, his commentary went unnoticed by the public and the general press. Hannan's remarks appeared in the July 19 issue of the *Clarion Herald,* a weekly newspaper for Catholic parishioners. In a human-rights-themed tract for his regular column, "The Archbishop Speaks," Hannan bemoaned how "there have been a number of flagrant invasions and disregard for human rights." He suggested how "as persons believing in the dignity of every man and woman (born and unborn), our faith in God impels us to express again our belief in human dignity."[55] Hannan then rebuked Communist oppression of religion and criticized the use of deadly force by police in Baton Rouge. In his final paragraph, located after a page jump, the archbishop pivoted to another topic:

> Meanwhile, the last report on the fire of the Up Stairs Lounge reveals that now 32 victims had been claimed by this disaster. The report and opinion of the fire chief that arson could have been or probably was involved makes all the more deplorable this holocaust of human lives. In the spirit of deep Christian concern and compassion, we offer prayers for the repose of the souls of the victims and the consolation of their bereaved families and friends. We pray also that the loss of their lives will lead to effective measures to prevent similar tragedies.[56]

With these four sentences, delivered nearly one month after the fire, Hannan openly acknowledged the catastrophe. His up-to-date citation of the number of dead, his use of the word "holocaust" (a term favored by the *States-Item*), and his mention of arson demonstrated a fluency with current events that suggested a man who followed the news closely. His examination of the fire within the context of human rights was also telling. While avoiding the word "homosexual," Hannan finally expressed sentiments that Troy Perry had spent the week of June 24 begging for him to say. But the timing had a nullifying effect. Decades later, gay and lesbian activists would ask Archbishop Hannan to apologize for never issuing a statement of sympathy after the fire. To these criticisms, Hannan, who would die and be interred at St. Louis Cathedral in September 2011, responded by denying his silence—once even speculating that a subordinate, "who thought he knew my mind," wrongly turned the MCC away from St. Louis Cathedral. Hannan, however, would never cite his July 19 column in these disavowals, which had a strange way of simultaneously absolving and implicating him.[57]

HARDLY PLACATED AT the time was a select cluster of the New Orleans gay community. These newly outed gays, roused by the St. Mark's memorial and calling themselves the Gay People's Coalition (GPC), met with police to tame speculation and dispel fears of "vigilante action" surrounding the alleged racial profile of the Up Stairs Lounge arsonist. The GPC then posted a "Rumor Control" statement in Quarter bars: "There is no truth whatsoever to recent rumors of an identified suspect in the case of the Up Stairs Lounge fire."[58] The GPC also petitioned the mayor's Human Relations Committee (HRC) with a proposal for organizing a "Taskforce on Gay Problems":

> On June 24, the gay community faced the worst tragedy in its history—and the community-at-large responded only with embarrassed silence.

> But the time for silence and embarrassment is ended.[59]

Perhaps Mayor Landrieu, a lifelong Catholic, read Hannan's words in the *Clarion Herald*, or perhaps he had merely been biding his time to expend some capital. On Monday, August 6, the New Orleans Human Relations Committee agreed to an hourlong meeting with the Gay People's Coalition. Considering that chairman Monsignor Arthur T. Screen, a Catholic priest answering to Archbishop Hannan, ordinarily set the HRC agenda, it's clear that a high-ranking advisor like Landrieu vouched for the GPC to get the group on the calendar. Hearing testimony from MCC pastor Lucien Baril, Bill Rushton, and a lesbian spokesperson named Celeste Newbrough, the HRC then passed a resolution to devote six months of city-funded study to issues faced by local homosexuals. "The idea," said an anonymous committee spokesperson, "is to get people to see that homosexuals are not just freaks they see on the street, but people they work with and respect."

The HRC also announced a local strategy to "get as many gay people as possible to declare that they are gay," while qualifying that "this will either cause a great deal of embarrassment or cause them to be accepted." Afterward, the proposed budget for the "Taskforce on Gay Problems," which would pass in front of the mayor's desk, received approval to move forward. Perhaps Landrieu had been moved by a tragic event, though not so moved as to align himself with homosexual activists in public, which remained beyond the reach of a politician facing a reelection campaign the next year. Within weeks, Landrieu also announced a Veterans Outreach Program to "locate and aid the veteran" in New Orleans.[60] A compassionate and forward-thinking leader of citizens, he was also a man of his times.

Emboldened by this win, the Gay People's Coalition grew in numbers and expanded operations. Sharing a temporary headquarters with the MCC of New Orleans on Magazine Street, GPC volunteers started the city's first gay telephone switchboard for emergencies. Additionally, they established a gay counseling committee to provide psychological services, opened a gay health clinic on North Rampart Street, and started a newspaper called *Causeway*. Sponsors from the MCC church and the National New Orleans Memorial Fund continued to support these projects, which were the first such services to be offered by homosexuals for homosexuals in New Orleans.[61]

On August 15, in Atlanta, Troy Perry delivered a "State of the Church" address to the more than a thousand gay and lesbian delegates gathered for the MCC's Fourth General Conference. He took a moment to eulogize the Up Stairs Lounge and called "the blaze that wiped out over one-third of the New Orleans congregation" a test of faith and an exemplar of spiritual "refiner's fire." Devastated, yet motivated, conference members seized on this message and used it to push for gay-to-lesbian outreach. MCC delegates voted to incorporate gender-inclusive language into their church charter and then elected the first female minister to their Board of Elders.[62]

At this conference, Paul Breton ran into Lucien Baril. They rekindled their friendship and discussed the memorial fund. "It seems all is under control there," Breton wrote in a letter to Morty Manford.

"According to Lucien, no family has of yet contacted him for assistance either with funerals or other financial needs." Baril, Breton observed, was displaying a unique flair for pastoring. Indeed, Baril spoke to *The Advocate* on multiple occasions about his efforts to place a plaque in memory of the fire victims at a public cemetery. A gay Hawaiian had carved and mailed a commemorative wooden plate in memoriam of the victims, which Baril put on display in his rectory.[63] The rising profile of New Orleans had made his church the proverbial talk of the gay world.

On September 11, 1973, Baril offered candid remarks to Joan Treadway, a *Times-Picayune* journalist writing a groundbreaking, six-part series on homosexuality. According to Baril, congregant numbers were up in his church, jumping "from about six to ten, to thirty-five to fifty." The Up Stairs Lounge fire, despite culling his congregation back in June, now served as a fund-raising tool and an evocative springboard. The MCC of New Orleans was resilient, Baril insisted, and no fire survivors or families, he reiterated, had yet come forward with requests for monetary assistance.[64]

The Advocate printed updates on the rising tally of the memorial fund, which topped $5,000 by July 26 and $15,000 by October 4, with the final amount being $17,299.20. "We are building a national sense of belonging out of this," wrote Morris Kight to Up North Chicago leader Jack David, who had sent $1,500 from the Windy City. Miami held a "Warehouse VIII Benefit" in early August and gifted $1,370. Friends of Smokey's Den in rural Springfield, Illinois, gave $308. The Anik Homophile Organization of Toronto gave $42. Reverend John Gill dispatched to Los Angeles all of the moneys collected in New Orleans and deposited for safekeeping by Lucien Baril, totaling $1,109.48. "Never have we had such a thing on which to build Gay Solidarity," Kight responded.[65]

A gay activist in California petitioned John Tunney, his Democratic senator in Washington. "On June 24, 1973, a tragic fire claimed the lives of over thirty people in the Upstairs [sic] Lounge in the New Orleans French Quarter," read the letter. "Since that time, it has been extremely difficult, if not impossible, to secure comprehensive and/or accurate information regarding the subsequent investigation of that holocaust." Rather than ignore the communiqué, Tunney passed it along to Senator Russell B. Long of Louisiana. Long conferred with the Louisiana state fire marshal, who informed both senators that while the fire "is in the investigative stage all documents contained in the file are naturally not subject to public purview."[66] Thus were even two U.S. senators denied the ability to learn more about the case.

CHAPTER 13

Downfall

September 1973–November 1974

By early fall, there was increasing evidence that the tragedy had roused a cadre of gay New Orleanians in ways unthinkable just a season before. For example, Lucien Baril's successes at being an activist minister led to his becoming a featured face and voice of gay life in New Orleans. In late July, Baril had taped a thirty-second "free speech message" for the Gay People's Coalition (GPC), which aired in prime-time hours on WWL. Following that came a ten-minute taped interview on a public access UHF station, plus a ninety-minute gab session with radio host Joe Culotta. Aware of Baril's ability to captivate, Bill Rushton campaigned for the GPC to join the Citizens United for Response Broadcasting, a consortium of more than thirty civil rights groups.[1]

Baril developed plans for a public service announcement to promote gay tourism. The proposed script, which would likely have been censored due to federal broadcast restrictions, read:

> I like New Orleans.
> Do you know what I like about New Orleans so much?
> It's the Gay life here.
> You can get any queer you want
> for a day
> for a week
> for a weekend
> Even 10 minutes, if you have no time.
> Gay is Great . . .[2]

In his enthusiasm, Baril ventured to fantasize that this ad would be sponsored not by the GPC but by the New Orleans Chamber of Commerce, a conservative lobbying group that advocated for downtown corporations.

The boom fell on Baril quickly. While attending the August MCC conference in Atlanta, a church elder from Dallas shook hands with him and thought that the eccentric New Orleans minister looked somehow familiar. Upon further consideration, the Texan recognized Baril to be a person known as Richard Green, a con artist from the Dallas area. Baril, it turned out, was an impostor with experience inserting himself into trusting groups. "He was a funny little, nelly little fat man," recalled Ricky Everett. "Young. And he had that charm that just kind of caught everybody." As so many gay men took on aliases in this era, it was easy for a convicted swindler to blend in. Suddenly, it became terrifyingly clear why Baril had seized leadership of a distracted MCC. With donations pouring into the wounded congregation, Baril had ready access to the MCC church coffers.[3]

Alarmed, the MCC church elder alerted Troy Perry and called the authorities. Baril, adept at reading situations, fled. The pastor, styling himself after Alfred Hitchcock and claiming to be of Russian Orthodox descent, absconded from the MCC rectory on Magazine Street with the church treasury. From late June to September, Baril had also been in charge of an undetermined amount of money in the National New Orleans Memorial Fund's local checking account. Perhaps New Orleans's philanthropy had been greater than existing records indicate. The $1,109.48 check from New Orleans, sent by John Gill to *The Advocate* and mentioned earlier, was likely a partial sum; the rest will probably never be accounted for, given that Baril kept the records.[4]

Following his disappearance, Baril was removed as a trustee of the memorial fund, and his name was disassociated from the national MCC church body and the New Orleans GPC. The circumstances of Baril's exposure and ejection remained hush-hush: Troy Perry and fellow leaders probably wished to avoid highlighting the mistake of giving Baril responsibilities. Perhaps they hoped to limit the legal fallout of Baril's misappropriations, which could tie up donations in an inquiry and prevent the money from reaching fire victims. In the

defense of Troy Perry and John Gill, the appearance of an out personality like Lucien Baril, willing to be photographed and quoted, must
have seemed like a godsend to gay leaders seeking assistance on the
morning of June 25, 1973.[5]

Nevertheless, Baril's actions now jeopardized their emergency efforts, including the memorial fund and the existence of the
now-penniless MCC of New Orleans. Writing Paul Breton, Morty
Manford made oblique mention of Lucien Baril: "Troy and I had dinner Sunday night and spoke a bit about happenings in New Orleans."
Breton responded: "I talked with Troy over the weekend. He clued
me in as to what was happening in New Orleans. It's an unfortunate
situation, but on the other hand, it's easy to see how something like
that can happen within our community." Absent a financial infusion,
the MCC of New Orleans faced the prospect of eviction from 1373–75
Magazine Street, thus losing every penny invested into the converted
residence by Bill Larson, the deceased pastor. With Baril's unmasking, faith in the MCC evaporated, and membership rolls for the local
church dwindled from fifty to below fifteen. The national MCC Board
of Elders downgraded New Orleans back to the status of a "mission."[6]
The congregation was now crippled, through fire and embezzlement.

Deacon Courtney Craighead attempted to step in and steady the
flock, but his efforts couldn't find footing. He was still processing his
own trauma and would do so for decades. Stung twice in quick succession, by the fire and his parents, Courtney suppressed his agony. "He
had pain at home," observed Henry Kubicki. Courtney developed a
habit of stockpiling his garbage and bottling his urine, according to
Henry. Henry felt that his friend was "crashing the religious rail" and
hoarding: two behaviors now closely associated with memory fixation
and post-traumatic stress disorder (PTSD), although such diagnoses
did not exist in 1973. Even Vietnam vets of this era would be emascu-
lated for displaying outward symptoms of post-traumatic stress, and
PTSD wouldn't be listed in the American Psychiatric Association's
Diagnostic and Statistical Manual until 1980.[7]

As a result, Courtney never received a medical diagnosis for his
behavior. No counseling services would be offered to fire survivors at

Charity Hospital, and Courtney did not seek them out personally for fear that a psychologist would diagnose his "homosexual disorder" and use legal loopholes to commit him to a facility. The talented deacon, college educated and licensed as a radio technician, soldiered on with what Henry called a "pittance of a job." Courtney worked as a janitor, mopping up messes at the Cenacle Retreat House in Metairie, Louisiana, for not much more than minimum wage. It was a protracted act of self-sabotage, of sadness seeking its own level. All was not dour, however, for the deacon. He relished the prospect of the 1974 Carnival season, and he obsessively prepared his Mardi Gras costume. In close to every facet, Courtney Craighead lived a life too distracted in these months to help a struggling church.[8]

It shouldn't be surprising, then, that New Orleans congregants appealed to national leaders for help. In the GPC's *Causeway* newspaper, Richard Vincent, a Dallas pastor assigned to rescue the flock, assessed that "a preliminary check of the Church records indicated an indebtedness of almost $2000." Vincent stated that "the first goals would be to seek funds to pay off all outstanding debts," in spite of the goodwill donations that the church had received after the fire. "Until different facilities are located," noted the story, "the MCC-New Orleans will continue meeting at its present location."[9] Within weeks, however, the bottom fell out, and Bill Larson's congregation lost the building.

TAKING ADVANTAGE OF the opportunity to jab the New Orleans Emergency Task Force in the wake of Baril's exposure, an anonymous man in New Orleans claimed that he had written a $10,000 check for Up Stairs Lounge victims, which he said that a trustee of the memorial fund had endorsed. "But never did we receive such a sum," Morris Kight would later write, "and our many calls for a photocopy of the check before and after failed, because we could never find the person." It should be noted that there is no record of a check for $10,000 in the receipts journal for the national fund, which received an outside audit. Nevertheless, the anonymous man or men would continue to call up New Orleans radio shows to voice the same complaint. "Often the shows were run by homophobes," Kight noted, "who would then tell of how horrible it all was that we should do that." Ray Broshears, a gay minister in San Francisco, also made accusations against fund trustees. The assault on the gay leaders escalated, during which many who had, or had not, given to the memorial fund felt justified in heaving brickbats at Morris Kight and Troy Perry. A gay Louisianan wrote *The Advocate* to censure its coverage of the fire, which he claimed was harming his ability to heal. Another letter from Tampa ripped into Perry, accusing the minister of wasting America's time during a TV appearance.[10]

Between July and September, it had appeared that Up Stairs Lounge would inspire a unified gay rights movement in America. Lucien Baril's embezzling and disappearance, however, provided ammunition to critics and brought an ignominious end to the New Orleans Emergency Task Force. More gay gathering places would come under attack, some within weeks. The MCC of San Francisco church burned to the ground, and a gay meetinghouse in Hawaii was destroyed by fire for the fifth time in two years. On October 2, the Indianapolis Police Department sent officers into an MCC prayer meeting and pronounced the faithful under arrest for "frequenting a dive"; Reverend John Gill flew to Indiana to lend his assistance.[11]

In New Orleans, the Gay People's Coalition dissolved shortly after losing its headquarters in the MCC building. Without GPC volunteers to petition officials, the proposed city-funded "Taskforce on Gay Problems" vanished from the Human Relations Committee agenda. City business resumed with its usual vigor. After several meetings between an architect and the mayor's office, the handsome Louis Armstrong Memorial Park, patterned on the Tivoli Gardens of Copenhagen, received approval from the City Planning Commission, with a $5.9 million budget.[12] In November Moon Landrieu easily won renomination for the 1974 mayoral election, taking 407 of 419 precincts with almost 70 percent of the vote.

TWO MONTHS AFTER New Orleans police closed their case, deputy state fire marshals finally found the time to pursue the lead about

Roger Dale Nunez having been stopped in a car in Morgan City. Tracing the car's license plates to Abbeville, the investigators contacted the local sheriff's office and confirmed the car's registered address of 305 South Valery Street, Roger's mother's house.[13]

On September 18, authorities issued a subpoena to question Roger and picked him up. Considering that investigators thought it necessary to serve a subpoena, it's clear that neither the local sheriff nor the fire marshals were aware of the outstanding warrant for Roger's parole violation. This warrant authorized more than just Roger's presence for questioning; it demanded his arrest. The New Orleans Police Department, whose headquarters were across the street from the courthouse where the warrant was issued, also seemed to be out of the loop on this discrepancy, but the NOPD wasn't participating in this roundup anyway.[14]

Roger soon sat in the company of arson investigators at the Abbeville sheriff's office. After a few inquiries, the fire marshals asked him if he would be willing to take a polygraph. Roger agreed. Because the Abbeville sheriff did not store such equipment on-site, investigators exploited a loophole by taking the suspect into custody and driving him more than a hundred miles to access a polygraph machine—from a rural police station to NOPD headquarters. Undoubtedly, this change of venue gave the fire marshals a psychological edge. They made Roger wait over a lengthy drive. Reaching the police station and ascending into the bunkerlike chambers of the Detective Bureau, the marshals found an empty interrogation room and sat the suspect in a chair. A police polygraphist stood at the ready to confirm or deny the veracity of Roger's words.[15]

As the deputy state fire marshals prepared to conduct the interrogation, neither Charles Schlosser nor Sam Gebbia, the NOPD detectives assigned to the Up Stairs Lounge case, made themselves available. Nor did any other detective pop into the room and participate, though this was the "Detective Bureau." This interview of Roger Nunez would remain absent from all police documents of the Up Stairs Lounge investigation, despite the NOPD's insistence in its "General Case Report" that "any future developments in this matter will be covered in a Supplemental Report." NOPD detectives would never find themselves able to question Roger Nunez while he lived or compile a "supplemental report," even though he walked into their offices and identified himself, while a nearby court demanded that he stand before a judge.[16] This wanted man, for whom they had searched the city since July 7, went ignored on their doorstep. The failure to acknowledge him reveals the NOPD in dereliction of the basic functions of a law enforcement agency, whereby "officers of the court" have a sworn duty to serve court orders such as warrants. Furthermore, Roger's going unnoticed in these circumstances calls into question whether he received preferential treatment from police, perhaps due to some unseemly aspect of the Up Stairs Lounge case, and challenges the sincerity of NOPD efforts to find a culprit for what amounted to thirty-two homicides. No deadlier incident would strike New Orleans in 1973.

The fire marshal investigators finally conducted an unimpeded interview of Roger from 6:25 to 6:55 p.m. on September 18. Since his release from Charity Hospital, Roger had been living in Abbeville and working as a deckhand at a place called D&B Boat Rentals. While at the boat company, Roger claimed to have survived an offshore accident. "I got a hit on the head, pretty bad," he told the investigators, "and that's what started me having more frequent seizures, than normal." Roger had left Charity with metal braces on his jaw and claimed to have traveled out of town no more than two or three times: once to a nearby orthodontist, who removed the braces, and once for a religious meeting in a town called Grand Coteau, home of a nunnery and a famous Catholic shrine for healing. He did not recall the documented trip to Morgan City.[17]

Roger recalled seeing Gene Davis around ten days after the fire, which would have been around July 7, something Davis did not mention in his July 9 statement to the NOPD. And Roger just could not piece together his visit to the Up Stairs Lounge on June 24, though he'd already admitted this to the fire marshals on July 2.[18] "No, sir" and "I don't know" were his preferred answers:

Q: Were you in the Upstairs [sic] Lounge on Sunday, June 24, 1973?
A: I could have been, sir. I don't remember for sure. I have been there before on Sundays for what the Beer Bust was.

Q: Were you there between the hours of five and seven fifty,
P.M.?

A: I don't know sir.

Q: Did you have a fight in the Upstairs Lounge on Sunday,
June 24, 1973, sometime before 6:30 p.m. and 7:00 p.m.?

A: I don't think so. I could have. I don't know for sure.

Q: Do you know if there was a fire there?

A: Yes, sir, I do know there was a fire there.

Q: Do you know who set the fire?

A: No, sir, I do not.

Q: Did you set the fire?

A: Oh, no, sir.[19]

Puzzlingly, Roger did not remember owning the 1966 Plymouth
Fury registered in his name or driving the car in July. Additionally, he
did not remember transferring ownership of the vehicle to his mother
shortly before she moved to Dallas, which had just happened in early
September. Fire marshals found and produced a bill of sale for Roger's
purchase of the Fury. They found Roger's application for a Louisiana
driver's license, in which he denied having a history of epilepsy, a condition that Roger admitted to in reference to his accident with D&B
Boat Rentals. They also found Roger's act of donation, which gifted
the car to his mother, all of which he disavowed from memory.[20]

Concerning the night of the fire, Roger couldn't recall being with
Mark Allen Guidry inside the Up Stairs Lounge and claimed not to
know Mark Allen Guidry's full name. He wasn't sure how he had
broken his jaw, although he was certain that it was not in a fight: "It's
not my nature to fight. I never fight." Roger's previous statement to
the fire marshals on July 2 about "a fight with three Negroes on Iberville Street . . . who took his wallet and knocked him down" was not
recollected. With regard to the fire scene on Iberville Street, Roger
said that he could not remember those late hours or recognize the
name Buddy Rasmussen.[21]

With his boat injury, mentioned but unverified near the middle of
the interview,[22] Roger provided justification for memory gaps, which

he cited often. Yet how could he forget owning a car for a period of several months but remember his employment at D&B Boat Rentals, where he had driven that car on workdays? How could Roger recall precisely how he had experienced an accident at D&B Boat Rentals involving a broken cable but forget the circumstances of another injury that had put him in the hospital? For an impaired human being with random access to memory, Roger did seem to recollect details that would help his position while being unable to recollect details that might draw him into entanglements.

Unhappy with the interview, the marshals signaled that it was now time for Roger Dale Nunez to face the lie detector. But the police polygraphist informed them that he couldn't perform such a test. He explained that he wouldn't be able to get an accurate read because of the suspect's epilepsy. The anticonvulsant medication in Roger's system, Dilantin, lowered stress and blood pressure to such a degree that a lie detector was ineffective. With that, the deputy state fire marshals were done.[23] They drove Roger all the way back to Abbeville. The investigators had finally had their day with him, but they had little to show for it.

In October, the Louisiana state fire marshals found another way to test Roger's truthfulness. The solution was an investigatory tool called the Dektor Psychological Stress Evaluation (PSE), a voice-mediated test billed as effective even for people with epilepsy. The Dektor PSE was designed to hear stress in vocal chords when the brain was forced to contradict a statement it knew to be false. Fire marshal investigators again drove to Abbeville, once more without NOPD counterparts. There, in the suspect's hometown, they commenced a Dektor PSE test for Roger, who by this stage had retained the services of a local attorney. Roger often spoke unevenly.[24] His voice possessed a pitchy, neurasthenic quality.

To get a baseline for stress levels, Roger spoke into an ultrasensitive microphone and was instructed to answer both yes and no to direct questions. According to the fire marshal report, "Mr. Nunez showed stress to pertinent questions about the case." When investigators instructed him to answer no to the question "Did you set the fire at the

Up Stairs Lounge?," Roger's stress levels spiked, and the test administrator made the note, "Stress indiacting [sic] that he is lying. He does
have knowledge of the crime." When instructed to answer "No" to the
question "Did you set the fire in the stairway?," Roger's stress levels
spiked again, and the administrator wrote, "Stress indicating that he
is lying. Hard Stress." Roger would answer just thirteen questions—
lasting fewer than ten minutes—before his attorney advised him to
end the assessment.[25] They rose abruptly and left.

Although Roger's Dektor PSE might seem damning, the results
only provided a semiempirical measurement of stress in his vocal
chords. Because the PSE required a trained Dektor administrator to
interpret the data, the test was prone to subjective interpretation, much
like the polygraph, and therefore difficult to present as legal evidence.[26]

AT ABOUT THE same time, a small uprising took place in America's
mental health establishment. When seventeen thousand psychologists
assembled in Montreal for the American Psychological Association's
1973 convention, gay and lesbian psychologists made themselves visible to their colleagues for the first time. An organization called the
Association of Gay Psychologists, heretofore operating behind closed
doors, took the radical step of holding an open forum and set forth an
agenda that "homosexuality be recognized as a viable alternative lifestyle rather than as a sickness." This advocacy reflected a fundamental
pivot for a clinical field that had at best contributed to homosexual
stigma and, at worst, used that stigma to turn "sexual psychopaths"
into permanent patients or human test subjects, à la the electrode
experiments of Dr. Robert Heath at Tulane University.[27]

Shortly after the revolt of psychologists, psychiatrists followed suit.
That December, the board of trustees of the American Psychiatric
Association approved a proposal to remove homosexuality as a mental illness in the *Diagnostic and Statistical Manual (DSM)*, the medical volume cited by not just doctors but also preachers and politicians
as reason to oppress homosexuals. "In the past," the resolution noted,

"homosexuals have been denied civil rights in many areas of life on the ground that because they suffer from a 'mental illness' the burden of proof is on them to demonstrate their competence, reliability or mental stability." The psychiatrists had also considered strong counterarguments. While a significant proportion of homosexuals, the proposal noted, are satisfied with their orientations, another proportion of homosexuals wish to be treated.[28]

Given this rationale, the proposal to remove homosexuality created, with the same stroke, a new condition: sexual orientation disturbance, defined as "individuals whose sexual interests are directed primarily toward people of the same sex."[29] For some gay activists, the delisting of homosexuality on the *DSM* represented a milestone. For others, it was a Pyrrhic victory, which ensured that clinically assisted attempts to convert homosexuals into heterosexuals would go forward with the same moral and legal impunity.

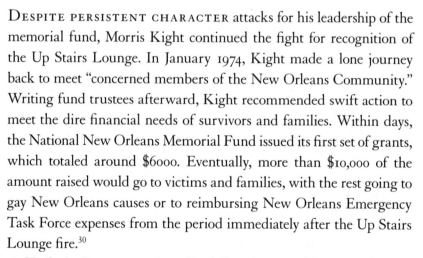

DESPITE PERSISTENT CHARACTER attacks for his leadership of the memorial fund, Morris Kight continued the fight for recognition of the Up Stairs Lounge. In January 1974, Kight made a lone journey back to meet "concerned members of the New Orleans Community." Writing fund trustees afterward, Kight recommended swift action to meet the dire financial needs of survivors and families. Within days, the National New Orleans Memorial Fund issued its first set of grants, which totaled around $6000. Eventually, more than $10,000 of the amount raised would go to victims and families, with the rest going to gay New Orleans causes or to reimbursing New Orleans Emergency Task Force expenses from the period immediately after the Up Stairs Lounge fire.[30]

Up Stairs Lounge survivors Fred Sharohway and Eugene Thomas, who'd scalded themselves by running down the burning staircase, received $618.15 and $718, respectively, most of which went directly to creditors. Survivor Michael Scarborough, who amassed a staggering $4900 in hospital bills during his long months in care, received $300 for personal expenses; he would be counseled to declare bankruptcy to clear his debts. Jeanne Gosnell, who remained bedridden and isolated at home following her release from the U.S. Public Health Service Hospital, received $171.50 to install a phone line in her apartment so that she could reach the outside world.[31]

Up Stairs Lounge victim John Golding's widow, Jane, received $360 to pay the private school tuition for her son John Jr. The night of the fire, Jane had stayed awake in front of the television watching the news coverage with her three children, whom she had alerted to the emergency. She repeatedly telephoned Charity Hospital, but they didn't have answers. She and John had lived a charade as a happy "Ozzie and Harriet"–type couple, but the circumstances of his death in a gay bar laid bare the family secret. When the reality set in, Jane went ghostly white and fell over in medical shock. Her daughter, who was studying to be a medical tech, had to elevate her mother's feet and cover her in blankets until she came to. "I fell asleep praying," recalled John Jr. "At the time, I was a religious little fellow, just praying, 'Oh let this be a mistake, let Dad come home.'"[32]

Afterward, people snickered around Jane, and she was forced to pull John Jr. from public school when bullies began to prey on him—a tall gangly youth, now without a father, who hadn't yet been taught to defend himself. Administrators turned a blind eye, and Jane feared what would happen if playground peers discovered the "queer" circumstances of the death of the boy's father. Jane hoped and prayed that a new set of classmates at a new Catholic middle school wouldn't bother young John about his family.[33]

In spite of Lucien Baril's questionable stewardship of donations intended for the fire survivors, Morris Kight sent a letter on behalf of trustees of the memorial fund to the former pastor, who by then had returned to his old name, Richard Green, and was facing legal troubles in Dallas. In the letter, Kight sounded sympathetic. He expressed love and appreciation for Baril's actions after the fire. "Without your deep Christian and brotherly concern," wrote Kight, "our work would have been far more difficult, if not impossible."[34] It seems probable that, given the timing of the communiqué and the distribution of grants to victims, this letter was an attempt to ensure that Baril didn't cause future problems.

———————— ꙮ ————————

EMBOLDENED BY THE FAILURE of arson investigators to prove their case against him, Roger Dale Nunez had moved back to New Orleans by January 1974, shortly before Mardi Gras season and right before his twenty-seventh birthday. He reported his work accident to the federal government and began receiving disability checks. Roger also sought psychiatric help at U.S. Public Health Service Hospital, where a physician treated him for conversion hysteria—a catch-all disorder through which various physical conditions, such as blindness or seizures, can manifest out of psychological stress.[35]

Roger used his welfare checks to pay rent in a downtown flophouse called the Imperial Hotel and, on the side, have some fun. His tenure in the hotel coincided with the building becoming a halfway house funded by the Catholic archdiocese. At the Imperial, Roger shared a room with a thirty-five-year-old cook named Ralph Forest. He befriended and then received the loving affections of this slightly older man, who was eager to please him sexually, financially, and otherwise. They made frequent love in what Forest called a "fifty-fifty proposition" of giving and receiving.[36]

In December of 1973, Phil Esteve, the owner of the Up Stairs Lounge, opened a new gay watering hole called the Post Office. Located on St. Louis Street in the French Quarter, it was the heir to his ill-fated bar. "Much of the same kind of funky décor—complete with elevated dance floor—that pervaded the Up-stairs is in evidence at The Post Office," read one notice. Buddy Rasmussen resumed his old position, working as Esteve's bartender and manager, and former Up Stairs patrons like Michael Scarborough and Ricky Everett soon became regular faces.[37] Life had to go on.

Post Office patrons continued the ritual of holding hands and singing "United We Stand" at the close of each evening. Formerly, the song had been an affirmation of togetherness; now, it seemed like a dirge that dampened the atmosphere. Still, even with "United We Stand" playing and men with burn scars crooning in tears, Roger Dale Nunez had the unabashed temerity to show up at the Post Office with his boyfriend. Fortunately for them, regulars like Michael Scarborough were not there on the nights they visited.[38]

That Mardi Gras, February 26, 1974, Roger Dale Nunez took a break from the costumes and bead "throws." He spotted Sister Mary Stephen Ledet, a middle-aged member of a Roman Catholic order, in the lobby of the Imperial Hotel and approached her. The nun had been watching parades and laughing. She had sauntered into the hotel to explore her new place of mission. Ledet, wearing her traditional habit, must have seemed like a representation of the Blessed Mother to Roger, who had grown up religious. Roger introduced himself and asked Sister Mary Stephen Ledet to counsel him. To Ledet, Roger must have appeared as a wounded soul, and she obliged. The two sat and communed on Fat Tuesday, even though Ash Wednesday—the time of sobriety and reflection—was but hours away.[39]

Roger confessed to Ledet of his "conflicting impulses" toward other men, which led her to give the advice that "no matter how low you are, you can always make something of yourself." The two became friends, in the way that clergy can sometimes blindly define friendship. "She said he was a mixed up human being," the fire marshals wrote after an interview with Ledet on November 20, 1974. "And he always said she expected more of him than he could give the world." Ledet began to regularly counsel Roger on the phone and in person, and Roger began calling her by the pet name Mawa, baby talk for "mama." "He didn't, he didn't like to er, to be gay and that er, threw him," Ledet later admitted to the authorities, with some amount of embarrassment. "His problems all stemmed from that, you know," she continued, "he couldn't, he, he reached the point where he couldn't accept himself for what he was." Roger soon gained the confidence to speak about a haunting event. "She said he made a statement to her that they had taken him in for questioning about the Up Stairs Lounge," the fire marshals would later report.[40]

Roger told an appalling story to Ledet, presuming that anything he said would be protected within a spiritual "vow of secrecy" similar to that of a priest hearing confessions. "She said he tried to impress her, as if he wasn't masculine," the fire report continued, "and that she thought that's how it [the subject of the Up Stairs Lounge] came in, that he tried to impress her that he did something, that they thought he had done something now, you know, big." Roger affirmed to Sister Mary Stephen Ledet that he, in words she seemingly admitted later on to Fire Superintendent William McCrossen, "torched the Up Stairs Lounge."[41]

But it was also a confession that she would flatly deny to state fire marshal investigators when they questioned her in 1974, in an official capacity. Evidently, as Ledet later explained to McCrossen, she felt that she had reason to protect the man who once baby-talked her, who would tell a childless woman, "You're my Mawa." After Roger made his admission, Ledet vowed to never tell another soul about what he said. She believed that Roger had mistakenly confessed to a capital crime with the belief that his words would fall within the Catholic sacrament of reconciliation, a theologically and somewhat legally protected act of contrition that only a Catholic priest can administer. Because the Roman Catholic Church believed reconciliation to be a divine ritual, a plea for secrecy or forgiveness in relation to that sacrament held utmost gravity. It seems that reconciliation, even when bungled, offered Roger Dale Nunez a kind of holy insurance policy.[42]

Under a different set of circumstances, Roger confessed to his boyfriend that he had set the Up Stairs Lounge fire. He first broached the subject with Ralph Forest after Mardi Gras day (around the time he confessed to Ledet) and affirmed the story again on a random night when the two were drinking at Wanda's on Iberville Street. The proximity of Wanda's to the ruins of the Up Stairs Lounge would make it a logical setting for an inebriated disclosure: Roger could see down the street and remember what happened there. "A friend of mine by the name of Roger Nunez," Ralph Forest later told the fire investigators, "has admitted to me several times under the influence of alcohol that he had started the fire at the Up Stairs Lounge. When I questioned him when he was sober regarding the fire, he wouldn't admit it."[43]

As to how Roger started the fire, Ralph Forest recalled: "According to what he told me and this was just once, that he used lighter fluid purchased from Walgreens." Each time that Roger told this story to his lover, Forest couldn't tell whether Roger wanted him to be glad or sad that he had gotten away with a heinous crime. His lover tended to make the admission matter-of-factly. When asked by the fire marshal why he had not immediately gone to the police or other authorities with such information, Forest explained, "Because I didn't believe that he had done it and also because I still had feelings toward him."[44]

On March 7, 1974, John P. BonneCarrere, a state probation officer assigned to Roger Dale Nunez's case, finally found his missing parolee. BonneCarrere wrote a letter to Judge Shea of the Orleans Parish Criminal Court describing the encounter: "I informed your honor that we had located the subject and that he had recently undergone brain surgery and we therefore did not effect his arrest at this time. The subject was under the mistaken impression that he had not been on probation."[45] Impressively, it seems that Roger appealed to BonneCarrere for compassion due to health reasons and won sympathy from a member of the criminal justice system with a legal responsibility to serve the warrant.

RALPH FOREST REMAINED steadfast in his love for Roger, despite the confessions of firesetting, even as the younger man's health deteriorated. Roger underwent a risky and ultimately unsuccessful brain surgery to remove a frontal lobe tumor at the U.S. Public Health Service Hospital in April 1974, and Forest nursed and supported him afterward. After weeks of painful recovery, Roger rose from their bed and promptly informed Ralph that their relationship was over. Roger, according to Forest, moved from their room in Lafayette Square to an apartment on Iberville. Attempting to start fresh, perhaps invigorated by his surgery or inspired by Sister Mary Stephen Ledet's teachings, Roger romantically pursued a woman more than twenty years his senior.[46]

Roger Nunez and Elaine Wharton Bassett met by chance when he was babysitting the child of a Wanda's bartender in New Orleans East.

This friend of Roger's had a small cottage that offered a stunning view of Lake Pontchartrain over the lip of the levee across the street. Bassett happened to live two doors down from where Roger was babysitting.[47] In a neighborly way, she must have come over to visit.

Elaine Wharton Bassett—a vibrant, financially independent fifty-year-old—was immediately drawn to the young suitor. Perhaps she fell in love with him. Perhaps she felt sorry for him. Perhaps she wanted to mother him or be his angel. In any combination of these ways, Bassett became spellbound. Judging by the timing of their union, any preambles to old-fashioned courtship gave way to passion. Curiously, it seems that the couple didn't find time to "test the waters" in bed during their wooing. Roger called friends—even Ralph Forest—to celebrate this newfound love. To Sister Mary Stephen Ledet, it must have seemed like the ultimate conversion; a man who'd been in a homosexual relationship in March and April had straightened out his life and found heterosexual bliss. Roger Dale Nunez married Elaine Wharton Bassett on May 17, 1974, at the Algiers Courthouse, just across the river from the French Quarter.[48]

With their nuptials in place, they proceeded to the boudoir, where Roger admitted his homosexuality to his new bride and also told her that he was impotent. With these words, Roger dashed the hopes of the woman to whom he just pledged lifelong fidelity. It's difficult to discern whether Roger had believed that the recitation of marital vows would magically cure his homosexual tendencies—as Sister Mary Stephen Ledet may have hinted was possible through intercession of the divine—or if Roger had merely been attempting to deceive an older partner in love for financial benefit. Bassett, no doubt, was devastated by Roger's wedding-night confession. Mercifully, she did not seek an annulment and allowed her young, ill, unemployed spouse to move into a trailer in her backyard while they sorted out their future plans.[49]

In a demonstration of stoic commitment to her new spouse, Bassett then took the dramatic step of changing her legal name to Elaine Bassett Nunez. During the months that Roger lived in her backyard, he also continued to receive his monthly Social Security disability check of $146, which proved to be insufficient for his expenditures. Subsequently, he began forging checks in his wife's name and cashing them at Pirate's Den, another Iberville Street bar. Indeed, he continued to drink near the ruin of the Up Stairs Lounge as the first anniversary of the catastrophe approached. This anniversary went largely unobserved.[50] The MCC of New Orleans, after all, barely kept a foothold in town.

A few people, however, would try to remember what happened. In one of the memorial fund's last attempts to keep the memory of the fire alive, trustees disbursed some $200 so survivor Jeanne Gosnell could fly to Los Angeles and be a guest of honor in the reinstated Christopher Street West parade for Gay Pride. As a scarred survivor, with at least 60 percent of her body still healing, Gosnell rode down Hollywood Boulevard in a layered dress and sun hat. She attended a rally in honor of the Up Stairs Lounge victims at De Longpre Park (Los Angeles, in fact, appears to be the only city to hold a public Up Stairs Lounge memorial in 1974). Although Gosnell couldn't say much to the crowd—it was still too difficult to talk about the death of Luther Boggs—she conveyed in few words the extent of the suffering, the lives lost, and her six months in the hospital. The tragedy, Gosnell observed, "seemed to bring us all together."[51]

Later that summer, on August 15, a New Orleanian who had taken a risk by offering help to Troy Perry during the last week of June 1973 died of metastatic lung cancer in the French Quarter. Clay Shaw had perished at sixty. Earlier in 1974, Shaw had suffered a blood clot to his brain and underwent a surgery that rendered one side of his body paralyzed. The condition had forced him to resign from his coveted post at the French Market Corporation, a job he'd assumed courageously—given the efforts it took, following his trial, to hold his head up high. According to an obituary printed in the *Pittsburgh Post-Gazette,* Shaw died with a $5 million civil lawsuit pending against former New Orleans district attorney Jim Garrison. With the primary litigant deceased, that case now couldn't proceed.[52]

Clay Shaw's obituary made the front page of the *Times-Picayune.* The city's paper of record took stock of the man as "one of the founders of International Trade Mart and the man acquitted of charges of conspiring to assassinate John F. Kennedy." *The New York Times*

called him "the businessman who was acquitted of plotting to assassinate President Kennedy after one of the nation's more sensational trials," while mentioning the accusations of homosexuality. Indeed, Jim
Garrison's crusade marred Shaw's reputation in death. None of these
obituaries would recognize Shaw's gesture of compassion for the Up
Stairs Lounge victims. Even in his most vulnerable condition, Shaw
had attempted to help others.[53]

———————— ⚬ ————————

As 1974 PROGRESSED, Roger's condition worsened. In between bouts
of partying, passing bad checks in his wife's name, and recuperating in
the backyard trailer, he had a stay at a mental health institution in Man-
deville, Louisiana. He scheduled yet another round of brain surgeries
for early fall. At some point, Elaine Bassett Nunez must have decided
that she'd had enough of her young husband. Public notice for the sep-
aration of their marriage appeared in the *Times-Picayune* on September
12. As the divorce proceedings went on, Roger continued to occupy the
trailer behind her residence, never once sleeping in the house.[54]

On the early morning of November 15, Roger Dale Nunez took
his own life by mixing Dilantin, his epilepsy medication, with three
vials of barbiturates and guzzling it all down with six cans of beer.
His soon-to-be ex-wife found him on the floor of a backyard shed and
called the police when she could not revive him. The coroner pronounced him dead on sight at 12:30 p.m. With no small amount of
grace, Elaine Bassett Nunez notified Ralph Forest, a man she knew
loved her husband, of the premature death, and Forest called Sister
Mary Stephen Ledet. Both were devastated by the news.[55]

An autopsy would reveal a "thick walled cystic lesion of dura" in
the "right front area" of Roger's brain. In fact, Roger Dale Nunez had
a skull-based tumor growing in his cerebral cortex, despite clear sur-
gical attempts to alleviate it. Such lesions could have contributed to a
vast range of anomalous behaviors. The autopsy provided proof of a
mental disturbance, revealing a body and a mind at war. After Roger's death, a grief-stricken Ralph Forest wandered, brokenhearted,

throughout the French Quarter. He made his way to the Post Office, finding owner Phil Esteve behind the bar. Esteve at first listened sympathetically as Forest confided that his lover had died. Then the customer mentioned the man's name.[56]

Overhearing the conversation, Michael Scarborough exclaimed, "Is it true? Is he dead?"

"Yes," Forest answered.

"That is the one that set the Up Stairs Lounge [fire], you know," Scarborough said, before sharing his own story about a perished lover: Glenn Green.[57]

Pressured by several Up Stairs Lounge survivors gathered at the Post Office that day, Forest admitted that Roger had confessed to him about setting the fire, on multiple occasions. Phil Esteve later called the state fire marshal's office, which sought Forest for questioning.[58] The New Orleans Police Department never took the same step.

Rodger Dale Nunez—his legal name was restored in the end—received a Catholic funeral service, well attended by friends and locals, at the countryside St. Anne Church. Blood relations in Abbeville, it seems, emerged to reclaim their own, and the parish priest received special thanks from the family afterwards: "We will always remember your thoughtfulness in our time of need." Roger was buried with military honors (a courtesy denied World War II vet Ferris LeBlanc, who had seen battlefield time) in the Nunez family plot at Harrington Cemetery in Forked Island, Louisiana. His remains were interred in an elegant marble cairn beside the grave of his uncle Shelton. His gravestone, recognizing his Specialist 4th Class status during the Vietnam War, received a regular setting of fresh flowers.[59]

Roger died as he lived—in a state of obscurity, concealment, and confusion. He was a lovable yet unloving man, a grifter who twisted the charity of others, someone who took people into his confidence and then scared them with his disclosures.[60] Roger did not have an obituary or a public death notice in the *Times-Picayune* or any other major newspaper; only Abbeville publications took note. He did not receive a traditional jazz funeral in New Orleans, and it could be said that few drank to his memory.

Years later, Miss Fury, a drag queen who worked at Wanda's on Iberville Street, came forward with a story that Roger had also confessed to setting the Up Stairs Lounge fire to her as she bartended. "He'd only meant to cause a little fire and some smoke," she told historian Johnny Townsend. "He'd only meant to scare everybody." Roger closed his eyes to the world having never admitted on the record what he, in private, confessed to at least three individuals: the negligent homicide of thirty-two people. Up Stairs Lounge survivor Stewart Butler offered Roger a small pardon: "I doubt he could have had any idea, when he set the fire, what was going to happen."[61]

Former *New York Times* reporter Roy Reed, without naming Roger Nunez, postulated on what the arsonist might have felt. "It occurs to me that the guy or the guys who were responsible for this, who had to have been in the neighborhood when the fire broke out, must have realized what they had done, that the fire that they had set had killed these people in the most horrible way imaginable," he said. "I've tried to put myself in the mind or minds of those two guys, and I can't even imagine the nightmares that they might have had from those few minutes of unmanageable rage, when they impulsively lit that fire, and had the rest of their lives to regret it. You have to wonder whether a suicide might have been connected to it."[62]

Above all, Roger's legacy was more rascal than rogue. He proved to be a misunderstood intelligence who relied upon a practiced display of weakness to manipulate great acts of compassion from ex-friends, ex-employers, ex-counselors, and ex-lovers, as well as parole officers and policemen. Some would rather perjure themselves than harm him. Consumed by agony, he revisited that agony on his fellow invisibles. He was almost pathological in his desire to get what he could from situations, harming others whether or not he had been provoked. Roger was also, paradoxically, a deeply religious soul who believed that the holiness of his intentions counterweighted his choices.[63] Given the preponderance of evidence, one cannot say conclusively that his life was the only one he took.

CHAPTER 14

Rally Forth

November 1974–1979

W hile gay activism in New Orleans virtually collapsed,[1] the power of Gay Liberation swelled into a national movement that displayed its strength in manifest ways.

The municipalities of Seattle, Minneapolis, Washington, D.C., Berkeley, California, and Austin, Texas, for example, all passed ordinances to prevent discrimination against homosexuals. The states of Massachusetts, Ohio, Arkansas, and North Dakota had rolled back sodomy laws and decriminalized same-gender sex.[2] Meanwhile, an enlisted serviceman in the air force decided to test the military's ban on homosexuality by coming out, in writing, to his commanding officer. "After some years of uncertainty, I have arrived at the conclusion that my sexual preferences are homosexual as opposed to heterosexual," wrote Sergeant Leonard Matlovich. As a consequence, Matlovich, who had been honored with a Bronze Star and a Purple Heart during Vietnam, received a general discharge—not an honorable one—from the armed forces, ending his career with a note of reproach. Matlovich then reached iconic status when his face graced the cover of *Time* magazine with the headline "I Am a Homosexual."[3]

As mayors of Atlanta and Los Angeles proclaimed Gay Days in their cities, Mayor Moon Landrieu remained tightlipped as the closet of New Orleans reclaimed its former hold. In the French Quarter, gay "Southern Decadent" parties blossomed into masked street parades with grand marshals—the first public festivals for homosexuals in city history.[4] But these to-dos were minuscule compared with the biggest and most heralded celebration in town: the opening of the $163 million Superdome in 1975. Landrieu attended the ribbon-cutting ceremonies. Comedian Bob Hope hosted. Raquel Welch sang. Archbishop Philip Hannan gave the invocation to a crowd of more than forty thousand.[5]

About a mile away from the stadium, Deacon Courtney Craighead soldiered on as a provisional leader of the MCC of New Orleans. He continued the search for a new minister alongside fire survivor Ricky Everett.[6] In 1975, Courtney and Ricky selected Mary Morris, a pastor whom they hoped could stabilize the congregation.

Morris decided that her first act should be to realign the church with its tragic legacy. Overruling words of caution from her deacons, she hosted an anniversary service for the Up Stairs Lounge fire in June 1975. This was to be the first such memorial in New Orleans in two years, but Morris's efforts, though well intentioned, failed to gather support. She soon stepped aside. Ricky Everett was promoted to the role of deacon for a span but eventually grew tired of the disarray. He parted ways with the MCC of New Orleans when he felt that the church had lost all sense of direction. "The way the people wanted to run the church just was not what I considered led by the spirit of God," he explained. "They were trying what they thought was the right thing to do, but these people were more involved in doing Mardi Gras clubs and running the Mardi Gras clubs."[7]

Adept at turning life's corners, Ricky moved on from the spiritual home of his deceased best friend, Bill Larson. "You've got to. You can't sit back and have the attitude, 'I don't think I can do that, that's crazy,'" explained Ricky. "You just do it. That's all it is." He eventually relocated to the New Orleans suburbs and found success in myriad careers, from steamship operations and publishing companies to interior design firms. He fell in love with a man whom he called his "husband," although their union lacked legal status, and outlived the devastation of the man dying of a sudden heart attack. Eventually, Ricky found the strength to speak and preach about the terrible blaze.[8] Enduring tragedy had made him a consummate survivor.

———————⌣⩊⌣———————

IN JULY 1975, after two years of investigation, state fire marshal investigators presented the case for arson at the Up Stairs Lounge to Orleans Parish District Attorney Harry Connick (father of the famous crooner Harry Connick Jr.). Although the fire marshal conceded that the prime arson suspect was dead by suicide, investigators asked the DA to accept their conclusion that Roger Dale Nunez was the man who lit the blaze that killed thirty-two people. Deputy state fire marshals deemed this a fitting denouement. Since Roger was deceased, and the criminal justice system wasn't designed to try the accused postmortem, charges of manslaughter and/or negligent homicide could not be forthcoming as a result of Connick's sign-off.[9]

Investigators simply wanted closure, which Connick's review and endorsement would provide. However, Connick reviewed the case in full and declined to accept the fire marshal's conclusion. This act of dismissal, given without explanation, garnered little attention, even though an earlier *Times-Picayune* story announced that the DA was reviewing the arson case while noting how "millions of dollars in lawsuits were filed by relatives of those who died and persons injured in the blaze."[10]

Considering that injured parties were seeking civil damages from city and state agencies, and that acceptance of the fire marshals' findings would accelerate the release of relevant files, Connick's dismissal had the effect of leaving the Up Stairs Lounge investigation perpetually open—thereby making evidence more difficult to access by opposing attorneys. Such delays created a legal blockade, and opposing attorneys were compelled to sue agencies like the fire department simply to access their documents.[11]

As it happened, the New Orleans Fire Department had yet to issue a report on the Up Stairs Lounge in 1975, even though the National Fire Protection Association had published its findings the previous year. In that report, flame tests on the indoor-outdoor carpeting inside the bar conducted by the National Bureau of Standards (a federal agency) revealed the material to be "Class E," a category considered too flammable for use in a place of public assembly. Patrons had been standing on a fire hazard. This carpet, which transferred flames from the stairwell to the bar within seconds, had passed New Orleans fire safety inspections on multiple occasions.[12]

Such discoveries encouraged the injured parties seeking restitution, and more files from never-ending investigations had to be subpoenaed and submitted in privileged status with clerks of the court—presuming that those agencies seeking to avoid disclosures would be nonetheless transparent. (As a matter of record, the seven-page NOFD report, now available to the public, was a handwritten document dated "6/24–25/73." Casework ended the day after the fire, and little clerical time was devoted to preparing the report itself. Only a seven-page supplemental report, an NOFD summary of National Fire Protection Association conclusions, appears to have been typewritten at a later date.[13])

Bill Rushton and his writers faithfully reported the legal proceedings in the *Vieux Carré Courier* and *The Advocate*. "NOFD Public Relations Officer Richard Blackmon concedes that prompt reports were issued in three of the city's other major blazes in recent years," wrote Rushton. "The only 'official' Up Stairs fire document produced thus far, Blackmon says, is an internal memorandum from the Fire Chief to the city's Chief Administrative Officer, a memorandum protected from public inspection by state law."[14]

In sworn depositions, Anthony Guarino, owner of 604 Iberville (the building formerly rented by the Up Stairs Lounge), admitted to having run an illegal bookmaking operation to fund his real estate holdings. For reasons unexplained, opposing attorneys made inquiries as to whether Guarino had offered bribes to an agent of the Louisiana state fire marshal.[15]

EVEN AS INTEREST in the fire waned, and while evidence continued to be hoarded, questions persisted among family members and former lovers of the victims. Many of those inquiring had not seen or heard from estranged kin, like Ferris LeBlanc or Reggie Adams, for what felt like eons. Marc Schmitz, a classmate who had known and loved Reggie Adams back in Dallas, wrote their high school, Jesuit College Prep, to inquire about his whereabouts. On June 10, 1976, Schmitz received a response from a priest who knew them both: Reggie had died in a New Orleans fire nearly three years before.[16]

Around this time, Ernest "Dutch" Morial, the former Armstrong Park committee cochair serving on the state Court of Appeals, joined a three-judge panel reviewing $28 million in civil complaints brought by Up Stairs Lounge survivors and families against the City of New Orleans, the Louisiana Office of the State Fire Marshal, and Up Stairs Lounge owner Phil Esteve, among others. This class-action lawsuit, on appeal after being heard and dismissed by a state judge at the district level, claimed gross negligence by multiple parties for failure to maintain a safe building for bar patrons—a building that, with a small can of lighter fluid and a single spark, went up like a tinderbox.[17] Rather than settle for a lesser sum with each plaintiff, the city and the state resolved to fight these nineteen consolidated lawsuits and hope for a favorable outcome.

Officials would not be disappointed. In February 1977, the appeals court ruled two to one that plaintiffs could not sue city or state agencies for damages due to "failure to inspect or negligent inspection." In its ruling, the court cited an earlier case, involving a negligent dog-catcher and a roving dog with rabies, as precedent. Interestingly, the appeals court did not consider whether a failure to inspect the Up Stairs Lounge for more than two years prior to June 1973, a period of time in breach of state safety standards, or the failure to cite flammable carpeting during inspections might create a unique form of liability.[18] Fire inspectors thus received legal carte blanche for duties not performed or performed unsatisfactorily.

Shrewdly, Judge Morial distanced himself from accusations of harshness for a legal decision that would compare a deadly inferno to a rabid dog with a one-sentence dissent that took issue with "that part of the opinion which affirms the decision of the district court maintaining the defendants' exceptions of no right and/or no cause of action."[19] Even a progressive judge in 1977 could not expose himself further than to say that the Up Stairs Lounge victims had a right to sue someone—just not the public institutions with money. With his dissent, Morial upheld his reputation while assenting to a legal decision that saved his city and state a treasure trove of cash.

Thus, the state Court of Appeals denied plaintiffs like widow Jane Golding a requested $2 million (for the loss of John Golding's income) and Bud Matyi's daughter, Tina, a requested $500,000 (to secure the financial future that her deceased father could no longer provide for). For survivors and families, this court decision represented the final stake that vanquished their chances for any substantial recompense.[20] The civil court system would not redeem their grievances in the absence of criminal justice. "All we had to keep us going was Social Security," John Golding Jr. recalled about his mother's finances after his father's death. "So anything that we could have gotten from a lawsuit or from whatever party would have been extremely helpful. We were on the edge, and thank goodness that no major health issues or anything else came up."[21]

Freed from financial liabilities, the city and state carried on while Up Stairs Lounge owner Phil Esteve and building owner Anthony Guarino ended up settling with the plaintiffs for a total of $80,000 (a trivial sum once divided among the plaintiffs). Duane Mitchell and his brother, Stephen, whose mother and grandparents did not make efforts to participate in the lawsuit, received nothing from the settlement to offset the premature passing of their father, Mitch. "I've never seen a dime of it," Duane insisted. Over time, this sum somehow became worse than nothing to young Duane—large enough to put a price on a head and small enough to rot his trust in his fellow man.[22]

———— ✧ ————

YET GAY LIFE continued to thrive in the Quarter—a nexus for queer parties. Southern Decadence became an annual occasion, and Mardi Gras festivities hosted by Bill Rushton drew Christine Jorgensen, the transgender activist widely believed to be the first American to receive sexual reassignment surgery, and the legendary gonzo journalist Hunter S. Thompson. According to *Bob Damron's Address Book*, there were more than forty gay and lesbian hangouts in New Orleans in 1977, with twenty-seven owned and operated by homosexuals. Gay vacationers in search of light entertainment now took in "nellydrama" shows held at the Fatted Calf by the re-formed Up Stairs Theatre, although few attendees understood the "Up Stairs" being referenced. Out-of-towners in the mood for the kind of drag revues once performed at the Up Stairs Lounge now came to the Post Office, Phil Esteve's establishment, where female impersonators lip-synched to popular ballads. A few of these queens had even performed at the Up Stairs Lounge, but no melancholy remembrances would be forthcoming during crowd-pleasing shows. Bartender and manager Buddy Rasmussen, no doubt overwhelmed by memories of Adam Fontenot during these routines, abruptly quit his job in the middle of a shift.[23]

Reportedly, Buddy returned the next morning to toss his keys at Phil Esteve. "He was never the same after [the fire]," recalled Steven Duplantis. "I remember visiting with him somewhere and him just about breaking down and saying, 'There's so much more I coulda done, half my fault.'" Buddy never worked in another bar again. He withdrew farther from the crowds and began a career in a shipyard that lasted until his retirement in the 1990s. He would, however, be named Queen of Mardi Gras for the gay Krewe of Amon-Ra in 1983. Buddy eventually moved to a plot of land in the Arkansas countryside, a place of trees and sunny glades.[24]

As the Quarter's old guard maintained its predominant hold on the gay scene, Ed Martinez, now reporting for the weekly *Vieux Carré Star,* took umbrage with the status quo. In a 1978 cover story, Martinez broke the silence by asking his readers, "Where are the gay activists in New Orleans?" Martinez chided the lack of "militant gay activity" in his city, while citing the deep "ghettoization of gays" and the persistent lack of kinship between closeted and out communities. Turning to the Up Stairs Lounge as a patent example of the lack of progress, Martinez rued how "nothing could have given a gay community more reason to band together than that horrible tragedy." Yet, in his words, "after the fire at the Up Stairs Lounge, everything has returned to normal. Nothing to raise gay consciousness has happened."[25]

Phil Esteve was incensed by the story and called Martinez to give him a lecture. Esteve explained, in an on-the-record interview, that the historic fire's politicization and controversy demonstrated precisely why there was no need for gay activists in town. Eager to critique Troy Perry and Morris Kight's activities in 1973, Esteve harangued them for taking "the attitude that they were in New Orleans to tell the local community what should be done, not to try to help in a time of crisis." Calling Perry and Kight a "divisive force," Esteve voiced further doubts about the National New Orleans Memorial Fund by noting how "there was a feeling among the survivors that the funds that Kight was administrating were being mishandled, if not actually misappropriated." Esteve went on to postulate that "perhaps there is some correlation between the amount of gay activism in other cities and the degree of police harassment," noting what he interpreted as the success of New Orleans's "live and let live" relationship between homosexuals and police.[26] Human rights and visibility for homosexuals, in the mind of a man whose bar had burned to the ground without explanation, came secondary to homosexuals' ability to muddle through without attracting trouble.

Leagues away from New Orleans, national Gay Liberation groups continued their push for the expansion of civil rights for gays and lesbians. On January 18, 1977, the Dade County Commission, with jurisdiction over Miami, approved an ordinance to outlaw discrimination on the basis of sexual orientation. This legislation, heralded as a victory for gays in Florida, led to an unanticipated backlash from conservative Christians on a level not seen in American politics since Prohibition. Prior to the passage of this ordinance, Gay Liberation's greatest adversaries had been members of law enforcement, such as Los Angeles police chief Ed Davis or New Orleans police major Henry Morris. But, with the triumph in Dade County, Gay Liberation inspired a new political nemesis: the thirty-six-year-old Bible-thumping singer Anita Bryant.[27]

Bryant's antihomosexual Save Our Children coalition arrived on the scene as a veritable hurricane and effectively manipulated fears of pedophilia to push for an overturn of gay rights in Dade County. Bryant, who had been second runner-up at the 1959 Miss America pageant and was now the lipsticked spokeswoman for Florida orange juice, deftly used her media savvy to become the voice of an American public previously too mortified to discuss homosexuality. Within weeks, her campaign had garnered more than 64,000 signatures to put the question of gay nondiscrimination on the ballot, so that voters could decide whether to approve or repeal the ordinance.[28]

Bryant was winning, and winning handily, in a newfound game of identity politics. Frequently citing her four school-age kids as exemplars, Bryant claimed that the new law "discriminates against my children's rights to grow up in a healthy, decent community." Homosexual rights, in Bryant's view, were part of a conspiracy to corrupt the nation's young. Her fear of homosexuals preying upon children was founded in the faulty concept of "gay recruitment," or the idea that homosexuality was not a biological orientation but a debauched lifestyle that the vulnerable could be seduced into joining.[29]

With her folksy aphorisms, Bryant made a compelling case that since homosexuals can't reproduce, they need a continuous supply of fresh blood for their aberrant practices. No gesture of legitimization for gay citizens seemed too slight to escape her penchant for public shaming. When President Carter invited two dozen leaders from the National Gay Task Force, including Troy Perry, to the White House in March 1977, she issued sharp words: "I protest the action of the White House staff in dignifying these activists for special privilege with a serious discussion of their alleged 'human rights.'" That Carter stayed at Camp David while White House aide Midge Costanza met the gay leaders did not assuage her. "Behind the high-sounding appeal against discrimination in jobs and housing, which is not a problem to the 'closet' homosexual," she continued, "they are really asking to be blessed in their abnormal life style by the office of the President of the United States." With Carter's absence, Troy Perry privately rued that he missed an opportunity to tell a president about the Up Stairs Lounge fire.[30]

Bryant's crusade in metropolitan Miami triumphed on June 7 when voters repealed the gay nondiscrimination ordinance by a two-to-one margin. "Anita Wins, Gay Rights Defeated," read the front-page headline of the *Chicago Tribune*. St. Paul, Minnesota; Eugene, Oregon; Wichita, Kansas; and Seattle, Washington were all considering similar rollbacks. Mainstream Americans, it seemed, had beaten back sex radicals through the commonsensical voice of a mother figure. Jubilant, Anita Bryant danced before cameras at the victory rally and told *The New York Times*, "All America and all the world will hear what the people have said, and with God's continued help, we will prevail."[31]

Gay Liberation leaders rebounded with ire. Sensing weakness in an opposition built around one core personality, gay groups retaliated directly against Bryant and strategized ways to kneecap her where it counted: in her professional ability to reap rewards from her celebrity. The National Gay Task Force called for a universal boycott of orange juice. Seventy percent of Bryant's concert bookings canceled, and Bryant adapted by accepting what few performance opportunities she could get, including a Shriners' concert in Chicago and events in Southern cities like Houston and New Orleans. On June 14 in Chicago, three thousand Midwestern gay men and lesbians encircled the Shriners' concert at the Medinah Temple chanting "Pray for Anita." In Houston, two days later, eight thousand people marched with Troy Perry to an anti-Bryant rally outside the annual convention for the Texas State Bar Association at the Hyatt Regency, where she had booked her concert.[32]

In New Orleans, organizers had the benefit of national momentum to plan a fitting welcome for Bryant. Indeed, Gay Liberation's successes in Chicago and Houston helped closeted New Orleanians develop an appetite for politics. The city's Municipal Auditorium had already agreed to host Bryant as part of an orchestra series called the Summer Pops, so gay activists like Bill Rushton seized the opportunity for a political head-to-head. Rushton met with leaders of seven gay and lesbian organizations to found the Human Equal Rights for Everyone (HERE) coalition to oppose Bryant. Seven of the city's gay Carnival krewes joined. In this campaign, Rushton worked with the benefit of an "inside man" at the Municipal Auditorium in Roberts Batson, who managed the venue. "I knew I was gay from when I was eight," explained Batson, a gentleman cut from a similar cloth as Tennessee Williams. In a show of cross-movement solidarity, the National Organization for Women and the Southern Christian Leadership Conference also endorsed HERE.[33]

Rod Wagener, who, as most industry colleagues knew, lost Bud Matyi at the Up Stairs Lounge, risked the closet and his career by shepherding the passage of an American Federation of Television and Radio Artists (AFTRA) resolution to ban any union member from participating in the Bryant concert. This maneuver had potential to scuttle the concert because Bryant was an AFTRA member. Wagener, however, was abandoned by AFTRA allies, who reconvened under pressure to lift the ban. "No one really knew what they were voting on before," explained an anonymous board member who changed positions.[34]

Paul Killgore, a New Orleanian who'd attended the St. Mark's memorial service in 1973 but abhorred the political scene, got involved with HERE. "I was so incensed at the time," he recalled. HERE secured permits from City Hall for a protest rally, to be held at Jackson Square at 5:30 p.m. on Saturday, June 18, and Bill Rushton retrofitted an activist headquarters out of the *Vieux Carré Courier* offices. Through Rushton's diligence, HERE printed and mailed 8500 rally posters around the country. "Miami, come help us demonstrate for human rights," read one notice. "Housing will be provided. . . . For more information contact Bill Rushton." More than a thousand additional posters went up in local bathhouses and gay bars—the very businesses that had refused to post Troy Perry's Up Stairs Lounge memorial flyers four years earlier. For HERE organizers, Bryant put a name and a face on a previously featureless set of adversaries bearing an elusive prejudice. Such opposition, when cast in the open, made itself vulnerable to critique. Responding to the surge in activism, Leonard Matlovich, the discharged army sergeant who outshone even Troy Perry in national celebrity by 1977, agreed to come to New Orleans.[35]

June 18 arrived in New Orleans with a torrential storm—weather so inhospitable that HERE organizers wondered whether anyone would turn up for their event. With less than an hour to go, skies cleared, and more than two thousand demonstrators materialized in Jackson Square, as if out of nowhere. They emerged from restaurants and side streets into the rally point before St. Louis Cathedral. Alarmed at the mob of gays and lesbians amassed in front of their basilica, Catholic authorities phoned the city, and police snipers posted themselves at key vantage points. "They were on the roofs of the Pontablas, the Cabildo and the Presbytere," recalled gay activist Roger Nelson, noting the historic buildings that overlook Jackson Square. "They were on mounted patrol, in squad cars up and down the adjoining streets and at every gate to the park. I think they expected trouble. Instead they got peace."[36]

Leonard Matlovich took the bullhorn and spoke loudly, his presence lending power. He asked the protesters to follow his lead. A river of bodies surged out of Jackson Square down St. Ann Street toward the Municipal Auditorium. "Out of the closets and into the streets!" they shouted, conjuring a favored chant from pride parades. "Out of the closets and into the streets," shouted Stewart Butler and Alfred Doolittle. "As we're going along, kind of like the pied piper," recalled Paul Killgore, "there are these people joining us."[37]

Gay men strode down the so-called lavender line of St. Ann Street, which had invisibly cordoned off their folk from straight revelers for years. "Nervous eyes peered out of bars, while others braved the streets to follow the march," reported the *Picayune*. "Balconies all over the Quarter were lined with detached supporters of the movement." Protesters reached the barrier of Rampart Street and turned left, soon amassing at their destination.[38]

In a final act of intimidation, police officers attempted to scatter the crowd outside the Municipal Auditorium by threat of identification. They pulled out cameras, instead of nightsticks. "There are all of these policemen with these video cameras taping all of this video," recalled Paul Killgore. "All of these policemen taking these still photos of all of us that are participating. So, whatever happened with those, I will never know." But the multitude stayed put, shouting, "Hey, hey, ho, ho, Anita Bryant's got to go," with individuals raising their middle fingers at the officers pressing click, lighting up flashbulbs and threatening to "out" them for their impudence.[39]

Reporter Alan Citron, covering the event for the *Times-Picayune*, deemed the rally "the biggest gay rights protest in the city's history." Tapping reservoirs of courage, most of these thousands stood unaware of a smaller groundswell that had occurred just up Rampart Street, four years prior, at St. Mark's Methodist Church. Mourners of the Up Stairs Lounge had gathered there and faced other cameras.[40] From those leaps in 1973, trailblazers like Bill Rushton, Paul Killgore, and Stewart Butler had motivated others to take the same journey.

Inside the auditorium, Anita Bryant crooned patriotic ditties and chanced ironically on a cover of Judy Garland's ballad "Over the Rainbow." When the audience ceased applauding, chanting could be heard from revelers outside. During Bryant's New Orleans appearance, a Florida state official confirmed that Bryant might soon be losing her $100,000-a-year job promoting Florida oranges. "The whole thing is just a mess," averred Arthur Darling, director of publicity for the Florida Department of Citrus. Later that year, as if a summation of the Save Our Children fallout, Bryant would receive a pie to the face from a gay activist during a televised news conference.[41]

Roberts Batson still remembers hearing the clarion call of friends in protest as he managed the Anita Bryant concert—on the other side of police barriers. Batson eventually met Leonard Matlovich in person. "You've got to come out," Matlovich implored him. "You've got to come out because, now, your parents and friends and loved ones are voting against you because they don't know you're gay." The Municipal Auditorium would later award Batson for his "spirit of commitment and the will to accomplish," but he could never forget what Matlovich said. Batson would take greater pains to be self-identifying. He eventually left the auditorium and outed himself as a gay activist. "The most skilled and experienced [gay] men and women I knew wouldn't come forward and lead the way into the political arena, mostly because they wouldn't come out," wrote Batson of this period. "They would contribute quietly and from the background, they told me, if others would be out front."[42]

CHAPTER 15

Last Resort

1978–1993

Rod Wagener, who had taken a brave stance against Anita Bryant in 1977, suddenly couldn't get a daytime slot on WGSO, his radio station, despite strong ratings. Sidelined to a less desirable evening time, he eventually received a pink slip in what was called "an economic move." With his career at a standstill, Wagener decided to abandon all caution and run for a seat in the Louisiana House of Representatives, while still in the closet, as a liberal candidate. In the race, Wagener accused one opponent of being "anti-Black, anti-labor and anti-ERA [Equal Rights Amendment]." Despite his local celebrity, Wagener was trounced in the primary.[1]

The city moved past all the Bryant hoopla, as New Orleans, in the wake of trauma and tragedy, is wont to do. Times seemed to change nationally as Ronald Reagan was elected president in November 1980, and Jerry Falwell's Moral Majority, of the so-called Christian Right, rose to prominence. It seemed like a new breed of conservatism was blossoming as Southern and fiscal Democrats switched their allegiances. Meanwhile John Lennon was gunned down by a disturbed fan almost exactly two years after gay icon and San Francisco city supervisor Harvey Milk was murdered. New Orleans reentered the public imagination through Anne Rice's novel *Interview with the Vampire*, which introduced the world to a host of immortal characters haunting the Vieux Carré—a city so beautiful it could metaphorically eat you alive.[2]

Even as New Orleans was growing in legend, however, the city was losing population and economic power. The NBA franchise the New Orleans Jazz couldn't last more than five years in town before uprooting to Utah. Perceptually, the Big Easy needed a wholesome win, and it found one in 1980. After racking up more than $10 million in costs, Louis Armstrong Memorial Park finally opened. A lineup of jazz legends, from Count Basie to Dave Brubeck, convened at the unveiling, performing on stages nestled between artificial coves in the thirty-one-acre park. Armstrong's widow addressed a crowd of thousands, and former mayor Moon Landrieu and his successor, Ernest Morial, the former judge and the city's first black mayor, also made speeches.[3]

The same year that Louis Armstrong Memorial Park premiered to the public, Regina Soleto legally changed her name to Regina Adams—taking the surname of her murdered beau. It was a gesture meant to honor the love of her life and the role he'd played in her transformation. That way, she could always be his "queen."[4]

Shortly after the Armstrong Park showcase, a band of sixty homosexuals, including Stewart Butler and Roberts Batson, founded the Louisiana Lesbian and Gay Political Action Caucus, more popularly known as LAGPAC. At last, politics-averse New Orleans boasted a gay group working "through the political system to promote full equality and civil rights for all lesbians and gay men." LAGPAC's primary objectives were the repeal of all criminal statutes against sexual expression and the passage of a human rights ordinance protecting homosexuals. With national and regional outreach a priority, LAGPAC coordinated with the National Gay Task Force and the Houston Gay Political Caucus to establish a gay vote network.[5]

Concurrent with these forward strides, an internal memo passed hands at the Louisiana Office of the State Fire Marshal in Baton Rouge. This note, paperclipped to a folder, put an end to the investigation of the Up Stairs Lounge, which had dogged investigators and occupied state resources since the early morning of June 25, 1973. "This report was submitted to the Dist. Att'y," wrote the chief of the Arson Division. "The suspect at the time, Roger Nunez, has since committed suicide. There was no other evidence or information pointing to anyone other than the above mentioned person. The investigators were completely satisfied that he was the person who set the fire. No charges were ever accepted by the D.A., N.O., LA. It is requested that this file be closed." No one at LAGPAC, not even Stewart Butler, heard of the Up Stairs Lounge case's having reached an end, and the state certainly didn't call a press conference to announce it.[6] The final report on the fire, which included the Roger Nunez interview that took place in the NOPD Detective Bureau, was shipped to state archives and microfiched, with the original documents then destroyed. The seven-year search for answers ended not with a proverbial bang but a bureaucratic whimper.

The New Orleans Police Department, likewise, purged all functional memory of the Up Stairs Lounge tragedy. In 1980, the department elevated Henry M. Morris to the role of interim police superintendent of New Orleans. Under Morris, homosexual residents once again became targets of harassment. Anticrime patrols would stop more than one hundred male couples in the French Quarter without cause and force them to fill out "Field Identification Cards," which could be used to identify suspects for future lineups. On the weekend of April 24, 1981, more than ninety gay men and women—including LAGPAC cofounder Roberts Batson—were arrested. Police detained fifty-two men in one evening in a blitzkrieg effort that involved pulling a paddy wagon up to a well-known gay bar. At the station, police charged pedestrians with violation of "obstruction of free passage," legalese for blocking a sidewalk. A police commander publicly defended the use of this ordinance to "protect the merchants of the city and to alleviate any potential fire hazards."[7] These roundups highlighted the lack of progress made by local gays, despite high turnouts at events like the anti–Anita Bryant demonstrations.

LAGPAC rallied in response and demanded meetings with Police Chief Morris and New Orleans Mayor Morial. Both officials complied and claimed to be caught off-balance by the actions of police rank and file. However, reportedly Henry Morris at first defended the arrests by telling a LAGPAC representative, "Four or five of you on the street is okay, but there are just too many of you; you need to get off the streets."[8] LAGPAC leaders, of course, immediately compared this statement with Morris's "queer bar" comment from 1973, although they did not cite additional memories of the fire after retrieving that relevant detail. Charges were dropped, and Morial made the following statement: "It is and has been the official policy of this administration not to discriminate against anyone on the basis of . . . sexual orientation." Morris asked LAGPAC, in writing, to "strive to work together for future better Community relations" rather than "trying to specifically concentrate on past instances."[8]

Quietly, in an act of charity unbeknownst to LAGPAC members or City Hall, Roeling Mace and Vic Scalise, two local gay leaders, donated burial space—an expensive proposition in a city with limited room for elaborate death rites—to the MCC. Mace and Scalise allocated one slot in a communal crypt for the ashes of Bill Larson. The pastor's ashes had sat in an urn inside the MCC altar for the previous eight years, during which the itinerant church had often struggled. The fear of losing or misplacing his remains was always present, especially when the congregation relocated or new pastors took charge.[9] But this endowment would provide the fallen pastor with a permanent resting place.

The donors—who, it's worth noting, were founding members of the gay Mardi Gras Krewe of Amon-Ra, a group with which MCC Deacon Courtney Craighead and Buddy Rasmussen were affiliated—had evidently tired of waiting for the national MCC to fund this venture and acted independently. Bill Larson's ashes were entombed at New Orleans's St. Roch Cemetery #1 on September 9, 1981. Afterward, the pastor's crypt failed to receive a stone plate bearing his name, as the endowment did not make those funds available. Larson's grave would, thus, be an unmarked one—unknown, except for those who attended the small burial service or sought paper records.[10]

Although Bill Larson never held the title in his life, he was entered into cemetery rolls as "Rev. William R. Larson," his designation of "Reverend" reflecting a posthumous elevation[11] (although neither Troy Perry nor MCC elders explained when Larson was awarded the title). Here, in the annals of these burial grounds, Larson was recognized as he wished to be: an ordained minister and member of the clergy.

———————— ✧ ————————

LOCAL ATTITUDES TOWARD outness began to change as gays and lesbians advanced their status from invisibles to vocal members of the body politic. "Gay Fest," a celebration of homosexual pride, was held at Armstrong Park in 1981 and emceed by an aspiring come- dienne named Ellen DeGeneres. "It became much more tolerant," recalled Cabildo Gallery owner Joseph Bermuda in the Quarter, "but gays always were singled out." Leon Irwin III, the former Louisiana Democratic National Committeeman who by 1981 was chairman of the Downtown Development District for New Orleans, was outed on local TV when he was filmed soliciting a male prostitute as part of an investigative series called "Cruisin' the Streets." Consequently, Irwin spent a few sheepish weeks out of town, but he would neither be arrested nor shunned for the incident, which metamorphosed over time into another piece of New Orleans lore.[12]

Some gay men who shied away from activism felt compelled to get involved. Steven Duplantis joined LAGPAC in 1982 and ran for the office of treasurer—a reversal from his refusal to self-identify or give testimony about Roger Dale Nunez in 1973. For months after the fire, Steven had sat at his desk at Randolph Air Force Base wondering if this was the day that military policemen would usher him to his court- martial for fellating a fellow serviceman. His paperwork to transfer to the Louisiana Air National Guard was kept "in process" for months. Finally, Steven mustered the courage to press an audience with his commanding officer. "Okay, I know all about your paperwork," said the man tauntingly. Steven finally wrote an uncle, an air force gen- eral in the Pentagon, about the holdup. Days later, he miraculously received his transfer to the air guard—a reserve militia under state authority.[13] Thus did he escape his federal inquisitors.

Steven had long since moved back home to Lake Charles and mended relations with family, who learned to be accepting of his lifestyle. His weekend sprees with Stewart Butler and Alfred Doolittle—coinciding with his one-weekend-a-month duties at the

Louisiana Air National Guard station in New Orleans—became wilder and more convenient. At the culmination of his military career, Steven Duplantis would receive an honorable discharge for more than a decade of service.[14]

GAYS PLANTED CIVIC roots just in time to face an almost biblical pestilence. The local gay weekly *Impact* christened 1983 "The Year Many Would Like to Forget," the year of the AIDS (acquired immune deficiency syndrome) outbreak. Persistent rumors of a "Rare Cancer Seen in Forty-One Homosexuals" were reported in *The New York Times* as early as 1981; this metamorphosed into declarations of a "Homosexual Plague" by *Newsweek* in 1982. Alarm bells sounded in Louisiana with talk of "gay-related immune deficiency" (GRID), a name abandoned when the disease spread to heterosexuals and received the more familiar abbreviation AIDS.[15]

To conservative alarmists, this new illness confirmed everything that Anita Bryant had tried to forewarn. Although isolated cases of a disease attacking the immune system had been documented since the late 1960s, little federal funding had been allotted for studies that might have connected those cases, which had mostly involved homosexuals and other "undesirables." According to figures provided by the Centers for Disease Control at the time, eight reported cases of AIDS in 1979 swelled to more than twelve hundred by the end of 1982, with about a 60 percent death rate. One could rarely find a news story about homosexuality in this era that did not also include some degree of AIDS coverage.[16]

The first AIDS victims, often visually identifiable through purple Kaposi's sarcoma lesions, became what *Time* called "The New Untouchables," and the U.S. Public Health Service almost immediately began counseling gay men not to give blood donations. Between the delisting of "homosexuality" as a mental illness in 1973 and the AIDS outbreak, it thus took only a decade for gays to be restigmatized by the medical establishment. Blood drive efforts for gay emergencies, such as those for the Up Stairs Lounge victims, became a thing of the past.[17]

By April 1983, about five new AIDS cases were being reported every day in the United States, and five individuals in New Orleans had already died of the illness. "Gays' Disease Spreads to Heterosexuals," ran a particularly charged *Times-Picayune* headline. Crowd sizes in gay bars trickled off. The Canal Baths in New Orleans announced its closing after attendance fell. "We're throwing in the sponge," said the owner, attempting humor. Blood donation centers in New Orleans sat empty, as state officials told the *Times-Picayune* that people were "deathly afraid" of blood-borne illnesses. One study in the *Journal of the American Medical Association*, reported by the *Picayune*, concluded that children could get AIDS from "routine close contact" with infected members of a household.[18]

A gay and lesbian coalition called the NO/AIDS Task Force filed articles of incorporation in June 1983 to stem the tide of discrimination. That October, the new group sponsored a candlelight vigil in Jackson Square, and Mayor Ernest Morial participated as a keynote speaker. Indeed, the mayor took the podium and readily admitted, "There has been an unwillingness in certain quarters to do the research necessary to address this dreaded disease." His words encouraged activists to make further moves to beat back the silence. According to a 1984 survey, nearly 73 percent of gay New Orleanians remained closeted in the workplace, with more than 55 percent reporting that "it would be a problem at work if their sexual orientation were known."[19]

As the AIDS debate grew more heated, with some surveys suggesting that more than 40 percent of Americans favored limiting the civil rights of AIDS patients, the death toll mounted. Morty Manford and Leonard Matlovich wasted away and then perished. Activist Bill Rushton contracted the virus, which eventually killed him. His *Times-Picayune* obituary declared him dead of a "long bout of liver trouble," thereby closeting a gay pioneer in the grave. Up Stairs Lounge survivor Jason Guidry faced a quieter, but no less agonizing, fate. Bishop Finis Crutchfield, who bravely supported the Up Stairs Lounge victims at St. Mark's Methodist Church, contracted a mysterious illness and then succumbed. United Methodist Church leaders initially counseled his family not to discuss the cause, which was listed on the death certificate, a public document, as AIDS.[20]

Misinterpreting Morial's show of support as blanket sponsorship of the homosexual agenda, LAGPAC proposed an ordinance to expand human rights protections for gay men and lesbians. Stewart Butler and Roberts Batson lobbied the New Orleans City Council and created draft legislation by 1984. Washington, D.C., Mayor Marion Barry Jr. personally endorsed their work. Barry cited several instances of discrimination against homosexuals in a packet on New Orleans gay history. However, the handout conspicuously omitted the Up Stairs Lounge fire as such an event. Mayor Morial would never offer the same endorsement. LAGPAC's campaign became quashed when Archbishop Philip Hannan registered his condemnation. Hannan, a political heavyweight in a heavily Catholic city, sent letters of admonition to all City Council members. Additionally, the archdiocese alerted church groups, at least one Catholic elementary school, and many parish priests, with instructions to rally the laity.[21]

On April 12, 1984, the LAGPAC ordinance failed to pass, by a vote of three to three. Councilman James Singleton, unreachable on military leave, absented himself from having to cast the tiebreaking vote. Mayor Morial could not be reached for comment later, although a high-ranking official told the *Picayune* that, "if the mayor had pushed it, the ordinance would have passed easily." Councilman Joseph Giarrusso, a former New Orleans police chief who'd boasted of his officers making 217 "homosexual arrests" in 1965, voted no and claimed that the ordinance would result in "reverse discrimination" against heterosexuals.[22]

After LAGPAC's loss, Rod Wagener established a new political lobbying group for "human rights." Even though Wagener planned to advance a homosexual agenda, he evidently felt that the term "human rights" was more palatable for New Orleanians. Wagener christened his organization the George Steven Matyi Private Trust, misspelling the middle name of his dead lover. In its first three years, the trust spent $500,000 lobbying for gay causes. Wagener published a political

pamphlet on June 24, 1988—the fifteenth anniversary of the immola-
tion of Bud Matyi at the Up Stairs Lounge. In this report, Wagener
declined to cite the Up Stairs Lounge at all or invoke its memory to
highlight discrimination.[23] This can be taken as proof that Rod Wagener, like many, continued to suffer in code.

Building courage slowly, Wagener eventually found himself able
to declare his sexuality, albeit in an indirect way. He agreed to an
expansive, on-the-record interview about his shared past with Bud
Matyi to Johnny Townsend, a groundbreaking historian just beginning to research a book about the Up Stairs Lounge fire. "A people
cannot exist as a people without a history," Wagener told Townsend.
Wagener hoped to live long enough to see this book published, but he
would die in 1991—twenty years before Townsend's *Let the Faggots
Burn* appeared.[24]

Meanwhile, LAGPAC rallied back. In 1986, it proposed another
municipal ordinance, and the measure received sponsorship from
Johnny Jackson, a black councilman. Archbishop Hannan again
opposed the measure. On December 4, after hours of debate in which
more than 120 people spoke for and against, the ordinance was soundly
defeated by a vote of five to two—an even wider margin than in 1984.
Councilman Jackson pounded on his podium and asked, "Why is this
not a civil matter?" Councilman Joseph Giarrusso, voting no for a second time, lectured LAGPAC that it had failed to prove how homosexuals were subject to discrimination.[25]

In fact, no local law offering protections to homosexual residents
would pass until after Rich Magill, a close ally of Stewart Butler, dedicated two years to assembling data that disbelievers like Giarrusso
would accept. Magill's comprehensive and excoriating study on the
closet and homophobia, entitled *Exposing Hatred: A Report on the Victimization of Lesbian and Gay People in New Orleans, Louisiana*, was
published in 1991. In its eighty-nine pages, it delineated a campaign
of brutality against homosexuals in the so-called live-and-let-live Big
Easy. Nearly 80 percent of the survey respondents reported some
form of antigay victimization in their lives: rape, harassment, vandalism, police abuse, bomb threats, and arson.[26] In a move that surprised

many and angered a few, Magill chose to dedicate his study to a lost set of victims:

> Remembering the 32 people lost in the Up Stairs Lounge Fire on June 24, 1973 604 Iberville at Charters, French Quarter, New Orleans, Louisiana . . . [27]

This was the first attempt in nearly twenty years to bring the fire to wider attention. Beside each alphabetically listed victim, Magill included the person's age at time of death and a brief description. Indeed, the memory of the dead had lingered all this time. Magill knew that the fire remained an untended wound. For years, Stewart Butler tried to share his stories with those who would listen. The burnt-out shell of the Up Stairs Lounge had never been reoccupied by another bar. Empty for much of the 1980s, the space had only been recently converted into administrative offices for the Jimani tavern—still in business on the corner, one floor down.[28]

It was a dark history, certain to fester, which made Magill's decision to include the dedication a measure of last resort, but the effect of the fire's presentation in this report—up front, right after the title page—created a whole new consciousness. Running one's eyes over the thirty-two names was like gazing upon a row of gravestones. City officials were now forced to acknowledge that antigay bias existed and even came with a body count. With the Magill report in hand, Councilman Giarrusso expressed satisfaction. The City Council at last voted to approve an ordinance protecting sexual minorities.[29]

The latent memory of the Up Stairs Lounge had won the sympathy of a majority of elected leaders and helped secure new human rights protections. Yet, despite the resulting victory for gay citizens, there continued to be no public remembrances for the Up Stairs Lounge, even two years later, on the twentieth anniversary of the massacre. That back-alley bar on the border of the French Quarter remained in a condition that Deacon Courtney Craighead would later verbalize: in a historic closet.[30]

Second Line

June 22, 2003

The day arrived like a prodigal son, long absent from home, but it looked just like any other day of the week. Horses and buggies lined up in Jackson Square. Tourists headed to Café du Monde for morning beignets and café au laits. Residents watered plants on balconies, which drained to cobblestones below and gathered in puddles. The city, in its never-ending cycle of bloom and decay, seemed to be able to stanch the march of time, and yet renewal was in the air as Reverend Dexter Brecht readied himself for the fire's thirtieth anniversary.[1]

So much had happened since Dexter Brecht began his mission to revive the fire's history, by making the tragedy the centerpiece of his MCC service in 1995. Courtney Craighead did not volunteer to join his committee, as the deacon had hinted in an interview with reporter Mark Thompson from the *Times-Picayune*. Thompson had respected Courtney Craighead's request for anonymity as a source and quoted him merely as "a deacon," although there were no other deacons for the church, in the ensuing story.[2] Twenty-two years after the fire, it had still behooved Courtney to shield himself in such a manner.

Considering that his name had been published widely in the 1970s, a request for anonymity in the 1990s appeared like a token gesture masking deeper torment. Fire survivors like Courtney had managed on their own, in their own ways, and sometimes did not. Formerly a socialite who behaved like the grown-up version of the boy scout that he had been, Courtney had retreated for decades from bar life and thrown himself headlong into church ministry. "That was his real identity, as a deacon of MCC," said Reverend Brecht. "That's really who he wanted to be." Such pain, even when sublimated by prayer, would not vanish, and Courtney had engaged in many private counseling sessions with Brecht to cope.[3]

Nevertheless, with the story's publication in 1995, Courtney Craighead did begin to identify himself more readily with the past. "I think my continuing to talk about the event," recalled Brecht, "and holding him up as an example as one of our forebears in the development of queer culture in New Orleans made him more comfortable with being able to talk about it and be recognized." For the first time, the deacon called himself a "survivor" at public events. He gave an on-the-record interview to the *Times-Picayune* in 1998, during which he admitted how many "were, in effect, outed by the fire." These were meaningful signs to fellow congregants that their deacon deemed the fire less excruciating to remember. Even with this progress, Courtney chose to speak guardedly, telling the *Picayune* in this interview that the fire "should not be politicized."[4]

When a museum approached the deacon to give his testimony, Courtney agreed to do so under the condition that, according to the curator's notes, the tragedy was "not seen as a 'hate crime,'" and that the event didn't become "a media circus or political issue." This was a sentiment shared by many Up Stairs Lounge survivors, who were cautious about their pain being co-opted. "The Up Stairs Lounge was *not* a gay rights tragedy nor did it ever play a part in any gay rights movement," explained Ricky Everett. "The gay pride or gay rights thing was a lie perpetrated by Troy Perry at the time of the fire. He was attempting to use that tragedy to promote gay pride."[5] Indeed, MCC pastor Perry's role in the Up Stairs Lounge aftermath remained the subject of debate for decades.

Perhaps the combination of this desire to share with a fear of being hurt, a condition of inner struggle that William Faulkner once termed "the human heart in conflict with itself," explained why not one member of the MCC of New Orleans initially volunteered for Dexter Brecht's Up Stairs Lounge memorial committee. "There were a lot of broken people before the fire and after the fire," explained former congregant Henry Kubicki. Brecht was forced to move forward alone. "My feeling was that the church was at a place, at that time, where it really needed to embrace a sense of its calling," he recalled, "and have sort of a resurrection experience."[6]

And resurrected it had been. A small revolution had transpired under Reverend Brecht's watch. In 1998, two important events marked the fire's twenty-fifth anniversary, and the *Times-Picayune* devoted multiple pages to the tragedy and the purpose of its legacy. First, about one hundred people gathered at the U.S. Mint on June 23 for a state sponsored panel called "Remembering the Up Stairs Lounge Fire." The event was put together by Louisiana State Museum curator Wayne Phillips, who felt that the tragedy deserved a greater observance after its omission from his museum's 1991 exhibit. At the panel, Courtney Craighead openly recounted his experiences. Clancy DuBos recalled the story of walking into the burn wards of Charity Hospital as an eighteen-year-old intern for the *Times-Picayune*, and he also read a letter from his *Times-Picayune* mentor, John LaPlace, who had reported on the tragedy. LaPlace had kept a secret he now wished to unburden: "There is also an unwritten, personal chapter to this story—a chapter that I have shared with no one until today," he wrote. "You see, the Up Stairs Lounge several nights earlier had been but one of several stops on my regular pub crawl through the French Quarter."[7] With this admission, LaPlace at last confessed that he had been an Up Stairs Lounge patron, one long compelled to keep silent.

Then folks regrouped the next day in the grand ballroom of the Royal Sonesta Hotel on Bourbon Street. Supporters read messages of recognition from U.S. Congressman William Jefferson, a Louisiana Democrat, and a proclamation from the mayor of New Orleans. Reverend Troy Perry—back in New Orleans after an absence of at least a decade—led the benediction. "Before the fire it was okay to be gay on Bourbon Street," he preached, "but go two blocks in either direction, and you could get your head bashed in." In November 1997, Perry had been an honored guest at President Bill Clinton's White House Conference on Hate Crimes. There, Perry had submitted a report cataloguing twenty-six attacks on MCC congregations between 1973 and 1996. The worst of these incidents had caused the deaths of "the church pastor, an associate pastor and ten members of the congregation."[8] This was the story of the Up Stairs Lounge, successfully brought before a president of the United States for the first time.

His success in getting the message to President Clinton made Perry ready to face his Up Stairs Lounge legacy—and perhaps put the controversy to rest. Standing beside Perry in the ballroom, Dexter Brecht had thanked attendees for their visibility, so that "another Up Stairs Lounge fire can never go unnoticed again." For the second portion of the Up Stairs Lounge service, Troy Carter, the first black New Orleanian to represent the French Quarter on the City Council since Reconstruction, led the crowd onto Bourbon Street for a "jazz funeral," a traditional Creole mourning ritual. With its two-part "first line, second line" structure, a "jazz funeral" blended Catholic and voodoo death rites with the city's iconic music to symbolize New Orleans's unique relationship to this life and the next.[9]

Mourners of the Up Stairs Lounge marched behind Councilman Carter and a brass band. For the "first line," the band played a dirge called "Just a Closer Walk with Thee," while select members of the procession held up placards with victims' names. Troy Perry had the sign for Adam Fontenot. Dexter Brecht bore a placard for Glenn Green. Reaching the crossroads near the Jimani tavern, above which the Up Stairs Lounge once stood, mourners dropped flowers beside the unmarked side door. Despite Brecht's desire to place a metal plaque at the site, the building owner, Henry Granet, had voiced strong opposition (Granet was recovering from an injury when reached for this book and unable to comment on these details). So the faithful observed a moment of silence. "Let's go back now and celebrate our community!" Brecht then announced. Trumpet and trombone broke into upbeat ditties like "When the Saints Go Marching In," drawing a cheer. Handkerchiefs waved to bid farewell to the deceased. A "second line" then commenced.[10]

Recalling the twenty-fifth anniversary, Brecht said, "That was the first time that the community of New Orleans publicly, in a demonstrative way, acknowledged this event." The newspaper coverage, the symposium, and the jazz funeral had made a splash, undoubtedly, but Brecht still believed that only a permanent marker would make the memory of the fire endure. Brecht would not be satisfied so long as the attainment of a "living memorial"—Troy Perry's goal as early as June 25, 1973—remained elusive.[11]

In the new century, Brecht made yet another attempt to establish an Up Stairs Lounge monument. He formed a new committee and invited Jack Carrel, director of the Lesbian and Gay Community Center of New Orleans, to join. Brecht also welcomed Donald St. Pierre—an Uptown businessman who in 2002 had raised eyebrows by participating in a commitment ceremony with his lover. Rounding out the anniversary team, Brecht appointed Wil Coleman, a thirty-something MCC congregant and lightning-rod personality with a mohawk, as head of fund-raising. As Coleman was no stranger to rivalries among the city's gay cliques, Brecht must have sensed in Coleman a voice for the next generation, a person who might take on the role of being a public advocate for the tragedy. "What is this really about?" Coleman had asked Brecht. "Why don't you do the research?" Brecht beseeched. Dexter Brecht's memorial committee met throughout 2003 and eventually received city approval to place a bronze plaque on a portion of the municipal sidewalk.[12]

It goes without saying that, since 1995, when Dexter Brecht first spoke as champion of the Up Stairs Lounge, homosexuality had made the leap from fringe culture into the mainstream. By 2002, according to National Opinion Research Center surveys, nearly one-third of Americans believed homosexual relations to be "not wrong at all," a gain from the mid-1990s and a nearly a threefold increase from 1973. In 1995, Andrew Sullivan, the editor in chief of *The New Republic*, had published *Virtually Normal: An Argument about Homosexuality*, in which he contended that many gay and lesbian Americans would make legal, lifelong commitments if permitted to do so and that society would benefit. Ellen DeGeneres, a former New Orleanian and newly out lesbian, shook the world when her sitcom character came out of the closet on prime-time television in 1997, declaring herself to be gay before 42 million viewers. Yet setbacks were inevitable. The federal Defense of Marriage Act, enacted in 1996, had already precluded the possibility of same-sex marriage by barring federal recognition of such unions and allowing states the right to refuse to recognize the same-sex nuptials of other states, territories, and governments. Network execs canceled the *Ellen* show. An HIV-positive student at the University of Wyoming named Matthew Shepard was brutally murdered—lured, beaten, and left for dead—in October 1998, much like Fernando Rios in 1958 New Orleans. Unlike Rios, Shepard would be mourned by the nation.[13]

A SIZABLE CROWD buzzed in the reception hall of the Ritz-Carlton New Orleans on June 22, 2003. Reverend Brecht, his short-cropped gray hair reflecting the heartache of a long struggle, seemed radiant in their presence. Stewart Butler nodded back from his seat. Former fire chief William McCrossen sat nearby as an honored guest. His mere presence moved many, as if the eighty-nine-year-old ex-fireman was making not just a personal statement but also an act of atonement on behalf of city leaders from the 1970s. Guests Reverend Troy Perry and Reverend Bill Richardson, the long-retired minister of St. George's Episcopal Church, also stood at the ready to preach. Gazing at faces in the Ritz-Carlton, Richardson felt vindicated that the Up Stairs Lounge continued to matter to others.[14]

Ricky Everett, nonetheless, was absent. He still struggled with the onslaughts of memory and therefore stayed away from events like this one. Henry Kubicki lived in town and wanted to attend but couldn't, having contended with too much woe as a caregiver for Up Stairs Lounge survivors like Courtney Craighead, as well as for dying friends during the AIDS crisis.[15] Returning to the MCC, Henry knew, would bring back too many faces from the past.

Reverend Brecht began the service by evoking the dark times. The crowd recited a responsorial psalm: "O God, our help in ages past, our hope for years to come, our shelter from the stormy blast." Perry, deferring to Brecht, told the story of the "crisis week" in his eulogy. In response, the crowd said a hymn: "We shall not give up the fight we have only started." At the culmination of the service, Deacon Courtney Craighead led participants outside, toward the fire site. Others followed, single file. Courtney's transformation, epitomized by this act, moved Brecht deeply in that he "was there as a representative of folks that had actually been through it," a role that the deacon had once been reluctant to assume.[16]

Stewart Butler let his imagination wander as he headed with Courtney through the Vieux Carré, which seemed to yield to their shared grief. Puffs of flower and fern and the breath of banana trees from secret gardens and inner courtyards, hidden between buildings, wafted through passageways. Stewart could never forget that Sunday evening—walking those steps down Iberville to the inferno. Everyone, it seemed, avoided the sight of the Lounge after a few days. Not a single city official attended either of the two memorial services, Stewart recalled. Now, the New Orleans Police Department, the institution that never named or charged a culprit, was a corporate sponsor for Up Stairs Lounge events.[17]

Courtney Craighead held his hand up when he reached Iberville and Chartres, as if to quiet the procession. Health complications compelled Courtney to accept the occasional guidance of his companion, Charlene Pitre, who stood close by. Nearing the golden age of his life, Courtney Craighead had retired and discovered pride in being a gay deacon, a pride reflected in his willingness to express such tenderness on Iberville, where he once feared to be seen. Observing Courtney, both Brecht and Troy Perry could recall the words in the Gospels that Jesus spoke to raise a man who had been dead for three days: "Lazarus, come out!"[18] This was the very symbol that Brecht had invoked, and hoped for, in 1995. Within two years, however, Courtney Craighead would die prematurely, at the age of sixty-five. Funeral rites would be held on June 24, 2005, the thirty-second anniversary of the fire, at the House of Bultman funeral home—the site of Bill Larson's wake. Dexter Brecht and Henry Kubicki gave eulogies.[19] In a sense, the three original deacons of the MCC of New Orleans—Bill Larson, Mitch Mitchell, and Courtney Craighead—would finally rest in peace.

Brecht marshaled his emotions when they reached the location, an unmarked door near the corner where a small wedge of sidewalk lay beneath a flapping white sheet. "We were not supposed to be blocking the street," he recalled, "but we did spill out into the street at that point." Brecht stood between the covered object and the bar's old door, with Troy Perry to his right and Wil Coleman to his left—three generations of Up Stairs Lounge activists. Together, they lifted a veil to reveal gleaming bronze embedded in the sidewalk brick.[20] Upon the plaque shone thirty-two names held together by an upside-down triangle and set between two fleurs-de-lis with these words:

At this site on June 24, 1973 in the Upstairs Lounge, these thirty-two people lost their lives in the worst fire in New Orleans. The impact went far beyond the loss of individual lives, giving birth to the Lesbian, Gay, Bisexual and Transgender rights movement in New Orleans.[21]

Looking at the marker, Brecht had to catch his breath. "To actually see the plaque," he recalled, "to see it there." Brecht sprinkled holy water on the metal surface. Just as he did, well-wishers tossed yellow chrysanthemums, and someone read out the names. "This was our birthing process," Brecht told the crowd. "This was really where we became a people." With this dedication, the Up Stairs Lounge achieved new status. The fire became one of the first historically significant events in the gay rights movement—the other being the Stonewall riots—to receive a permanent monument in a public place by 2003. It had truly become a "living memorial," etched into the fabric of New Orleans. "It, somehow, refused to die almost," Brecht recalled.[22]

The plaque itself weighed several hundred pounds. Its dimensions were thirty inches by thirty inches. Pouring the bronze had cost about $2200, with the materials and labor to install it in the sidewalk totaling a few thousand extra. Yet, the marker had taken three decades to appear. This monument held unique meaning for the MCC, for families of the Up Stairs Lounge victims denied dignity and restitution, for those fire survivors lost to the subsequent AIDS epidemic, and for those inside the bar who had become ashes. It meant a great deal that the plaque could transmute what had once been an historic abyss, a source of unspeakable pain, into a story that others could remember.[23]

Members of the procession then returned to the Ritz-Carlton for a small luncheon. William McCrossen, weathered from the heat but nonetheless energized, spoke from his wheelchair. He apologized for the way the city had treated the victims and survivors of the fire. Stewart Butler respired audibly and put his head in his hands, as if relieved of a weight. No mayor of New Orleans had yet to make the same gesture as the fire chief. Although other officials issued proclamations, only McCrossen undertook the task of reckoning with his actions in person.[24]

Folding his hands, he offered to answer any questions. Someone asked if he knew the person responsible for the blaze, and McCrossen told a puzzling story about a woman who had visited him many years before. She said she was a Catholic sister, the retired fire superintendent told listeners, who forsook her vows and left the order. A pain had seemed to enfold her, and, for the shame, she was moving away. But she wanted to clear her conscience by telling authorities about a confession she had heard from a young man's lips. These chilling remarks, he related, had come from a confused soul who later took his own life. This young man, McCrossen revealed, had told her how he started the Up Stairs Lounge fire. Evidently, the fire chief had responded by hugging the woman and then letting her walk away.[25]

On that day in 2003, the octogenarian could not recall the name of the sister or of the young man who had confessed to her. However, these details seemed to match with Mary Stephen Ledet, who left the Sisters of Christian Charity in 1974 and moved to Florida, as well as with Roger Dale Nunez, who conferred with Sister Ledet before his suicide in November of that same year. It does indeed seem that Ledet chose to leave her religious order shortly after Roger's suicide. She eventually married and then died in 2007. As these interactions had happened decades before, McCrossen's narrative, as if from beyond, could provide no official closure. The *Times-Picayune*, covering the anniversary, would neglect to include any of this interlude. Yet with this telling, William McCrossen, who would himself die the following year, momentarily stunned his listeners. Many then leaped to their feet and hugged one another, as if finally given something like an answer.[26]

Sitting off to the side at the luncheon, Wil Coleman chatted amiably with Troy Perry. "I, of course, was familiar with Troy and what that church movement had built," Coleman recalled, "not just in New Orleans but beyond that." Coleman looked Perry in the eyes and said, "You know, someday, I hope I can do something that matters like you." Perry blushed and was deeply moved. He then pulled Coleman close and whispered something into his ear. "But you already have," the preacher said, aware that Coleman had played a major role in fund-raising for the plaque.[27]

Just four days later, in an event that seemed related existentially, the U.S. Supreme Court decriminalized homosexuality.[28] The decision *Lawrence v. Texas*, handed down on June 26, 2003, declared unconstitutional the sodomy laws that had rendered consenting sexual acts between members of the same gender illegal. The conservative justice Antonin Scalia, writing in dissent of the 6–3 ruling, leveled the accusation that the Court had "signed on to the so-called homosexual agenda." Overlooking the condescension in the phrase "so-called," Scalia was not incorrect, for the legalization of same-sex marriage was already winding its way through the courts and would be decided on June 26, 2015—twelve years to the day from *Lawrence v. Texas*. With decriminalization, the state-sponsored oppression of homosexual relations seemed all but deposed by decree, and homosexual citizens abandoned secrecy in greater numbers, even on corners like Iberville and Chartres (where men once ran up stairs to find refuge), speaking at last their names.

At this site on June 24, 1973 in the Upstairs Lounge, these thirty-two people lost their lives in the worst fire in New Orleans. The impact went far beyond the loss of individual lives, giving birth to the Lesbian, Gay, Bisexual and Transgender rights movement in New Orleans.

Mrs. Willie Inez Warren & Her Sons, Eddie Hosea Warren & James Curtis Warren
Luther Boggs, Rev. William R. Larson, Dr. Perry Lane Waters, Jr.
Horace "Skip" Getchell, Leon Richard Maples,
George Steven Matyi, James Wall Hembrick,
Larry Stratton, Unidentified White Male

Robert "Bob" Lumpkin, David Stuart Gary, Guy D. Anderson,
Joseph George "Mitch" Mitchell & Louis Horace Broussard,
Reginald Adams Jr., Joseph Henry Adams, Herbert Dean Cooley,
Glenn Richard "Dick" Green, Unidentified White Male

Joe William Bailey & Clarence Joseph McCloskey, Jr.
Adam Roland Fontenot, Ferris LeBlanc, Donald Walter Dunbar,
Kenneth Paul Harrington, Gerald Hoyt Gordon, John Thomas Golding, Sr.
Douglas Maxwell Williams, Unidentified White Male

Notes

Preface

1. Lizette Alvarez and Richard Pérez-Peña, "Orlando Gunman Attacks Gay Nightclub, Leaving Fifty Dead," *The New York Times*, June 12, 2016 (www.nytimes.com/2016/06/13/us/orlando-nightclub-shooting.html); Del Quentin Wilber, "The FBI Investigated the Orlando Mass Shooter for Ten Months—and Found Nothing," *Los Angeles Times*, July 14, 2016 (www.latimes.com/nation/la-na-fbi-investigation-mateen-20160712-snap-story.html); Gal Tziperman Lotan, Paul Brinkmann, and Rene Stutzman, "Witness: Omar Mateen Had Been at Orlando Gay Nightclub Many Times," *Orlando Sentinel*, June 13, 2016 (www.orlandosentinel.com/news/pulse-orlando-nightclub-shooting/os-orlando-nightclub-omar-mateen-profile-20160613-story.html).

2. Sky Swisher and Marc Freeman, "Court Records Shed Light on Orlando Shooter's Employment History," *Sun-Sentinel*, June 13, 2016 (www.sun-sentinel.com/local/palm-beach/fl-orlando-shooter-lucie-court-file-20160613-story.html); Charlotte Alter, "Ex-Wife Says Orlando Shooter Might Have Been Hiding Homosexuality from His Family," *Time*, June 15, 2016 (http://time.com/4369577/orlando-shooting-sitora-yusufiy-omar-mateen-gay/).

3. Caitlin Doornbos, "Autopsy: Pulse Shooter Omar Mateen Shot Eight Times," *Orlando Sentinel*, August 5, 2016 (www.orlandosentinel.com/news/pulse-orlando-nightclub-shooting/omar-mateen/os-pulse-shooting-mateen-autopsy-20160805-story.html).

4. Gideon Resnick and Justin Miller, "Forty-Nine Killed at Pulse Gay Club in Orlando; Deadliest Mass Shooting in U.S. History," *The Daily Beast*, June 12, 2016 (www.thedailybeast.com/49-killed-at-pulse-gay-club-in-orlando-deadliest-mass-shooting-in-us-history); Liam Stack, "Before Orlando Shooting, an Anti-Gay Massacre in New Orleans Was Largely Forgotten," *The New York Times*, June 14, 2016 (www.nytimes.com/2016/06/15/us/upstairs-lounge-new-orleans-fire-orlando-gay-bar.html); Jim Downs, "Before Orlando, There Was New Orleans," *The New York Times*, June 13, 2016 (www.nytimes.com/2016/06/13/opinion/orlando-and-the-history-of-anti-gay-violence.html).

5. Buddy Dyer, "City of Orlando Update 10:20 a.m.," CityofOrlando.net, June

12, 2016, www.cityoforlando.net/mayor/2016/06/city-of-orlando-update-1020-a
-m/; Rick Scott, "Gov. Scott: We Will Devote Every Resource Available to Assist
with Orlando Shooting," FLgov.com, June 12, 2016, www.flgov.com/2016/06/12/gov
-scott-we-will-devote-every-resource-available-to-assist-with-orlando-shooting/;
Daniel White, "Read President Obama's Speech Memorializing Shooting Victims
in Orlando," *Time*, June 16, 2016 (http://time.com/4372521/orlando-shooting-barack
-obama-speech/).

6. Stack, "Before Orlando Shooting"; Sheryl Gay Stolberg, "Orlando Attack Roils Gay
Community, Painfully Accustomed to Violence," *The New York Times*, June 12,
2016; Commieflirt, "[NSFW] The Body of Rev. Bill Larson Clings to a Window of
the UpStairs Lounge, a New Orleans Gay Bar Set on Fire Killing Thirty-Two People on the Last Day of Pride Weekend," Reddit, June 13, 2016, www.reddit.com/r
/HistoryPorn/comments/4nubnk/nsfw_the_body_of_rev_bill_larson_clings_to_a/.

7. Lauren Laborde, "Superdome Was Lit Up in Rainbow Colors Last Night," Nola.
com, June 14, 2016, https://nola.curbed.com/2016/6/14/11933194/superdome-new-
orleans-rainbow-colors-orlando; New Orleans Pride, "The Superdome is Rainbow
tonight in memory of the lives lost in the Upstairs Lounge Fire. Thank you to the
staff at the Superdome for granting our request to change the colors for one night,"
Facebook, June 24, 2016, www.facebook.com/NewOrleansPrideFestival/photos/
a.377728969336.156215.331001594336/10154336318569337/?type=3&theater.

8. George Chauncey, *Gay New York: Gender, Urban Culture, and the Making of the Gay
Male World, 1890–1940* (New York: Basic Books, 1994).

9. David Webster Cory, *The Homosexual in America* (New York: Greenberg, 1951), 11.

10. Elizabeth A. Armstrong, *Forging Gay Identities: Organizing Sexuality in San Francisco* (Chicago: University of Chicago Press, 2002), 54; Gary Teller, "I Give You My
Word as a Homosexual," *Vector*, January 1966, 1.

Introduction: History Reclaimed

1. Interview with Dexter Brecht, July 29, 2015; Mark Thompson, "Thirty-Two Killed
in Fire Remembered at Quarter Church," New Orleans *Times-Picayune*, June 26,
1995 (used with permission of the *Times-Picayune* and NOLA.com, © 2017 NOLA
Media Group, LLC, all rights reserved).

2. Michael Riley, "The No-Win Election," *Time*, November 25, 1991 (http://content.time
.com/time/magazine/article/0,9171,974345,00.html); Storer Rowley, "Edwards
Accused of Cover-up Scheme," *Chicago Tribune*, December 6, 1985 (http://articles
.chicagotribune.com/1985-12-06/news/8503240438_1_edwards-health-care-key-point);
"Vote for the Crook," Nola.com, December 14, 2011, http://photos.nola.com/tpphotos
/2011/12/175duke.html.

3. Dexter Brecht, email to author, December 5, 2015.

4. "Historic Crime Data 1990–2014," Nola.gov, www.nola.gov/getattachment/NOPD
/Crime-Data/Crime-Stats/Historic-crime-data-1990-2014.pdf/; "New Orleans Murder Rate on the Rise Again," NBCNews.com, August 18, 2005, www.nbcnews.com/id
/8999837/ns/us_news-crime_and_courts/t/new-orleans-murder-rate-rise-again/#
.WZIHI1Xdq7e1/.

5. Brecht to author, December 5, 2015.
6. "Convention Aspirants Announce Views," New Orleans *Times-Picayune*, August 15, 1972, 64.
7. Interview with Henry Kubicki, April 5, 2016; "Convention Aspirants Announce Views"; Brecht to author, December 5, 2015.
8. Dexter Brecht, "Christophobia?," *The Advocate*, March 8, 1994, 8.
9. John Gallagher, "Is God Gay?," *The Advocate*, December 13, 1994, 40.
10. John Gallagher, "When *The Advocate*'s 'God Is Gay' Cover Infuriated the World," *The Advocate*, April 3, 2015 (www.advocate.com/politics/religion/2015/04/03/when -advocates-god-gay-cover-infuriated-world).
11. Katharine Seelye, "Gingrich's Life: The Complications and Ideals," *The New York Times,* November 24, 1994 (www.nytimes.com/1994/11/24/us/gingrich-s-life-the -complications-and-ideals.html?pagewanted=all); Paul Boyer et al., *Enduring Vision: The History of the American People*, vol. 2, *Since 1865* (Boston: Cengage Learning, 2010), 743.
12. Frank Newport, "Homosexuality," Gallup, September 11, 2002 (www.gallup.com /poll/9916/homosexuality.aspx).
13. Gallagher, "When *The Advocate*'s 'God Is Gay' Cover."
14. Christianne Gadd, "*The Advocate* and the Making of a Gay Model Minority, 1967– 2007" (Ph.D. diss., Lehigh University, 2012), 16 (preserve.lehigh.edu/cgi/viewcontent .cgi?.article=2340&context=et2).
15. Dale Carpenter, *Flagrant Conduct: The Story of Lawrence v. Texas* (New York: W. W. Norton, 2012), 169.
16. Jonathan Katz, *Gay American History* (New York: Crowell, 1976), 24.
17. Martha Washington to Mercy Otis Warren, March 7, 1778, http://marthawashington .us/items/show/31.
18. "Freddy Mercury, Forty-Five, Lead Singer of the Rock Band Queen, Is Dead," *The New York Times*, November 25, 1991 (www.nytimes.com/1991/11/25/arts/freddie- mercury-45-lead-singer-of-the-rock-band-queen-is-dead.html); Joseph Berger, "Rock Hudson, Screen Idol, Dies at Fifty-Nine," *The New York Times*, October 3, 1985 (www. nytimes.com/1985/10/03/arts/rock-hudson-screen-idol-dies-at-59.html).
19. Cliff Jahr, "Elton John: Lonely at the Top," *Rolling Stone*, October 7, 1976 (www .rollingstone.com/music/news/elton-john-lonely-at-the-top-rolling-stones-1976 -cover-story-20110202; accessed February 2, 2011); Marjorie Garber, *Bisexuality and the Eroticism of Everyday Life* (New York: Routledge, 2000), 145; Bill Carter, "Elton John's Revised 'Candle,' for a Princess and Charity," *The New York Times*, September 7, 1997 (http://partners.nytimes.com/library/world/diana/090997diana-elton.html).
20. Robert Christgau, "Turkey Shoot," *The Village Voice*, September 24, 1993 (www. robertchristgau.com/xg/cg/ts93-93.php).
21. Allan Gold, "Rep. Frank Acknowledges Hiring Male Prostitute as Personal Aide," *The New York Times*, August 26, 1989 (www.nytimes.com/1989/08/26/us/rep-frank -acknowledges-hiring-male-prostitute-as-personal-aide.html?pagewanted=all).
22. Brecht interview, July 29, 2015; Henry Kubicki, "Henry Kubicki Account" (unpub- lished manuscript, November 14, 2013), LGBT Religious Archives Network (http:// exhibits.lgbtran.org/exhibits/show/upstairs-lounge-fire), Berkeley, Calif.
23. Brecht interview, July 29, 2016; A. Elwood Willey, "The Upstairs Lounge Fire," *NFPA*

Journal 68, no. 1 (1974): 16–20; Troy Perry and Nancy Wilson, "Report to the President for the White House Conference on Hate Crimes," November 1, 1997, LGBT Religious Archives Network (http://exhibits.lgbtran.org/exhibits/show/upstairs -lounge-fire).

24. Thompson, "Thirty-Two Killed."

25. Willey, "The Upstairs Lounge Fire," 16; "General Case Report," New Orleans Department of Police, August 30, 1973, 2–5, Upstairs Lounge Records, City Archives, New Orleans Public Library.

26. Eric Newhouse, "French Quarter Revelers Trapped," *The* [Portland] *Oregonian*, June 25, 1973, 1.

27. Gay People's Coalition to Human Relations Committee of New Orleans, July 25, 1973, National New Orleans Memorial Fund Collection, ONE National Gay and Lesbian Archives at the USC Libraries, Los Angeles; Roberts Batson, "Remembering the Up Stairs Lounge," *Impact* 23, no. 13 (June 19, 1998): 16–17 (read at Skylar Fein Upstairs Lounge Fire Collection, Historic New Orleans Collection).

28. Interview with Troy Perry, December 2, 2014.

29. Betty Friedan, "Up from the Kitchen Floor," *New York Times Magazine*, March 4, 1973.

30. Thompson, "Thirty-Two Killed"; Vincent Lee, "Gay Leaders Plan Aid for Victims of Bar Fire," New Orleans *Times-Picayune*, June 27, 1973, 14.

31. Buckshot, "Give . . . ," *The Advocate*, August 1, 1973.

32. Homophile Action League, "In the Movement," *Homophile Action League Newsletter*, October 1969, 8.

33. "Blame Shifted on All Sides for Fire Horror," *The New York Times*, March 28, 1911, 1; "Door Was Locked at Factory Fire," *The New York Times*, December 9, 1911, 3.

34. Eric Newhouse, "Bar Not Inspected in Two Years," New Orleans *Times-Picayune*, July 1, 1973, 4.

35. "Six Dead After Church Bombing," *The Washington Post*, September 16, 1963 (www.washingtonpost.com/wp-srv/national/longterm/churches/archives1.htm); John Herbers, "Birmingham Klansman Guilty in Dynamite Case," *The New York Times*, October 9, 1963, 28.

36. "Bombing Is Twenty-First at Birmingham," *The New York Times*, September 16, 1963, 26; "Need More Time to Study Triangle Fire," *The New York Times*, March 1, 1912, 22; "Alfred E. Smith Dies Here at Seventy," *The New York Times*, October 4, 1944, 1.

37. Clayton Delery, "Thieves, Queers and Fruit Jars: The Community and Media Responses to the Fire at the Up Stairs Lounge" (paper presented at the First Annual Louisiana Studies Conference, September 26, 2009); "General Case Report," NOPD, 58; Gareth Griffin, "Flames of Hate: The New Orleans Upstairs Lounge Fire, 24 June 1973" (M.A. thesis, University of Louisiana, 2008; courtesy of Royd Anderson).

38. Provosty A. Dayries, Superintendent of New Orleans Police Department, to "fellow police chiefs," July 24, 1958, Mary Meeh Morrison and Jacob H. Morrison Papers, Historic New Orleans Collection.

39. Scott Ellis, *Madame Vieux Carré: The French Quarter in the Twentieth Century* (Jackson: University Press of Mississippi, 2010), 71.

40. Robert Heath, "Pleasure and Brain Activity in Man," *The Journal of Nervous and Mental Disease* 154 (1972): 3–18; Charles Moan and Robert Heath, "Septal Stimulation for the Initiation of Heterosexual Behavior in a Homosexual Male," *Journal of Behavior Therapy and Experimental Psychiatry* 3 (1972): 23–30; *Diagnostic and Statistical Manual of Mental Disorders (DSM-II)*, 2d ed. (Washington, D.C.: American Psychiatric Association, 1968); Robert Colvile, "The 'gay cure' experiments that were written out of scientific history," *Mosaic*, July 5, 2016 (https://mosaicscience.com/story/gay-cure-experiments).

41. Heath, "Pleasure and Brain Activity in Man," 7.

42. The advertisement, headlined "Christians and Jews!," appeared on p. 51 of the April 8, 1973, issue.

43. Griffin, "Flames of Hate."

44. Tom W. Smith and Jaesok Son, "Trends in Public Attitudes About Sexual Morality," National Opinion Research Center, April 2013, 11 (www.norc.org/PDFs/sexmoralfinal_06-21_FINAL.PDF); Daniel Cappon, *Toward an Understanding of Homosexuality* (Englewood Cliffs, N.J.: Prentice-Hall, 1965), vii; Mike Wallace, "The Homosexuals," *CBS Reports*, March 7, 1967, available at www.youtube.com/watch?v=tu1r6igCODw; Tom W. Smith, Jaesok Son, and Benjamin Shapiro, "Trends in Public Attitudes About Civil Liberties 1972–2014," National Opinion Research Center, April 2015, 16–18 (www.norc.org/PDFs/GSS%20Reports/GSS_CivLib15_final_formatted.pdf).

45. Paul Atkinson, "Beer's Dilemma on Bridge Noted," New Orleans *Times-Picayune*, July 8, 1973, 48; Paul Breton, "United We Stand" (unpublished manuscript, August 1973), National New Orleans Memorial Fund Collection, ONE National Gay and Lesbian Archives.

46. Thompson, "Thirty-Two Killed."

47. Bill Rushton, "Fire Three: Who the Victims Were," *Vieux Carré Courier*, July 13–19, 1973, 6.

48. Ibid.; Perry and Wilson, "Report to the President," 2. Batson, "Remembering the Up Stairs Lounge," 16; Jerry McLeod, "Family Solves Mystery After Learning Uncle Died in Infamous Upstairs Lounge Fire Forty-Plus Years Ago in New Orleans," *New Orleans Advocate*, June 10, 2015 (www.theadvocate.com/new_orleans/entertainment_life/article_bf16d3d9-b8e7-5994-8066-6dc1fa27bca5.html).

49. "Six of Fifteen Injured in Serious Condition," New Orleans *States-Item*, June 25, 1973, A-6b; Brecht interview, July 29, 2015; Delery, "Thieves, Queers and Fruit Jars."

50. Robert Goss, "Silencing Queers at the Up Stairs Lounge: The Stonewall of New Orleans," *Southern Communication Journal* 74 (September 2009): 269–77.

51. Interview with Roberts Batson, May 18, 2016; interview with Johnny Townsend, March 31, 2015; David Cuthbert, "Where There Was Smoke," New Orleans *Times-Picayune*, June 20, 1998.

52. Floyd Getchell to Johnny Townsend, June 11, 1990, Johnny Townsend Collection, ONE National Gay and Lesbian Archives; Townsend interview; interview with Paul Killgore, June 14, 2016.

53. Interview with Wayne Phillips, June 14, 2016. The exhibit, "Devouring Elements," ran from December 1991 to December 1992.

54. Interview with Stewart Butler, July 20, 2014; Phillips interview.

55. Ken Weiss, "VCC Director Criticizes Disaster Area Rhetoric," New Orleans *Times-Picayune*, July 18, 1973, 40.

56. Cuthbert, "Where There Was Smoke."

57. John Pope, "Arsonist Never Found in Fire That Killed Thirty-Two," New Orleans *Times-Picayune*, June 26, 1988, 20; Susan Finch, "Fire of '73: Tragedy United Gays," New Orleans *Times-Picayune*, June 24, 1993.

58. Interview with Dexter Brecht, July 29, 2016.

59. Thompson, "Thirty-Two Killed."

60. Perry interview.

61. Thompson, "Thirty-Two Killed"; Bruce Nolan and Chris Segura, "Memorial for Fire Dead Has Forgiveness Theme," New Orleans *Times-Picayune*, June 26, 1973, 3.

62. Brecht interview, July 29, 2015; Brecht to author, December 5, 2015.

63. Thompson, "Thirty-Two Killed"; Brecht interview, July 29, 2015; Thompson interview.

64. Brecht interview, July 29, 2015; Thompson, "Thirty-Two Killed."

1: Brotherhood of Men

1. "General Case Report," New Orleans Department of Police, August 30, 1973, 29, Upstairs Lounge Records, City Archives, New Orleans Public Library; Henry Kubicki, "Henry Kubicki Account" (unpublished manuscript, November 14, 2013), LGBT Religious Archives Network (http://exhibits.lgbtran.org/exhibits/show/upstairs-lounge-fire), Berkeley, Calif.

2. "General Case Report," NOPD, 29, 26; interview with Stewart Butler, July 20, 2014.

3. Susan Fosberg, "It's a Faggot Bar—Did I Tell You?" *Vieux Carré Courier*, June 29, 1973, 7; Johnny Townsend, *Let the Faggots Burn: The Up Stairs Lounge Fire* (self-published through BookLocker.com, 2011), 102.

4. Interview with Richard Everett, August 25, 2015; Butler interview, July 20, 2014.

5. "Action Set to Curb Deviates," New Orleans *Times-Picayune*, July 23, 1958, 10.

6. Clayton Delery, email to author, December 14, 2016; "General Case Report," NOPD, 3.

7. "General Case Report," NOPD, 6; Butler interview, July 20, 2014.

8. Interview with Henry Kubicki, September 3, 2015; "Homosexuals in Revolt: A Major Essay on America's Newest Militants, the Activists of 'Gay Liberation,'" *Life*, December 31, 1971; Townsend, *Let the Faggots Burn*, 103.

9. Butler interview, July 20, 2014.

10. "General Case Report," NOPD, 2; interview with Henry Kubicki, September 5, 2015.

11. Interview with Richard Everett, September 30, 2016; Kubicki interview, September 5, 2015.

12. Interview with Ronald Rosenthal, June 14, 2016; Everett interview, September 30, 2016.

13. Interview with Steven Duplantis, March 11, 2016; Butler interview, July 20, 2014.

14. "General Case Report," NOPD, 4; Troy Perry and Thomas Swicegood, *Don't Be Afraid Anymore* (New York: St. Martin's, 1990), 79; "Notes on Fire Victims," Orle-

ans Parish Coroner's Office, 1973, Upstairs Lounge Records, City Archives, New Orleans Public Library; Townsend, *Let the Faggots Burn*, 172.

15. "General Case Report," NOPD, 5, 29.

16. "The Dome Inside and Out," New Orleans *States-Item*, July 30, 1973.

17. "Up, Up and Away," New Orleans *Times-Picayune*, August 1, 1969, 10.

18. Vincent Lee, "Ceremony Held at New Statue," New Orleans *Times-Picayune*, October 26, 1972, 3; "Youth, Fourteen, Shoots Five-Foot Alligator," New Orleans *Times-Picayune*, May 15, 1961, 29.

19. "Shaw to Leave Mart October 1," New Orleans *Times-Picayune*, August 27, 1965, 1; Scott Ellis, *Madame Vieux Carré: The French Quarter in the Twentieth Century* (Jackson: University Press of Mississippi, 2010), 71; Clarence Doucet and Donald Hughes, "JFK Death Suspect Free Under $10,000 Bond," New Orleans *Times-Picayune*, March 2, 1967, 1.

20. Curt Sprang, "Inside the Clay Shaw Trial," WGNO.com, November 23, 2013, http://wgno.com/2013/11/23/the-kennedy-assassination-spawned-all-kinds-of-conspiracy-theories/; James Phelan, "A Plot to Kill Kennedy? Rush to Judgment in New Orleans," *Saturday Evening Post*, May 6, 1967 (http://mcadams.posc.mu.edu/phelan.htm); "Heard Shaw, Oswald, Ferrie Plot JFK Killing, Says Russo," New Orleans *Times-Picayune*, March 15, 1967, 1, 16; "'Mystery Man' Revealed in Probe," *Ellensburg* [Wash.] *Daily Record*, March 3, 1967, 1; Nicholas Lemann, "The Case Against Jim Garrison," *GQ*, January 1992; Jack Anderson, "Jim Garrison Is Accused of Molesting Youth of Thirteen," *Gadsden* [Ala.] *Times*, February 25, 1970, 4.

21. David Bird, "Clay Shaw Is Dead at Sixty; Freed in Kennedy 'Plot,'" *The New York Times*, August 16, 1974, 32; Edward Epstein, "Epitaph for Jim Garrison: Romancing the Assassination," *The New Yorker*, November 30, 1992 (www.edwardjayepstein.com /archived/garrison_print.htm); "Ferrie, JFK-Probe Data Linked," *Gadsden Times*, February 21, 1967, 1; Nicholas Lemann, "The Rise and Fall of Big Jim G.," *Harvard Crimson*, February 6, 1974.

22. Interview with Roberts Batson, July 11, 2014; James Kirkwood, *American Grotesque* (New York: Simon & Schuster: 1968), 33.

23. "Justice, at Long Last," New Orleans *Times-Picayune*, March 2, 1969, 1; "Clay Shaw Suit Trial Date Set," New Orleans *Times-Picayune*, June 27, 1974, 2.

24. Clarence Doucet, "Garrison Charges Shaw with Lying During Trial," New Orleans *Times-Picayune*, March 4, 1969, 1; *Clay L. Shaw v. Jim Garrison*, U.S. Court of Appeals for the Fifth Circuit, July 31, 1972 (http://law.justia.com/cases/federal/ appellate-courts/F2/467/113/154362/).

25. Ellis, *Madame Vieux Carré*, 80; "John Lafitte: History and Mystery," National Park Service, www.nps.gov/jela/upload/Jean%20Lafitte%20pirate%20site%20bulletin.pdf; "Spring Fiesta Magic," New Orleans *Times-Picayune*, April 9, 1972, 199; "Clay Shaw Final Rites to Be Today," New Orleans *Times-Picayune*, August 16, 1974, 1.

26. "General Case Report," NOPD, 11.

27. Map of Vieux Carré Boundaries, Vieux Carré Commission, www.nola.gov/vcc /map/.

28. "Deaths of Seven Are Probed," New Orleans *Times-Picayune*, January 16, 1972, 1; interview with John Meyers, January 28, 2016; Frank Perez and Jeffrey Palmquist,

In Exile: The History and Lore Surrounding New Orleans Gay Culture and Its Oldest Gay Bar (Hurlford, Scotland: LL-Publications, 2012), 110–11.

29. Kevin Fox Gotham, "Tourism Gentrification: The Case of New Orleans' Vieux Carré (French Quarter)," *Urban Studies* 42, no. 7 (June 2005): 1099–1121; Ken Weiss, "Disaster Waiting to Happen: Quarter Firetrap Crackdown," New Orleans *Times-Picayune*, June 28, 1973, 7; Moon Landrieu, oral history interview with Mark Cave, May 12, 2009, New Orleans Life Story Project, Historic New Orleans Collection.

30. A. Elwood Willey, "The Upstairs Lounge Fire," *NFPA Journal* 68, no. 1 (1974): 16–20; Vieux Carré Commission Evaluation, April 1876, 141 Chartres Street (604 Iberville), https://stevenwarran.blogspot.com/2014_08_01_archive.html; Sanborn's Insurance Maps, April 1976. Special Collections Division, Tulane University Libraries, New Orleans.

31. Willey, "The Upstairs Lounge Fire," 17; "General Case Report," NOPD, 10.

32. "General Case Report," NOPD, 16; Kubicki, "Henry Kubicki Account"; Fosberg, "It's a Faggot Bar," 7; Wood Dunham, "French Quarter Bar Guide, Part III," *Vieux Carré Courier*, March 3, 1972, 5; Townsend, *Let the Faggots Burn*, 44; interview with Stewart Butler, August 4, 2015.

33. Dunham, "French Quarter Bar Guide"; Howard Jacobs, "Blight in 600 Block of Iberville Lifting," New Orleans *Times-Picayune*, October 19, 1970, 11; Butler interview, July 20, 2014.

34. Townsend, *Let the Faggots Burn*, 47.

35. Willey, "The Upstairs Lounge Fire," 16; "General Case Report," NOPD, 10.

36. Duplantis interview; "General Case Report," NOPD, 10.

37. Clayton Delery-Edwards, *The Up Stairs Lounge Arson: Thirty-Two Deaths in a New Orleans Gay Bar, June 24, 1973* (Jefferson, N.C.: McFarland, 2014), 43, 17; Fosberg, "It's a Faggot Bar," 7.

38. Bill Rushton, "Window in the Orange Glow," *Vieux Carré Courier*, June 29, 1973, 4; Delery-Edwards, *The Up Stairs Lounge Arson*, 17; Becky Bruns, "Guys and Dolls . . . A Play on Roles," New Orleans *Times-Picayune*, January 16, 1977, 82–83; "Damage Estimated at $75,000," New Orleans *Times-Picayune*, January 6, 1972, 22; "General Case Report," NOPD, 12; Kubicki, "Henry Kubicki Account"; "Lovers of the Old-Time Mellerdrammers . . . ," New Orleans *Times-Picayune*, May 15, 1971, 9.

39. "General Case Report," NOPD, 29; "Field Inspection Report," New Orleans Department of Safety and Permits, October 19, 1970, Johnny Townsend Collection, ONE National Gay and Lesbian Archives at the USC Libraries, Los Angeles; Townsend, *Let the Faggots Burn*, 47.

40. Everett interview, August 25, 2015; Townsend, *Let the Faggots Burn*, 245.

41. Everett interviews, August 25 and July 27, 2015; "General Case Report," NOPD, 60.

42. Butler interview, July 20, 2014. David Cuthbert, "Where There Was Smoke," New Orleans *Times-Picayune*, June 20, 1998; Everett interview, August 25, 2015; Bill Rushton, "Society Real Culprit in New Orleans Tragedy?," *The Advocate*, August 1, 1973.

43. "General Case Report," NOPD, 30; Perry and Swicegood, *Don't Be Afraid Anymore*, 80; Butler interview, July 20, 2014.

44. Robert McAnear, Facebook message to author, January 6, 2017.

45. Ibid.

46. Robert McAnear, Facebook message to author, January 9, 2017; McAnear to author, January 6, 2017.

47. Nick Lemann, "'Racial Purity' and the State: How They Can Change Your Color," *Vieux Carré Courier*, August 24, 1973, 1; A. J. Liebling, *The Earl of Louisiana* (Baton Rouge: Louisiana State University Press, 1970).

48. McAnear to author, January 6, 2017; Fosberg, "It's a Faggot Bar," 7; "Survivor Discovers Her True Friends," *The Advocate*, July 31, 1974, 8.

49. Interview with anonymous friend of sister of Clayton Delery, September 2015; Eric Newhouse, "Smokie," Associated Press, June 1973; Paul Breton, "United We Stand" (unpublished manuscript, August 1973), National New Orleans Memorial Fund Collection, ONE National Gay and Lesbian Archives; Delery-Edwards, *The Up Stairs Lounge Arson*, 32.

50. Interview with Richard Everett, August 10, 2015; Bill Rushton, "New Orleans Toll Thirty-Two; Arson Evidence Cited," *The Advocate*, August 1, 1973, 6; Delery-Edwards, *The Up Stairs Lounge Arson*, 17.

51. Townsend, *Let the Faggots Burn*, 241; Rushton, "New Orleans Toll."

52. *Gertrude's Notes* (Gertrude Stein Society newsletter), January 1977 (read at Rebels, Rubyfruit and Rhinestones Research Files, James T. Sears Papers, Duke University Libraries, Durham, N.C.); "Come Join," *Sunflower* (New Orleans Gay Liberation Front newspaper) 1, no. 1 (January 1971) (read at Rebels, Rubyfruit and Rhinestones Research Files); Bob Damron, *Bob Damron's Address Book*, 8th ed. (San Francisco: Bob Damron, 1972), 76–78.

53. Newhouse, "Smokie"; interview with Paul Killgore, January 17, 2016; interview with John Meyers, February 1, 2016.

54. "Blackmail Lawmaker in Homosexual Ring," *Chicago Tribune*, May 17, 1967, 11.

55. Newhouse, "Smokie"; Meyers interview, January 28, 2016.

56. Everett interview, August 25, 2015; Fosberg, "It's a Faggot Bar," 7; Townsend, *Let the Faggots Burn*, 278.

57. Townsend, *Let the Faggots Burn*, 278; photograph of Buddy Rasmussen, Johnny Townsend personal archive; Killgore interview, January 17, 2016; Fosberg, "It's a Faggot Bar," 7.

58. Dunham, "French Quarter Bar Guide"; Killgore interview, January 17, 2016.

59. Associated Press photograph by Jack Thornell, June 25, 1973.

60. Bill Rushton, "After the Fire Upstairs," *Vieux Carré Courier*, June 29, 1973, 4; Cuthbert, "Where There Was Smoke"; "General Case Report," NOPD, 29.

2: Sunday Service

1. Henry Kubicki, "Henry Kubicki Account" (unpublished manuscript, November 14, 2013), LGBT Religious Archives Network (http://exhibits.lgbtran.org/exhibits /show/upstairs-lounge-fire), Berkeley, Calif.; Clayton Delery-Edwards, *The Up Stairs Lounge Arson: Thirty-Two Deaths in a New Orleans Gay Bar, June 24, 1973* (Jefferson, N.C.: McFarland, 2014), 23.

2. Kubicki, "Henry Kubicki Account"; interview with Stewart Butler, July 20, 2014.

3. Delery-Edwards, *The Up Stairs Lounge Arson*, 35; floor plan of MCC of New Orle-

ans, drawn by Henry Kubicki and given to author December 11, 2016; Kubicki, "Henry Kubicki Account."

4. Delery-Edwards, *The Up Stairs Lounge Arson*, 38; MCC of New Orleans floor plan; Everett interview, August 10, 2015; interview with Henry Kubicki, January 21, 2016.

5. William Lairson, Kentucky Birth Index, Ancestry.com. While Bill Larson's birth certificate reads "Lairson," all of the government records from his time at the Butler County Children's Home use the spelling "Larison."

6. "Summary," Ohio Bureau of Social Work, 1929, Children's Home Association of Butler County Records, Ohio History Connection, Columbus, Ohio; Issackar Larison, Kentucky Death Records, Ancestry.com.

7. Roscoe Larison, Butler County Children's Home, 1930 United States Federal Census, Ancestry.com; "Children's Home Kiddies Delighted At Egg Hunt," *Hamilton* [Ohio] *Evening Journal*, March 28, 1932, 16; "970," Roscoe Larison, Butler County Children's Home, 1926, Children's Home Association of Butler County Records; "Larison, Summary," Butler County Children's Home, February 1932, Children's Home Association of Butler County Records; "Summary," Ohio Bureau of Social Work, 1929; "Accept Settlement for Child's Death," *Hamilton* [Ohio] *Evening Journal*, March 15, 1929, 24.

8. "Arrest Mother of Five at Shack on Dump," *Hamilton* [Ohio] *Daily News*, July 16, 1930, 3; "Troy Howell 51422," U.S. National Homes for Disabled Volunteer Soldiers, 1926, Ancestry.com; "Licensed to Wed," *Hamilton* [Ohio] *Evening Journal*, July 17, 1930, 15; "Summary," Ohio Bureau of Social Work, 1929; "Record of Child's Own Family," Butler County Children's Home, 2, Children's Home Association of Butler County Records; "966," Larison, Butler County Children's Home, Children's Home Association of Butler County Records.

9. Roscoe Larison, Butler County Children's Home, 1940 United States Federal Census, Ancestry.com; letter to Butler County Juvenile Court, July 1, 1941, Children's Home Association of Butler County Records.

10. William Lairson, World War II Army Enlistment Records, April 10, 1944, Ancestry.com; "Honorable Discharges Presented to Other Servicemen from Butler County," *Hamilton* [Ohio] *Journal and Daily News*, April 26, 1946, 13; "Nellie K. Cloyd and William Lairson Marry," *Hamilton Journal and Daily News*, September 1, 1945, 3; "Review Campaign at Grace Church," *Hamilton Journal and Daily News*, February 18, 1947, 14.

11. "Grace Fellowship," *Hamilton Journal and Daily News*, March 29, 1947, 9; "Nellie Lairson Files Petition for Decree," *Hamilton Journal and Daily News*, July 12, 1947, 13; "Larson" (paid death notice), New Orleans *Times-Picayune*, June 30, 1973, 19.

12. Johnny Townsend, *Let the Faggots Burn: The Up Stairs Lounge Fire* (self-published through BookLocker.com, 2011), 128; William Richardson, letter to the editor, *The Voice of Integrity* 1, no. 2 (Summer 1991), LGBT Religious Archives Network (http://exhibits.lgbtran.org/exhibits/show/upstairs-lounge-fire); David Solomon, "New Congregation Will Be Organized," New Orleans *Times-Picayune*, April 17, 1971.

13. David Solomon, "Song of Solomon," *Sunflower* 1, no. 3 (April 1971), 9 (read at Rebels, Rubyfruit and Rhinestones Research Files, James T. Sears Papers, Duke University Libraries, Durham, N.C.); "'Gay' Group Pickets Police HQ in Orleans," Baton Rouge *Advocate*, January 24, 1971.

14. "Gay Liberation Front Bars an Attempt to Seize County," *The New York Times*, November 5, 1970, 58; Steven Roberts, "Homosexuals in Revolt," *The New York Times*, August 24, 1970, 28; C. Fraser, "'Gay Ghettos' Seen as Police Targets," *The New York Times*, August 31, 1970, 28.

15. "'Gay' Group Pickets Police HQ."

16. Townsend, *Let the Faggots Burn*, 14; "Come Join," *Sunflower* 1, no. 1 (January 1971), 4 (read at Rebels, Rubyfruit and Rhinestones Research Files, Sears Papers); "Gay Liberation Group Marches," New Orleans *Times-Picayune*, January 24, 1971, 16.

17. Roger Nelson to James Sears, n.d. (c. 2001), Rebels, Rubyfruit and Rhinestones Research Files; "Gay Liberation Group Marches," 16; Waddell Summers, "Bowling Summer-ies," New Orleans *Times-Picayune*, October 29, 1968, 27.

18. Moon Landrieu, oral history interview with Mark Cave, May 12, 2009, New Orleans Life Story Project, Historic New Orleans Collection; "Gay Front Fails to Meet Mayor," New Orleans *Times-Picayune*, January 21, 1971.

19. "'Gay' Group Pickets Police HQ"; "Gay Front Fails to Meet Mayor."

20. Winston Lill, press release, February 11, 1971, Rebels, Rubyfruit and Rhinestones Research Files, Sears Papers.

21. "'Chaplain' Calls for Panel Talk with Homosexuals," New Orleans *Times-Picayune*, January 29, 1971; Kubicki, "Henry Kubicki Account"; Mary Gehman, "N.O. Women's Movement: A Comprehensive History," *Distaff*, October 1973, 8 (read at Louisiana Research Collection, Howard-Tilton Memorial Library, Tulane University, New Orleans).

22. Solomon, "New Congregation Will Be Organized."

23. Referring to homosexuality in print, of course, ran counter to the mores of the time. It would have been viewed as equally unorthodox for the word "Gay" to appear in the newspaper because it was then regarded as slang. Spelled with a capital "G" initially to distinguish it from the common usage of the word as a synonym for "happy" (the theme song of the 1960s animated TV series *The Flintstones* spoke of the titular family's having "a gay old time"), "Gay" was in common usage among homosexuals, but this definition was not found in any dictionary. Style guides for major publications, such as *The New York Times*, banned the word, and copy editors replaced it with the more clinical "homosexual" whenever the topic was unavoidable. No leading paper in the country would use "Gay" without enclosing it in quotation marks. *The New York Times* would not change its style to allow the word "Gay" in the sense of "homosexual" until 1987.

24. Dotson Rader, "The Gay Militants," *The New York Times*, October 3, 1971, 133.

25. Interview with Henry Kubicki, April 5, 2016.

26. Interview with Joseph Bermuda, March 31, 2015.

27. Kubicki, "Henry Kubicki Account"; interview with Henry Kubicki, September 4, 2015.

28. Kubicki, "Henry Kubicki Account."

29. "The Cover," *In Unity*, March 1972, 2, https://issuu.com/mccchurches/doc; Troy Perry and Thomas Swicegood, *Don't Be Afraid Anymore* (New York: St. Martin's, 1990), 78; Edward B. Fiske, "Homosexuals in Los Angeles, Like Many Elsewhere, Want Religion and Establish Their Own Church," *The New York Times*, February 15, 1970, 58.

30. Fiske, "Homosexuals in Los Angeles," 58; interview with Troy Perry, December 2, 2014; Perry and Swicegood, *Don't Be Afraid Anymore*, 25; Troy Perry, "Hear Rev. Troy D. Perry," *The Advocate*, October 2, 1968.

31. "Directory," *In Unity*, April 1972, 30–32, https://issuu.com/mccchurches/doc; James Birkitt, "Rev. Troy Perry: The Father of Marriage Equality" (self-published, 2013), http://ourhopemcc.com/wp-content/uploads/2013/07/MCCSame-SexMarriageDates-Part.pdf.

32. Paul Houston, "Homosexuals Get ACLU Aid in Fight for Parade Permit," *Los Angeles Times*, June 13, 1970, A1; Paul Houston, "Homosexuals Stage Hollywood Parade," *Los Angeles Times*, June 29, 1970, 3.

33. Joan Treadway, "Fifties Climate of Hostility to Gays Gone—What Now?," New Orleans *Times-Picayune*, September 16, 1973, 21.

34. John Reed, *Dixie Bohemia: A French Quarter Circle in the 1920s* (Baton Rouge: Louisiana State University Press, 2012).

35. Interview with Nicholas Lemann, April 15, 2015.

36. "Justice, at Long Last," New Orleans *Times-Picayune*, March 2, 1969, 1.

37. Interview with John Meyers, January 26, 2016; "A Dandy Mayor," New Orleans *Times-Picayune*, March 11, 1886, 4; "Mahoney Estate Disposal Puzzle," New Orleans *Times-Picayune*, February 23, 1949, 14; "John McDonogh," New Orleans *Daily Picayune*, December 30, 1898, 4.

38. Clayton Delery, *Out for Queer Blood: The Murder of Fernando Rios and the Failure of New Orleans Justice* (Jefferson, N.C.: Exposit/McFarland, 2017), 48.

39. Scott Ellis, *Madame Vieux Carré: The French Quarter in the Twentieth Century* (Jackson: University Press of Mississippi, 2010), 66; "Action Set to Curb Deviates," New Orleans *Times-Picayune*, July 23, 1958, 10.

40. Frank Perez and Jeffrey Palmquist, *In Exile: The History and Lore Surrounding New Orleans Gay Culture and Its Oldest Gay Bar* (Hurlford, Scotland: LL-Publications, 2012), 40, 39.

41. "Ousted Patron Reenters Tavern in Pickup Truck," New Orleans *Times-Picayune*, May 4, 1969, 158; "Man Arrested, Booked on Morals Offense," New Orleans *Times-Picayune*, October 17, 1964, 54; "1958 Brent Award," New Orleans *Times-Picayune*, October 10, 1958, 10.

42. Perez and Palmquist, *In Exile*, 38; John Lahr, *Tennessee Williams: Mad Pilgrimage of the Flesh* (New York: W. W. Norton, 2015).

43. Louis Kronenberger, "The Theater: New Play, Old Play," *Time*, April 1, 1957; Louis Kronenberger, "The Theater: New Play in Manhattan," *Time*, April 4, 1955; Tennessee Williams to Frank Merlo, 1957, Tennessee Williams Manuscripts, Correspondence, and Related Materials, Historic New Orleans Collection.

44. Ellis, *Madame Vieux*, 68; interview with Frank Perez, July 15, 2015.

45. Interview with Jane Place, May 12, 2016; Perez and Palmquist, *In Exile*, 190.

46. Bill Rushton, "Society Real Culprit in New Orleans Tragedy?," *The Advocate*, August 1, 1973.

47. Kubicki, "Henry Kubicki Account"; "Elysian Fields Parish of MCC New Orleans," *In Unity*, June 1971, 25, https://issuu.com/mccchurches/doc; Delery-Edwards, *The Up Stairs Lounge Arson*, 22; Butler interview, July 20, 2014.

48. Delery-Edwards, *The Up Stairs Lounge Arson*, 19; Eric Newhouse, "Smokie," Associated Press, June 1973; Townsend, *Let the Faggots Burn*, 248.

49. Townsend, *Let the Faggots Burn*, 204, 248; Bob Damron, *Bob Damron's Address Book*, 9th ed. (San Francisco: Bob Damron, 1973), 101.

50. Interview with Henry Kubicki, September 3, 2015; interview with John Meyers, February 1, 2016; Kubicki, "Henry Kubicki Account."

51. Becky Bruns, "Guys and Dolls . . . A Play on Roles," New Orleans *Times-Picayune*, January 16, 1977, 82; Kubicki, "Henry Kubicki Account"; Robert McAnear, Facebook message to author, January 6, 2017; interview with Richard Everett, August 25, 2015.

52. Everett interview, August 25, 2015.

53. Bill Rushton, "How the Media Saw It," *Vieux Carré Courier*, June 29, 1973, 5; program for *Egad, What a Cad*, Theatre of the Upstairs, June 12, 1971. Henry Kubicki personal archive; Everett interview, August 10, 2015; Kubicki, "Henry Kubicki Account."

54. Richardson, *The Voice of Integrity*; Townsend, *Let the Faggots Burn*, 35; "Directory," *In Unity*, August–September 1972, 27, https://issuu.com/mccchurches/doc.

55. "Convention Aspirants Announce Views," New Orleans *Times-Picayune*, August 15, 1972, 64; Kubicki, "Henry Kubicki Account."

56. Kubicki, "Henry Kubicki Account"; Valerie Haynes, "Memorial Rites Honor Lounge Blaze Victims," New Orleans *Times-Picayune*, June 23, 1975.

57. Kubicki interview, September 5, 2015; Everett interview, August 25, 2015; Eric Newhouse, "Church Slates Mourning for Victims of N.O. Fire," Baton Rouge *Morning Advocate*, June 26, 1973; "Roscoe Larison," Butler County Children's Home, 1936, Children's Home Association of Butler County Records, Ohio History Connection.

58. Kubicki, "Henry Kubicki Account"; Perry and Swicegood, *Don't Be Afraid Anymore*, 79; Roberts Batson, "Remembering the Up Stairs Lounge," *Impact* 23, no. 13 (June 19, 1998): 16 (read at Skylar Fein Upstairs Lounge Fire Collection, Historic New Orleans Collection); Kubicki interview, September 4, 2015; "Ax Falls on Socially Conscious Boston Minister," *The Advocate*, July 18, 1973, 17.

59. "Duane George Mitchell," *Birmingham News*, July 2, 1973, 43; Tom Frazer, "Sons of Fire Victim Sent Home—Unaware of Father's Death," New Orleans *States-Item*, June 26, 1973, A3; Delery-Edwards, *The Up Stairs Lounge Arson*, 39.

60. "Ex-Resident Killed in New Orleans Fire," Chicago *Daily Herald*, July 3, 1973, 36; "Guy Andersen," death notice, *The Des Plaines* [Illinois] *Herald*, July 3, 1973, 8; interview with Dexter Brecht, July 29, 2016; "Fire Victims: More than Just Names," *The Advocate*, August 1, 1973, 17.

61. Interview with Marc Schmitz, July 1, 2016.

62. "General Case Report," New Orleans Department of Police, August 30, 1973, 50, Upstairs Lounge Records, City Archives, New Orleans Public Library. In keeping with the times, friends at the bar would refer to Soleto as a drag queen. They used the term "cross-dresser" or "transsexual" only rarely. The word "trans-gender," as it was spelled then, and the concept of gender dysphoria as a medical phenomenon were not well understood—even by gay friends.

63. Damron, *Bob Damron's Address Book*, 9th ed., 101.

64. Interview with Robert Camina, July 2016; "General Case Report," NOPD, 50; Townsend, *Let the Faggots Burn*, 191.

65. Delery-Edwards, *The Up Stairs Lounge Arson*, 38.

66. Everett interview, August 25, 2015; Patsy Sims, *The Klan* (Lexington: University of Kentucky Press, 1996), 152–53.

67. Everett interview, August 25, 2015.

68. "Tonight's Movie Showcase," New Orleans *Times-Picayune*, June 24, 1973, 52; Harold Fairbanks, "Jan-Michael Denies 'Fag' Slur," *The Advocate*, November 8, 1972, 27.

69. Interview with Duane Mitchell, August 13, 2015; Frazer, "Sons of Fire Victim Sent Home," A3.

70. Mitchell interview, August 13, 2015.

3: Gay Liberation

1. Johnny Townsend, *Let the Faggots Burn: The Up Stairs Lounge Fire* (self-published through BookLocker.com, 2011), 170–71; Anonymous, *The Cajun Queen: A Complete Guide to New Orleans Gaydom* (New Orleans: Minotaur, Inc., 1974), 17; interview with David Williams, January 21, 2016; interview with Richard Everett, July 27, 2015.

2. Everett interviews, August 25, 2015, July 27, 2015, September 30, 2016, and August 10, 2015; interview with Ronald Rosenthal, June 14, 2016; Henry Kubicki, "Henry Kubicki Account" (unpublished manuscript, November 14, 2013), LGBT Religious Archives Network (http://exhibits.lgbtran.org/exhibits/show/upstairs-lounge-fire), Berkeley, Calif.

3. Everett interview, July 27, 2015.

4. Frank Perez and Jeffrey Palmquist, *In Exile: The History and Lore Surrounding New Orleans Gay Culture and Its Oldest Gay Bar* (Hurlford, Scotland: LL-Publications, 2012), 17; Frank Perez, email to author, December 6, 2016; "A Nineteenth Century Photo," *Clarion Herald*, June 28, 1973, 1; Don Gross, " 'My Name Is Nobody'—And Some People Agree," New Orleans *Times-Picayune*, June 25, 1973, 24.

5. Everett interview, July 27, 2015.

6. Eugene Davis, Statement to Louisiana Office of State Fire Marshal, October 1, 1973, 2, Skylar Fein Upstairs Lounge Fire Collection, Historic New Orleans Collection.

7. Ibid.; "Eugene C. Davis Services Monday," New Orleans *Times-Picayune*, June 3, 1984, 22; Clayton Delery-Edwards, *The Up Stairs Lounge Arson: Thirty-Two Deaths in a New Orleans Gay Bar, June 24, 1973* (Jefferson, N.C.: McFarland, 2014), 119; Townsend, *Let the Faggots Burn*, 213.

8. Delery-Edwards, *The Up Stairs Lounge Arson*, 120; "Vice Charges Okayed by DA: Obscenity, Eight Other Morals Cases Accepted," New Orleans *Times-Picayune*, October 8, 1958, 22; Dean A. Andrews, Orleans Parish Grand Jury testimony, June 28, 1967, http://mcadams.posc.mu.edu/russ/testimony/andrewsshaw3.htm.

9. "N.O. Bar Owner Sues NBC on Probe Report," New Orleans *States-Item*, August 13, 1968; "Two Persons Die in $50,000 Hotel Fire at Silver Dollar Hotel," New Orleans *Times-Picayune*, October 14, 1970, 8.

10. Davis, Statement to State Fire Marshal, 2; Mark Allen Guidry, Statement to Louisiana Office of State Fire Marshal, July 2, 1973, 4, Skylar Fein Upstairs Lounge Fire Collection, Historic New Orleans Collection.

11. Rodger Dale Nunez, New Orleans Police Department Arrest Register, April 4, 1973, Johnny Townsend Collection, ONE National Gay and Lesbian Archives at USC Libraries, Los Angeles; Cynthia Ann Savant, Statement to Louisiana Office of State Fire Marshal, August 1, 1974, 10, Louisiana State Archives, Baton Rouge (copy courtesy of Clayton Delery).

12. Rodger Dale Nunez, U.S. Army records, National Military Personnel Records Center, St. Louis, Mo.; Delery-Edwards, *The Up Stairs Lounge Arson*, 118; Will Peneguy, "Now Hear This," New Orleans *Times-Picayune*, April 20, 1973, 39; Maud O'Bryan, "Up and Down the Street," New Orleans *Times-Picayune*, March 24, 1968, 61; Clayton Delery, email to author, December 15, 2016.

13. Alex Heigl, "Courir de Mardi Gras: The Strangest Tradition You've Never Heard Of," *People*, March 4, 2014 (http://people.com/celebrity/courir-de-mardi-gras-referenced -on-true-detective/); Delery to author, December 15, 2016.

14. "TU Doctors Seek Cut in La. Infant Mortality," New Orleans *Times-Picayune*, September 30, 1979, 31; Delery to author, December 15, 2016.

15. Joseph Nunez and Rose Choate family tree, Our Family History, www.hpeterjr.us /familygroup.php?familyID=F29003&tree=1; Roger Dale Nunez, U.S. Navy enlistment application, June 1, 1964, National Military Personnel Records Center; "Official Report," Louisiana Office of State Fire Marshal, July 22, 1975, Louisiana State Archives.

16. Nunez, U.S. Navy enlistment application; Nunez, U.S. Army records.

17. Nunez, U.S. Army records.

18. Ibid; Rodger Dale Nunez, letter to the editor, *Abbeville Meridional*, February 18, 1965, 2.

19. Roger Dale Nunez, Record 814225, Louisiana Department of Public Safety, 1973, Louisiana State Archives; Rodger D. Nunez, District Court for the Parish of New Orleans fine record, December 4, 1972, Johnny Townsend Collection, ONE National Gay and Lesbian Archives; Nunez, NOPD Arrest Register, April 4, 1973; John BonneCarrere to Judge Frank Shea, Orleans Parish Criminal Court, August 7, 1973, Johnny Townsend Collection.

20. Davis, Statement to State Fire Marshal, 2; Guidry, Statement to State Fire Marshal, 4; Nunez, NOPD Arrest Register, April 4, 1973.

21. Forensic Laboratory Report, Coroner's Office Parish of Orleans, December 5, 1974, Louisiana State Archive (copy courtesy of Trevor Santos); Townsend, *Let the Faggots Burn*, 211.

22. Davis, Statement to State Fire Marshal, 2, 3; Guidry, Statement to State Fire Marshal, 4.

23. Davis, Statement to State Fire Marshal, 3.

24. Kubicki, "Henry Kubicki Account"; Henry Kubicki, email to author, July 2, 2016.

25. Kubicki, "Henry Kubicki Account"; "Grand Opening of Hotel Is Set," New Orleans *Times-Picayune*, July 17, 1972, 14; "Dollars and Sense of the Marriott," New Orleans *Times-Picayune Dixie Roto Magazine*, June 4, 1972, 26.

26. Interview with Henry Kubicki, September 4, 2015; "New Businesses in New

Orleans," New Orleans *Times-Picayune*, December 6, 1970, sect. 5, p. 27; interview with Gene Adams, April 18, 2016.

27. Interview with Henry Kubicki, April 5, 2016.

28. "Gay Rights Protections in the U.S. and Canada," National Gay Task Force, 1976, Rebels, Rubyfruit and Rhinestones Research Files, James T. Sears Papers, Duke University Libraries, Durham, N.C.; David K. Johnson, *The Lavender Scare* (Chicago: University of Chicago Press, 2004); "Douglas Dissents as Tribunal Upholds Ouster of Homosexual," *Chicago Tribune*, May 23, 1967, 4.

29. Kubicki interview, April 5, 2016; Kubicki, "Henry Kubicki Account."

30. Townsend, *Let the Faggots Burn*, 124; Dale Carpenter, *Flagrant Conduct: The Story of Lawrence v. Texas* (New York: W. W. Norton, 2012), 7.

31. Photograph, June 12, 1971, Henry Kubicki personal archive; Kubicki, "Henry Kubicki Account."

32. Interview with Stewart Butler, July 20, 2014; H. L. Mencken, "The Rev. Clergy," *Chicago Sunday Tribune*, April 4, 1927, 7; Perez and Palmquist, *In Exile*, 110.

33. Allan Katz, "Some Krewes Lowering the Color Barrier," New Orleans *States-Item*, May 4, 1973; Richard Campanella, *Bourbon Street: A History* (Baton Rouge: Louisiana State University Press, 2014), 187; Roberts Batson, "Ye Shall Know the Magic and the Magic Shall Set Ye Free!," *Impact*, February 16, 1996, 35 (read at Rebels, Rubyfruit, and Rhinestones Research Files, Sears Papers); Townsend, *Let the Faggots Burn*, 73.

34. Howard Smith, email to author, October 7, 2016; "A History of the Gay Krewes," *Impact*, February 1978, 3 (read at Rebels, Rubyfruit and Rhinestones Research Files).

35. Interview with Stewart Butler, July 20, 2014; interview with Steven Duplantis, March 11, 2016.

36. Ibid.

37. Duplantis interview.

38. Allen Bérubé, *Coming Out Under Fire: The History of Gay Men and Women in World War II* (Chapel Hill: University of North Carolina Press, 2010); Charles Kaiser, *The Gay Metropolis* (New York: Grove Press, 2007); John Lahr, *Tennessee Williams: Mad Pilgrimage of the Flesh* (New York: W. W. Norton, 2014).

39. W. F. Charles to Café Lafitte in Exile, April 26, 1966. I read this letter at the bar, where it remains on display.

40. Randy Wicker, "Gays Pour Through New York," *The Advocate*, July 18, 1973, 3; John Darnton, "Homosexuals March Down Seventh Avenue," *The New York Times*, June 25, 1973, 21.

41. Gerald Hansen, "Color, Joy in San Francisco," *The Advocate*, July 18, 1973, 3; Don Dunfee, "3000 Brave Heat for Chicago Pride Parade," *The Advocate*, July 18, 1973, 6; Mary Ann Cherry, "Gay Pride 1973" (unpublished manuscript, October 2012, available at http://morriskight.blogspot.com/2012/10/gay-pride-1973); Troy Perry and Thomas Swicegood, *Don't Be Afraid Anymore* (New York: St. Martin's, 1990), 77.

42. Delery-Edwards, *The Up Stairs Lounge Arson*, 39; "Ninety-Six Are Booked After Jeff Raid: Authorities Break Up 'Stag Party,'" New Orleans *Times-Picayune*, February 26, 1962, 9.

43. Perez and Palmquist, *In Exile,* 49.

44. "Jury Acquits Three Students Tried in Slaying of Guide," New Orleans *Times-Picayune*, January 24, 1959; "Injuries Fatal for Tour Chief," New Orleans *Times-*

Picayune, September 29, 1958, 1; Orleans Parish Criminal District Court, *State of Louisiana v. Alberto Calvo, David Drennan, and John Farrell* (docket 161-757), Louisiana State Archives; Clayton Delery, *Out for Queer Blood: The Murder of Fernando Rios and the Failure of New Orleans Justice* (Jefferson, N.C.: Exposit/McFarland, 2017), 88.

45. Perez and Palmquist, *In Exile*, 50; Roy Reed, "The Quarter, an Enchantress Who Always Keeps Her Secrets," *The New York Times*, July 11, 1972, 37; Duplantis interview.

46. Duplantis interview.

47. Ibid.; Butler interview, July 20, 2014.

48. Duplantis interview; Townsend, *Let the Faggots Burn*, 80; photograph of Stewart Butler and Alfred Doolittle embracing, February 1972, courtesy of Stewart Butler.

49. Butler interview, July 20, 2014; Duplantis interview.

50. Townsend, *Let the Faggots Burn*, 80; Butler interview, July 20, 2014; Duplantis interview.

51. Stewart Butler, "Carville Memories 1942–1949," *The Star* 64, no. 17 (January 2014): 6. (I am grateful to Stewart Butler for supplying me with a copy of this monthly newsletter from the National Hansen's Disease Program.)

52. Ibid.; Townsend, *Let the Faggots Burn*, 74.

53. Butler interview, July 20, 2014; Duplantis interview.

54. Ibid.

4: United We Stand

1. Interview with Richard Everett, August 25, 2015; Susan Fosberg, "It's a Faggot Bar—Did I Tell You?," *Vieux Carré Courier*, June 29, 1973, 7; Johnny Townsend, *Let the Faggots Burn: The Up Stairs Lounge Fire* (self-published through BookLocker .com, 2011), 276, 278.

2. "General Case Report," New Orleans Department of Police, August 30, 1973, 29, Upstairs Lounge Records, City Archives, New Orleans Public Library; interview with Steven Duplantis, March 11, 2016.

3. Duplantis interview; interview with Stewart Butler, July 20, 2014; A. Elwood Willey, "The Upstairs Lounge Fire," *NFPA Journal* 68, no. 1 (1974): 17; interview with Ronald Rosenthal, June 14, 2016.

4. Interview with Robert Vanlangendonck, August 11, 2015; "General Case Report," NOPD, 29, 23; interview with Duane Mitchell, August 13, 2015; interview with Richard Everett, July 27, 2015.

5. Rosenthal interview; Everett interviews, August 25, 2015, and September 30, 2016.

6. "Survivor Discovers Her True Friends," *The Advocate*, July 31, 1974, 8; Everett interview, August 25, 2015; Jim Downs, "The Horror Upstairs," *Time*, July 1, 2013 (http://time.com/4365509/the-horror-upstairs/); Townsend, *Let the Faggots Burn*, 143.

7. Interview with Stewart Butler, August 4, 2015; Henry Kubicki, "Henry Kubicki Account" (unpublished manuscript, November 14, 2013), LGBT Religious Archives Network (http://exhibits.lgbtran.org/exhibits/show/upstairs-lounge-fire), Berkeley, Calif.; "General Case Report," NOPD, 10–11; Townsend, *Let the Faggots Burn*, 131.

8. "Fire Victims: More than Just Names," *The Advocate*, August 1, 1973, 17; interview with John Golding Jr., November 6, 2017.

9. Interview with Golding; "Two Arrests Made on Moral Charges," New Orleans *Times-Picayune*, November 22, 1963, sect. 3, p. 4; "Grant Number Three: Mrs. John Golding," National New Orleans Memorial Fund, c. January 17, 1974, National New Orleans Memorial Fund Collection, ONE National Gay and Lesbian Archives at the USC Libraries, Los Angeles; Townsend, *Let the Faggots Burn*, 135.

10. "Orleans Parish Records of the Day," New Orleans *Times-Picayune*, December 6, 1968, 74; "Orleans, Jefferson Records of the Day," New Orleans *Times-Picayune*, June 22, 1972, 102.

11. Clayton Delery, email to author, December 14, 2016; George Painter, "Louisiana," *Gay and Lesbian Archives of the Pacific Northwest*, 2002, www.glapn.org/sodomy laws/sensibilities/louisiana.htm; "Orleans Parish Records," 74; interview with John Meyers, February 3, 2016.

12. Eric Newhouse, "Smokie," Associated Press, June 1973; "Fire Victims," 17; Rosenthal interview; Willey, "The Upstairs Lounge Fire," 17.

13. Bill Williams, "Country Music Nashville Scene," *Billboard*, July 14, 1973, 33; interview with Tina Matyi, October 29, 2016; Townsend, *Let the Faggots Burn*, 233, 234; "Week's Radio," New Orleans *Times-Picayune*, February 8, 1970, 28; "Groups to Hold Arthritis Talks," New Orleans *Times-Picayune*, May 19, 1974, 35; "Blues Give Way to C&W in St. Louis," *Billboard*, June 30, 1973, 45.

14. Townsend, *Let the Faggots Burn*, 236; Matyi interview; George Stephen Matyi, California Divorce Index, 1966–1984, Ancestry.com.

15. Townsend, *Let the Faggots Burn*, 237; "General Case Report," NOPD, 39.

16. Dan Gross, "'My Name Is Nobody'—And Some People Agree," New Orleans *Times-Picayune*, June 25, 1973, 24; Patrick Healy, "Showmen Blazing a Trail," *The New York Times*, March 28, 2013 (www.nytimes.com/2013/03/31/theater/showmen -who-inspired-the-nance.html); Jim Farber, "Growing Up Gay to a Glam Rock Soundtrack," *The New York Times*, November 3, 2016 (www.nytimes.com/2016/11/04 /fashion/mens-style/growing-up-gay-glam-rock-queen-bowie-freddie-mercury .html?_r=0); Josh Greenfield, "A Skeleton in Every Closet," *The New York Times*, April 30, 1967 (www.nytimes.com/books/98/03/01/home/vidal-washington.html).

17. Mark Allen Guidry, Statement to Louisiana Office of State Fire Marshal, July 2, 1973, 1, Skylar Fein Upstairs Lounge Fire Collection, Historic New Orleans Collection; Rodger Dale Nunez, Statement to Louisiana Office of State Fire Marshal, September 18, 1973, 9, Skylar Fein Upstairs Lounge Fire Collection; Duplantis interview; Eugene Davis, Statement to Louisiana Office of State Fire Marshal, October 1, 1973, 2, Skylar Fein Upstairs Lounge Fire Collection; Everett interview, August 25, 2015.

18. Duplantis interview; Guidry, Statement to State Fire Marshal, 1; "General Case Report," NOPD, 60.

19. "General Case Report," NOPD, 60, 23, 29; Duplantis interview; Clayton Delery-Edwards, *The Up Stairs Lounge Arson: Thirty-Two Deaths in a New Orleans Gay Bar, June 24, 1973* (Jefferson, N.C.: McFarland, 2014), 44.

20. Townsend, *Let the Faggots Burn*, 283.; Willey, "The Upstairs Lounge Fire," 17; Vanlangendonck interview; Duplantis interview.

21. Duplantis interview.

22. "General Case Report," NOPD, 60–61; interview with Mary David Mihalyfi, May 4, 2016.

23. Michael Scarborough, Statement to Louisiana Office of State Fire Marshal, July 16, 1973, 1, Skylar Fein Upstairs Lounge Fire Collection, Historic New Orleans Collection; Mihalyfi interview; interview with Naoma McCrae, May 12, 2016.

24. Scarborough, Statement to State Fire Marshal, 1–2; Duplantis interview; "General Case Report," NOPD, 22; Douglas Rasmussen, Statement to Louisiana Office of State Fire Marshal, July 18, 1973, 1, Skylar Fein Upstairs Lounge Fire Collection.

25. Duplantis interview; Butler interview, July 20, 2014.

26. "General Case Report," NOPD, 30

27. Ibid., 37.

28. Rasmussen, Statement to State Fire Marshal, 1; interview with Henry Kubicki, September 6, 2017; Troy Perry and Thomas Swicegood, *Don't Be Afraid Anymore* (New York: St. Martin's, 1990), 80.

29. "General Case Report," NOPD, 47–48.

30. Ibid.

31. Butler interview, July 20, 2014; Angus Lind, Lanny Thomas, and Walt Philbin, "Possible Arson Probed," New Orleans *States-Item*, June 25, 1973, 2; Delery-Edwards, *The Up Stairs Lounge Arson*, 45.

32. "General Case Report," NOPD, 29; Delery-Edwards, *The Up Stairs Lounge Arson*, 43, 35.

33. "General Case Report," NOPD, 17, 52–53; Vieux Carré Commission Evaluation, April 1876, 141 Chartres Street (604 Iberville), https://stevenwarran.blogspot.com/2014_08_01_archive.html; "Report of the Crime Laboratory," June 27, 1973, in supplemental materials to "Official Report," Louisiana Office of State Fire Marshal, July 22, 1975, Louisiana State Archives, Baton Rouge.

34. "General Case Report," NOPD, 31–33, 57; Royd Anderson. *The UpStairs Lounge Fire* (documentary film), Lake Oaks Studio, June 24, 2013; "Twenty-Nine Die in New Orleans as Flames Gut Lounge," Wilmington [Del.] *Evening Journal*, June 25, 1973, 2; Willey, "The Upstairs Lounge Fire," 19.

35. "General Case Report," NOPD, 57, 53, 19; Howard Jacobs, "9-1-1 Phone Number for Emergency Seen," New Orleans *Times-Picayune*, May 5, 1969, 15; "Police Reports," New Orleans *Times-Picayune*, April 22, 1973, 26; Bill Rushton, "After the Fire Upstairs," *Vieux Carré Courier*, June 29, 1973, 5; Lind, Thomas, and Philbin, "Possible Arson Probed," 2.

36. Anderson. *The UpStairs Lounge Fire*; Weather History of KMSY, June 1973, weatherunderground.com, www.wunderground.com/history/airport/KMSY/1973/6/24/Monthly History.html?req_city=&req_state=&req_statename=&reqdb.zip=&reqdb.magic=&reqdb.wmo=; interview with Joseph Bermuda, March 31, 2015.

37. Interview with Trevor Santos, November 19, 2015; Willey, "The Upstairs Lounge Fire," 19; "General Case Report," NOPD, 53.

38. Everett interview, September 30, 2016; Rosenthal interview; Willey, "The Upstairs Lounge Fire," 17; Lind, Thomas, and Philbin, "Possible Arson Probed," 2; Townsend, *Let the Faggots Burn*, 286.

39. "General Case Report," NOPD, 41, 27, 51; Willey, "The Upstairs Lounge Fire," 19, 17; John LaPlace and Ed Anderson, "Twenty-Nine Killed in Quarter Blaze," New Orleans *Times-Picayune*, June 25, 1973, 1 (and accompanying photo by Ronald LeBoeuf); Townsend, *Let the Faggots Burn*, 288.

40. "General Case Report," NOPD, 51, 27, 30, 23; David Cuthbert, "Where There Was Smoke," New Orleans *Times-Picayune*, June 20, 1998; Roberts Batson, "Holocaust," *Impact*, June 5, 1998, 12 (read at Rebels, Rubyfruit and Rhinestones Research Files, James T. Sears Papers, Duke University Libraries, Durham, N.C.); Willey, "The Upstairs Lounge Fire," 17.

41. "General Case Report," NOPD, 25, 27; Everett interview, September 30, 2016; Rosenthal interview; Santos interview, November 29, 2015.

42. Everett interview, August 25, 2015; Bill Rushton, "A Window in the Orange Glow," *Vieux Carré Courier*, June 29, 1973, 4; "Bar's Funky Décor, Clutter Created Instant Firestorm," *The Advocate*, August 1, 1973, 6; Willey, "The Upstairs Lounge Fire," 19; Rushton, "After the Fire Upstairs," 5; "General Case Report," NOPD, 27; Delery-Edwards, *The Up Stairs Lounge Arson*, 46.

43. Vanlangendonck interview; "Official Report," Louisiana Office of State Fire Marshal, July 22, 1975, 28; Delery-Edwards, *The Up Stairs Lounge Arson*, 46; Anderson, *The UpStairs Lounge Fire*.

44. "General Case Report," NOPD, 33; Walt Philbin, "First the Horror—Then the Leap," New Orleans *States-Item*, June 25, 1973, 6.

45. Vanlangendonck interview; "General Case Report," NOPD, 33.

46. "Survivor Discovers Her True Friends," 8; Delery-Edwards, *The Up Stairs Lounge Arson*, 47.

47. Philbin, "First the Horror—Then the Leap," 6; "New Orleans Fire Probe Launched," *Monroe* [La.] *News-Star*, June 25, 1973, 2.

48. Lind, Thomas, and Philbin, "Possible Arson Probed," 2; Willey, "The Upstairs Lounge Fire," 19; Delery-Edwards, *The Up Stairs Lounge Arson*, 47; Earl Thomas Grant, Records, National New Orleans Memorial Fund, c. 1974, National New Orleans Memorial Fund Collection, ONE National Gay and Lesbian Archives; Fred Sharohway Grant, Records, National New Orleans Memorial Fund, c. 1974, National New Orleans Memorial Fund Collection.

49. "General Case Report," NOPD, 30, 27; Rosenthal interview.

50. Willey, "The Upstairs Lounge Fire," 17; Rosenthal interview; "General Case Report," NOPD, 52.

51. "General Case Report," NOPD, 26, 11; Scarborough, Statement to State Fire Marshal, July 16, 1973, 5.

52. "General Case Report," NOPD, 30; Willey, "The Upstairs Lounge Fire," 17; Rosenthal interview.

53. Everett interview, August 25, 2015; "General Case Report," NOPD, 31.

54. "General Case Report," NOPD, 30; Everett interviews, August 25, 2015, and September 30, 2016.

55. Everett interviews, September 30, 2016, July 27, 2015, and August 10 and August 25, 2015; Rosenthal interview.

56. "General Case Report," NOPD, 25; Kubicki, "Henry Kubicki Account."

57. "General Case Report," NOPD, 30.

58. Ibid., 30–31; Willey, "The Upstairs Lounge Fire," 18; Everett interview, September 30, 2016.

59. "General Case Report," NOPD, 31, 20; Townsend, *Let the Faggots Burn*, 301.

60. "Supplemental Information," Fire Prevention Division of the New Orleans Fire

Department, fig. 1: Floor Plan of Upstairs Lounge, c. 1975, Johnny Townsend Collection, ONE National Gay and Lesbian Archives; "General Case Report," NOPD, 23; "Supplemental Information," NOFD, 1, c. 1975, Johnny Townsend Collection.

61. Willey, "The Upstairs Lounge Fire," 17; "General Case Report," NOPD, 8, 19.
62. Willey, "The Upstairs Lounge Fire," 17–18.
63. Batson, "Holocaust," 12; Susan Fosberg, "It's a Faggot Bar," *Vieux Carré Courier*, June 29, 1973, 7.
64. Fosberg, "It's a Faggot Bar," 7; "General Case Report," NOPD, 18; Willey, "The Upstairs Lounge Fire," 18; Davis, Statement to State Fire Marshal, 4; Jacqueline Bullard, Statement to Louisiana Office of State Fire Marshal, March 17, 1975, 2, Louisiana State Archives.
65. "General Case Report," NOPD, 8; interview with Milton Mary, August 22, 2016, courtesy of Tracking Fire, LLC.
66. Clayton Delery-Edwards, email to author, July 8, 2016; Downs, "The Horror Upstairs"; Lind, Thomas, and Philbin, "Possible Arson Probed," 2; Angus Lind, "Fire Bares the Grisly Face of Death," New Orleans *States-Item*, June 25, 1973, 6; Mihalyfi interview; Scarborough, Statement to State Fire Marshal.
67. "French Quarter Fire Toll Worst for New Orleans," *Monroe News-Star*, June 25, 1973, 2; interview with Trevor Santos, March 3, 2016; Vanlangendonck interview; interview with Sheri Wright, June 2016; Mary interview.
68. Bermuda interview.
69. "General Case Report," NOPD, 8; LaPlace and Anderson, "Twenty-Nine Killed," 1; "French Quarter Fire Toll Worst for New Orleans," 2; Perry Waters, Autopsy, Orleans Parish Coroner's Office, 1973, Upstairs Lounge Records, City Archive, New Orleans Public Library; Duane George Mitchell, Autopsy, Orleans Parish Coroner's Office, 1973, Upstairs Lounge Records; Mary interview.
70. Santos interview, March 3, 2016; Ed Tunstall, "'Up Stairs Lounge' Fire Is New Orleans' Worst," Wilmington [Del.] *Index-Journal*, June 25, 1973, 24; Lanny Thomas, "Fun . . . Drinks . . . Song . . . with Death at the Piano," New Orleans *States-Item*, June 25, 1973, 6; Townsend, *Let the Faggots Burn*, 143; "General Case Report," NOPD, 12; George Steven [sic] Matyi, Autopsy, Orleans Parish Coroner's Office, 1973, Upstairs Lounge Records; Inez Warren, Autopsy, Orleans Parish Coroner's Office, 1973, Upstairs Lounge Records; Rushton, "After the Fire Upstairs," 4; George Schwandt, "Holocaust in New Orleans," *The Advocate*, June 18, 1973, 9; Lind, "Fire Bares the Grisly Face of Death," 6.
71. "General Case Report," NOPD, 31; Cuthbert, "Where There Was Smoke."
72. Thomas, "Fun . . . Drinks . . . Song," 6.

5: Mayhem

1. Interview with Stewart Butler, July 20, 2014; Anonymous, *The Cajun Queen: A Complete Guide to New Orleans Gaydom* (New Orleans: Minotaur, Inc., 1974), 32; Johnny Townsend, *Let the Faggots Burn: The Up Stairs Lounge Fire* (self-published through BookLocker.com, 2011), 251.

2. Royd Anderson, *The UpStairs Lounge Fire* (documentary film), Lake Oaks Studio, June 24, 2013; Butler interview, July 20, 2014; Eugene Davis, Statement to Louisiana Office of State Fire Marshal, October 1, 1973, 4, Skylar Fein Upstairs Lounge Fire Collection, Historic New Orleans Collection.

3. Jacqueline Bullard, Statement to Louisiana Office of State Fire Marshal, March 17, 1975, 2, Louisiana State Archives, Baton Rouge.

4. Butler interview, July 20, 2014; "General Case Report," New Orleans Department of Police, August 30, 1973, 19, Upstairs Lounge Records, City Archives, New Orleans Public Library. I confirmed the number of steps from 704 Iberville Street to 604 Iberville.

5. "New Orleans Fire Probe Launched," *Monroe* [La.] *News-Star*, June 25, 1973, 2; Eric Newhouse, "Arson Eyed in New Orleans Fire," *Abilene* [Tex.] *Reporter News*, June 25, 1973; Paul Atkinson, "Obscenity Crackdown Begins," New Orleans *Times-Picayune*, June 28, 1973, 1; "General Case Report," NOPD, 34; Chris Segura, "Black, Empty Windows Stare," New Orleans *Times-Picayune*, June 26, 1973, 3.

6. Associated Press footage, "US Fire," June 25, 1973, aparchive.com; Sharon Swindall, "Tourist Recalls Nightmare," New Orleans *Daily Record*, June 27, 1973, 7; John LaPlace and Ed Anderson, "Twenty-Nine Killed in Quarter Blaze," New Orleans *Times-Picayune*, June 25, 1973, 1 (and accompanying photo by Ronald LeBoeuf); Townsend, *Let the Faggots Burn*, 297; interview with Milton Mary, August 22, 2016; Angus Lind, Lanny Thomas, and Walt Philbin, "Twenty-Nine Dead in Quarter Holocaust," New Orleans *States-Item*, June 25, 1973, 6.

7. Clayton Delery-Edwards, *The Up Stairs Lounge Arson: Thirty-Two Deaths in a New Orleans Gay Bar, June 24, 1973* (Jefferson, N.C.: McFarland, 2014), 49, 52; Townsend, *Let the Faggots Burn*, 303.

8. Lind, "Fire Bares," 6; "Yesterday's Dreams, Today's Ghosts," *The Advocate*, March 13, 1974, 12; Douglas Rasmussen, Statement to Louisiana Office of State Fire Marshal, July 18, 1973, 1, Skylar Fein Upstairs Lounge Fire Collection, Historic New Orleans Collection; Townsend, *Let the Faggots Burn*, 301; Associated Press footage, "US Fire"; interview with Robert Vanlangendonck, August 11, 2015.

9. Lind, "Fire Bares," 6; "Yesterday's Dreams, Today's Ghosts," *The Advocate*, March 13, 1974, 12; Douglas Rasmussen, Statement to Louisiana Office of State Fire Marshal, July 18, 1973, 1, Skylar Fein Upstairs Lounge Fire Collection, Historic New Orleans Collection; Townsend, *Let the Faggots Burn*, 301; Associated Press footage, "US Fire"; interview with Robert Vanlangendonck, August 11, 2015.

10. Lind, "Fire Bares," 6; Clayton Delery, email to author, July 8, 2016.

11. Butler interview, July 20, 2014; Lind, "Fire Bares," 6; Lanny Thomas, "Fun . . . Drinks . . . Song . . . with Death at the Piano," New Orleans *States-Item*, June 25, 1973, 6.

12. "French Quarter Fire Toll Worst for New Orleans," *Monroe News-Star*, June 25, 1973, 2; John LaPlace, "Scene of French Quarter Fire Is Called Dante's 'Inferno,' Hitler's Incinerators," New Orleans *Times-Picayune*, June 25, 1973, 1 (and accompanying photo by G. E. Arnold); Associated Press photograph of rescue worker leaning against charred window, June 24, 1973, aparchive.com.

13. Ed Tunstall, "N.O. Fire Fighter Urges High-Rise Sprinkler Law," Shreveport *Times*, November 25, 1973, 142; "General Case Report," NOPD, 18.

14. Sharon Swindall, "Rookie Fireman Describes Fire," New Orleans *Daily Record*, June

28, 1973, 1. "Fatality List, 604 Iberville" New Orleans Fire Department, June 24, 1973, 1–3, Johnny Townsend Collection, ONE National Gay and Lesbian Archives at the USC Libraries, Los Angeles; Tunstall, "N.O. Fire Fighter Urges," 142.

15. "General Case Report," NOPD, 19; interview with Joseph Bermuda, March 31, 2015; A. Elwood Willey, "The Upstairs Lounge Fire," *NFPA Journal* 68, no. 1 (1974): 18; LaPlace and Anderson, "Twenty-Nine Killed," 3.

16. Lind, Thomas, and Philbin, "Twenty-Nine Dead," 1; Willey, "The Upstairs Lounge Fire," 18–19.

17. "General Case Report," NOPD, 16–17; interview with Ronald LeBoeuf, April 15, 2015; photograph of fireman giving first aid by G. E. Arnold, Associated Press, June 24, 1973, aparchive.com.

18. Interview with Henry Kubicki, September 5, 2015; Henry Kubicki, "Henry Kubicki Account" (unpublished manuscript, November 14, 2013), LGBT Religious Archives Network (http://exhibits.lgbtran.org/exhibits/show/upstairs-lounge-fire), Berkeley, Calif.

19. Kubicki interview, September 5, 2015; Kubicki, "Henry Kubicki Account."

20. Interview with Ronald Rosenthal, June 14, 2016; interviews with Richard Everett, January 20, 2017, and August 25, 2015.

21. Kubicki interview, September 4, 2015; Michel Montaigne, *The Essays of Montaigne*, trans. George Ives (Cambridge: Harvard University Press, 1925), 13; Everett interview, August 25, 2015.

22. Interview with Dexter Brecht, July 29, 2015; Kubicki, "Henry Kubicki Account"; Thomas, "Fun . . . Drinks . . . Song," 6.

23. LaPlace, "Scene of French Quarter Fire Is Called," 2; report from CBS Evening News, June 26, 1973 (archived at http://exhibits.lgbtran.org/exhibits/show/upstairs -lounge-fire); videorecorded interview with Clancy DuBos, conducted by Royd Anderson, April 22, 2008 (courtesy of Royd Anderson); Frank Hayward to Winston Lill (memorandum), September 25, 1973, Records of Mayor Moon Landrieu, City Archives, New Orleans Public Library.

24. Lind, "Fire Bares," 6; Lind, Thomas, and Philbin, "Twenty-Nine Dead," 1.

25. LeBoeuf interview; Thomas, "Fun . . . Drinks . . . Song," 6; Newhouse, "Arson Eyed in New Orleans Fire"; report from CBS Evening News, June 26, 1973; Townsend, *Let the Faggots Burn*, 193.

26. Swindall, "Tourist Recalls Nightmare," 7; Newhouse, "Arson Eyed in New Orleans Fire."

27. Rasmussen, Statement to State Fire Marshal, 1; "General Case Report," NOPD, 24. 31; Davis, Statement to State Fire Marshal, 5.

28. Townsend, *Let the Faggots Burn*, 214.

29. "General Case Report," NOPD, 31.

30. Townsend, *Let the Faggots Burn*, 214.

31. "General Case Report," NOPD, 31; Rasmussen, Statement to State Fire Marshal, 1; "Official Report," Louisiana Office of State Fire Marshal, July 22, 1975, 27, Louisiana State Archives.

32. Delery-Edwards, *The Up Stairs Lounge Arson*, 125; "Official Report," State Fire Marshal, 27; Rasmussen, Statement to State Fire Marshal, 1.

33. "Official Report," State Fire Marshal, 27.

34. Interview with Roy Reed, September 24, 2014; Roy Reed, "1,500 Turned Back," *The New York Times*, March 10, 1965, 1.

35. Reed interview; Roy Reed, "Flash Fire in New Orleans Kills at Least Thirty-Two in Bar," *The New York Times*, June 25, 1973, 1.

36. Reed interview; Reed, "Flash Fire in New Orleans," 66.

37. Clancy DuBos, "A Front-Row View of Tragedy," *Gambit*, June 18, 2013, 23; Lind, Thomas, and Philbin, "Twenty-Nine Dead," 6; Clancy DuBos, "Blood, Moans: Charity Scene," New Orleans *Times-Picayune*, June 25, 1973, 1; DuBos interview with Anderson.

38. DuBos, "Blood, Moans," 1; Delery to author, July 8, 2016.

39. DuBos, "A Front-Row View," 23; DuBos, "Blood, Moans," 1; Lind, Thomas, and Philbin, "Twenty-Nine Dead," 6; Jim Downs, "The Horror Upstairs," *Time*, July 1, 2013 (http://time.com/4365509/the-horror-upstairs).

40. DuBos, "Blood, Moans," 2; Paul Breton, "United We Stand" (unpublished manuscript, August 1973), National New Orleans Memorial Fund Collection, ONE National Gay and Lesbian Archives; Bill Rushton, "New Orleans Toll Thirty-Two; Arson Evidence Cited," *The Advocate*, August 1, 1973, 2; "New Burn Unit Used at Charity," New Orleans *Times-Picayune*, June 28, 1973, sect. 7, p. 16.

41. DuBos, "Blood, Moans," 1; DuBos, "A Front-Row View," 23; DuBos interview with Anderson.

42. DuBos interview with Anderson; DuBos, "A Front-Row View," 23.

43. "General Case Report," NOPD, 7–8.

44. "General Case Report," NOPD, 8–9, 35–36, 50–51; Nolan Lewis and Helen Yarnell, "Pathological Fire-Setting (Pyromania)," *Nervous and Mental Disease Monograph* 82 (1952): 8–26; W. Hurley and T. M. Monahan, "Arson: The Criminal and the Crime," *The British Journal of Criminology* 9, no. 1 (January 1, 1969): 4–21; Robert McAnear, Facebook message to author, January 6, 2017; "Jeff Sheriff Affirms Firings," New Orleans *Times-Picayune*, January 15, 1972, 17.

45. Delery-Edwards, *The Up Stairs Lounge Arson*, 94; McAnear to author, January 6, 2017; "General Case Report," NOPD, 9, 18–19; "Inspection and/or Investigation Report," Fire Prevention Division of the New Orleans Fire Department, June 24–25, 1973, Johnny Townsend Collection, ONE National Gay and Lesbian Archives; "Official Report," State Fire Marshal.

46. "General Case Report," NOPD, 31–32, 24.

47. Tom Frazer, "Sons of Fire Victim Sent Home—Unaware of Father's Death," New Orleans *States-Item*, June 26, 1973, A3; interview with Duane Mitchell, August 13, 2015.

48. Interview with Duane Mitchell, August 14, 2015.

49. Ibid.; Frazer, "Sons of Fire Victim Sent Home," A3.

6: Call for Aid

1. "General Case Report," New Orleans Department of Police, August 30, 1973, 16–17, Upstairs Lounge Records, City Archives, New Orleans Public Library; Angus Lind, "Fire Bares the Grisly Face of Death," New Orleans *States Item*, June 25, 1973, 6.

2. "General Case Report," NOPD, 17; John LaPlace and Ed Anderson, "Twenty-

Nine Killed in Quarter Blaze," New Orleans *Times-Picayune*, June 25, 1973, 1; A. Elwood Willey, "The Upstairs Lounge Fire," *NFPA Journal* 68, no. 1 (1974): 17–18; "Supplemental Information," Fire Prevention Division of the New Orleans Fire Department, c. 1975, 1, Johnny Townsend Collection, ONE National Gay and Lesbian Archives at the USC Libraries, Los Angeles.

3. "General Case Report," NOPD, 49; "Report of the Crime Laboratory," June 27, 1973, in supplemental materials to "Official Report," Louisiana Office of State Fire Marshal, July 22, 1975, Louisiana State Archives, Baton Rouge.

4. "General Case Report," NOPD, 17; "Inspection and/or Investigation Report," Fire Prevention Division of the New Orleans Fire Department, June 24–25, 1973, 3, Johnny Townsend Collection.

5. LaPlace and Anderson, "Twenty-Nine Killed," 2; "General Case Report," NOPD, 11; "Fatality List, 604 Iberville," New Orleans Fire Department, June 24, 1973, 3, Johnny Townsend Collection.

6. "General Case Report," NOPD, 16–17; Ed Tunstall, "'Up Stairs Lounge' Fire Is New Orleans' Worst," Wilmington [Del.] *Index-Journal*, June 25, 1973, 24; "French Quarter Fire Toll Worst for New Orleans," *Monroe* [La.] *News-Star*, June 25, 1973, 2.

7. Ken Weiss, "Blaze Victims' Names Sought," New Orleans *Times-Picayune*, June 26, 1973, 3; Lind, "Fire Bares," 6; George Schwandt, "Holocaust in New Orleans," *The Advocate*, June 18, 1973, 9.

8. Robert McAnear, Facebook messages to author, January 6 and January 9, 2017; Townsend, *Let the Faggots Burn*, 305.

9. Robert McAnear, Facebook message to author, January 25, 2017; Townsend, *Let the Faggots Burn*, 305; McAnear to author, January 6, 2017.

10. Interview with Ronald Rosenthal, June 14, 2016; "General Case Report," NOPD, 21; interviews with Richard Everett, September 30, 2016, and August 25, 2015.

11. Everett interview, September 30, 2016; Rosenthal interview; Weiss, "Blaze Victims' Names Sought," 3.

12. Rosenthal interview.

13. Lind, Thomas, and Philbin, "29 Dead," 1.

14. Rosenthal interview; Angus Lind, Lanny Thomas, and Walt Philbin, "Twenty-Nine Dead in Quarter Holocaust," New Orleans *States-Item*, June 25, 1973, 1; LaPlace and Anderson, "Twenty-Nine Killed," 6.

15. Everett interviews, August 25, 2015, and September 30, 2016.

16. Everett interview, September 30, 2016; Bill Rushton, "After the Fire Upstairs," *Vieux Carré Courier*, June 29, 1973, 1; Rosenthal interview.

17. Rosenthal interview; interview with Dan Bugg, June 14, 2016; "Atlanta Church Chartered," *In Unity*, June–July 1972, 13–14, https://issuu.com/mccchurches/doc.

18. Interview with Steven Duplantis, March 11, 2016.

19. Ibid.

20. Ibid.

21. Ibid.; interview with Stewart Butler, July 20, 2014.

22. Duplantis interview.

23. Ibid.

24. Ibid.

25. Ibid.

26. Ibid.

27. Ibid.

28. Ibid.

29. Mary Ann Cherry, "Gay Pride 1973" (unpublished manuscript, October 2012, available at http://morriskight.blogspot.com/2012/10/gay-pride-1973); Craig Kaczorowski, "Mattachine Society," 2015, glbtq.com, www.glbtqarchive.com/ssh/mattachine _society_S.pdf.

30. Cherry, "Gay Pride 1973"; Daniel Winunwe Rivers, *Radical Relations: Lesbian Mothers, Gay Fathers, and Their Children in the United States Since World War II* (Chapel Hill: University of North Carolina Press, 2014); photograph of Cockapillar float, 1972, ONE National Gay and Lesbian Archives.

31. Jonathan Katz, *Gay American History* (New York: Crowell, 1976), 412; "Interviewing Morris Kight," *Causeway* (Gay People's Coalition of New Orleans newsletter), January 1974 (read at Rebels, Rubyfruit and Rhinestones Research Files, James T. Sears Papers, Duke University Libraries, Durham, N.C.).

32. Cherry, "Gay Pride 1973"; Randy Wicker, "Gays Pour Through New York," *The Advocate*, July 18, 1973, 5.

33. Arthur Evans, "National Structure Still Gays' Critical Need," *The Advocate*, August 1, 1973, 27; "Stonewall 'Historic'?," *The Advocate*, August 15, 1973, 16.

34. "Gays Just Watch L.A. Beating," *The Advocate*, July 18, 1973, 22.

35. "Four Policemen Hurt in 'Village' Raid," *The New York Times*, June 29, 1969, 33; William Yardley, "Storme DeLarverie, Early Leader in the Gay Rights Movement, Dies at Ninety-Three," *The New York Times*, May 29, 2014 (www.nytimes.com/2014/05/30 /nyregion/storme-delarverie-early-leader-in-the-gay-rights-movement-dies-at-93.html); K. Stormé DeLarverie, "Storme on Stonewall," Stonewall Veterans' Association, www.stonewallvets.org/StormeDeLarverie.htm; interview with Brendan Flaherty, November 12, 2016.

36. Flaherty interview.

37. Yardley, "Storme"; "Police Again Rout Village Youths," *The New York Times*, June 30, 1969, 22; "Hostile Crowd Dispersed near Sheridan Square," *The New York Times*, July 3, 1969, 19.

38. Rosenthal interview.

39. Dudley Clendinen and Adam Nagourney, *Out for Good: The Struggle to Build a Gay Rights Movement in America* (New York: Simon & Schuster, 2001); Bugg interview; "Directory," *In Unity*, August–September 1972, 27, https://issuu.com/mcchurches /doc.

40. Troy Perry and Thomas Swicegood, *Don't Be Afraid Anymore* (New York: St. Martin's, 1990), 78.

41. Ibid., 77.

42. Ibid.; interview with Troy Perry, December 2, 2014.

43. Perry and Swicegood, *Don't Be Afraid Anymore*, 78; Troy Perry and Nancy Wilson, "Report to the President for the White House Conference on Hate Crimes," November 1, 1997, 2, LGBT Religious Archives Network (http://exhibits.lgbtran .org/exhibits/show/upstairs-lounge-fire), Berkeley, Calif.; Perry interview; "Directory," *In Unity*, June–July 1972, 27, https://issuu.com/mcchurches/doc.

44. Perry interview.

45. Perry and Swicegood, *Don't Be Afraid Anymore*, 80.

46. Perry interview.

47. "Homosexuals in Revolt," *Life*, December 31, 1971; "The Militant Homosexual," *Newsweek*, August 23, 1971, 45–48; Perry interview.

48. Perry and Swicegood, *Don't Be Afraid Anymore*, 80; Wicker, "Gays Pour Through New York," 5; Cherry, "Gay Pride 1973."

49. "Re: Gay Activist Alliance," Federal Bureau of Investigation, March 17, 1972, posted on GLIB.com, www.glib.com/fbi_gaa_06-10-2002_docs.html#2; Bruce Lambert, "Morty Manford, Forty-One, a Lawyer and Early Gay Rights Advocate," *The New York Times*, May 15, 1992 (www.nytimes.com/1992/05/15/nyregion/morty-manford-41-a-lawyer-and-early-gay-rights-advocate.html); Eric Pace, "Official Accuses Maye of Assault," *The New York Times*, April 25, 1972, 11.

50. "Maye Cleared of Harming Homosexual," *The New York Times*, July 6, 1972, 38; Pace, "Official Accuses Maye of Assault," 11.

51. Cherry, "Gay Pride 1973"; "Aid Mounts for New Orleans," *The Advocate*, August 15, 1973, 22.

52. Paul Breton, "United We Stand" (unpublished manuscript, August 1973), National New Orleans Memorial Fund Collection, ONE National Gay and Lesbian Archives; Perry interview.

53. "General Case Report," NOPD, 37–38, 30.

54. Ibid., 37.

55. Ibid., 38, 46–47.

56. John Gill, transcript of phone interview with *The Advocate*, 4:30 a.m. PST, June 25, 1973, New Orleans Upstairs Bar Fire/Advocate Records, ONE National Gay and Lesbian Archives.

57. Anonymous, *The Cajun Queen: A Complete Guide to New Orleans Gaydom* (New Orleans: Minotaur, Inc., 1974), 17.

58. Bill Rushton, "Fire Tragedy Confused Both Straights, Gays," *The Advocate*, July 18, 1973, 9; "Miss Lill and Mr. Craige Plan June 30 Wedding," New Orleans *Times-Picayune*, June 15, 1973, sect. 4, p. 6; Winston Lill to Robert Hess, June 29, 1973, Records of Mayor Moon Landrieu, City Archives.

59. Rushton, "New Orleans Toll," 15; Morris Kight, transcript of phone interview with *The Advocate*, June 27, 1973, New Orleans Upstairs Bar Fire/Advocate Records; John LaPlace, "Endless Lines of Blood Donors Flock to Charity," New Orleans *Times-Picayune*, January 8, 1973, 2.

60. Gill, transcript of *Advocate* interview, June 25, 1973; Veterans Administration to Thomas L. Baril, February 6, 1974, National New Orleans Memorial Fund Collection, ONE National Gay and Lesbian Archives; Henry Kubicki, "Henry Kubicki Account" (unpublished manuscript, November 14, 2013), LGBT Religious Archives Network (http://exhibits.lgbtran.org/exhibits/show/upstairs-lounge-fire); Lucien Baril, transcript of phone interview with *The Advocate*, 4:30 a.m. PST, June 25, 1973, New Orleans Upstairs Bar Fire/Advocate Records.

61. Duplantis interview; interview with Stewart Butler, July 20, 2014.

62. Ibid.

63. Duplantis interview.

64. Kubicki interview, September 5, 2015; Kubicki, "Henry Kubicki Account."

65. Kubicki interview, September 5, 2015; LaPlace and Anderson, "Twenty-Nine Killed," 1.
66. Kubicki interview, September 5, 2015.
67. Ibid.; Kubicki, "Henry Kubicki Account."
68. Kubicki interview, September 5, 2015; Butler interview, March 11, 2016.

7: Liberation Descends

1. Bill Rushton, "How the Media Saw It," *Vieux Carré Courier*, June 29, 1973, 5; Bill Rushton, "Fire Tragedy Confused Both Straights, Gays," *The Advocate*, July 18, 1973, 2; "Twenty-Nine Died in Suspicious Flash Fire," *The Irish Times*, June 26, 1973, 7; David Wigg, "Twenty-Nine Killed in New Orleans Cocktail Bar Fire," *The Times* (London), June 26, 1973, 5; "Fire Sweeps Bar, Kills Twenty-Nine in N. Orleans," *International Herald Tribune*, June 26, 1973, 4; "Blaze in New Orleans Bar; Twenty-Nine Die," *The Sydney Morning Herald*, June 26, 1973, 5.
2. Eric Newhouse, "French Quarter Revelers Trapped," *The* [Portland] *Oregonian*, June 25, 1973, 1; "N.O. Lounge Fire Kills Twenty-Nine Persons," Baton Rouge *State-Times*, June 25, 1973, 1; Wigg, "Twenty-Nine Killed in New Orleans," 5; John LaPlace and Ed Anderson, "Twenty-Nine Killed in Quarter Blaze," New Orleans *Times-Picayune*, June 25, 1973, 1; Clancy DuBos, "Blood, Moans: Charity Scene," New Orleans *Times-Picayune*, June 25, 1973, 1; John LaPlace, "Scene of French Quarter Fire Is Called Dante's 'Inferno,' Hitler's Incinerators," New Orleans *Times-Picayune*, June 25, 1973, 2; Rushton, "How the Media," 5; interview with Clancy DuBos, May 18, 2016.
3. LaPlace and Anderson, "Twenty-Nine Killed," 1; LaPlace, "Scene of French Quarter Fire," 1; Roberts Batson, "Out of the Ashes," *Impact*, July 3, 1998, 14 (read at Rebels, Rubyfruit, and Rhinestones Research Files, James T. Sears Papers, Duke University Libraries, Durham, N.C.); DuBos interview, May 18, 2016.
4. "Twenty-Nine Die in Bar Fire," *Los Angeles Times*, June 25, 1973, 1; "Bar Fire Kills Twenty-Nine in French Quarter," *Newsday*, June 25, 1973, 3; "Twenty-Nine Die in New Orleans Fire," *Chicago Tribune*, June 25, 1973, 1.
5. Roy Reed, "Flash Fire in New Orleans Kills at Least Thirty-Two in Bar," *The New York Times*, June 25, 1973, 1; "Flee Fire, Plunge to Death," *Chicago Tribune*, November 30, 1972, 1.
6. "Twenty-Nine Die in New Orleans Fire," 1; "Gay Liberation Stages March to Civic Center," *Chicago Tribune*, June 28, 1970, 27.
7. Reed, "Flash Fire in New Orleans," 66; Michelangelo Signorile, "Out at *The New York Times*: Gays, Lesbians, AIDS and Homophobia Inside America's Paper of Record," *The Huffington Post*, November 28, 2012, www.huffingtonpost.com/2012/11/28/new-york-times-gays-lesbians-aids-homophobia_n_2200684.html; "Four Policemen Hurt in 'Village' Raid," *The New York Times*, June 29, 1969, 33; "Hostile Crowd Dispersed near Sheridan Square," *The New York Times*, July 3, 1969, 19.
8. Reed, "Flash Fire in New Orleans," 1, 66; "Flash Fire Kills Twenty-Eight in New Orleans Bar," *The Washington Post*, June 25, 1973, 1, 22.

9. Interview with Roy Reed, September 24, 2014; Rushton, "How the Media," 5.

10. Rushton, "Fire Tragedy Confused," 9; videorecorded interview with Clancy DuBos, conducted by Royd Anderson, April 22, 2008 (courtesy of Royd Anderson); Henry Kubicki, "Henry Kubicki Account" (unpublished manuscript, November 14, 2013), LGBT Religious Archives Network (http://exhibits.lgbtran.org/exhibits /show/upstairs-lounge-fire), Berkeley, Calif.; Johnny Townsend, *Let the Faggots Burn: The Up Stairs Lounge Fire* (self-published through BookLocker.com, 2011), 40; Bill Rushton, "After the Fire Upstairs," *Vieux Carré Courier*, June 29, 1973, 6; Susan Fosberg, "It's a Faggot Bar—Did I Tell You?," *Vieux Carré Courier*, June 29, 1973, 7; Clayton Delery-Edwards, *The Up Stairs Lounge Arson: Thirty-Two Deaths in a New Orleans Gay Bar, June 24, 1973* (Jefferson, N.C.: McFarland, 2014), 72; Bill Rushton, "Society Real Culprit in New Orleans Tragedy?," *The Advocate*, August 1, 1973, 7.

11. Robert McAnear, Facebook message to author, January 9, 2016; Lanny Thomas, "Have Labels Overshadowed Twenty-Nine Deaths?," New Orleans *States-Item*, June 28, 1973, 16; interview with Joseph Bermuda, March 31, 2015.

12. "Behavior: The Homosexual. Newly Visible, Newly Understood," *Time*, October 31, 1969 (http://content.time.com/time/subscriber/article/0,33009,839116-1,00.html); Silas House, "Deliver Me from *Deliverance*: Finally, a Hollywood Movie Gets Appalachian People Right," *Salon*, October 25, 2015, www.salon.com/2015/10/25/deliver_me _from_deliverance_finally_a_hollywood_movie_gets_appalachian_people_right/.

13. "Film Fare," *Vieux Carré Courier*, June 8, 1973, 15; Thomas Borstelmann, *The 1970s: A New Global History from Civil Rights to Economic Inequality* (Princeton, N.J.: Princeton University Press, 2011), 106.

14. Rushton, "Fire Tragedy Confused," 9; Rushton, "After the Fire Upstairs," 1.

15. Rushton, "After the Fire Upstairs," 1; "Families Urged to Appeal LA Welfare Payment Cuts," New Orleans *Times-Picayune*, July 19, 1973, 46; Mary Gehman, "N.O. Women's Movement: A Comprehensive History," *Distaff*, October 1973, 9 (read at Louisiana Research Collection, Howard-Tilton Memorial Library, Tulane University, New Orleans).

16. "Sniper Shoots Firemen," *Chicago Daily Defender*, January 8, 1973, 10; James H. Gillis, "Relations Law Being Studied by N.O. Council," New Orleans *Times-Picayune*, September 8, 1967, 1; "Nominees for Human Relations Committee," 1972, Records of the Human Relations Committee, City Archives, New Orleans Public Library; Philip Hannan to Arthur Screen, August 29, 1972, Records of the Human Relations Committee; HRC Answer Desk pamphlet, 1973, Vieux Carré Courier Collection, Earl K. Long Library, University of New Orleans; Leonard Moore, *Black Rage in New Orleans: Police Brutality and African American Activism* (Baton Rouge: Louisiana State University Press, 2010).

17. John E. Rousseau, "Mobile Answer Desk Now Serves Five Neighborhoods," *Louisiana Weekly*, January 15, 1972; interview with Troy Perry, December 2, 2014.

18. Perry interview; Troy Perry and Thomas Swicegood, *Don't Be Afraid Anymore* (New York: St. Martin's, 1990), 81.

19. Rushton, "After the Fire Upstairs," 1; Sharon Swindall, "Dead Man Was Pastor to Other Fire Victims," New Orleans *Daily Record*, June 26, 1973, 1.

20. Bill Rushton, "New Orleans Toll Thirty-Two; Arson Evidence Cited," *The Advocate*, August 1, 1973, 2; interview with Florence Jumonville, April 9, 2015.

21. Interview with Brendan Flaherty, November 12, 2016; interview with David Williams, January 21, 2016.

22. "966," Larison, Children's Home Association of Butler County Records, Ohio History Connection, Columbus, Ohio; Mrs. Ada Hill, "College Corner: F and S Club Holds Meeting," Hamilton [Ohio] *Daily News Journal*, January 21, 1971, 18; "Boli Issued Decree to Nellie Lairson," Hamilton [Ohio] *Journal—The Daily News*, September 9, 1947, 7; "Larison," Butler County Children's Home, 1936–1941, 3–4, Children's Home Association of Butler County Records.

23. "Larison," Butler County Children's Home, 1936–1941, 3–4; "Roscoe," Butler County Children's Home, 1936, Children's Home Association of Butler County Records; "Indian Legend Portrayed: Children's Home Cast, Resplendent in Red Paint and Feathers, Appears Before 200," Hamilton [Ohio] *Daily and News Journal*, June 26, 1935, 9; "Roscoe Larison," Butler County Children's Home, 1940, Children's Home Association of Butler County Records; "Grace Methodist Program Sunday," Hamilton [Ohio] *Daily and News Journal*, June 18, 1942, 13.

24. "Entertainer There," *Hamilton Daily News Journal*, June 24, 1951, 6.

25. Interview with Naoma McCrae, May 12, 2016; interview with Mary David Mihalyfi, May 4, 2016.

26. Interview with Skip Bailey, August 21, 2015; Jerry McLeod, "Family Solves Mystery After Learning Uncle Died in Infamous Upstairs Lounge Fire Forty-Plus Years Ago in New Orleans," *New Orleans Advocate*, June 10, 2015 (www.theadvocate.com/new_orleans/entertainment_life/article_bf16d3d9-b8e7-5994-8066-6dc1fa27bca5.html).

27. Perry and Swicegood, *Don't Be Afraid Anymore*, 81; Rushton, "After the Fire Upstairs," 1.

28. Interview with Ronald Rosenthal, June 14, 2016.

29. Swindall, "Dead Man Was Pastor to Other Fire Victims," 8; Rosenthal interview; interview with John Meyers, February 3, 2016.

30. Interview with Paul Killgore, June 14, 2016; Meyers interview, February 3, 2016.

31. Interview with Rene Sirois, February 7, 2017; interview with Larry Bagneris, August 24, 2015.

32. Killgore interview, June 14, 2016.

33. Perry and Swicegood, *Don't Be Afraid Anymore*, 81–86; interview with Henry Kubicki, September 4, 2015.

34. Lucien Baril, transcript of phone interview with *The Advocate*, 4:30 a.m. PST, June 25, 1973, New Orleans Upstairs Bar Fire/Advocate Records, ONE National Gay and Lesbian Archives at the USC Libraries, Los Angeles; John Gill, transcript of phone interview with *The Advocate*, 4:30 a.m. PST, June 25, 1973, New Orleans Upstairs Bar Fire/Advocate Records; Troy Perry, transcript of phone interview with *The Advocate*, June 26, 1973, New Orleans Upstairs Bar Fire/Advocate Records; Kubicki interview, September 4, 2015.

35. Kubicki interview, September 4, 2015; William Richardson, letter to the editor, *The Voice of Integrity* 1, no. 2 (Summer 1991), LGBT Religious Archives Network (http://exhibits.lgbtran.org/exhibits/show/upstairs-lounge-fire); Perry and Swicegood, *Don't Be Afraid Anymore*, 81; interview with Richard Everett, July 27, 2015; "List of Persons Identified or Presumed Dead," New Orleans Police Department Criminal Investigation Division, July 27, 1973, Vieux Carré Courier Collection, Earl K. Long Library; Eric Newhouse, "Smokie," Associated Press, June 1973.

36. Perry and Swicegood, *Don't Be Afraid Anymore*, 86; hotel receipts, rooms 1003 (Paul Breton) and 1004 (Morty Manford), National New Orleans Memorial Fund Collection, ONE National Gay and Lesbian Archives.

37. "Aid Mounts for New Orleans," *The Advocate*, August 15, 1973, 22; Perry and Swicegood, *Don't Be Afraid Anymore*, 86; Charlie Ferguson, oral history interview with Mark Cave, May 7, 2009, New Orleans Life Story Project, Historic New Orleans Collection.

38. Angus Lind, Lanny Thomas, and Walt Philbin, "Twenty-Nine Dead in Quarter Holocaust," New Orleans *States-Item*, June 25, 1973, 1; Rushton, "How the Media," 5.

39. Rushton, "How the Media," 5; Baril, transcript of *Advocate* interview, June 25, 1973; Lind, Thomas, and Philbin, "Twenty-Nine Dead," 1, 6.

40. Bagneris interview, August 24, 2015; Jervis Anderson, *Bayard Rustin: Troubles I've Seen* (New York: HarperCollins, 1997), 17–18; Eric Pace, "Bayard Rustin Is Dead at Seventy-Five; Pacifist and a Rights Activist," *The New York Times*, August 25, 1987, 30.

41. Lind, Thomas, and Philbin, "Twenty-Nine Dead"; Perry and Swicegood, *Don't Be Afraid Anymore*, 87.

42. LaPlace and Anderson, "29 Killed," 1; Bill Rushton, "Forgetting the Fire," *Vieux Carré Courier*, July 6, 1973, 1, 6; Clayton Delery, "Thieves, Queers and Fruit Jars: The Community and Media Responses to the Fire at the Up Stairs Lounge" (paper presented at the First Annual Louisiana Studies Conference, September 26, 2009); Robert McAnear, Facebook message to author, January 6, 2017.

43. Perry interview; Frank Straughan, "Phases of a Man Called 'Moon': Mayor Landrieu and Race Relations in New Orleans, 1960–1974" (M.A. thesis, University of New Orleans, 2011); Moon Landrieu, oral history interview with Mark Cave, September 15, 2009, New Orleans Life Story Project, Historic New Orleans Collection.

44. "New Orleans Mayor Moon Landrieu on MTP June 18, 1972," *Meet the Press*, NBCNews.com, June 18, 1972, www.nbcnews.com/video/meet-the-press/38923238 #38923238; "Mayor Offers Sympathy, Prayers, Thanks in Fire," New Orleans *Times-Picayune*, December 1, 1972, 11; "Landrieu Leaves After Fire News," New Orleans *Times-Picayune*, November 30, 1972, 1.

45. Landrieu, oral history, September 15, 2009; Delery, "Thieves, Queers, and Fruit Jars"; J. E. Bourgoyne, "Searched Well, Says Giarrusso," New Orleans *Times-Picayune*, January 9, 1973, 1, 3; "N.O. Mourning Is Proclaimed," New Orleans *Times-Picayune*, January 10, 1973, 9; "N.O. in Tribute to Blood Banks," New Orleans *Times-Picayune*, January 17, 1973, 7.

46. Delery, "Thieves, Queers, and Fruit Jars"; "Fire Sweeps Bar, Kills Twenty-Nine in New Orleans," 4; Wigg, "Twenty-Nine Killed in New Orleans," 5.

47. Jeff Taylor, *Politics on a Human Scale: The American Tradition of Decentralism* (Lanham, Md.: Lexington Books, 2013), 239; Straughan, "Phases of a Man Called 'Moon'"; interview with Moon Landrieu, December 13, 2014; Moon Landrieu, oral history with Mark Cave, May 12, 2009, New Orleans Life Story Project, Historic New Orleans Collection.

48. Landrieu interview; Landrieu, oral history, May 12, 2009; Straughan, "Phases of a Man Called 'Moon.'"

49. Interviews with Roberts Batson, July 11, 2014, and September 13, 2017; "No Post Offer Given to Irwin," New Orleans *Times-Picayune*, August 23, 1970, 13; interview

with Clancy DuBos, September 5, 2017; Dan Baum, *Nine Lives: Death and Life in New Orleans* (New York: Spiegel & Grau, 2010), 68; Winston Lill, "Must Invite List," June 29, 1973, Records of Mayor Moon Landrieu, City Archives.

50. "Democrats Elect Edwards' Choices," *Monroe* [La.] *News-Star*, February 21, 1972, 2; "State Democrats Show New Unity," *Monroe News-Star*, September 14, 1973, 2; Landrieu, oral history, September 15, 2009; interview with Moon Landrieu, December 18, 2014; Roberts Batson, "Claiming Our Past" (column 5), *Impact*, c. July–August 1994 (read at Rebels, Rubyfruit and Rhinestones Research Files, Sears Papers).

51. Delery, "Thieves, Queers, and Fruit Jars"; Don Lewis, "Tragedy Fund Is Established," New Orleans *Times-Picayune*, January 13, 1973, 1; Rushton, "Forgetting the Fire," 1.

52. Scrapbook 4, March–July 1973, Moon Landrieu Collection, Special Collections, Monroe Library, Loyola University, New Orleans; Moon Landrieu to Internal Revenue Service, June 22, 1973, Moon Landrieu Collection; Moon Landrieu to Gerhard Sigle, June 4, 1973, Records of Mayor Moon Landrieu, City Archives.

53. Paul Atkinson, "Beer's Dilemma on Bridge Noted," New Orleans *Times-Picayune*, July 8, 1973, 48; Ken Weiss, "N.O. Area Has Active Fourth," New Orleans *Times-Picayune*, July 5, 1973, 2; Landrieu, oral history, September 15, 2009.

54. Scott Ellis, *Madame Vieux Carré: The French Quarter in the Twentieth Century* (Jackson: University Press of Mississippi, 2010), 185; Robin Riley to Hans-Henrik Holm, June 11, 1973, Records of Mayor Moon Landrieu, City Archives; Winston Lill to Charles Ferguson, telefax, June 28, 1973, Records of Mayor Moon Landrieu.

55. Perry and Swicegood, *Don't Be Afraid Anymore*, 87; Paul Breton, "United We Stand" (unpublished manuscript, August 1973), National New Orleans Memorial Fund Collection, ONE National Gay and Lesbian Archives; Chris Segura, "Black, Empty Windows Stare," New Orleans *Times-Picayune*, June 26, 1973, 3; Chris Segura, "Devastating French Quarter Fire Probed by Three Agencies," New Orleans *Times-Picayune*, June 26, 1973, 3 (and accompany photograph by Robert T. Stoiner); Rushton, "Forgetting the Fire," 6.

56. Perry and Swicegood, *Don't Be Afraid Anymore*, 88; Perry interview; Morris Kight, transcript of phone interview with *The Advocate*, June 27, 1973, New Orleans Upstairs Bar Fire/Advocate Records, ONE National Gay and Lesbian Archives.

57. Rushton, "After the Fire Upstairs," 5; George Schwandt, "Holocaust in New Orleans," *The Advocate*, June 18, 1973, 9; Perry, transcript of *Advocate* interview, June 26, 1973.

58. Perry, transcript of *Advocate* interview, June 26, 1973; interviews with Richard Everett, September 20, 2016, and August 25, 2015.

59. WWL-TV New Orleans editorial transcript, June 25, 1973, National New Orleans Memorial Fund Collection, ONE National Gay and Lesbian Archives; Delery-Edwards, *The Up Stairs Lounge Arson,* 168.

60. "Upstairs Lounge Fire Network News Coverage," Youtube.com, September 4, 2007, www.youtube.com/watch?v=cvvRJNQolYM.

8: Visions

1. Bruce Nolan and Chris Segura, "Memorial for Fire Dead Has Forgiveness Theme," New Orleans *Times-Picayune*, June 26, 1973, 3; Troy Perry and Thomas Swicegood, *Don't Be Afraid Anymore* (New York: St. Martin's, 1990), 89; Henry Kubicki, "Henry Kubicki Account" (unpublished manuscript, November 14, 2013), LGBT Religious Archives Network (http://exhibits.lgbtran.org/exhibits/show/upstairs-lounge-fire), Berkeley, Calif.

2. "'We Knew Them as People,' Pastor Tells Gay Mourners," New Orleans *States-Item*, June 26, 1973, 3; Ed Brown, "A Brief History of St. George's" (unpublished manuscript, January 20, 2011; courtesy of Ed Brown); W. E. B. Du Bois, "Relations of Negroes to Whites in the South," *The Social Theory of W. E. B. Du Bois*, ed. Phil Zuckerman (New York: Sage Publications, 1965), 50.

3. Nolan and Segura, "Memorial for Fire Dead," 3; "'Pray for Those Who Did This,'" *The Advocate*, July 18, 1973, 8; interview with Ronald Rosenthal, June 14, 2016; Johnny Townsend, *Let the Faggots Burn: The Up Stairs Lounge Fire* (self-published through BookLocker.com, 2011), 36; interview with Richard Everett, August 30, 2016.

4. Townsend, *Let the Faggots Burn*, 35; William Richardson, letter to the editor, *The Voice of Integrity* 1, no. 2 (Summer 1991), LGBT Religious Archives Network (http://exhibits.lgbtran.org/exhibits/show/upstairs-lounge-fire); interview with Henry Kubicki, September 4, 2015.

5. Richardson, *The Voice of Integrity*.

6. "'Pray for Those Who Did This,'" 8.

7. Eric Newhouse, "Arson Squads Probe Rubble of Bar; Gay Group Plans Day of Mourning," *Mobile* [Ala.] *Press*, June 26, 1973; "'Pray for Those Who Did This,'" 8; "'We Knew Them as People,'" 3; interview with Richard Everett, August 30, 2016.

8. Troy Perry, transcript of phone interview with *The Advocate*, June 26, 1973, New Orleans Upstairs Bar Fire/Advocate Records, ONE National Gay and Lesbian Archives at the USC Libraries, Los Angeles; interview with John Meyers, February 3, 2016.

9. Cynthia Ann Savant, Statement to Louisiana Office of State Fire Marshal, August 1, 1974, 10–12, Louisiana State Archives, Baton Rouge (courtesy of Clayton Delery); Clayton Delery-Edwards, *The Up Stairs Lounge Arson: Thirty-Two Deaths in a New Orleans Gay Bar, June 24, 1973* (Jefferson, N.C.: McFarland, 2014), 130.

10. Savant, Statement to State Fire Marshal.

11. Ibid.; Rodger Dale Nunez, New Orleans Police Department Arrest Register, April 4, 1973, Johnny Townsend Collection, ONE National Gay and Lesbian Archives; Marine Casualty Report, U.S. Coast Guard Marine Board of Investigation, October 7, 1971, dco.uscg.mil.

12. Kubicki interview, September 4, 2015; interview with Dexter Brecht, July 29, 2015; Angus Lind, "Fire Bares the Grisly Face of Death," New Orleans *States-Item*, June 25, 1973, 6; Newhouse, "Church Slates"; "New Orleans Fire Probe Launched," *Monroe* [La.] *News-Star*, June 25, 1973, 2; "Church Deacon Believes 'Gay Bar' Flash

Fire Product of Arsonist," Fremont [Calif.] *Argus*, June 26, 1973, Joseph P. Manguno, "Deacon in Tavern Blames Arsonist," *Boston Herald American*, June 26, 1973.

13. Kubicki interview, September 4, 2015; Joseph Courtney Craighead, World War II draft card, Ancestry.com; Townsend, *Let the Faggots Burn*, 127.

14. Kubicki interview, September 4, 2015; Townsend, *Let the Faggots Burn*, 127.

15. Perry and Swicegood, *Don't Be Afraid Anymore*, 80; Paul Breton, "United We Stand" (unpublished manuscript, August 1973), National New Orleans Memorial Fund Collection, ONE National Gay and Lesbian Archives; Chris Segura, "Devastating French Quarter Fire Probed by Three Agencies," New Orleans *Times-Picayune*, June 26, 1973, 1; "General Case Report," New Orleans Department of Police, August 30, 1973, 2, Upstairs Lounge Records, City Archives, New Orleans Public Library; "McCloskey," *The Times-Picayune*, June 28, 1973, 14. Although 816 N. Gayoso St. is a valid street address in New Orleans, I could find no record of forty-eight-year-old Clarence McCloskey's having lived there. A casual review of phone books reveals that address to be the residence of McCloskey's dad, Clarence McCloskey Sr., a sixty-nine-year-old retiree with a working phone. The unlikely notation that the *Times-Picayune* would fail to perform this due diligence in reporting a death suggests a degree of intentionality in their error.

16. Captain Edwin Holmes, New Orleans Fire Department, email to author, November 15, 2017 (Holmes confirmed Bernard McCloskey's employment as a New Orleans fireman from 1956 until 1983); Supplemental Lists, Orleans Parish Coroner, 1973, Upstairs Lounge Records; "McCloskey" (paid death notice), New Orleans *Times-Picayune*, June 28, 1973, 14.

17. "General Case Report," NOPD, 39; Townsend, *Let the Faggots Burn*, 312; George Stephen Matyi, California Divorce Index, 1966–1984, ancestry.com; interview with Tina Matyi, October 29, 2016; Supplemental Lists, Orleans Parish Coroner, 1973, Upstairs Lounge Records.

18. Perry and Swicegood, *Don't Be Afraid Anymore*, 80; Everett interview, September 30, 2016; Breton, "United We Stand."

19. "New Charity Burn Unit Aids Fire Victims," New Orleans *States-Item*, June 27, 1973; Segura, "Devastating French Quarter Fire Probed," 3.

20. "Yesterday's Dreams, Today's Ghosts," *The Advocate*, March 13, 1974, 12, 16.

21. Morris Kight, Special Visiting Permit to Charity Hospital, June 26, 1973, Kight (Morris) Papers and Photographs, ONE National Gay and Lesbian Archives; interview with Troy Perry, December 2, 2014; Morris Kight, transcript of phone interview with *The Advocate*, June 27, 1973, New Orleans Upstairs Bar Fire/Advocate Records, ONE National Gay and Lesbian Archives.

22. Perry and Swicegood, *Don't Be Afraid Anymore*, 93; Larry Stratton, Autopsy, Orleans Parish Coroner's Office, 1973, Upstairs Lounge Records, City Archives; Perry interview; James Hambrick, Autopsy, Orleans Parish Coroner's Office, 1973, Upstairs Lounge Records, City Archives.

23. Townsend, *Let the Faggots Burn*, 1; Perry and Swicegood, *Don't Be Afraid Anymore*, 93; Luther Boggs, Autopsy, Orleans Parish Coroner's Office, 1973, Upstairs Lounge Records; Luther Thomas Boggs, World War II draft card, Ancestry.com; Breton, "United We Stand."

24. "Arson Assumption in N.O. Fire Eyed," Baton Rouge *Morning Advocate*, June 27,

1973; Perry interview; Bill Rushton, "Forgetting the Fire," *Vieux Carré Courier*, July 6, 1973, 1.

25. Rushton, "Forgetting the Fire," 1; Breton, "United We Stand"; Chris Segura, transcript of phone interview with *The Advocate*, June 26–27, 1973, New Orleans Upstairs Bar Fire/Advocate Records, ONE National Gay and Lesbian Archives; George Schwandt, "Holocaust in New Orleans," *The Advocate*, June 18, 1973, 2.

26. Bill Rushton, "How the Media Saw It," *Vieux Carré Courier*, June 29, 1973, 5; Breton, "United We Stand"; Schwandt, "Holocaust," 2.

27. Bill Rushton, "After the Fire Upstairs," *Vieux Carré Courier*, June 29, 1973, 5; "Arson Assumption"; Bill Rushton, "Fire Tragedy Confused Both Straights, Gays," *The Advocate*, July 18, 1973, 9; Rushton, "How the Media," 5.

28. Townsend, *Let the Faggots Burn*, 136; Winston Lill to Doug Augustin, June 26, 1973, Records of Mayor Moon Landrieu, City Archives; Winston Lill to Jay Handelman (memorandum), June 26, 1973, Records of Mayor Moon Landrieu, City Archives.

9: Fun House

1. Troy Perry and Thomas Swicegood, *Don't Be Afraid Anymore* (New York: St. Martin's, 1990), 93; interview with Troy Perry, December 2, 2014; Morris Kight, "New Orleans Community Disaster Relief Committee" diagram, c. June 26, 1973, Kight (Morris) Papers and Photographs, ONE National Gay and Lesbian Archives at the USC Libraries, Los Angeles.

2. Kight, "New Orleans Community Disaster Relief Committee" diagram; Troy Perry, transcript of phone interview with *The Advocate*, June 26, 1973, New Orleans Upstairs Bar Fire/Advocate Records, ONE National Gay and Lesbian Archives.

3. Royd Anderson. *The UpStairs Lounge Fire* (documentary film), Lake Oaks Studio, June 24, 2013; Clayton Delery-Edwards, *The Up Stairs Lounge Arson: Thirty-Two Deaths in a New Orleans Gay Bar, June 24, 1973* (Jefferson, N.C.: McFarland, 2014), 60; Paul Breton, "United We Stand" (unpublished manuscript, August 1973), National New Orleans Memorial Fund Collection, ONE National Gay and Lesbian Archives.

4. A. Elwood Willey, "The Upstairs Lounge Fire," *NFPA Journal* 68, no. 1 (1974): 18; "General Case Report," New Orleans Department of Police, August 30, 1973, 29–31, Upstairs Lounge Records, City Archives, New Orleans Public Library; Johnny Townsend, *Let the Faggots Burn: The Up Stairs Lounge Fire* (self-published through BookLocker.com, 2011), 319.

5. Lanny Thomas, "Have Labels Overshadowed Twenty-Nine Deaths?," New Orleans *States-Item*, June 28, 1973, 16; Chris Segura, "Black, Empty Windows Stare," New Orleans *Times-Picayune*, June 26, 1973, 3; Bill Rushton, "Forgetting the Fire," *Vieux Carré Courier*, July 6, 1973, 6; interview with Ulysses Robertson, August 7, 2017.

6. Rushton, "Forgetting the Fire," 6; Morris Kight, transcript of phone interview with *The Advocate*, June 27, 1973, New Orleans Upstairs Bar Fire/Advocate Records, ONE National Gay and Lesbian Archives; Eric Newhouse, "Smokie," Associated Press, June 1973.

7. Segura, "Black, Empty Windows Stare," 3.
8. Thomas, "Have Labels Overshadowed."
9. Ibid.; Tom W. Smith and Jaesok Son, "Trends in Public Attitudes About Sexual Morality," National Opinion Research Center, April 2013, 11 (www.norc.org/PDFs /sexmoralfinal_06-21_FINAL.PDF).
10. "General Case Report," NOPD, 29, 3, 50–51; Delery-Edwards, *The Up Stairs Lounge Arson,* 73; Cynthia Ann Savant, Statement to Louisiana Office of State Fire Marshal, August 1, 1974, Louisiana State Archives, Baton Rouge (courtesy of Clayton Delery).
11. "Gays Begin Relief Funds for Upstairs Fire Victims," New Orleans *Daily Record,* June 27, 1973, 1; Vincent Lee, "Gay Leaders Plan Aid for Victims of Bar Fire," New Orleans *Times-Picayune,* June 27, 1973, 14; Kight, transcript of *Advocate* interview, June 27, 1973.
12. "Gays Begin Relief Funds," 1; Perry interview; "Dallas Attorney Slain; Challenges Sex Laws," *The Advocate,* August 1, 1973, 14; Lee, "Gay Leaders," 14; Anderson. *The UpStairs Lounge Fire.*
13. Breton, "United We Stand"; Martin St. John, "'A Part of Our Souls Was Ignited . . . ,'" *The Advocate,* August 1, 1973, 1, 16–17.
14. "Tragedy in New Orleans" (Up Stairs Lounge flyer), 1973, National New Orleans Memorial Fund Collection, ONE National Gay and Lesbian Archives; "National Day of Mourning" (Up Stairs Lounge flyer), 1973, National New Orleans Memorial Fund Collection; "The 'Upstairs Tragedy' Continues," *Gay Community News,* July 5, 1973, 1.
15. Interview with Henry Kubicki, September 5, 2015; interviews with Richard Everett, September 30, 2016, and July 27, 2015; Henry Kubicki, "Henry Kubicki Account" (unpublished manuscript, November 14, 2013), LGBT Religious Archives Network (http://exhibits.lgbtran.org/exhibits/show/upstairs-lounge-fire), Berkeley, Calif.
16. Kubicki interview, September 5, 2015; Everett interviews, July 27, 2015, and September 30, 2016; interview with Ronald Rosenthal, June 14, 2016.
17. Everett interviews, August 25, 2015, September 30, 2016, and July 27, 2015.
18. Ibid.
19. Interview with Clancy DuBos, May 18, 2016; Charlie Ferguson, oral history interview with Mark Cave, May 7, 2009, New Orleans Life Story Project, Historic New Orleans Collection; Bill Rushton, "New Orleans Toll Thirty-Two; Arson Evidence Cited," *The Advocate,* August 1, 1973, 1; "Press Club's Dedication Held," New Orleans *Times-Picayune,* August 1, 1973, 67.
20. Lee, "Gay Leaders," 14; Bill Rushton, "Fire Tragedy Confused Both Straights, Gays," *The Advocate,* July 18, 1973, 2; Bruce Nolan and Chris Segura, "Memorial for Fire Dead Has Forgiveness Theme," New Orleans *Times-Picayune,* June 26, 1973, 3.
21. Interview with Milton Mary, August 22, 2016; interview with Ronald LeBoeuf, April 15, 2015.
22. Perry and Swicegood, *Don't Be Afraid Anymore,* 94; Chris Segura, "'Positive Identifications' Made for Nine Fire Victims," New Orleans *Times-Picayune,* June 27, 1973, 3.
23. Breton, "United We Stand."
24. Edwin Edwards to A. T. Screen, June 10, 1970, Records of the Human Relations Committee, City Archives; Breton, "United We Stand."

25. Breton, "United We Stand."
26. Ibid.; Segura, " 'Positive Identifications' Made," 3.
27. Perry and Swicegood, *Don't Be Afraid Anymore*, 91; Rushton, "New Orleans Toll," 6; interview with Meyers, January 26, 2016.
28. Ed Martinez, "The Fire at the Lounge: Where Was Mercy?," *Nola Express*, July 27, 1973; Perry interview; Perry and Swicegood, *Don't Be Afraid Anymore*, 91; interview with Brendan Flaherty, November 12, 2016.
29. Scott Ellis, *Madame Vieux Carré: The French Quarter in the Twentieth Century* (Jackson: University Press of Mississippi, 2010), 68; interview with Roberts Batson, July 11, 2014; Perry and Swicegood, *Don't Be Afraid Anymore*, 92; Delery-Edwards, *The Up Stairs Lounge Arson*, 79; Perry interview; Check signed by Morris Kight, Security Pacific National Bank—Wilshire & Union Branch. 1973, National New Orleans Memorial Fund Collection, ONE National Gay and Lesbian Archives; National New Orleans Memorial Fund, sample legal letter, 1973, National New Orleans Memorial Fund Collection.

10: Firetraps

1. Interview with Troy Perry, December 2, 2014; "Blaze Victims' Memorial Set," New Orleans *Times-Picayune*, June 30, 1973, 11; " 'Pray for Those Who Did This,' " *The Advocate*, July 18, 1973, 8; William Richardson, letter to the editor, *The Voice of Integrity* 1, no. 2 (Summer 1991), LGBT Religious Archives Network (http://exhibits.lgbtran.org/exhibits/show/upstairs-lounge-fire), Berkeley, Calif.
2. Richardson, *The Voice of Integrity*; "Morality in Media Issues Letter Urging Involvement," New Orleans *Times-Picayune*, April 8, 1973, 12.
3. Richardson, *The Voice of Integrity*.
4. Ibid.; Troy Perry and Thomas Swicegood, *Don't Be Afraid Anymore* (New York: St. Martin's, 1990), 95.
5. Richardson, "An Important Statement from the Rector," St. George's Episcopal Church, June 28, 1973, LGBT Religious Archives Network (http://exhibits.lgbtran .org/exhibits/show/upstairs-lounge-fire/gallery?response-to-tragedy).
6. Richardson, *The Voice of Integrity*; Perry and Swicegood, *Don't Be Afraid Anymore*, 95; Paul Breton, "United We Stand" (unpublished manuscript, August 1973), National New Orleans Memorial Fund Collection, ONE National Gay and Lesbian Archives at the USC Libraries, Los Angeles; Perry interview.
7. Martinez, "The Fire at the Lounge: Where Was Mercy?," *Nola Express*, July 27, 1973; Breton, "United We Stand"; Bill Rushton, "Forgetting the Fire," *Vieux Carré Courier*, July 6, 1973, 1.
8. Peter Finney, "Archbishop Hannan, Paratroop Chaplain and Kennedy Counselor, Dies at Ninety-Eight," *Today's Catholic News*, September 29, 2011 (www.todays catholicnews.org/2011/09/archbishop-hannan-paratroop-chaplain-and-kennedy -counselor-dies-at-98/); Philip Hannan, *The Archbishop Wore Combat Boots: From Combat to Camelot to Katrina* (Huntington, Ind.: Our Sunday Visitor, 2010), 196–243; "Condolences to Victims' Families Offered by Archbishop Hannan," New Orleans *Times-Picayune*, November 30, 1972, 3; Elmo Romagosa,

"Shepherd Tends to His Flock," *Clarion Herald*, January 11, 1973, 1; "Archbishop Hannan's Legacy: Catholic Charities Archdiocese of New Orleans," Archdiocese of New Orleans, September 30, 2011, www.arch-no.org/articles/archbishop -hannans-legacy-catholic-charities-archdiocese-of-new-orleans-1.

9. Bill Rushton, "New Orleans Toll Thirty-Two; Arson Evidence Cited," *The Advocate*, August 1, 1973, 2; Breton, "United We Stand"; interview with John Meyers, February 3, 2016.

10. Breton, "United We Stand"; Perry and Swicegood, *Don't Be Afraid Anymore*, 96; Perry interview.

11. Clayton Delery-Edwards, *The Up Stairs Lounge Arson: Thirty-Two Deaths in a New Orleans Gay Bar, June 24, 1973* (Jefferson, N.C.: McFarland, 2014), 79; David Bird, "Clay Shaw Is Dead at Sixty; Freed in Kennedy 'Plot,'" *The New York Times*, August 16, 1974, 32; Moon Landrieu, oral history interview with Mark Cave, September 15, 2009, New Orleans Life Story Project, Historic New Orleans Collection; "Planned French Market Rejuvenation Is Praised," New Orleans *Times-Picayune*, March 17, 1972, 21; "News Release," City Hall, July 12, 1973, Records of Mayor Moon Landrieu, City Archives, New Orleans Public Library; Perry interview.

12. Delery-Edwards, *The Up Stairs Lounge Arson*, 79.

13. Ken Weiss, "Disaster Waiting to Happen: Quarter Firetrap Crackdown," New Orleans *Times-Picayune*, June 28, 1973, 1; "VCC Blamed for French Quarter Firetraps," New Orleans *States-Item*, June 28, 1973, 3.

14. "VCC Blamed for French Quarter Firetraps," 3; Rushton, "Forgetting the Fire," 6; Weiss, "Disaster Waiting to Happen," 1, 7; Bob Damron, *Bob Damron's Address Book*, 8th ed. (San Francisco: Bob Damron, 1972), 76–78.

15. Weiss, "Disaster Waiting to Happen," 7; "VCC Blamed for French Quarter Firetraps," 3; Rushton, "Forgetting the Fire," 6.

16. "Two Persons Die in $50,000 Hotel Fire at Silver Dollar Hotel," New Orleans *Times-Picayune*, October 14, 1970, 8; Bob Damron, *Bob Damron's Address Book*, 9th ed. (San Francisco: Bob Damron, 1973), 101; George Schwandt, "Holocaust in New Orleans," *The Advocate*, June 18, 1973, 1; Paul Atkinson, "Obscenity Crackdown Begins," New Orleans *Times-Picayune*, June 28, 1973, 1; Ed Jackson, "Obscenity Ruling Turns Back Clock—and Then Some," *The Advocate*, July 18, 1973, 4; "Court Resolves Obscenity Suits," New Orleans *Times-Picayune*, July 7, 1973, 7.

17. "General Case Report," New Orleans Department of Police, August 30, 1973, 49, Upstairs Lounge Records, City Archives.

18. "Six More Victims of Fire Identified, Coroner Says," New Orleans *Times-Picayune*, June 29, 1973, 9; Angus Lind, Lanny Thomas, and Walt Philbin, "Twenty-Nine Dead in Quarter Holocaust," New Orleans *States-Item*, June 25, 1973, 1; list of persons identified or presumed dead, New Orleans Police Department, July 27, 1973, Vieux Carré Courier Collection, Earl K. Long Library, University of New Orleans; Supplemental Lists, Orleans Parish Coroner, 1973, Upstairs Lounge Records.

19. "Six More Victims of Fire Identified," 9; "Thirtieth Bar Blaze Victim Dies; Eight Remain Unidentified," New Orleans *States-Item*, June 29, 1973; Adam Fontenot, Autopsy, Orleans Parish Coroner's Office, 1973, Upstairs Lounge Records; Johnny Townsend, *Let the Faggots Burn: The Up Stairs Lounge Fire* (self-published through

BookLocker.com, 2011), 319; "History of Sacred Heart Parish," sacredheartvp
.com, http://sacredheartvp.com/about/parish-history/; Adam Roland Fontenot,
findagrave.com, www.findagrave.com/cgi-bin/fg.cgi?page=gr&GRid=82606301.

20. Breton, "United We Stand"; Townsend, *Let the Faggots Burn*, 319.

21. Interview with Mary David Mihalyfi, May 4, 2016.

22. Ibid.; Glenn Richard Green, Autopsy, Orleans Parish Coroner's Office, 1973,
    Upstairs Lounge Records.

23. Mihalyfi interview; "Services," "Relatives and Friends," and "Newspaper Notices"
    pages of Glenn Green funeral album, 1973 (courtesy of Mary David Mihalyfi);
    "General Case Report," NOPD, 60.

24. "Hambrick" (paid death notice), New Orleans *Times-Picayune*, June 29, 1973, 24;
    interview with Sheri Wright, June 2016; James Hambrick, Autopsy, Orleans Parish
    Coroner's Office, 1973, Upstairs Lounge Records.

25. Wright interview; "Thirtieth Bar Blaze Victim Dies"; "Hambrick" (paid death
    notice), 24.

26. "Larson" (paid death notice), New Orleans *Times-Picayune*, June 30, 1973, 19; Wil-
    liam Ros Larson, Autopsy, Orleans Parish Coroner's Office, 1973, Upstairs Lounge
    Records; Sharon Swindall, "Dead Man Was Pastor to Other Fire Victims," New
    Orleans *Daily Record*, June 26, 1973, 1; Vincent Lee, "Gay Leaders Plan Aid for Vic-
    tims of Bar Fire," New Orleans *Times-Picayune*, June 27, 1973, 14; Lanny Thomas,
    "Fun . . . Drinks . . . Song . . . with Death at the Piano," New Orleans *States-Item*,
    June 25, 1973, 6; Eric Newhouse, "Arson Squads Probe Rubble of Bar; Gay Group
    Plans Day of Mourning," *Mobile* [Ala.] *Press*, June 26, 1973; "Fire Victims, Funeral
    Home," Orleans Parish Coroner's Office, 1973, Upstairs Lounge Records.

27. Perry and Swicegood, *Don't Be Afraid Anymore*, 93; "Troy R. Howell Rites Thurs-
    day," *Hamilton* [Ohio] *Daily News Journal*, October 27, 1953, 2.

28. "Summary," Ohio Bureau, 1929, Children's Home Association of Butler County
    Records, Ohio History Connection, Columbus, Ohio; "Roscoe Larison," Butler
    County Children's Home, 1938, Children's Home Association of Butler County
    Records; "Larison," Butler County Children's Home, 1936–1941, 5, Children's Home
    Association of Butler County Records; "Dickens' Characters Portrayed At Pro-
    gram In Children's Home," *Hamilton* [Ohio] *Daily and News Journal*, December 22,
    1937, 28; "Children's Home Kiddies Also Hunt Eggs," *Hamilton* [Ohio] *Daily and
    News Journal*, April 10, 1939, 14; Roscoe Larison, Certificate of Confirmation, First
    Reformed Church, 1939, Children's Home Association of Butler County Records;
    "Roscoe Larison" (weekly reports), Butler County Children's Home, 1940, Children's
    Home Association of Butler County Records; "Entertainer There," *Hamilton Daily
    News Journal*, June 24, 1951, 6; "Larson" (paid death notice), 19.

29. Wm. Roscoe Lairson to Butler County Children's Home, February 21, 1947, Chil-
    dren's Home Association of Butler County Records.

30. Perry and Swicegood, *Don't Be Afraid Anymore*, 25; "Twenty-Nine Persons Die
    in Blaze Destroys New Orleans Bar," *Hamilton* [Ohio] *Journal-News*, June 25,
    1973, 2; "Re: The Rev. William (Bill) Ros Larson," National New Orleans Memo-
    rial Fund, January 17, 1973, National New Orleans Memorial Fund Collection,
    ONE National Gay and Lesbian Archives; Delery-Edwards, *The Up Stairs Lounge
    Arson*, 90.

31. House of Bultman to Gay Community Services Center (letter), May 13, 1974, National New Orleans Memorial Fund Collection; Breton, "United We Stand"; Lucien Baril, transcript of phone interview with *The Advocate*, 4:30 a.m. PST, June 25, 1973, New Orleans Upstairs Bar Fire/Advocate Records, ONE National Gay and Lesbian Archives.

32. Delery-Edwards, *The Up Stairs Lounge Arson*, 176; Veterans Administration to Thomas L. Baril, March 6, 1973, National New Orleans Memorial Fund Collection; Paul Breton to Morris Kight, March 21, 1974, National New Orleans Memorial Fund Collection.

33. Townsend, *Let the Faggots Burn*, 313; interview with Richard Everett, September 30, 2016; "Larson" (paid death notice), 19.

11: In Memoriam

1. Troy Perry and Thomas Swicegood, *Don't Be Afraid Anymore* (New York: St. Martin's, 1990), 96.

2. Ellen Blue, *St. Mark's and the Social Gospel: Methodist Women and Civil Rights in New Orleans, 1895–1965* (Knoxville: University of Tennessee Press, 2014), 20, 165; Claude Sitton, "Crowd of Racists Heckles Minister," *The New York Times*, December 5, 1960, 1, 38.

3. Blue, *St. Mark's and the Social Gospel*, 212; Perry and Swicegood, *Don't Be Afraid Anymore*, 96; "Blaze Victims' Memorial Set," New Orleans *Times-Picayune*, June 30, 1973, 11; Clayton Delery-Edwards, *The Up Stairs Lounge Arson: Thirty-Two Deaths in a New Orleans Gay Bar, June 24, 1973* (Jefferson, N.C.: McFarland, 2014), 80; B. A. Robinson, "The United Methodist Church and Homosexuality Decisions by Church Conferences and Courts from 1972 to 1996," August 21, 2014, ReligiousTolerance.org, www.religioustolerance.org/hom_umc6.htm.

4. "Blaze Victims' Memorial Set," 11; Paul Breton, "United We Stand" (unpublished manuscript, August 1973), National New Orleans Memorial Fund Collection, ONE National Gay and Lesbian Archives at the USC Libraries, Los Angeles.

5. Breton, "United We Stand"; Perry and Swicegood, *Don't Be Afraid Anymore*, 97; interview with John Meyers, February 3, 2016.

6. Meyers interview, February 3, 2016.

7. Interview with Stewart Butler, July 20, 2014; interview with Richard Everett, September 30, 2016; Henry Kubicki, "Henry Kubicki Account" (unpublished manuscript, November 14, 2013), LGBT Religious Archives Network (http://exhibits.lgbtran. org/exhibits/show/upstairs-lounge-fire), Berkeley, Calif.; Breton, "United We Stand"; Eric Newhouse, "Memorial Services for N.O. Blaze Victims," Baton Rouge *Morning Advocate*, July 2, 1973; Martin St. John, "'A Part of Our Souls Was Ignited . . . ,'" *The Advocate*, August 1, 1973, 16; interview with Paul Killgore, January 17, 2016.

8. Delery-Edwards, *The Up Stairs Lounge Arson*, 82; Bill Rushton, "Fire Three: Who the Victims Were," *Vieux Carré Courier*, July 13–19, 1973, 6; Killgore interview, January 17, 2016; Butler interview, July 20, 2014.

9. Butler interview, July 20, 2014; Everett interview, September 30, 2016; Kubicki, "Henry Kubicki Account"; interview with Henry Kubicki, September 5, 2015

10. Interview with Steven Duplantis, March 11, 2016; Lucien Baril, transcript of phone call with *The Advocate*, September 14, 1973, New Orleans Upstairs Bar Fire/Advocate Records, ONE National Gay and Lesbian Archives.

11. Chris Segura, "Cleric Says Oppression Problem for Homosexuals," New Orleans *Times-Picayune*, July 2, 1973, 14; Newhouse, "Memorial Services for N.O. Blaze Victims"; Rushton, "Forgetting the Fire," 6; "Morality in Media Issues Letter Urging Involvement," New Orleans *Times-Picayune*, April 8, 1973, 12; Emily Yoffe, "Bishop Denies 'Brotherhood' to the End," *Chicago Tribune*, December 3, 1987 (http:// articles.chicagotribune.com/1987-12-03/features/8703300793_1_rev-troy-perry -metropolitan-community-churches-gay-bar); Perry and Swicegood, *Don't Be Afraid Anymore*, 98; Breton, "United We Stand."

12. Breton, "United We Stand."

13. Ibid.; Segura, "Cleric Says Oppression Problem," 14.

14. Breton, "United We Stand"; interview with Henry Kubicki, September 4, 2015; Perry and Swicegood, *Don't Be Afraid Anymore*, 99.

15. Breton, "United We Stand"; "Resolution," LSUNO Young Democrats, June 28, 1973, Vieux Carré Courier Collection, Earl K. Long Library, University of New Orleans.

16. Ed Martinez, "The Fire at the Lounge: Where Was Mercy?," *Nola Express*, July 27, 1973; Bill Rushton, "New Orleans Toll Thirty-Two; Arson Evidence Cited," *The Advocate*, August 1, 1973, 2.

17. Breton, "United We Stand"; "Two Hundred Attend Service for Lounge Victims," New Orleans *States-Item*, July 2, 1973; Segura, "Cleric Says Oppression Problem," 14; Newhouse, "Memorial Services for N.O. Blaze Victims."

18. Butler interview, July 20, 2014; Killgore interview, January 17, 2016.

19. Breton, "United We Stand"; Segura, "Cleric Says Oppression Problem," 14; Martinez, "The Fire at the Lounge"; St. John, "'A Part of Our Souls,'" 16; Rushton, "Forgetting the Fire," 6.

20. Segura, "Cleric Says Oppression Problem," 14; Kubicki interview, September 5, 2015; Newhouse, "Memorial Services for N.O. Blaze Victims"; Breton, "United We Stand"; Killgore interview, January 17, 2016.

21. Killgore interview, January 17, 2016; Butler interview, July 20, 2014; Breton, "United We Stand"; Perry interview; Rushton, "Fire Three," 6; Segura, "Cleric Says Oppression Problem," 14; Martinez, "The Fire at the Lounge."

22. Interview with Henry Kubicki, September 4, 2015; Killgore interview, January 17, 2016; Martinez, "The Fire at the Lounge"; Perry interview; Newhouse, "Memorial Services for N.O. Blaze Victims."

23. Interview with Royd Anderson, September 2, 2017; Delery-Edwards, *The Up Stairs Lounge Arson*, 143; WDSU-New Orleans, "Film Log June 2, 1973, to December 31, 1974" (courtesy of Royd Anderson).

24. "Rev. Perry Will Speak," New Orleans *Times-Picayune*, July 16, 1977, 32; St. John, "'A Part of Our Soul,'" 1; Tom Taylor, "The Impossible Dream," *In Unity*, June 1974, 19, https://issuu.com/mcchurches/doc; Jackie M. Blount, *Fit to Teach: Same-Sex Desire, Gender, and School Work in the Twentieth Century* (Albany: SUNY Press, 2005), 138; Lillian Faderman, *The Gay Revolution: The Story of the Struggle* (New York: Simon & Schuster, 2015); Perry interview; Perry and Swicegood, *Don't Be Afraid Anymore*, 29.

25. Breton, "United We Stand"; Morris Kight to Lucien Baril, January 18, 1974, National New Orleans Memorial Fund Collection, ONE National Gay and Lesbian Archives; Morty Manford to Bill Rushton, July 11, 1973, Vieux Carré Courier Collection, Earl K. Long Library; Gay People's Coalition to Human Relations Committee, July 25, 1973, National New Orleans Memorial Fund Collection.

12: Deliverance

1. Martin St. John, "'A Part of Our Souls Was Ignited . . . ,'" *The Advocate*, August 1, 1973, 1; Paul Breton, "United We Stand" (unpublished manuscript, August 1973), National New Orleans Memorial Fund Collection, ONE National Gay and Lesbian Archives at the USC Libraries, Los Angeles; "Parade," *The New Yorker*, July 11, 1970, 19; "The Militant Homosexual," *Newsweek*, August 23, 1971, 45–48.
2. St. John, "'A Part of Our Souls,'" 1; Roberts Batson, "Errors in Up Stairs Lounge Story," *Gambit* 19, no, 25 (June 23, 1998): 6; interview with John Meyers, January 26, 2016.
3. Vicki Eaklor, Robert R Meek, and Vern L Bullough, *Bringing Lesbian and Gay Rights into the Mainstream: Twenty Years of Progress* (Abingdon, U.K.: Routledge, 2006), 86; "Memorial Services . . . San Francisco" and "The Seattle MCC," *Advocate* notes, July 1, 1973, New Orleans Upstairs Bar Fire/Advocate Records, ONE National Gay and Lesbian Archives; St. John, "'A Part of Our Souls,'" 16; Grace Lichtenstein, "Homosexuals in New York Find New Pride," *The New York Times*, October 25, 1977, 39; "Ecumenical Memorial Service" (official leaflet), July 1, 1973, New Orleans Upstairs Bar Fire/Advocate Records.
4. Jim Kepner, "Memorial Remarks for Those Gays Burned to Death Last Sunday in the Upstairs Bar in New Orleans," July 1, 1973, New Orleans Upstairs Bar Fire/Advocate Records; "Join the Rest," *Advocate* notes, July 1973, New Orleans Upstairs Bar Fire/Advocate Records.
5. St. John, "'A Part of Our Souls,'" 1; National Day of Mourning Memorial Service" (official leaflet), July 1, 1973, New Orleans Upstairs Bar Fire/Advocate Records.
6. "General Case Report," New Orleans Department of Police, August 30, 1973, 54, Upstairs Lounge Records, City Archives, New Orleans Public Library; Louisiana Office of State Fire Marshal, July 22, 1975, 20, Louisiana State Archives, Baton Rouge.
7. "Official Report," State Fire Marshal, 20.
8. Ibid., 12–20.
9. Ibid., 20; "General Case Report," NOPD, 54, 37–38.
10. "General Case Report," NOPD, 54–55.
11. Ibid., 55; "Official Report," State Fire Marshal, 29; "New Burn Unit Used at Charity," New Orleans *Times-Picayune*, June 28, 1973, sect. 7, p. 16.
12. "General Case Report," NOPD, 55, 52; C. Helmstaedter, C. E. Elger, and M. Lendt, "Postictal Courses of Cognitive Deficits in Focal Epilepsies," *Epilepsia* 35, no. 5 (September 1994): 1073–78.
13. "Notes on Fire Victims," Orleans Parish Coroner's Office, 1973, Upstairs Lounge Records, City Archives; interview with Duane Mitchell, August 14, 2015.
14. Tom Frazer, "Sons of Fire Victim Sent Home—Unaware of Father's Death," New

Orleans *States-Item*, June 26, 1973, A3; Mitchell interview, August 14, 2015; "Three More Fire Victims Named," New Orleans *States-Item*, June 30, 1973.

15. Mitchell interview, August 14, 2015; "Duane George Mitchell" (paid death notice), *Birmingham News*, July 2, 1973, 43.

16. Ibid.

17. Ibid.; "Broussard, Louis Horace," Acadia Genealogical and Historical Society, www.theusgenweb.org/la/acadia/obitalpha/Obits_B18.html.

18. Mitchell interview, August 14, 2015; "Duane George Mitchell," 43.

19. Mitchell interview, August 14, 2015.

20. Eric Newhouse, "Bar Not Inspected in Two Years," New Orleans *Times-Picayune*, July 1, 1973, 4.

21. A. Elwood Willey, "The Upstairs Lounge Fire," *NFPA Journal* 68, no. 1 (1974): 16–20; Elaine Tyrrell to Elwood Willey, December 12, 1973, LGBT Religious Archives Network (http://exhibits.lgbtran.org/exhibits/show/upstairs-lounge-fire), Berkeley, Calif; "NOFD Officials Rebut AP Story," New Orleans *Times-Picayune*, July 3, 1973, 6.

22. Newhouse, "Bar Not Inspected," 4; "Quarter Violations Count Passes 1,000 Mark," New Orleans *Times-Picayune*, July 21, 1973, 7; George Schwandt to Rob Cole, July 8, 1973, New Orleans Upstairs Bar Fire/Advocate Records, ONE National Gay and Lesbian Archives.

23. Ken Weiss, "Five Quarter Buildings Ordered Repaired or Demolished," New Orleans *Times-Picayune*, July 29, 1973, 14; Moon Landrieu to Frank Incaprera, July 9, 1973, Records of Mayor Moon Landrieu, City Archives; Robin Riley to Hans-Henrik Holm, June 11, 1973, Records of Mayor Moon Landrieu; Moon Landrieu to Carroll Trosclair, July 9, 1973, Records of Mayor Moon Landrieu; Moon Landrieu, "To the Readers of *Living Magazine*," July 9, 1973, Records of Mayor Moon Landrieu; Bill Rushton, "Forgetting the Fire," *Vieux Carré Courier*, July 6, 1973, 1.

24. "Official Report," State Fire Marshal, 58, 22, 29–30; Rodger Dale Nunez, Statement to Louisiana Office of State Fire Marshal, September 18, 1973, 4–5, Skylar Fein Upstairs Lounge Fire Collection, Historic New Orleans Collection; "General Case Report," NOPD 55.

25. "Official Report," State Fire Marshal, 29, 58; Cynthia Ann Savant, Statement to Louisiana Office of State Fire Marshal, August 1, 1974, Louisiana State Archives (copy courtesy of Clayton Delery).

26. "Official Report," State Fire Marshal, 58, 22, 29–30; "General Case Report," NOPD, 55.

27. "General Case Report," NOPD, 55, 52, 58; "Official Report," State Fire Marshal, 22; Nunez, Statement to State Fire Marshal, 4–5.

28. "General Case Report," NOPD, 58–59; Nunez, Statement to State Fire Marshal, 12; Charles Aldinger, "Teeth Only Way to Identify Victims of Fire," *Jennings* [La.] *Daily News*, June 25, 1973, 8.

29. "Arson Assumption in N.O. Fire Eyed," Baton Rouge *Morning Advocate*, June 27, 1973; "Probe Slated in Shakedown," New Orleans *Times-Picayune*, July 10, 1973, 10; Bob Ussery, "Charge Brings Suspension for Police Officer," New Orleans *Times-Picayune*, July 7, 1973, 3; Glenn Helton, "Police Probe Shakedown," New Orleans *States-Item*, July 7–8, 1973; Bob Ussery, "Police Officer Is Reinstated," New Orleans *Times-Picayune*, July 27, 1973, 1.

30. "General Case Report," NOPD, 41; Boggs, Autopsy; interview with Troy Perry, December 2, 2014; "Yesterday's Dreams, Today's Ghosts," *The Advocate*, March 13, 1974, 12.

31. Jay Handelman, memorandum, July 9, 1973, Records of Mayor Moon Landrieu, City Archives; Paul Atkinson, "Landrieu Attacks Property Tax Plan," New Orleans *Times-Picayune*, July 12, 1973, 1, 3; Bill Rushton, "Fire Three: Who the Victims Were," *Vieux Carré Courier*, July 13–19, 1973, 6.

32. Rushton, "Fire Three," 6; Atkinson, "Landrieu Attacks," 3.

33. Larry Stratton, Autopsy, Orleans Parish Coroner's Office, 1973, Upstairs Lounge Records, City Archives.

34. Breton, "United We Stand"; Stratton, Autopsy; "General Case Report," NOPD, 41, 5; Larry Dean Stratton, memorial 112770954, findagrave.com.

35. "General Case Report," NOPD, 59; "Official Report," State Fire Marshal, 22, 29; Nunez, Statement to State Fire Marshal, 8.

36. Interview with Tina Matyi, October 29, 2016; Johnny Townsend, *Let the Faggots Burn: The Up Stairs Lounge Fire* (self-published through BookLocker.com, 2011), 312.

37. Townsend, *Let the Faggots Burn*, 312; Matyi interview; George Steven [sic] Matyi, Autopsy, Orleans Parish Coroner's Office, 1973, Upstairs Lounge Records, City Archives; Inez Warren, Autopsy, Orleans Parish Coroner's Office, 1973, Upstairs Lounge Records; "General Case Report," NOPD, 12.

38. Matyi interview.

39. "Morty Manford Tour" (press release), July 20, 1973, National New Orleans Memorial Fund Collection, ONE National Gay and Lesbian Archives; "Gay Coalition of Denver" (press release), July 19, 1973, National New Orleans Memorial Fund Collection; "Chicago Gays to Raise Funds for New Orleans Fire Victims" (press release), July 17, 1973, National New Orleans Memorial Fund Collection, "Chicago Gays Mobilize to Aid Fire Victims," *Chicago Gay Crusader*, August 1973, 1.

40. "Morty Manford Tour"; Paul Breton to Dick Michaels, September 7, 1973, National New Orleans Memorial Fund Collection; "Fund," *Causeway*, January 1974, 7–8 (read at Rebels, Rubyfruit and Rhinestones Research Files, James T. Sears Papers, Duke University Libraries, Durham, N.C.); Morris Kight, transcript of phone call with *The Advocate*, September 12, 1973, New Orleans Bar Fire/Advocate Records, ONE National Gay and Lesbian Archives; Ed Belew, "Re: Blood Account" (telephone message dictated and transcribed for Morris Kight), November 2, 1976, National New Orleans Memorial Fund Collection.

41. New Orleans Memorial Fund Receipts Journal, National New Orleans Memorial Fund Collection, ONE National Gay and Lesbian Archives; "Gay Pride Day," *The Advocate*, July 18, 1973, 1; "It's Our Concern," *The Advocate*, July 18, 1973, 1.

42. Bill Rushton, Gay People's Coalition notes. Vieux Carré Courier Collection, Earl K. Long Library, University of New Orleans; Roberts Batson, "Remembering the Up Stairs Lounge," *Impact* 23, no. 13 (June 19, 1998): 16 (read at Skylar Fein Upstairs Lounge Fire Collection, Historic New Orleans Collection); Breton, "United We Stand"; "Fire Victims, Funeral Home," Orleans Parish Coroner's Office, 1973, Upstairs Lounge Records, City Archives.

43. Rushton, "Fire Three," 6; Unknown (Body #18), Autopsy, Orleans Parish Coroner's Office, 1973, Upstairs Lounge Records, City Archives, Unknown (Body

#22), Autopsy, Orleans Parish Coroner's Office, 1973, Upstairs Lounge Records; Unknown (Body #28), Autopsy, Orleans Parish Coroner's Office, 1973, Upstairs Lounge Records.

44. "Three More Fire Victims Named"; Jerry McLeod, "Family Solves Mystery After Learning Uncle Died in Infamous Upstairs Lounge Fire Forty-Plus Years Ago in New Orleans," *New Orleans Advocate*, June 10, 2015 (www.theadvocate.com/new _orleans/entertainment_life/article_bf16d3d9-b8e7-5994-8066-6dc1fa27bca5.html); interview with Skip Bailey, August 21, 2015.

45. Bailey interview; "Three More Fire Victims Named"; McLeod, "Family Solves Mystery"; Rushton, "Fire Three," 6; Royd Anderson, *The UpStairs Lounge Fire* (documentary film), Lake Oaks Studio, June 24, 2013.

46. McLeod, "Family Solves Mystery"; Unknown (Body #18), Autopsy; Unknown (Body #22), Autopsy; Unknown (Body #28), Autopsy.

47. Interview with John Meyers, January 26, 2016; Henry Kubicki, "Henry Kubicki Account" (unpublished manuscript, November 14, 2013), LGBT Religious Archives Network (http://exhibits.lgbtran.org/exhibits/show/upstairs-lounge-fire).

48. Batson, "Errors in Upstairs Lounge Story"; Howard Smith, email to author, October 7, 2016; Edwin Edwards, email to author, January 27, 2017.

49. "General Case Report," NOPD, 60.

50. Ibid., 61, 47; Delery-Edwards, *The Up Stairs Lounge Arson*, 112.

51. "General Case Report," NOPD, 61; Eugene Davis, Statement to Louisiana Office of State Fire Marshal, October 1, 1973, 4, Skylar Fein Upstairs Lounge Fire Collection, Historic New Orleans Collection; Jacqueline Bullard, Statement to Office of Louisiana State Fire Marshal, March 17, 1975, 2–3, Louisiana State Archives.

52. "General Case Report," NOPD, 63, 61; "Official Report," State Fire Marshal, 22; interview with Steven Duplantis, March 11, 2016.

53. "General Case Report," NOPD, 64, 17, 31–33, 63; Willey, "The Upstairs Lounge Fire," 16.

54. Bill Rushton, "Mystery Unravels in New Orleans Bar Fire," *The Advocate*, October 22, 1975 (read at Johnny Townsend Collection, ONE National Gay and Lesbian Archives); John BonneCarrere to Judge Frank Shea of Orleans Parish Criminal Court, April 11, 1974, Johnny Townsend Collection; John BonneCarrere to Judge Frank Shea of Orleans Parish Criminal Court, August 7, 1973, Johnny Townsend Collection.

55. Philip Hannan, "The Archbishop Speaks," *Clarion Herald*, July 19, 1973, 3.

56. Ibid.

57. Ibid.; Angus Lind, Lanny Thomas, and Walt Philbin, "Twenty-Nine Dead in Quarter Holocaust," New Orleans *States-Item*, June 25, 1973, 1; Lanny Thomas, "Lounge Fire Probe Goes On," New Orleans *States-Item*, June 27, 1973, 1; Susan Finch, "Fire of '73: Tragedy United Gays," New Orleans *Times-Picayune*, June 24, 1993; Dennis Hevesi, "Philip Hannan, Ninety-Eight, Dies; New Orleans Archbishop," *The New York Times*, September 30, 2011 (www.nytimes.com/2011/09/30/us/archbishop-philip-m-hannan-dies-at-98.html).

58. "Fire Four: The Slight Latin and Rumor Control," *Vieux Carré Courier*, July 20, 1973, 3.

59. "HRC to Attack Gay Problems," New Orleans *Times-Picayune*, August 8, 1973, 17.

60. Ibid.; Delery-Edwards, *The Up Stairs Lounge Arson*, 144; Joan Treadway, "Gay Community Surfaces," New Orleans *Times-Picayune*, September 11, 1973, 13; "Human Relations Committee Minutes of Monday, October 1, 1973 Meeting," October 1, 1973, Records of the Human Relations Committee, City Archives; "New Orleans Voters Renominate Mayor," *The New York Times*, November 11, 1973, 34; "News Release Public Relations Office, City Hall," August 24, 1973, Records of Mayor Moon Landrieu, City Archives.

61. Treadway, "Gay Community Surfaces," 13; Bill Rushton, "Aug. 7 release," August 7, 1973, Vieux Carré Courier Collection, Earl K. Long Library; "Grant Number Four," National New Orleans Memorial Fund, January 17, 1974, National New Orleans Memorial Fund Collection, ONE National Gay and Lesbian Archives.

62. Troy Perry, "State of the Church," report presented to MCC General Conference, August 15, 1973, LGBT Religious Archives Network (http://exhibits.lgbtran.org /exhibits/show/upstairs-lounge-fire); Perry and Swicegood, *Don't Be Afraid Anymore*, 113; Tom Taylor, "The Impossible Dream," *In Unity*, June 1974, 19, https:// issuu.com/mccchurches/doc.

63. Paul Breton to Morty Manford, September 8, 1973, National New Orleans Memorial Fund Collection; Lucien Baril, transcript of phone call with *The Advocate*, September 14, 1973, New Orleans Upstairs Bar Fire/Advocate Records, ONE National Gay and Lesbian Archives; "Outlook Brightens for Fire Victims," *The Advocate*, October 10, 1973, 6.

64. Joan Treadway, "No Mardi Gras Magic: Gay Community Surfaces in Tragedy," New Orleans *Times-Picayune*, September 11, 1973, 13.

65. "Fund Nudges $5000 Mark," *The Advocate*, August 15, 1973, 22; "Benefits Boost N.O. Fund," *The Advocate*, November 14, 1973; "First Gay Dollars Reach New Orleans Fire Victims," *The Advocate*, February 13, 1974, 2; Morris Kight to Jack David, September 20, 1973, National New Orleans Memorial Fund Collection; "Aid Mounts for New Orleans," *The Advocate*, August 15, 1973, 2; Kight, transcript of *Advocate* interview, September 12, 1973; Memorial Fund Receipts Journal; John Gill to Morris Kight, September 12, 1973, National New Orleans Memorial Fund Collection, Morris Kight to John Gill, September 16, 1973, National New Orleans Memorial Fund Collection.

66. Edward Belew to John Tunney, September 27, 1973, Russell Long to Raymond Oliver, October 5, 1973, and Raymond Oliver to Russell Long, November 2, 1973, all in supplemental materials to "Official Report," Louisiana Office of State Fire Marshal, July 22, 1975, Louisiana State Archives.

13: Downfall

1. Press release, Gay People's Coalition, October 12, 1973, Vieux Carré Courier Collection, Earl K. Long Library, University of New Orleans; Roger Nord to Bill Rushton, July 23, 1973, Vieux Carré Courier Collection.

2. Public-service announcement script, Gay People's Coalition, 1973, Vieux Carré Courier Collection.

3. Clayton Delery, email to Troy Perry, January 4, 2010 (courtesy of Clayton Del-

ery and Troy Perry); interview with Richard Everett, August 10, 2015; Johnny Townsend, *Let the Faggots Burn: The Up Stairs Lounge Fire* (self-published through BookLocker.com, 2011), 109; interview with Henry Kubicki, September 5, 2015; Henry Kubicki, "Henry Kubicki Account" (unpublished manuscript, November 14, 2013), LGBT Religious Archives Network (http://exhibits.lgbtran.org/exhibits /show/upstairs-lounge-fire), Berkeley, Calif.

4. Delery to Perry, January 4, 2010; Kubicki, "Henry Kubicki Account"; John Gill to Morris Kight, September 12, 1973, National New Orleans Memorial Fund Collection, ONE National Gay and Lesbian Archives at the USC Libraries, Los Angeles.

5. "Fund," *Causeway*, January 1974, 7–8 (read at Rebels, Rubyfruit and Rhinestones Research Files, James T. Sears Papers, Duke University Libraries, Durham, N.C.); Everett interview, August 10, 2015; Troy Perry, transcript of phone interview with *The Advocate*, June 26, 1973, New Orleans Upstairs Bar Fire/Advocate Records, ONE National Gay and Lesbian Archives.

6. MCC New Deal," *Causeway*, February 1974, 5 (read at Rebels, Rubyfruit and Rhinestones Research Files); Morty Manford to Paul Breton, October 16, 1973, National New Orleans Memorial Fund Collection; Paul Breton to Morty Manford, October 24, 1973, National New Orleans Memorial Fund Collection; "New Church Building from Ashes of Tragedy," *The Advocate*, February 13, 1974, 10.

7. Interview with Henry Kubicki, September 4, 2015; Matthew J. Friedman, "PTSD History and Overview," U.S. Department of Veterans Affairs, www.ptsd.va.gov/ professional/ptsd-overview/ptsd-overview.asp.

8. Kubicki interview, September 4, 2015; Kubicki, "Henry Kubicki Account."

9. "MCC New Deal."

10. Morris Kight, memorandum to ONE National Gay and Lesbian Archives, March 11, 1984, National New Orleans Memorial Fund Collection; New Orleans Memorial Fund Receipts Journal, National New Orleans Memorial Fund Collection; "Aid Mounts for New Orleans," *The Advocate*, August 15, 1973, 22; J. B. Gautreaux to *The Advocate*, July 17, 1973, New Orleans Upstairs Bar Fire/Advocate Records, ONE National Gay and Lesbian Archives; Lewis Rio, "Perry on TV," *The Advocate*, August 15, 1973.

11. Gerald Hansen, "Arsonists Torch San Francisco MCC," *The Advocate*, August 15, 1973, 1; "Gay Meeting Place Burned Out," *The Advocate*, October 24, 1973, 1, 22; "Indianapolis Police Hit MCC Meet," *The Advocate*, October 24, 1973, 1, 22.

12. Interview with Roberts Batson, May 18, 2016; "Human Relations Committee Meeting of November 5/73," November 5, 1973, Records of the Human Relations Committee, City Archives, New Orleans Public Library; Paul Atkinson, "Park to Honor Satchmo OK'd," New Orleans *Times-Picayune*, July 26, 1973, 1.

13. "General Case Report," New Orleans Department of Police, August 30, 1973, 64, Upstairs Lounge Records, City Archives; "Official Report," Louisiana Office of State Fire Marshal, July 22, 1975, 29, Louisiana State Archives, Baton Rouge; Rodger Dale Nunez, Statement to Louisiana Office of State Fire Marshal, September 18, 1973, 8, Skylar Fein Upstairs Lounge Fire Collection, Historic New Orleans Collection.

14. "Official Report," State Fire Marshal, 30; John BonneCarrere to Judge Frank Shea, Orleans Parish Criminal Court, Johnny Townsend Collection, ONE National Gay

and Lesbian Archives; John BonneCarrere to Judge Frank Shea, Orleans Parish Criminal Court, August 7, 1973, Johnny Townsend Collection.

15. "Official Report," State Fire Marshal, 30; Nunez, Statement to State Fire Marshal, 13.

16. Clayton Delery-Edwards, *The Up Stairs Lounge Arson: Thirty-Two Deaths in a New Orleans Gay Bar, June 24, 1973* (Jefferson, N.C.: McFarland, 2014), 125; "General Case Report," NOPD, 64; BonneCarrere to Shea, April 11, 1974.

17. Nunez, Statement to State Fire Marshal, 13, 5–6, 8; Jerel Giarrusso, "Bayou Country Offers Everything from Sweet Potatoes to Mansions," New Orleans *Times-Picayune*, August 21, 1988, F2.

18. Nunez, Statement to State Fire Marshal, 12, 11; "General Case Report," NOPD, 59; "Office Report," State Fire Marshal, 20.

19. Nunez, Statement to State Fire Marshal, 2.

20. Nunez, Statement to State Fire Marshal, 8, 4; "Office Report," State Fire Marshal, 32.

21. Nunez, Statement to State Fire Marshal, 11, 7, 3; "Office Report," State Fire Marshal, 22.

22. Nunez, Statement to State Fire Marshal, 6.

23. "Office Report," State Fire Marshal, 30.

24. John Jenkins, "A 'Lie Detector' That Often Lies: 'Voice Stress' Analyzers Are Accurate Less than Half the Time, Experts Say," *The Washington Post*, September 2, 1979 (www .washingtonpost.com/archive/opinions/1979/09/02/a-lie-detector-that-often-liesvoice -stress-analyzers-are-accurate-less-than-half-the-time-experts-say/fb9a3aad-cab7-4225 -a8ad-20d16ce79a50/?utm_term=.5bfb7c31f02f); Delery-Edwards, *The Up Stairs Lounge Arson*, 122; "Official Report," State Fire Marshal, 36; Nunez, Statement to State Fire Marshal.

25. "Official Report," State Fire Marshal, 36; Delery-Edwards, *The Up Stairs Lounge Arson*, 127; Roger Nunez, Dektor PSE 1, October 1973, Louisiana State Archives.

26. Jenkins, "A 'Lie Detector' That Often Lies."

27. "New Gay Role Felt as Psychologists Convene," *The Advocate*, October 16, 1973, 6; Robert Heath, "Pleasure and Brain Activity in Man," *The Journal of Nervous and Mental Disease* 154 (1972): 7.

28. American Psychiatric Association, "Homosexuality and Sexual Orientation Disturbance: Proposed Change in DSM-II, 6th Printing, page 44," November 1973, psychiatryonline.com/DSMPDF/DSM-II_Homosexuality_Revision.pdf.

29. Ibid.

30. Morris Kight to Fund Trustees, January 17, 1974, National New Orleans Memorial Fund Collection, ONE National Gay and Lesbian Archives; Paul Breton to Morty Manford, February 13, 1974, National New Orleans Memorial Fund Collection; Note on grant amounts to victims, National New Orleans Memorial Fund, January 17, 1974, National New Orleans Memorial Fund Collection.

31. "Grant Number Four," National New Orleans Memorial Fund, January 17, 1974, National New Orleans Memorial Fund Collection; "Grant Number Five," National New Orleans Memorial Fund, January 17, 1974, National New Orleans Memorial Fund Collection; "Medical Bills Submitted to the National New Orleans Memorial Fund," National New Orleans Memorial Fund, 1974, National New Orleans Memorial Fund Collection; "Grant Number Nine," National New Orleans Memo-

rial Fund, January 17, 1974, National New Orleans Memorial Fund Collection; interview with Mary David Mihalyfi, May 4, 2016; "Grant Number Six," National New Orleans Memorial Fund, January 17, 1974, National New Orleans Memorial Fund Collection.

32. "Grant Number Three: Mrs. John Golding," National New Orleans Memorial Fund, c. January 17, 1974, National New Orleans Memorial Fund Collection; Townsend, *Let the Faggots Burn*, 309; Frank Perez and Jeffrey Palmquist, *In Exile: The History and Lore Surrounding New Orleans Gay Culture and Its Oldest Gay Bar* (Hurlford, Scotland: LL-Publications, 2012), 43; interview with John Golding Jr., November 6, 2017.

33. Interview with Golding; Delery-Edwards, *The Up Stairs Lounge Arson*, 148.

34. National New Orleans Memorial Fund to Lucien Baril, January 18, 1974, National New Orleans Memorial Fund Collection.

35. Ralph Spencer Forest, Statement to Louisiana Office of State Fire Marshal, November 19, 1974, 1, Skylar Fein Upstairs Lounge Fire Collection, Historic New Orleans Collection; "Official Report," State Fire Marshal, 50–51, 30; Elaine Wharton (Bassett) Nunez, Statement to Louisiana Office of State Fire Marshal, December 9, 1974, 1–2, Louisiana State Archives; Patrik Vuilleumier, "Hysterical Conversion and Brain Function," *Progress in Brain Research* 150 (2005): 309–29.

36. Forest, Statement to State Fire Marshal, 2–5.

37. "The Post Office," *Causeway*, December 1973, 2 (read at Rebels, Rubyfruit and Rhinestones Research Files, Sears Papers); Townsend, *Let the Faggots Burn,* 321; Forest, Statement to State Fire Marshal, 11, 6.

38. Delery-Edwards, *The Up Stairs Lounge Arson,* 130; Forest, Statement to State Fire Marshal, 6.

39. Forest, Statement to State Fire Marshal, 10; "Official Report," State Fire Marshal, 51.

40. Ibid.; Mary Stephen Ledet, Statement to Louisiana Office of State Fire Marshal, November 20, 1974, 3–4, Skylar Fein Upstairs Lounge Fire Collection, Historic New Orleans Collection.

41. Delery-Edwards, *The Up Stairs Lounge Arson*, 136; "Official Report," State Fire Marshal, 51.

42. Ibid.; Forest, Statement to State Fire Marshal, 10.

43. Forest, Statement to State Fire Marshal, 1–3; "Official Report," State Fire Marshal, 51.

44. Forest, Statement to State Fire Marshal, 2, 5, 8.

45. BonneCarrere to Shea, April 11, 1974.

46. Forest, Statement to State Fire Marshal, 2–4, 12; (Bassett) Nunez, Statement to State Fire Marshal, 1.

47. (Bassett) Nunez, Statement to State Fire Marshal, 1.

48. Ibid.; Forest, Statement to State Fire Marshal, 12.

49. (Bassett) Nunez, Statement to State Fire Marshal, 1.

50. Ibid.; Delery-Edwards, *The Up Stairs Lounge Arson*, 130.

51. "Invoice for National New Orleans Memorial Fund," June 22, 1974, National New Orleans Memorial Fund Collection, ONE National Gay and Lesbian Archives;

"Narrative of Support," June 22, 1974, National New Orleans Memorial Fund Collection; "Survivor Discovers Her True Friends," *The Advocate*, July 31, 1974, 8.

52. Interview with Troy Perry, December 2, 2014; David Bird, "Clay Shaw Is Dead at Sixty; Freed in Kennedy 'Plot,'" *The New York Times*, August 16, 1974, 32; "Clay Shaw Final Rites to Be Today," New Orleans *Times-Picayune*, August 16, 1974, 1; "Clay L. Shaw of JFK Case Is Dead at Sixty," *Pittsburgh Post-Gazette*, August 16, 1974, 4.

53. "Clay Shaw Final Rites," 1; Perry interview.

54. (Bassett) Nunez, Statement to State Fire Marshal, 1–2; Rodger Dale Nunez, Coroner's Office Day Record, November 16, 1974, in supplemental materials to "Official Report," Louisiana Office of State Fire Marshal, July 22, 1975, Louisiana State Archives, Baton Rouge; "Court Records," New Orleans *Times-Picayune*, September 12, 1974, sect. 4, p. 3.

55. "Case Report," New Orleans Police Department, November 15, 1974, 1–2 (read at Rebels, Rubyfruit and Rhinestones Research Files, Sears Papers); Nunez, Coroner's Office Day Record; Forest, Statement to State Fire Marshal, 12, 10; (Bassett) Nunez, Statement to State Fire Marshal, 1.

56. Rodger Dale Nunez, Autopsy, Orleans Parish Coroner's Office, November 15, 1974, in supplemental materials to "Official Report," State Fire Marshal; Forest, Statement to State Fire Marshal, 6.

57. Forest, Statement to State Fire Marshal, 6.

58. Ibid., 6–7.

59. "Rodger Dale Nunez," obituary, *Kaplan Herald*, November 20, 1974, 8; "OUR SINCERE AND HEARTFELT THANKS," *Abbeville Meridional*, December 5, 1974, 21; Nunez, Coroner's Office Day Record; Rodger D. Nunez, memorial 95376662, findagrave.com.

60. "Official Report," State Fire Marshal, 51.

61. Townsend, *Let the Faggots Burn*, 219; Forest, Statement to State Fire Marshal, 1; Delery-Edwards, *The Up Stairs Lounge Arson*, 136; interview with Stewart Butler, August 4, 2015.

62. Interview with Roy Reed, September 24, 2014.

63. Townsend, *Let the Faggots Burn*, 219, 213; "Official Report," State Fire Marshal, 51; Forest, Statement to State Fire Marshal, 1, 3-4; BonneCarrere to Shea, April 11, 1974; "General Case Report," NOPD, 55.

14: Rally Forth

1. Interview with Roberts Batson, May 18, 2016.

2. "Gay Rights Protections in the U.S. and Canada," National Gay Task Force, 1976, Rebels, Rubyfruit and Rhinestones Research Files, James T. Sears Papers, Duke University Libraries, Durham, N.C.; George Painter, "Massachusetts," *Gay and Lesbian Archives of the Pacific Northwest*, 2002, www.glapn.org/sodomylaws/sensibilities/massachusetts.htm; George Painter, "Ohio," *Gay and Lesbian Archives of the Pacific Northwest*, 2002, www.glapn.org/sodomylaws/sensibilities/ohio.htm; George Painter, "Arkansas," *Gay and Lesbian Archives of the Pacific Northwest*, 2002,

www.glapn.org/sodomylaws/sensibilities/arkansas.htm; George Painter, "North Dakota," *Gay and Lesbian Archives of the Pacific Northwest*, 2002, www.glapn.org/sodomylaws/sensibilities/north_dakota.htm.

3. "I Am a Homosexual," *Time*, September 8, 1975, 32–36; "Gay Activist Leonard Matlovich, Forty-Four, Is Buried with Full Military Honors," *Chicago Tribune*, July 3, 1988 (http://articles.chicagotribune.com/1988-07-03/news/8801120440_1_homosexuals-in-concentration-camps-congressional-cemetery-gay-rights-activists).

4. Neil Swan, "Gay Pride Rally Without Incident," *Atlanta Constitution*, June 27, 1976, 7B; Patrick Buchanan, "A Somber View of Gay Pride Week," *Chicago Tribune*, July 1, 1976, 20 (http://archives.chicagotribune.com/1976/07/01/page/20/article/buchanan); Frank Perez and Jeffrey Palmquist, *In Exile: The History and Lore Surrounding New Orleans Gay Culture and Its Oldest Gay Bar* (Hurlford, Scotland: LL-Publications, 2012), 192.

5. Merikaye Presley, "Bob Hope Will Host Grand Opening Gala at Superdome," New Orleans *Times-Picayune*, August 1, 1975, 1; Paul Atkinson, "Superdome to Open Doors in 1975," New Orleans *Times-Picayune*, January 12, 1975, 160; Nancy Weldon, "Best of Hope, Lamour—and Savalas," New Orleans *Times-Picayune*, August 30, 1975, 6; "Dome Close Up View Today," New Orleans *Times-Picayune*, August 3, 1975, 1.

6. Henry Kubicki, "Henry Kubicki Account" (unpublished manuscript, November 14, 2013), LGBT Religious Archives Network (http://exhibits.lgbtran.org/exhibits/show/upstairs-lounge-fire), Berkeley, Calif.

7. Valerie Haynes, "Memorial Rites Honor Lounge Blaze Victims," New Orleans *Times-Picayune*, June 23, 1975; interviews with Richard Everett, August 10 and August 25, 2015; Kubicki, "Henry Kubicki Account."

8. Interviews with Richard Everett, January 20, 2017, and July 27, 2015.

9. Kenneth Weiss, "Blaze Report Is Near," New Orleans *Times-Picayune*, June 25, 1975, 18; correspondence file between Deputy State Fire Marshal Edward Hyde and Orleans Parish District Attorney Harry Connick, 1975, Louisiana State Archives, Baton Rouge; interview with Trevor Santos, November 19, 2015.

10. Clayton Delery-Edwards, *The Up Stairs Lounge Arson: Thirty-Two Deaths in a New Orleans Gay Bar, June 24, 1973* (Jefferson, N.C.: McFarland, 2014), 135; correspondence file between Hyde and Connick, 1975; Weiss, "Blaze Report Is Near," 18.

11. "Up Stairs Fire," *Vieux Carré Courier*, September 11, 1975, 2 (read at Rebels, Rubyfruit and Rhinestones Research Files, Sears Papers); correspondence file between Deputy State Fire Marshal Edward Hyde and Orleans Parish District Attorney Harry Connick, 1975–1980, Louisiana State Archives; Bill Rushton, "Mystery Unravels in New Orleans Bar Fire," *The Advocate*, October 22, 1975 (read at Johnny Townsend Collection, ONE National Gay and Lesbian Archives at the USC Libraries, Los Angeles).

12. Rushton, "Mystery Unravels in New Orleans Bar Fire"; National Bureau of Standards to Elwood Willey, December 12, 1973, LGBT Religious Archives Network (http://exhibits.lgbtran.org/exhibits/show/upstairs-lounge-fire); "Inspection and/or Investigation Report," Fire Prevention Division of the New Orleans Fire Department, December 4, 1970, and Inspection and/or Investigation Report, Fire Prevention Division of the New Orleans Fire Department, October 15, 1970, both in Johnny Townsend Collection.

13. Rushton, "Mystery Unravels in New Orleans Bar Fire"; "Inspection and/or Investigation Report," Fire Prevention Division of the New Orleans Fire Department, June 24–25, 1973, Johnny Townsend Collection; "Supplemental Information," Fire Prevention Division of the New Orleans Fire Department, c. 1975, Johnny Townsend Collection.

14. Rushton, "Mystery Unravels in New Orleans Fire."

15. Ibid.

16. Interview with Skip Bailey, August 21, 2015; interview with Marc Schmitz, July 1, 2016; Joseph Rivoire to Marc Schmitz, June 10, 1976 (courtesy of Marc Schmitz).

17. Johnny Townsend, *Let the Faggots Burn: The Up Stairs Lounge Fire* (self-published through BookLocker.com, 2011), 178; *Francis Dufrene v. Anthony Guarino et al.*, Court of Appeals of Louisiana, Fourth Circuit, January 12, 1977; Ken Weiss, "VCC Director Criticizes Disaster Area Rhetoric," New Orleans *Times-Picayune*, July 18, 1973, 40.

18. *Dufrene v. Guarino*; Eric Newhouse, "Bar Not Inspected in Two Years," New Orleans *Times-Picayune*, July 1, 1973, 4.

19. *Dufrene v. Guarino*.

20. Townsend, *Let the Faggots Burn*, 178–79; interview with Tina Matyi, October 29, 2016.

21. Interview with John Golding Jr., November 6, 2017.

22. Townsend, *Let the Faggots Burn*, 179; interview with Duane Mitchell, August 14, 2015.

23. "Christine Jorgensen," *Gertrude's Notes* (Gertrude Stein Society newsletter), March 1977 (read at Rebels, Rubyfruit and Rhinestones Research Files, Sears Papers); John McQuiston, "Christine Jorgensen, Sixty-Two, Is Dead; Was First to Have a Sex Change," *The New York Times*, May 4, 1989; Becky Bruns, "Guys and Dolls . . . A Play on Roles," New Orleans *Times-Picayune*, January 16, 1977, 82; Townsend, *Let the Faggots Burn*, 320.

24. Townsend, *Let the Faggots Burn*, 320–21; interview with Steven Duplantis, March 11, 2016.

25. Ed Martinez, "Where Are the Gay Activists in New Orleans," *Vieux Carré Star*, April 7, 1977, 1 (read at Rebels, Rubyfruit and Rhinestones Research Files).

26. "Esteve Says There's No Need for Gay Activists," *Vieux Carré Star*, April 14, 1977, 1, 7 (read at Rebels, Rubyfruit and Rhinestones Research Files).

27. "Gay Rights Protections"; "Bias Against Homosexuals Is Outlawed in Miami," *The New York Times*, January 19, 1977, 14; "Battle over Gay Rights," *Newsweek*, June 6, 1977, 16–24; "County in Florida Has Sex Problem," Harlingen [Tex.] *Valley Morning Star*, March 27, 1970; Paul Houston, "Homosexuals Stage Hollywood Parade," *Los Angeles Times*, June 29, 1970, 3; Angus Lind, Lanny Thomas, and Walt Philbin, "Twenty-Nine Dead in Quarter Holocaust," New Orleans *States-Item*, June 25, 1973, 1.

28. Joel Greenberg, "Singer Opens Drive to Repeal Gay Law," *Miami Herald*, February 12, 1977; "Battle over Gay Rights," 16; "Anita Bryant—Call from the Lord," *Oakland Tribune*, May 6, 1977.

29. Perry Deane Young, *God's Bullies: Power Politics and Religious Tyranny* (New York: Holt, Rinehart and Winston, 1982); "Bias Against Homosexuals Is Outlawed in Miami," 14; Morton Kondracke, "Anita Bryant Is Mad About Gays," *The New*

Republic, May 7, 1977, 13–14; Jean O'Leary and Bruce Voeller, "Anita Bryant's Crusade," *The New York Times*, June 7, 1977, 35.

30. Kondracke, "Anita Bryant Is Mad About Gays"; "Anita Bryant Scores White House Talk with Homosexuals," *The New York Times*, March 28, 1977, 56; interview with Troy Perry, December 2, 2014; "Gay Panel Talks with Carter Officials," Newport News *Daily Press*, March 27, 1977, A2; Lillian Faderman, *The Gay Revolution: The Story of the Struggle* (New York: Simon & Schuster, 2015).

31. B. Drummond Ayres, "Miami Votes 2 to 1 to Repeal Law Barring Bias Against Homosexuals," *The New York Times*, June 8, 1977, 1; Timothy McNulty, "Anita Wins, Gay Rights Defeated," *Chicago Tribune*, June 8, 1977, 1; Nathanial Sheppard, "Law on Homosexuals Repealed in St. Paul," *The New York Times*, April 26, 1978, 1; Faderman, *The Gay Revolution*; "Voting Against Gay Rights," *Time*, May 22, 1978 (http://content.time.com/time/magazine/article/0,9171,91947,00.html); "Officers Attack Gay Rights," *Walla Walla Evening Bulletin*, August 8, 1978.

32. Ivan Sharpe, "Angry Gays March Through S.F.," *San Francisco Examiner*, June 8, 1977, 1; "The Nation: The Gaycott Turns Ugly," *Time*, November 21, 1977 (http://content.time.com/time/magazine/article/0,9171,915719,00.html); Thomas Tobin, "Bankruptcy, Ill Will Plague Bryant," *St. Petersburg Times*, April 28, 2002 (www.sptimes.com/2002/04/28/State/Bankruptcy__ill_will_.shtml); Millie Ball, "'I'd Rather My Child Be Dead than Homo,'" New Orleans *Times-Picayune*, June 19, 1977, 3; Jane Fritsch and Derrick Blakley, "Eight Arrested as 3,000 Protest Anita Bryant's Shriner Show Here," *Chicago Tribune*, June 15, 1977, 2; "3,000 in Houston Protest Anita Bryant Appearance," *The New York Times*, June 17, 1977, 12; Alan Citron, "Anti-Anita Forces Hold Silent Protest," New Orleans *Times-Picayune*, July 18, 1977, 1; Robert McQueen, "First-Hand from Houston: Bearing Witness to Our Humanity," *The Advocate*, July 27, 1977, 10–11; "2500 Marched in New Orleans, as Many as 8000 in Houston," *Vieux Carré Star*, June 30, 1977, 1 (read at Rebels, Rubyfruit and Rhinestones Research Files, Sears Papers); interview with Larry Bagneris, August 24, 2015.

33. "At Ease," *Vieux Carré Courier*, June 2, 1977; interview with Roberts Batson, July 11, 2014; George Hager, "Anita Bryant Pops Booking Stirs Protest," New Orleans *Times-Picayune*, May 14, 1977, 26; Alan Robinson, personal diaries, Alan Robinson Papers, Louisiana Research Collection, Howard-Tilton Memorial Library, Tulane University, New Orleans; "Anita Bryant," *Vieux Carré Courier*, May 19, 1977, 19; Roberts Batson, "Claiming Our Past" (column 19), *Impact*, May 12, 1995, 18 (read at Rebels, Rubyfruit and Rhinestones Research Files); "Batson Wins Award," *Impact*, August 1978, 1 (read at Impact Records, Louisiana Research Collection); "Demonstrate for Human Rights" (rally poster), June 1977, Rebels, Rubyfruit, and Rhinestones Research Files.

34. Townsend, *Let the Faggots Burn*, 312; "Rod Wagner" [sic], *Gertrude's Notes*, March 1978 (read at Rebels, Rubyfruit and Rhinestones Research Files); "AFTRA Adopts Bryant Motion," New Orleans *Times-Picayune*, May 16, 1977, 14; Batson, "Claiming Our Past" 19; "Blacklist Anita Bryant?," New Orleans *Times-Picayune*, May 17, 1977, 12; "Anita Bryant Boycott Is Killed," New Orleans *Times-Picayune*, May 26, 1977, 5.

35. Killgore interview, January 17, 2016; "No Violence, Anita Demonstrators Told,"

New Orleans *States-Item*, June 17, 1977, 4; "Friday Bulletin," HERE, June 1977, Rebels, Rubyfruit and Rhinestones Research Files; "Miami Come Help Us," HERE, June 1977, Rebels, Rubyfruit and Rhinestones Research Files; Paul Breton, "United We Stand" (unpublished manuscript, August 1973), National New Orleans Memorial Fund Collection, ONE National Gay and Lesbian Archives; "The Lavender Hill Mob Takes on Anita Bryant," New Orleans *Figaro*, June 29, 1977, 29 (read at Rebels, Rubyfruit and Rhinestones Research Files).

36. "The Lavender Hill Mob Takes on Anita Bryant," 29; Batson interview, July 11, 2014; "2500 Marched at New Orleans," 1; Killgore interview, January 17, 2016; "Demonstrate for Human Rights"; Roger Nelson to James Sears, c. 2001, Rebels, Rubyfruit and Rhinestones Research Files.

37. "The Lavender Hill Mob Takes on Anita Bryant," 29; Killgore interview, January 17, 2016; Alan Citron, "'Out of Closets, into Streets' Is Gay Protest Rally Cry," New Orleans *Times-Picayune*, June 19, 1977, 3; Ralph Blumenthal, "March Is Staged by Homosexuals," *The New York Times*, June 26, 1972, 21; interview with Stewart Butler, July 20, 2014.

38. Frank Perez, "The Lavender Line: Jerry Menefee, St. Ann, and Bourbon," *Ambush*, July 19, 2016 (www.ambushmag.com/is1516/images/1516main6-10.pdf); Citron, "'Out of the Closets, into Streets' Is Gay Protest Rally Cry," 3; "The Lavender Hill Mob Takes on Anita Bryant," 29.

39. Killgore interview, January 17, 2016; Lovell Beaulieu, "No Incidents at Anita Protest," New Orleans *Times-Picayune*, June 19, 1977, 3; Batson interview, July 11, 2014.

40. Citron, "'Out of Closets, into Streets' Is Gay Protest Rally Cry," 3; Chris Segura, "Cleric Says Oppression Problem for Homosexuals," *The Times-Picayune*, July 2, 1973, 14.

41. Delery-Edwards, *The Up Stairs Lounge Arson*, 141; Batson interview, July 11, 2014; "Anita May Lose OJ Job," New Orleans *Times-Picayune*, June 19, 1977, 1; Vecsey, "Secular Bookings Off, Anita Bryant Sings at Revivals," 18.

42. Batson interview, July 11, 2014; "Batson Wins Award," 1; Roberts Batson, "Gay Politics," *Impact*, June 23, 1995, 30 (read at Rebels, Rubyfruit and Rhinestones Research Files).

15: Last Resort

1. "Anita Bryant Performance Causes Stir in New Orleans," Fort Myers *News-Press*, May 25, 1977, 47; "Rod Wagner" [sic], *Gertrude's Notes*, March 1978 (read at Rebels, Rubyfruit and Rhinestones Research Files, James T. Sears Papers, Duke University Libraries, Durham, N.C.); "Whatever Happened to . . . ," New Orleans *Times-Picayune*, March 18, 1979, 195; Kim Chatelain, "Thirteen Candidates Vie for Alliance Support," New Orleans *Times-Picayune*, August 15, 1979, 4; Paul Atkinson, "Glaudi, Wagener Clash at Political Forum," New Orleans *Times-Picayune*, September 8, 1979, 4; "Most Incumbents Rise," New Orleans *Times-Picayune*, October 28, 1979, 12.

2. Dudley Clendinen, "'Christian New Right's' Rush to Power," *The New York Times*, August 18, 1980, 31; Joe Darby, "Vampire Story Serious Novel," New Orleans *Times-Picayune*, August 1, 1976, 170,

3. Arthur Roane, "Reversal Sought on Jazz Ruling," New Orleans *Times-Picayune*, August 22, 1979, 19; Kelly Tucker, "A Memorial to Satchmo," New Orleans *Times-Picayune*, April 11, 1980, special Jazz Fest section, p. 9; Ed Anderson, "Giarrusso Replacement, Taxes on Morial's Mind," New Orleans *Times-Picayune*, November 14, 1977, 1.

4. Johnny Townsend, *Let the Faggots Burn: The Up Stairs Lounge Fire* (self-published through BookLocker.com, 2011), 304; interview with Robert Camina, July 2016.

5. "The State of the Caucus," LAGPAC, August 1981, Alan Robinson Papers, Louisiana Research Collection, Howard-Tilton Memorial Library, Tulane University, New Orleans; "By-laws," LAGPAC, August 18, 1980, Alan Robinson Papers; "Dear LAGPAC Members and Friends," LAGPAC, January 1981, Stewart Butler Papers, Louisiana Research Collection; "Membership Form," LAGPAC, 1981. Alan Robinson Papers; "Minutes," LAGPAC, October 25, 1980, Alan Robinson Papers; "Charged with Obstruction of Free Passage," n.d., Alan Robinson Papers.

6. Frank Locascio, memorandum to William Roth and John Fischer, 1980, in supplemental materials to "Official Report," Louisiana Office of State Fire Marshal, July 22, 1975, Louisiana State Archives, Baton Rouge; "Official Report," Louisiana Office of State Fire Marshal, July 22, 1975, 6, Louisiana State Archives; interview with Stewart Butler, July 20, 2014.

7. "Gays Seeking Equal Rights Form Crescent City Coalition," New Orleans *Times-Picayune*, October 19, 1981, 16; interview with Roberts Batson, July 11, 2014; "For Immediate Release" (press release), LAGPAC, May 5, 1981, Rebels, Rubyfruit and Rhinestones Research Files, Sears Papers; "Police Raids Net 101 Arrests," *Impact*, May 1981 (read at Rebels, Rubyfruit and Rhinestones Research Files); "Mass Arrests of Gays Spark Reaction," *Figaro*, May 4, 1981 (read at Rebels, Rubyfruit, and Rhinestones Research Files); "Charged with Obstruction of Free Passage"; "Police Explain Last Month's Actions," *Impact*, May 1981 (read at Rebels, Rubyfruit and Rhinestones Research Files).

8. "Dear Members and Friends," LAGPAC, July 23, 1982, Alan Robinson Papers; "Charged with Obstruction of Free Passage"; "Gay and Lesbian Town Meeting," LAGPAC, July 8, 1981, Rebels, Rubyfruit and Rhinestones Research Files; "Charges Are Dropped!," *Impact*, July 1981 (read at Rebels, Rubyfruit, and Rhinestones Research Files); Henry Morris to Roberts Batson, 1981, Stewart Butler Papers, Louisiana Research Collection.

9. Frank Perez, "Metropolitan Community Church," *Ambush*, April 9, 2016, 12 (www.ambushmag.com/is916/images/916main11-15.pdf); Clayton Delery-Edwards, *The Up Stairs Lounge Arson: Thirty-Two Deaths in a New Orleans Gay Bar, June 24, 1973* (Jefferson, N.C.: McFarland, 2014), 176; "Larson Rev. William R.," Interment Records of St. Roch Cemeteries 1 & 2, 1981, http://files.usgwarchives.net/la/orleans/cemeteries/roch/book/1981.txt; Henry Kubicki, "Henry Kubicki Account" (unpublished manuscript, November 14, 2013), LGBT Religious Archives Network (http://exhibits.lgbtran.org/exhibits/show/upstairs-lounge-fire), Berkeley, Calif.

10. Howard Smith, email to author, October 10, 2016; Wally Sherwood, "Former Olympus King Passes Away," *Ambush*, July 19, 2005 (www.ambushmag.com/is1505/sherwoods.htm); Townsend, *Let the Faggots Burn*, 321; Perez, "Metropolitan Com-

munity Church," 12; "Larson Rev. William R."; Delery-Edwards, *The Up Stairs Lounge Arson*, 176.

11. Kubicki, "Henry Kubicki Account"; "Larson Rev. William R."

12. Interview with Joseph Bermuda, March 31, 2015; "Ordinances," New Orleans *Times-Picayune*, January 14, 1981, 70; interview with Roberts Batson, September 13, 2017.

13. "Candidates for LAGPAC Board of Directors" (newsletter), LAGPAC, November 19, 1982, Alan Robinson Papers, Louisiana Research Collection; interview with Steven Duplantis, March 11, 2016.

14. Duplantis interview.

15. "1983—The Year Many People Would Like to Forget," *Impact*, July 1983 (read at Rebels, Rubyfruit and Rhinestones Research Files, Sears Papers); "Rare Cancer Seen in Forty-One Homosexuals," *The New York Times*, July 3, 1981, 20; " 'Homosexual Plague' Strikes New Victims," *Newsweek*, August 23, 1982, 10; John Pope, "Deadly AIDS No Longer Stranger to La.," New Orleans *Times-Picayune*, May 10, 1987, 29; "Gay Parades Dedicated to AIDS Victims," New Orleans *Times-Picayune*, June 27, 1983, 29.

16. W. Pate McMichael, "The Pre-Pandemic Puzzle," *St. Louis Magazine*, August 2007; Todd Summers and Jennifer Kates, *Trends in U.S. Government Funding for HIV/AIDS Fiscal Years 1981 to 2004* (The Henry J. Kaiser Family Foundation, March 2004; https://kaiserfamilyfoundation.files.wordpress.com/2013/01/issue-brief-trends-in-u -s-government-funding-for-hiv-aids-fiscal-years-1981-to-2004.pdf); "Acquired Immunodeficiency Syndrome (AIDS) Weekly Surveillance Report—United States," Centers for Disease Control, December 22, 1983, www.cdc.gov/hiv/pdf/reports /surveillance/cdc-hiv-surveillance-report-1983.pdf; Kathleen Mulvihill, "AIDS: Mystery Disorder," New Orleans *Times-Picayune*, April 11, 1983, 38.

17. "Acquired Immunodeficiency Syndrome (AIDS) Weekly Surveillance Report"; Evan Thomas, "The New Untouchables," *Time*, September 23, 1985 (http://content.time .com/time/magazine/article/0,9171,959944,00.html); "U.S. Urges Homosexual Men Not to Give Blood Donations," *Chicago Tribune*, March 4, 1983, 12 (http:// archives.chicagotribune.com/1983/03/04/page/12/article/u-s-urges-homosexual -men-not-to-give-blood-donations).

18. "Patients Advised Transfusions Risky Because of AIDS," New Orleans *Times-Picayune*, April 15, 1983, 3; "AIDS Has Killed Five in State," New Orleans *Times-Picayune*, April 23, 1983, 23; "Gays' Disease Spreads to Heterosexuals," New Orleans *Times-Picayune*, October 30, 1982, 65; John Pope, "AIDS Scare Closing Bathhouse," New Orleans *Times-Picayune*, November 23, 1985, 19; "Fear That Blood Has AIDS Blamed as Donations Fall," New Orleans *Times-Picayune*, July 9, 1983, 25; "Heterosexual Contact May Spread AIDS, Study Says," New Orleans *Times-Picayune*, May 19, 1983, 6.

19. "Articles of Incorporation," NO/AIDS Task Force, June 28, 1983, Rebels, Rubyfruit and Rhinestones Research Files, Sears Papers; "Meeting!," *NO/AIDS Task Force News*, September 1983, Alan Robinson Papers, Louisiana Research Collection; Gayle Ashton, "AIDS March Turns Heads in Quarter," New Orleans *Times-Picayune*, October 9, 1983, 2; Rich Magill, *Exposing Hatred: A Report on the Victimization of Lesbian and Gay People in New Orleans, Louisiana* (New Orleans: LAGPAC, 1991), 2.

20. Robert Steinbrook, "The Times Poll: 42 Percent Would Limit Civil Rights in AIDS Battle," *Los Angeles Times*, July 31, 1987 (http://articles.latimes.com/1987 -07-31/news/mn-217_1_aids-virus); "N.O. Architecture Critic Bill Rushton, Thirty-Nine, Dies," New Orleans *Times-Picayune*, August 11, 1987, 18; Kubicki, "Henry Kubicki Account"; "Two Hundred Attend Service for Lounge Victims," New Orleans *States-Item*, July 2, 1973; "Church Leaders Urged Family Not to Confirm Bishop Died of AIDS," Associated Press, May 25, 1987; Emily Yoffe, "Bishop Denies 'Brotherhood' to the End," *Chicago Tribune*, December 3, 1987 (http:// articles.chicagotribune.com/1987-12-03/features/8703300793_1_rev-troy-perry -metropolitan-community-churches-gay-bar).

21. "Anti-Discrimination Ordinance Committee Meeting" (meeting notes), LAGPAC, February 21, 1983, Rebels, Rubyfruit and Rhinestones Research Files; "The New Orleans Gay Civil Rights Ordinance" (report), LAGPAC, 1984, Rebels, Rubyfruit and Rhinestones Research Files; Marion Barry to "Public Official," LAGPAC, 1984, Rebels, Rubyfruit and Rhinestones Research Files; "Gay Civil Rights Ordinance Debated," *Impact*, March 16, 1984, 1 (read at Rebels, Rubyfruit and Rhinestones Research Files); Patricia Behre and Frank Donze, "Catholic Groups Waging Battle Against Gay-Rights Ordinance," New Orleans *Times-Picayune*, March 8, 1984, 1.

22. Frank Donze, "City Council Kills Ordinance on Gay Rights," New Orleans *Times-Picayune*, April 13, 1984, 1, 4; "N.O. Gay Ordinance Fails to Pass," *Impact*, April 20, 1984, 1 (read at Rebels, Rubyfruit and Rhinestones Research Files); Frank Donze, "Support Fell Through, Gay Rights Leaders Say," New Orleans *Times-Picayune*, April 14, 1984, 4; "Vice Squad Arrests Total 1,443 in 1965," New Orleans *Times-Picayune*, February 4, 1966, 50.

23. Townsend, *Let the Faggots Burn*, 314; "A Minority Agenda for the Decade of the 1990s," George Steven Matyi Private Trust, June 24, 1988, Johnny Townsend Collection, ONE National Gay and Lesbian Archives at the USC Libraries, Los Angeles.

24. Townsend, *Let the Faggots Burn*, 314; Rod Wagener to Johnny Townsend, August 9, 1990, Johnny Townsend Collection.

25. Philip Batiste, "A Defeat for the City," New Orleans *Times-Picayune*, December 11, 1986, 26; James Gill, "Gays and the Ending of Prejudice," New Orleans *Times-Picayune*, November 9, 1986, 27; Sheila Grissett-Welsh, "Civil Rights Measure Rejected," New Orleans *Times-Picayune*, December 5, 1986, 1; interview with Stewart Butler, August 4, 2015; Frank Perez, "Rich Magill Exposes Hatred," *Ambush*, June 11, 2013 (www.ambushmag.com/is1213/images/1213main26-30.pdf).

26. Perez, "Rich Magill Exposes Hatred"; Magill, *Exposing Hatred*, 1.

27. Magill, *Exposing Hatred*, iii.

28. Ibid.; Butler interview, August 4, 2015; Delery-Edwards, *The Up Stairs Lounge Arson*, 168.

29. Butler interview, August 4, 2015; Magill, *Exposing Hatred*, iii; Perez, "Rich Magill Exposes Hatred."

30. Susan Finch, "Fire of '73: Tragedy United Gays," New Orleans *Times-Picayune*, June 24, 1993; Mark Thompson, "Thirty-Two Killed in Fire Remembered at Quarter Church," New Orleans *Times-Picayune*, June 26, 1995.

Coda: Second Line

1. Interview with Dexter Brecht, January 19, 2017.
2. Mark Thompson, "Thirty-Two Killed in Fire Remembered at Quarter Church," New Orleans *Times-Picayune*, June 26, 1995 (used with permission of the *Times-Picayune* and NOLA.com, © 2017 NOLA Media Group, LLC, all rights reserved); Dexter Brecht, email to author, December 15, 2015; interview with Mark Thompson, January 21, 2016.
3. Joseph P. Manguno, "Deacon in Tavern Blames Arsonist," *Boston Herald American*, June 26, 1973; interview with Henry Kubicki, September 4, 2015; Brecht interviews, January 19, 2017, and July 29, 2015.
4. Brecht interview, July 29, 2015; David Cuthbert, "Where There Was Smoke," New Orleans *Times-Picayune*, June 20, 1998.
5. Wayne Phillips, notes for "Remembering the Up Stairs Lounge Fire," 1998 (courtesy of Wayne Phillips); Richard Everett, email to author, August 26, 2015.
6. William Faulkner, "Banquet Speech," Nobel Prize, December 10, 1950, www.nobelprize.org; Brecht interview, July 29, 2015; interview with Henry Kubicki, September 5, 2015.
7. Roberts Batson, "Out of the Ashes," *Impact*, July 3, 1998 (read at Rebels, Rubyfruit, and Rhinestones Research Files, James T. Sears Papers, Duke University Libraries, Durham, N.C.); Cuthbert, "Where There Was Smoke"; interview with Wayne Phillips, June 14, 2016.
8. Bruce Nolan, "Service Remembers Upstairs Fire Victims," New Orleans *Times-Picayune*, June 25, 1998, B1; Rip and Marsha Naquin-Delain, "Upstairs Fire Twenty-Fifth Anniversary Memorial," *Ambush*, June 1998 (ambushmag.com/is1498/hot.htm); Brecht interview, July 29, 2015; "Upstairs Lounge Fire Memorial" (program), MCC of New Orleans, June 24, 1998, Skylar Fein Upstairs Lounge Fire Collection, Historic New Orleans Collection; Troy Perry and Nancy Wilson, "Report to the President for the White House Conference on Hate Crimes," November 1, 1997, 2, LGBT Religious Archives Network (http://exhibits.lgbtran.org/exhibits/show/upstairs-lounge-fire), Berkeley, Calif.
9. Interview with Troy Perry, December 2, 2014; Nolan, "Service Remembers Upstairs Fire Victims," B1; Batson, "Out of the Ashes"; Nick Spitzer, "Love and Death at Second-Line," *Southern Spaces*, February 20, 2004 (https://southernspaces.org/2004/love-and-death-second-line).
10. Batson, "Out of the Ashes"; Nolan, "Service Remembers Upstairs Fire Victims," B1; "Upstairs Lounge Fire Memorial"; interview with Roberts Batson, May 18, 2016; Brecht interview, July 29, 2015.
11. Brecht interview, January 19, 2017; "'We Knew Them as People,' Pastor Tells Gay Mourners," New Orleans *States-Item*, June 26, 1973.
12. Brecht interview, January 19, 2017; Eileen Loh Harrist, "Just Married?," *Gambit*, 2002 (www.bestofneworleans.com/gambit/just-married/Content?oid=1242206); interview with Wil Coleman, November 20, 2015.
13. Thompson, "Thirty-Two Killed"; Tom W. Smith and Jaesok Son, "Trends in Public Attitudes About Sexual Morality," National Opinion Research Center, April 2013, 11 (www.norc.org/PDFs/sexmoralfinal_06-21_FINAL.PDF); Rich-

ard Bernstein, "A Stand on Homosexuality for Both Left and Right," *The New York Times*, September 6, 1995 (www.nytimes.com/books/97/08/17/home/18419 .html); "Yep, I'm Gay," *Time*, April 14, 1997 (http://content.time.com/time/specials /2007/article/0,28804,1704183_1704257_1704513,00.html); Michael Winerip, "Gay Support Holds for Clinton in Middle America," *The New York Times*, September 22, 1996, 22; Bill Carter, "ABC Is Canceling *Ellen*," *The New York Times*, April 25, 1998 (www.nytimes.com/1998/04/25/arts/abc-is-canceling-ellen.html); "Gay Man Beaten and Left for Dead," *The New York Times*, October 10, 1998, 9; Tom Kenworthy, "Gay Wyoming Student Succumbs to Injuries," *The Washington Post*, October 13, 1998 (www.washingtonpost.com/archive/politics/1998/10/13/gay-wyoming-student-succumbs-to-injuries/ba23fb55-c545-4ab0-b446-515ab22d899c /?utm_term=.53457d529eee).

14. Toni Pizanie, "Why?," *Ambush*, June 3, 2003 (www.ambushmag.com/is1103/sappho .htm); Keith O'Brien, "Final Witness," New Orleans *Times-Picayune*, July 2, 2003, E1; interview with Stewart Butler, July 20, 2014; Brecht interview, January 19, 2017; "Refined from the Ashes" (program), MCC of New Orleans, June 22, 2003, Skylar Fein Upstairs Lounge Fire Collection, Historic New Orleans Fire Collection.

15. Interview with Richard Everett, January 20, 2017; interview with Henry Kubicki, April 7, 2016.

16. "Refined from the Ashes"; Coleman interview; Clayton Delery-Edwards, *The Up Stairs Lounge Arson: Thirty-Two Deaths in a New Orleans Gay Bar, June 24, 1973* (Jefferson, N.C.: McFarland, 2014), 176; Brecht interview, January 19, 2017; Phillips, notes for "Remembering the Upstairs Lounge Fire"; Thompson, "Thirty-Two Killed."

17. Butler interview, July 20, 2014; Delery-Edwards, *The Up Stairs Lounge Arson*, 168; Paul Breton, "United We Stand" (unpublished manuscript, August 1973), National New Orleans Memorial Fund Collection, ONE National Gay and Lesbian Archives at the USC Libraries, Los Angeles; "General Case Report," New Orleans Department of Police, August 30, 1973, Upstairs Lounge Records, City Archives, New Orleans Public Library; "Upstairs Lounge Fire Memorial," 1998, Skylar Fein Upstairs Lounge Fire Collection.

18. Brecht interview, January 19, 2017; Wally Sherwood, "Former Olympus King Passes Away," *Ambush*, July 19, 2005 (www.ambushmag.com/is1505/sherwoods .htm); Manguno, "Deacon in Tavern Blames Arsonist"; Butler interview, July 20, 2014; Perry interview.

19. Thompson, "Thirty-Two Killed"; Sherwood, "Former Olympus King Passes Away"; Kubicki interview, September 5, 2015.

20. Brecht interview, January 19, 2017; Perry interview; Coleman interview; O'Brien, "Final Witness," E1.

21. Laine Kaplan-Levenson, "Arson at the UpStairs Lounge," WWNO.org, July 28, 2016 (http://wwno.org/post/arson-upstairs-lounge).

22. Brecht interview, January 19, 2017; Delery-Edwards, *The Up Stairs Lounge Arson*, 176; O'Brien, "Final Witness," E1.

23. Brecht interview, January 29, 2017; O'Brien, "Final Witness," E1; Toni Pizanie, "Upstairs Fire Memorial," *Ambush*, April 22, 2003 (www.ambushmag.com/is803 /Sappho.htm); interview with Tina Matyi, October 29, 2016; interview with Mary David Mihalyfi, May 4, 2016.

24. Interview with Carole Cotton Winn, March 5, 2018; Brecht interview, January 19, 2017; Delery-Edwards, *The Up Stairs Lounge Arson*, 135; Butler interview, July 20, 2014.

25. Delery-Edwards, *The Up Stairs Lounge Arson*, 136; Brecht interview, January 19, 2017.

26. Delery-Edwards, *The Up Stairs Lounge Arson*, 136; interview with Skylar Fein, July 24, 2015; Ralph Spencer Forest, Statement to Louisiana Office of State Fire Marshal, November 19, 1974, 1, Skylar Fein Upstairs Lounge Fire Collection, Historic New Orleans Collection; "Stephen Ledet," Social Security Claims, November 15, 2007, Ancestry.com; O'Brien, "Final Witness," E1; Brecht interview, January 19, 2017.

27. Tragically, after serving as an Up Stairs Lounge spokesperson for more than a decade through his public remembrances and his "Together, you and I" workshop at religious conferences, Wil Coleman passed away in October 2017 due to health complications related to HIV/AIDS. He was only fifty; Coleman interview; Perry interview; Brecht interview, January 19, 2017.

28. Linda Greenhouse, "The Supreme Court: Homosexual Rights; Justices, 6–3, Legalize Gay Sexual Conduct in Sweeping Reversal of Court's '86 Ruling," *The New York Times*, June 27, 2003 (www.nytimes.com/2003/06/27/us/supreme-court -homosexual-rights-justices-6-3-legalize-gay-sexual-conduct.html).

Acknowledgments

Although I was the vessel through which *Tinderbox* took form, a team of allies seemed to circle this project from the beginning, as if to guard its creation.

First, I must recognize my husband, Ryan Leitner, to whom I dedicate this book. Through Ryan's strength I found the strength to write and finish this work—testimony of a world that predated us but, in many ways, created us too.

I owe a great deal to my editor, Robert Weil, as well as to two of my former Columbia Journalism School professors, Nicholas Lemann and Samuel G. Freedman. At a lunch, Bob and Nick discussed the Up Stairs Lounge fire as an underexplored event, one that someone needed to write a book about. In a subsequent email exchange between Nick and Sam, my name was mentioned, opening the way to my taking on this project. I must also thank Jim Adams, who graciously proofread the resulting book proposal; Jeff Ferzoco, who created the elegant map at the beginning of this book; and Trent Duffy, who copyedited the final draft.

An equal, if not greater, debt of gratitude is owed to the survivors and families of the fire. Stewart Butler, Steven Duplantis, Ricky Everett, John Golding Jr., Tina Marie Matyi, Mary David Mihalyfi, Duane Mitchell, and Ronnie Rosenthal all spoke with me on the record for this book, often for many hours. All gave a wide range of access and bravely recounted their experiences without asking for editorial control. I also appreciate the witnesses and advocates who spoke to me about those weeks in 1973: Joseph Bermuda, Clancy DuBos, Mark Allen Guidry, Lynn Jordan, Paul Killgore, Henry Kubicki, Ronnie LeBoeuf, Milton Mary, Naoma McCrae, John Meyers, Troy Perry, and Roy Reed. Dexter Brecht and Wil Coleman provided the much needed context of recent history, without which this book would have lacked a sense of legacy.

Writing a work of history invariably involves standing on the shoulders of those who came before. So I must recognize Clayton Delery, author of the award-winning *The Up Stairs Lounge Arson*, for his tireless mentorship while I examined the very same subject. Clayton could have easily turned me away as an annoying usurper treading on his terrain. Instead, treating me as an equal and a friend, he gave me early tips, scanned and emailed documents, encouraged me when I doubted myself, and even lent me his notes. His actions taught me an unforgettable lesson: a work of history does not hinge on self-glamorization.

In a similar vein, I must recognize Royd Anderson, creator of the documentary *The Up Stairs Lounge Fire*; Johnny Townsend, author of *Let the Faggots Burn*; Frank Perez, co-author of *In Exile*; Janet Allured, author of *Remapping Second-Wave Feminism*; Skylar Fein, the artist and activist behind the trailblazing exhibition "Remember the Upstairs Lounge"; and Sheri Wright, director of the forthcoming documentary *Tracking Fire*. All not only graciously spent time with me but also shared evidence that they had gathered through their tireless research. In addition, each permitted me an inside look at their interview style and subjects. Although we were not able to connect to the same degree, I must also thank Robert Camina, whose award-winning documentary *Upstairs Inferno* succeeded in raising the profile of the fire more than any other project before or since.

Writing a book is actually deeply humbling in practice, one that involves drawing on the resources of friends and family members. During my four years of research on *Tinderbox* in New Orleans, I stayed generously often at free or reduced rent for extended periods of time—on the day bed in the sunroom of my good friends Gareth Veitch, Miriam Matasar, and Scott Morrison. Their faith in my ability to write a book about the Up Stairs Lounge made possible the detailed and highly localized research that gave birth to *Tinderbox*. I could not have undertaken this book without their hospitality and daily sacrifice of privacy. The delightful Kelsey Green also put me up on several occasions. In addition, my sister Annie and brother-in-law Paul Garchar hosted me in Columbus, Ohio, during my research into Bill Larson's past.

The rest of my family also deserves acknowledgment. My father taught me to love the slog of writing and sat with me many a late evening as I struggled to write my first essays. My mother taught me to examine cultures from different angles. My aunt Donna encouraged a sensitive boy not to be embarrassed about loving poetry. My uncle Charlie demonstrated to me, by example, that it was possible to write a book that matters. My sister Lauren taught me how to organize projects. And Billy, my brother, taught me about never giving up.

I appreciate being taken under the wings, so to speak, of several esteemed French Quarter personages, including the celebrated LGBTQ+ historian Roberts Batson, the famed Sazerac mixologist Neil Racoma at the Hotel Monteleone, and the cherished staff and management of Boucherie on Carrollton Avenue.

I am in awe of the great constellation of archivists and librarians who not only maintain troves of documents but helped guide me to the ones cited in this book. My heartfelt thanks and praise go to the staff of the Historic New Orleans Collection; the Earl K. Long Library at the University of New Orleans; the Louisiana Research Collection of Tulane University, especially Leigh Miller; ONE National Gay and Lesbian Archives at the University of Southern California Libraries; the Duke University Library Archives; the Ohio History Connection; the Sexual Minorities Archives; and the History Project of Boston. As our civilization has painfully learned from gaps in our vision of antiquity, history is lost to us without our great archives—those stores of knowledge maintained in perpetuity for our enrichment.

About the Research

As a journalist by training, I began my research into the Up Stairs Lounge fire by relocating to New Orleans and sleuthing through the primary source documentation preserved in local archives. Through this process, I discovered that, in the great diaspora of people and knowledge of New Orleans after Hurricane Katrina, certain documents had found their way to archives located around the country, and I made plans to visit those other repositories.

Simultaneously, I reviewed and collected secondary sources from the early 1970s, such as newspaper stories, and read or reviewed any account of the tragedy that had already been told through an academic paper, book, art exhibition, or film. Microfiche became a font of historic gold. With this foundation, I then reached out to the authors, academics, and artists—experts who had engaged with this history.

Through this initial process, I was able to assemble a list of the historic figures involved in this tragedy and use publicly available databases to determine whether these figures were alive. If I found that they were dead, I worked to find information about their burial, gravesite, and the circumstances of their death. If I found that they were alive, I attempted to contact them through phone, email, or letter.

When a person responded and contacted me, I engaged him or her as both an informed professional and as a student of the subject matter. I described the book and requested an interview. These on-the-record interviews generally lasted forty-five to sixty minutes. While sometimes there was just one interview per subject, other figures required as many as seven separate sessions, all conducted from a historical rather than an activist angle.

I let interviewees know that I had ears to hear whatever they had to share. I wanted to understand social nuance. I encouraged any explication of the context of the time period. The transcriptions of these interviews became living documents, material I could cross-check against primary sources and that I could mine for quotations incorporated into the text.

If a historic figure didn't respond to my initial overtures, or if someone responded merely to decline participating in this project, I searched for any source that might contain that person's testimony in a previous account; if I was successful, I acquired the appropriate permissions to use their words.

I have to observe that about midway through the process of writing the book, the Pulse nightclub shooting occurred in Orlando. Many of the historic figures who had been on the fence about granting an interview reached out in those weeks after the June 2016 mass shooting, urgently wanting to have their testimony included. This made some aspects of the drafting of this text challenging, because I was suddenly faced with the task of distilling and slotting the new data into a narrative structure that had already taken root. It became something of an improvisation to not just accept but also to celebrate and integrate each new revelation into the fabric of the work.

Illustration Credits

Index

About the Author

Robert W. Fieseler is a recipient of the Pulitzer Traveling Fellowship and the Lynton Fellowship in Book Writing. He graduated co-valedictorian from the Columbia University Graduate School of Journalism. *Tinderbox* is his first book.

Fieseler's stories have been published by *Narratively* and *The Big Roundtable*, among other places, and been recognized in roundups of best nonfiction by *The Atlantic*. His essays have appeared in *Columbia Journal*, the *River Teeth* blog, and elsewhere. In other lives, Fieseler studied English and history at the University of Michigan and worked as a bookseller for Borders, the now-defunct retailer.

When he received the opportunity to write *Tinderbox*, Fieseler moved into the guestroom of his friends in New Orleans to soak in the city's culture. A proud gay American, Fieseler married his longtime partner at Walden Pond and lives in Boston, Massachusetts.